The Jacksonian Heritage

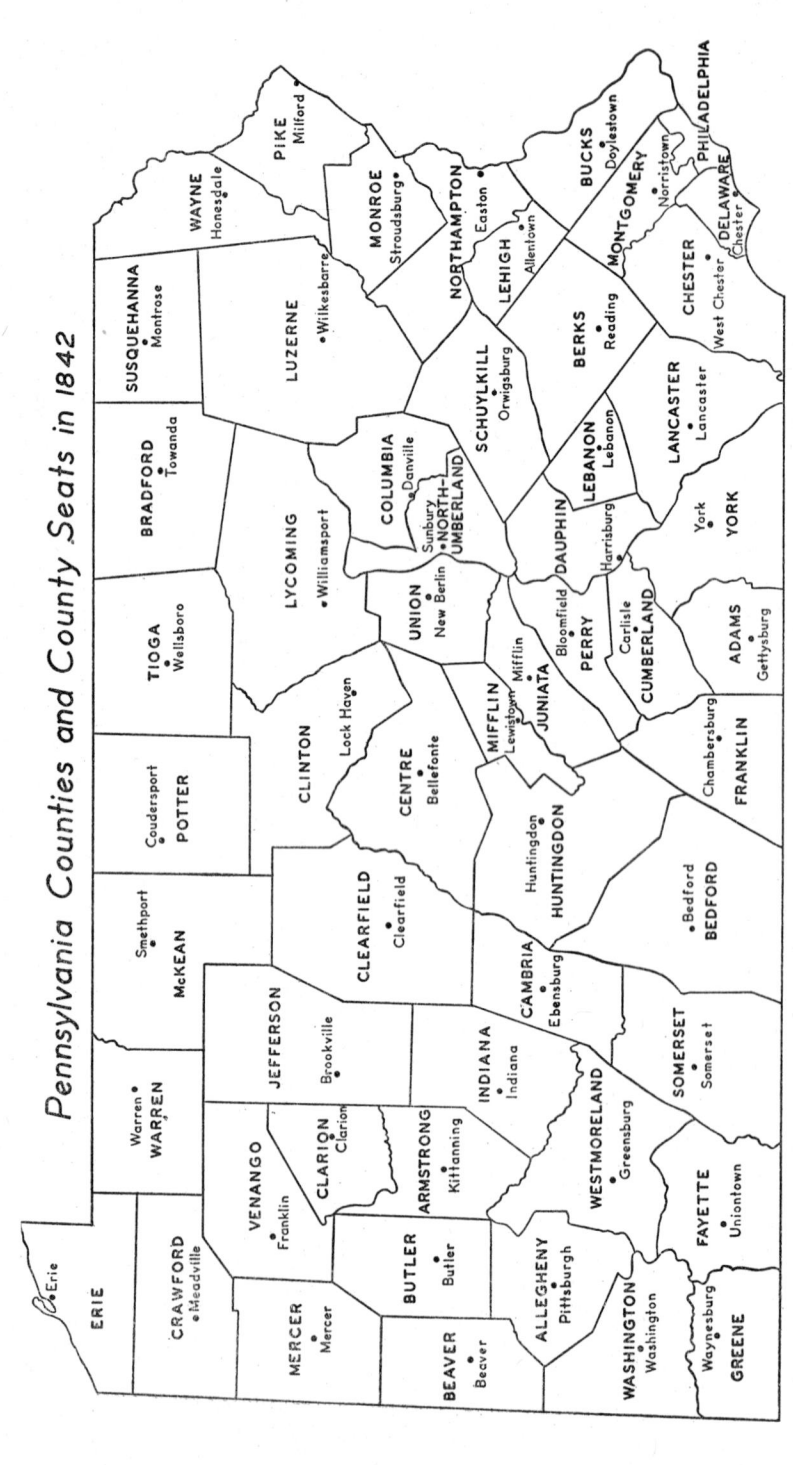

The Jacksonian Heritage
Pennsylvania Politics
1833-1848

BY
CHARLES MCCOOL SNYDER

COMMONWEALTH OF PENNSYLVANIA
THE PENNSYLVANIA HISTORICAL AND
MUSEUM COMMISSION
Harrisburg, Pennsylvania
1958

THE PENNSYLVANIA HISTORICAL AND MUSEUM COMMISSION

Frank W. Melvin, *Chairman*

James B. Stevenson, *Vice Chairman*

Frances Dorrance
Maurice A. Mook
Thomas F. Murphy *(deceased)*
Charles H. Boehm, *ex officio*
  Superintendent of Public Instruction

J. Bennett Nolan
John W. Oliver
Grace A. Rankin
Mrs. Lawrence M. C. Smith

Members from the General Assembly

Leroy E. Chapman, *Senator*
E. Gadd Snider, *Representative*

Israel Stiefel, *Senator*
Norman Wood, *Representative*

Trustees Ex Officio

George M. Leader, *Governor of the Commonwealth*
Charles C. Smith, *Auditor General*
Robert F. Kent, *State Treasurer*

Administrative Staff

Sylvester K. Stevens, *Executive Director*
William N. Richards, *Executive Assistant*
Earle W. Newton, *Director*
Bureau of Museums, Historic Sites, and Properties
Sanford W. Higginbotham, *Director*
Bureau of Research, Publications, and Records

Preface

ANOTHER study of the Jackson Era requires no apology. While the scene at Washington has been described many times, the history of the states in this period remains a fertile field for research. Issues emanating from the nation's capital had repercussions in the states; and local issues, in turn, sometimes reached the halls of Congress and the White House.

This work is an evaluation of this cause and effect in Pennsylvania between 1833 and 1848. It begins with the impact of Jackson's veto of the recharter of the Second Bank of the United States and closes with the Whig triumph in the State and national elections of 1848.

Jackson's challenging veto of the Bank Bill was only the starting point of this controversy in Pennsylvania. Philadelphia was the home of the Bank, and Pennsylvanians were proud of it. Yet the fortunes of politics plunged it into the vortex of party strife; and before the issue receded, the Bank received a State charter and precipitated a political furor seldom equaled in the State's history.

During this era the Democratic party, with Jackson's prestige to bolster it, was the dominant political organization. But Democratic discord enabled a coalition of Antimasons and Whigs to elect a Governor and at times to control the legislature. Party strife boiled over briefly to produce the famous "Buckshot War."

During the 1840's the tariff tended to overshadow other issues. The unparalleled expansion of business enterprise during this decade was identified with protection and the Tariff of 1842; and the tariff issue shaped the elections of 1844, 1846, and 1848. Each ton of coal mined and each furnace lighted in the State weakened the force of agrarianism and strengthened the power of business. The Walker Tariff of 1846 tipped the balance to give the Whigs a temporary ascendancy in 1848.

Few of Pennsylvania's politicians in this era became national figures. Exceptions were James Buchanan, George M. Dallas, Simon Cameron, and Thaddeus Stevens. Of this quartet, Buchanan merits greatest emphasis here. He was the most prominent Democrat and his party's choice for President in two elections. Dallas was Buchanan's chief rival for preferment, and was elected to the Vice Presidency in 1844. Cameron played the game of politics to the hilt, but lacked stature in his party, then the Democratic. But he managed to combine Whig and dissident Democratic votes to win election to the United States

PREFACE

Senate in 1845. Stevens enjoyed a brief taste of power as an Antimasonic legislative leader and adviser to Governor Ritner, but his power declined with Antimasonry. He entered upon a new career as a Whig Congressman in 1848.

Though not a part of a formal series, this work is one of several dealing with Pennsylvania politics and inspired by Dr. Roy F. Nichols of the University of Pennsylvania. Not properly a part of this group is Theodore Thayer's *Pennsylvania Politics and the Growth of Democracy, 1740-1776*,[1] which presents a brief survey of the struggle for home rule waged by the Colonial Assembly against the Proprietor. Robert L. Brunhouse in his book, *The Counter-Revolution in Pennsylvania, 1776-1790*,[2] describes the conservative reaction against the radicalism of the Revolutionary era and its culmination in the adoption of the Constitution of 1790. Harry M. Tinkcom's *Republicans and Federalists in Pennsylvania, 1790-1801: A Study in National Stimulus and Local Response*[3] analyzes the State's reaction to national and international issues stemming from the creation of the Federal Union and the rise of forces which produced the Republican and Federalist parties. Sanford W. Higginbotham's *The Keystone in the Democratic Arch: Pennsylvania Politics, 1800-1816*,[4] studies the era of Republican hegemony in the State until its disintegration in 1816. The last of these monographs, speaking chronologically, is Philip S. Klein's *Pennsylvania Politics, 1817-1832: A Game Without Rules*,[5] which describes the factional rivalries through a decade of flux and disorder to the creation of a new partisan division based on national issues.

This book pursues the nascent National Republicans, Democrats, and Antimasons through an era shaped by the heritage of Jackson.

I am grateful for many favors from the staffs of the Historical Society of Pennsylvania, the Library of Congress, the Library of the University of Pennsylvania, the Library Company of Philadelphia, the Free Library of Philadelphia, the American Philosophical Society, the Historical Society of Western Pennsylvania, the Lancaster County Historical Society, the Wyoming Historical and Geological Society, the Carnegie Library of Pittsburgh, the Haverford College Library, the

[1] Pennsylvania Historical and Museum Commission, Harrisburg, 1953.
[2] Pennsylvania Historical and Museum Commission, Harrisburg, 1942.
[3] Pennsylvania Historical and Museum Commission, Harrisburg, 1950.
[4] Pennsylvania Historical and Museum Commission, Harrisburg, 1952.
[5] Historical Society of Pennsylvania, Philadelphia, 1940.

PREFACE

Pennsylvania Historical and Museum Commission, the Bucknell University Library, the Danville Public Library, and the Milton *Evening Standard*. To Dr. Frank P. Boyer of Mifflinburg, Merrill Linn of Lewisburg, and Norris S. Barratt of Germantown thanks are due for the use of private collections.

I would like to acknowledge encouragement given by Dr. Cyrus Karraker and Dr. J. Orin Oliphant of Bucknell University and assistance and guidance from Dr. Roy F. Nichols. Thanks go to the Pennsylvania Historical and Museum Commission and to Dr. S. K. Stevens, Executive Director, for making possible the printing of this book and especially to Dr. Sanford W. Higginbotham and Donald H. Kent of its staff for their work as editors. I am further indebted to the Historical Society of Pennsylvania and the Historical Society of Dauphin County for permission to reproduce paintings and engravings from their collections, and to the Pennsylvania Department of Commerce and the Pennsylvania Historical and Museum Commission for photographic reproductions of these portraits. The Commission also provided the map used as a frontispiece.

Finally, I am grateful to my wife, Mary Burrowes Snyder, for her countless favors in the completion of this book.

Contents

	PREFACE	v
I.	THE SETTING	3
II.	JACKSON AND THE WHIGS, 1833-1834	35
III.	THE "WOLVES" AND THE "MUHLS," 1834-1835	50
IV.	JOSEPH AND HIS BRETHREN, 1835-1836	68
V.	NOURISHMENT FOR THE "MONSTER," 1836-1837	82
VI.	THE CONSTITUTION OF 1838	96
VII.	THE DEPRESSION, BANKING, AND THE BUCKSHOT WAR, 1837-1838	112
VIII.	PORTER AT THE HELM, 1839-1840	136
IX.	THE REDEMPTION OF CREDIT AND THE REPUDIATION OF PORTER, 1840-1843	151
X.	THE CAMPAIGN OF 1844	171
XI.	PENNSYLVANIA INTERESTS AND THE WALKER TARIFF, 1845-1847	187
XII.	THE ELECTION OF 1848 AND THE PASSING OF DEMOCRATIC SUPREMACY	204
	APPENDIX	221
	BIBLIOGRAPHY	231
	INDEX	243

Illustrations

MAP
(Frontispiece)
Pennsylvania Counties and County Seats in 1842

PENNSYLVANIA PORTRAITS
(On insert between pages 150 and 151)

Governor George Wolf
Governor Joseph Ritner
Governor David Rittenhouse Porter
Governor Francis Rawn Shunk
Governor William Freame Johnston
George Mifflin Dallas
James Buchanan
Nicholas Biddle
Thaddeus Stevens
Henry Augustus Philip Muhlenberg
Simon Cameron
David Wilmot

The Jacksonian Heritage

CHAPTER I

The Setting

SECTIONS

PENNSYLVANIA in 1832 reflected the arbitrary and impulsive manner in which Charles II had parceled out his vast domain in America. The Southeast enjoyed the blessings accruing from the fortuitous combination of fertile soil in proximity to tidewater. Roads converged upon Philadelphia, the metropolis, the outlet for foreign trade, the market for domestic produce, the intellectual and cultural center of the area. But across the Piedmont the Susquehanna Valley drained into the Chesapeake Bay in Maryland, and before the advent of railroads Baltimore appeared to be the natural outlet. Along the northern tier of counties the valleys opened into New York and were separated from the central portions of the State by the Appalachian highlands. Most remote from the other regions was the West, isolated by the broad Appalachian Plateau. Drained by the Ohio and its tributaries, the Monongahela in the south and the Allegheny in the north, this area centering at Pittsburgh at the forks of the Ohio looked westward and southwestward to the Mississippi and New Orleans for markets. Harrisburg, the State capital, situated on the east bank of the Susquehanna, was a town of 4,500, distinguished from other river towns only by its political significance as a county town and the seat of the government of the State.

Pennsylvania thus lacked geographic and economic unity, a situation contributing inevitably to political sectionalism. Aaronsburg in Centre County, located at the geographic center of the State, remains today a village of a single street with a broad central square and a tradition that it was to become the political center.

Pennsylvania offered contrasts between the old and the new. The Southeast presented a picture of order and stability. Families with roots reaching back for five and six generations were not uncommon, and the natural increase in population produced an exodus to the west and north, and, as industrialization advanced, to the towns. In 1830 twelve counties in this region occupying about one-seventh of the area held one-half of the people of the State. This density of population gave the Southeast a potency in politics denied to other areas, though it was frequently dissipated by factional strife.

The newness was also worn from the face of the countryside in the central portions of the State. A frontier, settled by the Scotch-Irish in the decades immediately preceding and following the Revolution, it had been filled in by the overflow from the German counties of Lancaster, Berks, and Lebanon to the southeast. A visitor who followed the main-traveled roads would have accepted the region as the home of the former, but a peddler who penetrated into the side roads would have discovered that "Pennsylvania Dutch" was the spoken word in many sections. The Scotch-Irish had also crossed the Alleghenies into the southwestern corner of the State prior to the Revolution, and in 1832 the log cabin in Pennsylvania was a relic of generations gone by.

By way of contrast the northern portions of the State from east to west exhibited the rawness of the frontier. Bypassed during the early decades of the Republic because there were broader valleys and more accessible farm lands to the south, this region was now entering upon a process of transition. While forests retreated before the blows of the axeman and farmers occupied the fertile regions, capitalists speculated in land and organized companies to mine and transport coal to meet an ever growing demand.

Society

Pennsylvania in this era continued to mirror the racial diversity which had characterized the Colonial period, though the American environment was imperceptibly blending and modifying. In the Southeast, particularly in Philadelphia, Bucks, Montgomery, Delaware, and Chester counties, the English element predominated. As farmers, craftsmen, and merchants they contributed to Philadelphia's rise as a commercial center. Collectively they were creditors and exerted a conservative influence in the area and in the State. They supplied the membership of the professions, and occupied many appointive posts in federal, state, and local government. Scattered through the area were people of Welsh, Scotch-Irish, Negro, German, French, and Dutch stock. None was sizable enough to alter the prevailing English pattern.

Beyond the counties adjacent to Philadelphia lay the German belt, including Lancaster, York, Berks, Lebanon, Northampton, Lehigh, Dauphin, Schuylkill, and Union counties. Further west and north in Allegheny, Armstrong, Bedford, and Washington, and in Cumberland, Huntingdon, Mifflin, and Centre counties were scattered communities of Germans who had emigrated from the original settlements. Rustic, frequently unlettered, and handicapped by a language barrier in their relations with other national groups, they tended to be apathetic toward politics unless prodded into action by threats to their security—taxation, for example—or the attraction of a German name on the ballot. The German element furnished more than its share of Governors prior to 1832 and a German nominee continued to be a political asset to a party in the years which followed.

The Scotch-Irish, widely dispersed across the valleys of the interior, the Appalachian Plateau, and the Ohio watershed, constituted the third major element in the population. In need of capital, transportation, schools, and other services from the State, they turned to politics for aid. As party leaders, organizers, and managers they were unsurpassed.

> Their dramatic instincts, their flair for politics, their adherence to an organized Presbyterian church that demanded trained leaders and afforded a place of congregation, their imagination and boldness, all aided in giving them an incommensurate weight in early politics. . . . Their political influence was vastly greater than their numbers would seem to indicate.[1]

Mingling with the Scotch-Irish along the northern tier, particularly in Luzerne, Bradford, Susquehanna, and Tioga counties, were citizenry of New England stock and natives of New York who entered the State from the north and east. Isolated from the main streams of migration which flowed from Philadelphia westward, they were more responsive than other Pennsylvanians to political currents emanating from New York and New England.

Finally, mention should be made of the Irish in the Philadelphia area. Of little significance in the early 1830's, the Irish vote loomed more and more important a decade later as immigration mounted. By the early 1840's politicians had evolved a pattern: neglect during the months of political quiescence, then a spirited campaign for the Irish vote during the weeks before election.

Town and Country

Pennsylvania was predominantly rural in 1832, the majority of its one and one-third million citizens residing on farms or in villages. In the entire State there were but three cities, and two of these had populations under 20,000. Philadelphia with about 200,000 residents,

[1] Russell J. Ferguson, *Early Western Pennsylvania Politics* (Pittsburgh, 1938), 10-11.

including the unincorporated districts of the county, was without a rival in the State. The second city of the nation and a thriving commercial community since the decade of its founding, its markets were the most celebrated in the Union. They extended on Market Street from the Delaware River to Eighth Street, and on market days an array of stalls and wagons lined the curbstones for six or seven blocks further west. The number and size of its banks made it the financial center of the State, and towering over the others in size and prestige was the Bank of the United States, housed in a replica of the Parthenon on Chestnut Street. Noted for many years for the variety of its shops and crafts, Philadelphia was beginning to feel the impact of the Industrial Revolution, particularly upon its fringes: at Dyottsville in Kensington, a glass factory employed about three hundred hands; at Manayunk on the east bank of the Schuylkill, a region overgrown with trees and bushes in 1819, newly erected factories were producing cotton and woolen yarns, flour, paper, and iron products.[2] It was also the entrepôt for the foreign trade of the State. In contrast with the expansion in population and industry, however, the volume of trade was almost stationary.[3] Merchants looked to the State to relieve them from the disadvantage resulting from the completion of the Erie Canal, which had given their rivals in New York City an all-water route to the West. But Philadelphia's pre-eminence was not limited to the countinghouse.

Though it was no longer the political hub of the State, its tradition of leadership through the Colonial era, the Revolution, and the formative years of the republic endured. The radicalism of the Revolutionary War had yielded to conservatism during the decades which followed, but on election day Democratic majorities in the unincorporated districts tended to offset the National Republican pluralities in the city. Finally, Philadelphia was the cultural center of the State. It filled the professions and learned societies, and exercised leadership through the press.

Pittsburgh, the second city of the State, had a population of about 20,000 and occupied a position in the West comparable to Philadelphia in the East. Situated at the forks of the Ohio where the east-west traffic "took to water," it was known throughout America and Europe

[2] Rebecca Eaton, *A Geography of Pennsylvania* (Philadelphia, 1835), 74; Eli Bowen, *The Pictorial Sketch-Book of Pennsylvania* (Philadelphia, 1852), 42; Victor S. Clark, *History of Manufactures in the United States*, 2 vols. (Washington, 1916-1928), I, 549-552.
[3] Robert G. Albion, *The Rise of New York Port* (New York, 1939), 402.

as the "Gateway to the West." It was also a manufacturing community, where dozens of items, particularly metalwares which were too bulky to be carried across the mountains economically, were produced. It was sometimes likened to Birmingham by English travelers, who seldom failed to record the pall of smoke hanging over it. By 1832 it had nine foundries, eight rolling mills, nine rail factories, eight glass houses, and a newly erected row of coke ovens at the base of Coal Hill. Bridges across the Monongahela and Allegheny rivers extended its suburbs westward and northward, and in 1834 the completion of the Pennsylvania State Works linked it by rail and water to the Susquehanna Valley.[4] Activity was everywhere, but change did not modify the underlying conservatism of the city in politics. Federalism remained triumphant there as late as 1820, and prominent Federalists, such as William Wilkins, continued to exert a powerful influence through the decade of the 1830's.

In contrast with Pittsburgh, Lancaster, the third city in the State, bore an air of permanency and stability. A marketing point in the fertile "Garden of America," its growth had been gradual, paralleling that of the countryside. By 1832 it had a population of a little more than 7,000, a courthouse and jail, an almshouse, a market house, three banks, two insurance offices and a cotton mill, a college, an academy and a public school, a museum, and eleven churches.[5] Except for its size it resembled the larger county towns in the older sections of the State. Similar to Philadelphia and Pittsburgh, it exerted a conservative influence in politics. A stronghold of Federalism, it had scarcely gone over to the Democrats, strengthened by the popularity of Jackson, when it was engulfed by Antimasonry.

In addition to its cities, Pennsylvania had many incorporated boroughs. Reading, with a population almost equal to Lancaster, manufactured boots and shoes, farm machinery, and stoneware, and was particularly noted for it hats. Situated upon the recently completed Schuylkill Canal with easy access to coal and iron, it was at the threshold of a new era. Easton and York were about the size of Harrisburg, others were even smaller. Significant for the future were such villages as Mauch Chunk (now Jim Thorpe), erected by the Lehigh Coal and Navigation Company to house its workers on a site covered with forest less than a decade before, and Pottsville with a population of

[4] Leland D. Baldwin, *Pittsburgh: The Story of a City* (Pittsburgh, 1938), 191-221; F. Frank Crall, "A Half-Century of Rivalry between Pittsburgh and Wheeling," *Western Pennsylvania Historical Magazine*, XIII (October, 1930), 242-244.
[5] William F. Worner, *Old Lancaster, Tales and Traditions* (Lancaster, 1927), 175.

8   THE JACKSONIAN HERITAGE

2,400 made up largely of Scots, Irish, Welsh, and English miners who had emigrated to work in the anthracite pits. Six years earlier it had been a village of five houses.

Boroughs and cities with populations of 5,000 or over made up approximately 15 per cent of the citizenry of the State. The remainder lived on farms or in villages and small towns which complemented the needs of a rural society. A traveler might expect to find a general store, tavern, gristmill, blacksmith and cobbler shops, a church or two, and possibly a post office. In the county seats, he might observe also carriage and wagon shops, and perhaps a foundry, print shop, lawyers' and doctors' offices, and, of course, the courthouse and jail. Such a scattered and isolated society dependent upon unimproved country roads for communication presented problems which tested the ingenuity of the politician. They were difficult to reach and to organize for the support of a cause or a candidate, and once molded into a pattern they resisted change. A party machine in the modern sense was impractical.

ECONOMIC PATTERN

The typical Pennsylvanian was a farmer. The census of 1840 indicates that approximately 60 per cent of the workers of the State were engaged in agriculture and that they exceeded the number employed in manufacturing and trade by a ratio of two to one.[6] While the "dirt" farmers were slow to grasp developments in scientific farming, they improved upon the methods of their forebears by practicing the rotation of crops and the application of fertilizers, and they compared favorably with the husbandmen in other states. Visitors were struck with the neat and substantial appearance of the buildings and fences, the pride in the barn, the comfort and shelter provided for the livestock, and the order and convenience of the whole domestic arrangement.[7] Crops were generally diversified, distance from markets and inadequate transportation contributing to discourage specialization. In 1840 Pennsylvania farmers led the nation in the production of rye; their wheat crop was exceeded only by Ohio; their oats, second only to New York. They ranked second, also, in orchard produce and butter.[8] In the Philadelphia area, however, they concentrated on truck gardening; in Lancaster they found tobacco a lucrative cash crop; and

[6] *Sixth Census or Enumeration of the Inhabitants of the United States . . . in 1840* (Washington, 1841), 138-186.
[7] Charles B. Trego, *A Geography of Pennsylvania* (Philadelphia, 1843), 112.
[8] *Statistical View of the United States, . . . Being a Compendium of the Seventh Census . . .* (Washington, 1854), 171.

in the counties in the Southwest, particularly in Washington County, they specialized in sheep raising.

Conscious of the need for more adequate transportation, the farmer supported internal improvements by the State in the form of roads and canals when they facilitated the carrying of his produce to market, but his sense of thrift and his adherence to the Jeffersonian ideal of a government confined to the maintenance of peace and justice made him critical of expenditures in regions remote from his own locality. Farmers in the southern and southeastern counties, with access to markets, saw in the improvements only competition, debts, and taxes, whereas farmers in central and western counties and along the lines of projected improvements gave them their enthusiastic approval. Farmers usually gave lip service to the protective tariff with its promise of more extensive American markets, and sheep growers were ardent champions of protection for wool.

Manufacturing was expanding rapidly in the 1830's, though the value of the products of the home and shop exceeded those of the factory. Traditional establishments which offered employment to substantial numbers of workers included leather goods, distilled and fermented liquors, flour milling, printing and bookbinding, carriages and wagons, machinery, bricks and lime, cotton and woolen goods, iron forges, bloomeries, and rolling mills.[9] The utilization of machinery foreshadowed far-reaching modifications in the economic pattern. While woolen manufacture in Philadelphia continued in households and shops, eight mills averaging more than 100,000 yards per year were operating in nearby Delaware County; and growth in the size of mills was accompanied by a tendency to concentrate in particular areas.[10] By 1840, for example, more than two-thirds of the cotton spindles in the State were operating within thirty miles of Philadelphia.[11] Ironmaking revealed a similar trend. Before 1800 it had extended up the Schuylkill and Susquehanna valleys and even into the Juniata region and to Pittsburgh, and by 1840 production in all forms of iron exceeded New York, the State's closest rival, by more than three times.[12]

[9] *Sixth Census*, 138-186; Trego, *Geography, passim;* Clark, *History of Manufactures*, I, 497-570.
[10] *Ibid.*, 567.
[11] *Ibid.*, 549-552.
[12] *Ibid.*, 497-501. See also Arthur C. Bining, "The Rise of Iron Manufacture in Western Pennsylvania," *Western Pennsylvania Historical Magazine*, XVI (October, 1933), 235-256.

Meanwhile, specialization was evident in the Pittsburgh area, where in three years before 1830 the output of rolled iron trebled, and where eight mills were annually rolling 6,000 tons of blooms, and in the towns along the Schuylkill—Norristown, Phoenixville, Reading, and Pottsville. The use of anthracite in the blast furnace was demonstrated at the latter in 1839; a decade later others of this type were in production at Lebanon, Easton, Phoenixville, Safe Harbor, and Harrisburg.[13] The growth of industry strengthened the demand for more adequate transportation. Manufacturers lent their support to the movement for a State-constructed and State-operated system of improvements— the need for cheap transportation offsetting any misgivings that the State was entering an area which should be reserved for private enterprise.[14] It also reinforced the doctrine of protectionism to which Pennsylvanians had already subscribed.

The rise of the coal trade in this era was also significant. A mere novelty prior to 1820 when the Lehigh Coal and Navigation Company marketed 365 tons of anthracite, operations were extended during the next decade to the Schuylkill and Lackawanna fields. In 1830, a total of 174,734 tons was mined, and by 1840, despite the Panic of 1837, the volume had multiplied fivefold.[15] Mining directed the flow of capital into areas hitherto undeveloped, stimulated the lethargic export trade of Philadelphia, and precipitated a flurry of canal and railroad projects. It made a financial success of the Schuylkill Navigation Company and induced New York financiers to construct the Delaware and Hudson Canal. It also produced an extension of the State Works along the West Branch and the North Branch of the Susquehanna.

Of the phenomena attending the transition from an agrarian to a mercantile economy, none aroused the interest of contemporaries more than developments in transportation. The responsibility of the State for promoting improvements in roads had been recognized from the time of the Revolution. The General Assembly had constructed and operated highways and bridges, chartered turnpike companies, and frequently engaged in mixed enterprise by purchasing blocks of stock in the latter.[16] Corporate organization, supplementing the State system, began in the Philadelphia area in 1791 and spread westward. The turnpike was soon the most prevalent form of corporate activity in the State.

[13] Bowen, *Pictorial Sketch-Book*, 55-107, 181-182.
[14] Louis Hartz, *Economic Policy and Democratic Thought: Pennsylvania, 1776-1860* (Cambridge 1948), 128-142.
[15] Bowen, *Pictorial Sketch-Book*, 226.
[16] Hartz, *Economic Policy*, Chap. III.

By the decade of the 1820's highways were competing with canals for public favor. Numerous canal companies were chartered, and by 1832 the Union Canal linking the Schuylkill with the Susquehanna, the Schuylkill Navigation Company, the Lehigh Navigation Company, and the Delaware and Hudson Canal were in operation. But pressure arising from the interstate competition for the western trade, meanwhile, moved the State to undertake a gigantic program of public works. Philadelphia businessmen and civic leaders in 1824 founded the Pennsylvania Society for the Promotion of Internal Improvements for the purpose of uniting the eastern and western sections of the State by a canal. They flooded the press with literature, sponsored a canal convention at Harrisburg in 1825, and carried the issue to the legislature. They enlisted warm advocates in the West and along the proposed line of improvements, and by 1826 were able to commit the State to the "Public" or "State Works," the most ambitious of which was the Pennsylvania Canal, with a railroad from Philadelphia to Columbia on the Susquehanna, a canal from that point northward along the Susquehanna and westward along the Juniata to Hollidaysburg, a railroad to provide a portage across the Alleghenies, and a canal along the Kiskiminetas and Allegheny rivers to Pittsburgh.

Despite the tremendous cost entailed, it proved to be the beginning rather than the end of the State's plunge into the canal business. The need to reconcile opinion in regions remote from the main line, added to the flush of optimism generated by the opening of the Erie Canal which led advocates of the Pennsylvania State Works to anticipate that "the tolls will support the government, and educate every child in the commonwealth,"[17] induced the State to undertake the construction of the Delaware Canal in the East, the West and North Branch divisions along the Susquehanna, and the Beaver and French Creek canals in the West, and to give financial aid to dozens of new road building projects and several railroads.

The venture proved to be far more extensive and costly than the most sanguine of its original proponents could have anticipated, and by 1836 expenditures totaled more than $22,000,000. "The system," Mathew Carey observed, "was moulded by the prevalence of local interests, in violation of the plain dictates of sound policy."[18] Much of the work was done hastily and inadequately. Freshets destroyed dams and washed out banks, and repairs sometimes held up traffic

[17] *Ibid.*, 138, quoting Pennsylvania, *House Journal, 1824-25*, II, 284.
[18] Mathew Carey, *Brief View of the System of Internal Improvement of the State of Pennsylvania* (Philadelphia, 1831), 18.

for weeks in the spring. Receipts never equaled the costs of operation, and the legislature was pressed annually to find funds for maintenance and interest as well as new construction. The Panic of 1837 produced a financial crisis and transformed enthusiasm for the Public Works into disillusionment. The failures, however, should not obscure the contributions of the improvements to Philadelphia and Pittsburgh and other communities on the paths of the canals, and to the farmers who now had cheap transportation for their bulky commodities, not to overlook the opportunities for contractors and laborers.

Though the program had at least the perfunctory support of all parties at the outset, its impact upon policies was nevertheless significant. The Canal Convention of 1825 divided upon sectional considerations, and a similar split occurred in the legislature, where "Main Line Men" confronted "Branch Men." Representatives of counties along the Southern Tier and in the Northwest and Schuylkill areas, regions distant from the system, lined up against the project unless they were rewarded with appropriations for improvements in their own districts. The result was both an intense and prolonged contest in "logrolling," which tended to monopolize the attention of the legislature year after year. Improvements were valued by the local politicians for their vote-getting potentialities, and rival leaders vied for the support of the laborers engaged on the projects. Charges and counter-charges of "colonization" stemming from the latter became familiar components of the election scene.

Pennsylvanians in the 1830's were also promoting numerous railroad projects, particularly in the coal regions, but with the exception of a few short lines built by mining companies and the Philadelphia and Reading Railroad Company, they remained in the planning stage until the decade of the 1840's.

Banking in 1832 was characterized by decentralization and extreme fluctuation. Pressure from the interior for relief from what was regarded as the credit despotism of Philadelphia had produced the Banking Act of 1814, which had incorporated forty-one banks with a capital totaling $17,000,000 and touched off an orgy of speculation. The Panic of 1819 left numerous failures in its wake, and by 1822 eleven of those chartered in 1814 had closed their doors, and several others were unable to make specie payments. By 1830 there were thirty-three banks in the State, of which eleven, with more than two-thirds of the aggregate banking capital, were in Philadelphia.[19] Jackson's quarrel

[19] *Hazard's Register of Pennsylvania*, VII (1831), 60.

THE SETTING

with the Bank of the United States revived this rural-city division and stimulated the rise of a radical antibank group, with the result that petitions for bank charters precipitated furious encounters in the legislature between the bank men, abetted by lobbyists or "borers," and the antibank radicals.[20]

Government

A visitor to the State capital at Harrisburg in the 1850's recorded his impressions as follows:

> The capitol stands on a handsome sloping elevation, rising in the northeast end of town. ... The capitol grounds are enclosed with an iron-rail fence, and laid out in handsome gravel walks, shaded with numerous trees, which are still young and in vigorous growth. The main building is one hundred and eighty feet in length by eighty feet in width, and two stories in height. It is a plain but substantial brick building, sufficiently characteristic of our old commonwealth. A large circular portico, faced with six heavy stone columns, constitutes the front entrance to the building. In the interior is a large rotunda, with a high dome overarching, from which is entered the Senate Chamber on the left, and the Hall of the Representatives on the right.[21]

The government functioned here under the Constitution of 1790, which had been adopted during the flood tide of the counter-revolution to replace the radical Constitution of 1776.[22] The extensive powers which it granted to the executive cast the government in a conservative mold.

The Governor was elected for a term of three years and might serve a maximum of nine years in twelve. The first three executives held office for three consecutive terms, but after the retirement of Simon Snyder in 1817 none was able to reach this goal. The Governor held the veto power and could be overridden only by a two-thirds vote of both houses of the legislature. Executives during the 1830's and 1840's did not hesitate to invoke this prerogative, using it frequently to block charters for banking and manufacturing and to defeat a variety of other private bills. The most distinctive feature of the governorship was the appointive power, which was truly regal in its proportions. Authorized to appoint all officers whose offices were established by the constitution or should be provided subsequently

[20] See Chapters V and VII.
[21] Eli Bowen, *Locomotive Sketches . . . from Philadelphia to Pittsburg* (Philadelphia, 1854), 73.
[22] See Robert L. Brunhouse, *The Counter-Revolution in Pennsylvania, 1776-1790* (Harrisburg, 1942).

by law except those otherwise provided for, the Governor had at his disposal the naming of the Secretary of the Commonwealth, the Attorney General, the Adjutant General, the Escheator General, the Auditor General, the Surveyor General, the Secretary of the Land Office, and the State Librarian; the judiciary, including judges, justices of the peace and aldermen, notaries public, registers, recorders, clerks of the courts, sheriffs, and coroners; miscellaneous officers, such as auctioneers, inspectors and measurers; and commissioners, such as the Canal Commissioners and administrators of State institutions. It made the executive a power in every community in the State; it was also a staggering responsibility, since he was compelled to rely upon the judgment of local politicians for many of the appointments, and it created a situation which was often more conducive to schism than harmony. Had this power not been curbed by the Constitution of 1838, it might have become a source of political strength in the years which followed, but in the 1830's parties were too loosely knit to use it effectively.

During the period covered by this study there were four Governors, George Wolf of Easton, Joseph Ritner of Washington County, David R. Porter of Huntingdon County, and Francis R. Shunk of Pittsburgh. Thus, none came from the Philadelphia area, and only one from the region east of the Susquehanna.[23] Of the four, all but Porter, who was of Scotch-Irish extraction, were of German stock, a testimonial to the potency of a German name in a State-wide election. None was adept at organization or manipulation of party machinery, or could be considered a party leader, though Ritner was the perennial Antimasonic candidate for the gubernatorial office.

The legislature, officially the General Assembly, consisted of two houses, the Senate and the House of Representatives. The latter with a membership of one hundred was elected annually by districts. A small, rural county typically chose one, while Philadelphia city and county in 1832 elected seven and eight respectively. The Senate had thirty-three members; Senators were elected for four-year terms with approximately one-fourth retiring annually. The majority of the districts elected one member each; several, two; and Philadelphia County, three. Districts were apportioned every seven years in accordance with the number of taxables. The constitution anticipated the possibility

[23] Shunk had lived in Harrisburg until a short time before his election as Governor. William F. Johnston, who became Governor in 1848 when Shunk resigned, was also from western Pennsylvania. He has been omitted from this discussion since he served so briefly in this period.

THE SETTING

of gerrymandering by requiring that counties forming a district be adjoining and that no county be divided in order to form a senatorial district, but the provision did not discourage the majority party from using it to its advantage. The Antimasons, for example, made the apportionment of 1836 a masterpiece of gerrymandering.[24]

Among the occupational groups in the legislature the farmers were the most numerous, consistently making up about 50 per cent of the membership. Merchants, mechanics, and lawyers usually totaled from 10 to 15 per cent respectively. The House of Representatives of 1837, a rather typical body, had the following distribution:[25]

Farmers	48
Mechanics	16
Lawyers	14
Merchants	11
Physicians	2
Gentlemen	2
Miller	1
Artist	1
Accountant	1
Innkeeper	1
Engineer	1
Surveyors	2

The frequent elections encouraged a large turnover of membership in the House and placed a premium upon organization and continuity, while the small proportion of lawyers in bodies frequently beset by legal technicalities gave them a prominence beyond their numbers.

The ethnic background of the legislators reflected the various nationalities resident in the State. The German contingent was sizable enough to warrant the publishing of the House and Senate journals in German, but in numbers as well as in leadership they yielded to the Scotch-Irish, who found the political atmosphere of Harrisburg congenial to their interests and talents. Legislators met in joint session for the election of United States Senators and the State Treasurer, the parties generally meeting first in caucus to seek agreements upon candidates; and while the party convention had replaced the legislative caucus as the means of nominating candidates for Governor and electors for the Electoral College, legislators often occupied seats in these conventions and participated actively in the proceedings. The public took

---

[24] See Chapter IV.
[25] Mechanics included cabinetmakers, carpenters, hatters, millwrights, printers, tanners, blacksmiths, silver platers, and shoemakers. *Niles' Register*, LI (February 11, 1837), 384.

a keen interest in the deliberations of the legislature. Proceedings were rushed to Philadelphia via the "cars" upon the completion of the Philadelphia and Columbia Railroad in 1834 and published in the dailies less than forty-eight hours after their occurrence in Harrisburg. Larger papers employed reporters to supplement the debates. Interpretations were apt to be biased and given to extremes. A legislator who exerted leadership upon controversial issues could expect rough handling in the columns of the opposition press.

The judiciary of the State consisted of a Supreme Court and local courts, including courts of quarter sessions, oyer and terminer and general jail delivery, courts of common pleas, orphans' courts, registers' courts, and magistrates' courts. There were three justices of the Supreme Court, one Chief Justice and two Associate Justices. They held court in five districts. By 1832 courts of common pleas had been set up in sixteen districts; each was presided over by a president judge, who was assisted in each county in his circuit by a panel of three or four associate judges. The ascendancy of the Scotch-Irish here was similar to that in the legislature. Appointed to hold office during good behavior, judges enjoyed their tenure with little interference from the public during the 1830's. This contrasted with the previous decades when impeachments were not uncommon.[26] However, there was a growing repugnance to appointments for life, and the demand that judges serve for limited terms, coupled with the pressure to make justices of the peace and other local officers elective, contributed substantially to the calling of the constitutional convention in 1837.[27]

In 1832 Pennsylvania elected twenty-eight Congressmen to the House of Representatives. This was an increase of two over the previous decade and required an apportionment which augmented the districts from eighteen to twenty-five. In the absence of a decisive shift in political hegemony during the previous decade there was little excuse for the kind of gerrymandering which had marked the apportionment of 1822, when Democratic-Republicans had arranged the districts so as to minimize Federalist strength. The apportionment of 1832 merely reflected the more rapid growth of the western than the eastern counties.[28]

United States Senators were elected by the General Assembly in joint session after nominations had been made previously in the two houses.

[26] See Philip S. Klein, *Pennsylvania Politics, 1817-1832: A Game Without Rules* (Philadelphia, 1940), 30-32.
[27] See Chapter VI.
[28] See the Appendix for apportionment of 1832.

Both bodies habitually drew up long lists of nominees with the result that many ballots were occasionally required to obtain a majority of the whole number for a candidate. In 1833, for example, when Democrats failed to reach an agreement upon a candidate, an election could not be consummated during the entire session.[29] Party leaders made strenuous efforts to avoid such contests by caucusing prior to the balloting, but they were not always successful. In fact, the failure of such a caucus enabled Simon Cameron to vault into the Senate in 1845.[30] Products of "logrolling" and compromise, successful candidates in this era were generally commonplace and carried little weight in Washington. Among the personnel, which included William Wilkins, Samuel McKean, Daniel Sturgeon, Simon Cameron, and James Buchanan, only the latter distinguished himself at the national capital.[31]

Pennsylvanians also held hundreds of appointive posts which stemmed from Washington. The most coveted of these, membership in the President's cabinet, seldom came their way, however, since executives hesitated to face the wrath of the dissatisfied elements which inevitably accompanied such appointments. Jackson retained William J. Duane as his Secretary of the Treasury for a few months in 1833 for the purpose of "removing" government deposits in the Bank, but ignored the State's claims thereafter. Van Buren avoided naming a Pennsylvanian to his cabinet until the closing months of his term when he appointed Henry D. Gilpin as Attorney General. Harrison refused to decide between the quarreling Whigs and Antimasons in 1840, though Tyler, anxious to obtain support wherever he could find it, took two of the State's politicians into his fold and had a third rejected by the Senate.[32]

It was not until 1845 when Polk named Buchanan as Secretary of State that a Pennsylvanian played a prominent role in a presidential administration. The State fared better in the courts than in the cabinet, supplying an Associate Justice to the Supreme Court throughout this era. Henry Baldwin, a Jackson appointee, served until his death in 1846, and Polk was prepared to appoint another resident of the State in his place, but it required persistence since his first nominee

[29] See page 31.
[30] See pages 188-189.
[31] Sturgeon was twice elected due to disagreements over men who were more prominent than he. Cameron's reputation was made a decade later after he had abandoned the Democratic party for the Republican party.
[32] Walter Forward, Secretary of the Treasury, 1841-1843; William Wilkins, Secretary of War, 1844-1845. James M. Porter was rejected as Secretary of War in 1844; see page 170.

was rejected by the Senate due to a factional dispute among the Democrats. He finally secured the confirmation of a second nominee, Robert C. Grier.[33] Appointive offices of a local character varied from the collectorship of the port of Philadelphia, desired for the patronage which it controlled, and the postmastership of Philadelphia, almost equally attractive, to the smallest of the more than nine hundred postmasterships.[34] Positions valued highly included Naval Yard offices in Philadelphia, directorship of the United States Mint, district judgeships, attorneyships, and marshalcies. From the highest to the lowest, they were regarded as the spoils of victory, to reward those who had labored but had not received positions from the State. The list of officeholders included a considerable proportion of the elder politicians and hangers-on. The supply never equaled the demand.

The Electorate

If the extensive authority of the Governor exerted a conservative influence, the franchise tended to offset it. Few males were disqualified from voting by the constitutional provision which made eligibility dependent upon the payment of a State or county tax.[35] In fact, it approached a universal, male franchise even before the Constitution of 1838 guaranteed "white" manhood suffrage, and years before restrictive provisions were deleted from the constitutions of neighboring states. This broad electorate affected the politics of the State from the start. It discouraged the concentration of power in the hands of small groups. Henry Adams, writing of the State as it was about 1800, gave particular emphasis to this.

> The only true democratic community then existing in the eastern States, Pennsylvania was neither picturesque nor troublesome. The State contained no hierarchy like that of New England; no great families like those of New York; no oligarchy like the planters of Virginia and South Carolina.[36]

Albert Gallatin noted similarly with pardonable pride:

> In Pennsylvania not only we have neither Livingstons nor Rensselaers, but from the suburbs of Philadelphia to the banks of the Ohio I do not know of a single family that has any extensive influence. An equal distribution of property has rendered every

---

[33] See pages 192-193.

[34] Thomas F. Gordon, *A Gazetteer of the State of Pennsylvania* (Philadelphia, 1832), 503-508. The author lists 968 in 1830.

[35] Article III, Sec. 1.

[36] Henry Adams, *History of the United States of America*, 9 vols. (New York, 1889-1891), I, 114-115.

individual independent, and there is among us true and real equality.[37]

On election day voters generally turned out in force despite the difficulties in transportation. Gubernatorial elections usually attracted the greatest numbers; that of 1835, for example, brought out 65 per cent of the electorate to the polls.[38] Inspectors checked the voters against the tax lists; the device was simple and generally effective, but subject to abuse in the cities, particularly Philadelphia. The coalition of Whigs and Antimasons imposed a registration law upon Philadelphia in 1836 for the expressed purpose of preventing alleged "importations" on election days.[39] Democrats maintained that this was a mere subterfuge designed to restrain the laborer from voting, since registration would place a hardship upon him by taking him from his work. They repealed the law at the earliest opportunity.

POLITICAL METHODS

The local unit of political organization was the county. In each, groups of officeholders, federal, State, and local, acted as nuclei to perform the mundane tasks during slack seasons, to take the initiative in launching campaigns, and to participate in the patronage if success crowned their efforts. Typical activities included correspondence with committees in other counties, maintenance of local newspapers, preparations for celebrations, particularly the Fourth of July and, among the Democrats, Jackson Day on the eighth of January, and organization of committees of vigilance to scrutinize the movements of opponents in order to avoid trickery during campaigns and on election days.

They also assumed the leadership in making nominations for offices. The procedure was simple and informal. They would issue the call for a meeting, now termed a convention, but differing little from the traditional caucus which was in bad repute with the public, prepare a ticket in advance, and usually secure its acceptance from the assembled party members. The process was not without serious weaknesses, however. All too frequently factions called the conventions on short notice and at times and places unsatisfactory to their rivals. The organization of the meeting was also subject to abuses. A clique sometimes

---

[37] Quoted, *ibid.,* 115.
[38] Taxables in 1835 numbered 309,421. *Pennsylvania Archives,* 4th Series, 12 vols. (Harrisburg, 1900-1902), VI, 641. The total vote was 200,629. *Hazard's Register,* XVI (1835), 341.
[39] See page 74.

arrived early by arrangement, seized the platform, proceeded with the business, and, if necessary, locked the doors. Such an incident occurred in Reading in 1834 as Democrats prepared for the gubernatorial nomination of the following year. A participant, reporting the incident to Governor Wolf, noted,

> By the time I had obtained the key to the public-room, the stairs had been crowded and the reverend Gentleman [Henry A. Muhlenberg] in the midst of them. As soon as I had opened the door, they rushed in the room, Muhlenberg among them as pale as death, and before ten persons could [enter] the room, James Donagan, with his usual boldness nominated Muhlenberg chairman.[40]

Dissidents retaliated by holding a second convention, nominating a rival list, and declaring the previous meeting irregular. Lacking machinery to iron out such situations, disagreements often persisted long after the incidents which provoked them had lost their significance. With all of its faults, however, the convention system provided a means of registering opinion at the grass roots which would otherwise have been ignored.

State-wide party organization was almost as loose and as informal as in the counties; the vigorous sectionalism, based on geographic, economic, and social factors, mentioned above, precluding a close-knit structure. The Antimasons maintained a central standing committee which provided for a systematic exchange of views and the calling of conventions. The Democrats and National Republicans lacked even such a simple arrangement. Among the officeholders the Deputy Secretary of the Commonwealth was regarded as the unofficial adviser to the Governor upon political matters. The office was usually reserved for a personal friend of the executive who had promoted his candidacy. Governor Wolf appointed his son-in-law, Henry Buehler; Ritner named Joseph Wallace, the chairman of the Antimasonic Central Committee; and Porter chose Henry Petriken, an editor and an original Porter man, for this post. But there was no party chairman, no treasury, and no permanent party organization. The parties usually reserved March 4 as the date for conventions to nominate candidates for Governor, to select delegates to national conventions, to choose slates of nominees for presidential electors, and to transact other party

---

[40] Jacob Marshall to George Wolf, August 14, 1834, Secretary of the Commonwealth, Minutes and Papers, Miscellaneous, Division of Public Records, Pennsylvania Historical and Museum Commission. Democratic opponents of Wolf were backing Muhlenberg for the nomination. See Chapter III.

business. The date was convenient in that it fell prior to the adjournment of the legislature. It was also early enough to permit a full-fledged campaign before the State elections in October and late enough to avoid traveling in the dead of winter.

State conventions by 1832 had become systematized to the extent that membership was apportioned to districts in accordance with their representation in the legislature, but this did not guarantee that the machinery would operate smoothly. Due to the failure of the local conventions, mentioned above, the State conventions were frequently beset with the problem of admitting one of two delegations, both claiming legitimacy. When a contest was close and disputed delegations numerous, the outcome of this preliminary issue was decisive in determining the ultimate nomination. In 1835 such a dispute divided the Democrats into two warring factions, each supporting its respective nominee for Governor, resulting in the election of an Antimason.[41] In 1844 a similar split was narrowly averted.[42] There were more successes than failures, however, and the nominations were generally reached after considerable "horse-trading" in the convention and not as a result of dictation from a machine or boss.

It is difficult for contemporary Americans to appreciate the zest for the political fray which was characteristic a century ago. Campaigns were both spirited and colorful, and occasionally hysterical.

In the forefront of the contest was the press. Newspapers were almost universally identified with politics. Many sprouted during the heat of the campaign only to wither during the dormant months which followed. Those which survived the tests of time commonly owed their existence to printing contracts derived from their political connections. Thus a campaign was often a fight for survival, a struggle in which editors castigated their own fraternity as savagely as they belabored the opposition candidates. Few holds were barred. Ridicule heaped upon nominees would today be regarded as scurrilous and libelous. The threat of libel suits was commonplace, but there were few prosecutions. Occasionally, newspapers enriched their accounts with cartoons. In fact, in the campaign of 1838 drawings of Ritner in unflattering poses gave the papers a modern tabloid effect.[43] Printers also issued numerous extra editions, handbills, broadsides, and biographies. All in all, their contributions to the campaign were unsurpassed by other media of expression.

[41] See pages 56-58.
[42] See pages 181-182.
[43] See page 129.

Rallies, demonstrations, parades, and oratory were of course universal. Leaders took pains to gather and edit the toasts prior to their presentation and to publicize every gathering as a multitude. Strangely enough, when compared with a modern election, the candidates remained on the side lines, confining their activities to letter-writing, since the tradition that the office sought the man deterred them from taking the stump.[44]

Because of the lack of co-ordination, the small circulations and the independence of the newspapers, and the diversity of sectional interests, there was considerable variation in the campaign from place to place. Opposition to the Bank of the United States in 1834, for example, was a rallying force among Democrats in the West, but a source of embarrassment to their associates in the Philadelphia area. The situation was a challenge to local politicians and editors, and the skill which they displayed in accepting and rejecting or reconciling national, State, and local issues spelled the difference between victory and defeat.

Political Parties

By 1832 parties as distinguished from factions were emerging after a long era of Democratic-Republican supremacy had virtually extinguished the party system. The Democratic-Republicans had swept into power in 1799, forecasting the Jeffersonian Revolution which followed a year later. Their victory was not the result of organization or a common cause, but was a protest against Federalism, associated with privilege, entrenched power, and taxes on homes and whiskey. It also reflected a class and sectional cleavage. They were strongest in the rural West, weakest in the commercial East. Their extended tenure resulted from a combination of factors which are difficult to appraise individually. It was due in part to the weakness of the Federalists and their early decline nationally. Possibly their greatest strength was their identification with the "will of the people" from 1799 onward. Among an electorate based upon virtual manhood suffrage, equalitarian slogans had a tremendous appeal, and farmers and artisans traditionally supported the party at the polls regardless of changing issues and candidates. In the era after the War of 1812 Democratic-Republicans came to the support of such Hamiltonian principles as the protective tariff, internal improvements constructed by the federal and State governments, and the Second Bank of the United States. They remained

[44] See pages 185-186.

flexible, however. They absorbed the enlarged functions of government without eliminating those who dissented, and maintained their identity with the popular will.

A party so comprehensive could not long remain meaningful in terms of a practical program, and it soon mirrored the geographic, economic, and social divisions among the citizenry. By 1820 the confusion over party names was so extreme that newspapers abandoned their efforts to link the candidates for Governor to any party. Rival factions were termed simply "Hiesterites" and "Findlayites."[45] The presidential election of 1824 revealed similar tendencies. There were friends of Crawford, Adams, Calhoun, Clay, and Jackson, but no parties worthy of the name, though Jackson and Calhoun had aggressive factional support.

> It was not until the spring of 1828 that the people of Pennsylvania finally relinquished all former partisan affiliations and took their places under the standards of Jackson and Adams. It was only then that county politicians generally adopted the presidential issue as the basis of their local division. The tickets were headed by the names of two presidential candidates for the first time in a score of years, and the terms Federalist and Democrat or the names of rival candidates for governor ceased temporarily to be the guiding lines of county political division.[46]

Upon the restoration of the two-party system in 1828 the Jackson party or Democrats assumed a dominant position in the State, the popular vote for President showing 101,652 ballots for Jackson and 50,848 for Adams. The returns did not divulge, however, that the Jackson men were divided into two hostile camps—the Calhoun or "Eleventh Hour Men," and "Amalgamation Men" or "Original" Jackson Men. The former was headed by Samuel D. Ingham, Jackson's Secretary of the Treasury until he became a casualty of the Jackson-Calhoun imbroglio. Since they adhered to Calhoun as long as he remained in the field for the Presidency in the election of 1828, and then made a last-minute switch to Jackson, they were dubbed "Eleventh Hour Men" by their rivals, the "Original" Jackson Men, who were the Republicans and former Federalists who endorsed Jackson in 1824.[47] Because of

---

[45] For Joseph Hiester and William Findlay, see Klein, *Pennsylvania Politics*, 109.
[46] *Ibid.*, 251.
[47] Joining in the cry of "bargain and sale" against Adams and Clay, this group had continued to campaign for the "Old Hero" until his election in 1828.

their diverse origins the latter, in turn, were called "Amalgamators" by the Calhoun-Ingham faction.

Upon the election of Jackson the two groups competed for leadership. The struggle was frequently bitter; and resulting enmities endured to embarrass the Democratic party for more than a decade. The immediate advantages were gained by the Calhoun men. Ingham took a seat in the cabinet; George Wolf with Ingham's backing defeated Isaac D. Barnard, the candidate of the Amalgamation Men, for the gubernatorial nomination after a heated contest; and George M. Dallas, with the support of the Calhoun forces, was elected to the United States Senate. But the fall of Calhoun in Washington undermined the influence of his supporters in the State. Ingham retired from the cabinet, discredited. His organization collapsed, and Wolf and his confederates were left to shift for themselves.[48]

Having overthrown the Calhoun party in the State, Jackson further distracted his partisans by naming Van Buren as his choice for Vice President in 1832 and ultimate successor to the Presidency. He could have given his blessing to no one less acceptable. Calhoun men charged Van Buren with plotting their leader's downfall, and few Democrats dissented from the view that he was a fawning politician and the head of a corrupt political machine. Accordingly, they closed their ears to the call for a national convention and proceeded to make their own nomination for Vice President. They would not be pacified and cast their thirty electoral votes for William Wilkins of Pittsburgh, colleague of Dallas in the Senate. With Van Buren in the Vice Presidency, however, they found their position embarrassing, and an about-face distasteful. But short of bolting the party, they had no alternative except to fall in line.

Jackson's opposition to the recharter of the Bank of the United States was another damaging blow to Democratic unity. The Bank was scarcely a controversial issue in the State. It had been chartered by the Democratic-Republican party and had been accepted in time by all political factions. In fact, its prestige had never been higher than at the moment Jackson issued his veto message. Only two months before, Wolf had affixed his signature to a joint resolution of the legislature, adopted unanimously, expressing confidence in the Bank. In the Pennsylvania congressional delegation, both National Republicans and Jackson men had supported the recharter bill and with but

[48] For the origins and the activities of the rival Jackson factions, see Klein, *Pennsylvania Politics*.

two exceptions had voted for its passage.[49] The veto, delivered in the heat of the gubernatorial campaign of 1832, placed Wolf in an unenviable position; he could afford to repudiate neither Jackson nor the Bank. The harassed executive sought refuge in silence, trusting that his record would attract the voters regardless of their attitude toward the recharter.

It is difficult to appraise Jackson's influence upon the election. In 1829 Wolf carried Philadelphia by a safe margin, and the vigor with which he supported the Public Works led him to anticipate a larger majority in 1832. But these services were lost upon the National Republicans, who abandoned him for Ritner, the Antimasonic candidate, in their frenzy to destroy anyone tinged with Jacksonism, and Wolf lost the city by 1,400 votes. In a letter to a close friend, he bitterly assailed the National Republicans for linking his name and candidacy to Jackson, and had nothing but contempt for the argument which they had advanced, that

> to put down Jackson it was necessary to put down Wolf. I never have when a candidate taken any measures to promote my own election. I never coupled myself with Andrew Jackson. The people did that of their own accord without consulting me. I had neither lot nor part in the matter but it has had its effect to greatly injure if not destroy altogether my election.[50]

His forebodings upon the outcome of the election in the State proved to be unnecessarily pessimistic, but his prediction that the National Republicans would desert him proved to be accurate.

The presidential election a month later clearly demonstrated that Jackson could withstand the shock of an encounter with Calhoun, the foisting of an unpopular vice presidential candidate upon the party, and an assault upon the Bank. But he did not leave the battle unscathed, his margin decreasing from approximately 51,000 to 24,000 votes, and his followers emerged from the victory divided and confused. Many Jackson men echoed the sentiments of Henry King, a member of Congress and confidant of the Governor. Writing of the gulf which separated what he regarded as Pennsylvania interests from those emanating from Washington, he complained,

> The *Telegraph* is for nullification and free trade . . . and the *Globe* which at least ought to pay some regard to the interests,

[49] Adam King of York County voted in the negative; Henry A. Muhlenberg of Berks did not vote. *Niles' Register*, XLVI (March 8, 1834), 18.

[50] Wolf to Roberts Vaux, October [10], 1832, Vaux Papers, Historical Society of Pennsylvania.

> the wishes—and if you will call them so—the prejudices of Pennsylvania—is anti-tariff, anti-Union and opposed to the Supreme Court and the Bank of the United States. And yet this is the organ of our party at the seat of the National Government. We are attached to "Old Hickory"—but I do not exactly comprehend why for that reason we should be used in this way—every . . . Pennsylvania policy treated with scorn.[51]

Wolf had won a re-election by 91,335 votes to 88,165 by avoiding commitments upon the Vice Presidency, the national convention, and the Bank recharter. But time was running out; he would have to run with the hare or hunt with the hounds. Could Jackson men in Pennsylvania harmonize their "prejudices" with the Jackson-Van Buren leadership in Washington?

The National Republican party, beginning as a faction among the Democratic-Republicans and evolving into the Whig party, had its origins in the campaign of 1824, the Jackson-Adams controversy which accompanied the latter's Presidency, and the issues growing out of Jackson's two terms of office. At the outset of Adams' administration his followers were woefully deficient in organization, and their plight was not eased by Adams who refused to use the patronage to build a party. Yet forces were at work molding an anti-Jackson organization. The violence with which the Jackson managers assaulted the President turned the federal officeholders as well as the Clay men to the defense. Many Pennsylvanians were suspicious of the southern influence, particularly that of Virginia, in the Jackson movement, fearing that it might prove inimical to internal improvements and manufacturing. The contest over the Woolens Bill weakened Jackson, especially in the West. Ritner, soon to become the Antimasonic nominee for Governor, was among those who deserted Jackson when the Woolens Bill met defeat. On the positive side, Adams' support of internal improvements and protection gained friends for him among the leaders of the Shulze administration and the conservative elements of the population.[52] By 1828

> the outstanding names of Pennsylvania were at the service of the Adams party. The most distinguished ministers of the gospel, educators, authors, editors, merchants, bankers, coal and iron barons, scientists, statesmen and philanthropic citizens were on the side of the Administration.[53]

---

[51] King to Wolf, February 15, 1832, George Wolf Political Correspondence, Historical Society of Pennsylvania.
[52] John Andrew Shulze, Governor, 1823-1829.
[53] Klein, *Pennsylvania Politics*, 226-227.

They did not add up to victory on election day, but Adams' electors polled majorities in Beaver and Erie counties in the west, Adams in the south, and Bucks and Delaware in the east.

National Republicans continued to enroll recruits during Jackson's first term as they dropped from the ranks of the Democrats, victims of the factional strife and the controversies surrounding his administration. The collapse of the Calhoun party and the rise of Van Buren, the Maysville Road and Bank vetoes produced new contingents of volunteers. In fact, the National Republicans might have built a formidable opposition party if their growth had not been cut short by the unexpected emergence of a third party, Antimasonry.

Pennsylvania historians have likened the Antimasonic movement to the mass frenzy which produced the witchcraft trials in Salem in the seventeenth century.[54] It might be looked upon, also, as a manifestation of the ferment which characterized the second quarter of the nineteenth century. People who were stirred by the emotional appeal of abolitionism, temperance, perfectionism, evangelism, and democracy were apt to feel an affinity for the tenets of Antimasonry. Popular resentment toward Masonry in Pennsylvania antedated the rise of political Antimasonry. Democratic citizens, particularly among the Scotch-Irish, mechanics, and farmers, saw in Masonry the symbol of an outmoded aristocracy, a state within the state, which operated behind the cloak of secrecy to further the well-being of its members. In their eyes, Masons appeared to hold a virtual monopoly upon the professions and public offices and to exert an undue influence upon the execution of the law and the functioning of the courts. The mere pardoning of a convict in Pittsburgh was sufficient to produce the rumor that it had been effected by Masonic influence. "It was even said that criminals in the dock had been seen to give the signal of distress to Masons in the jury box."[55] Quakers and Germans belonging to pietistic sects disliked the oath-taking and ritual observed by the order. A committee of Presbyterians objected to a society which embraced "with equal affection the Pagan, the Turk, and the Christian,"[56] and five churches in Pittsburgh refused to permit the use of their buildings for a Masonic

[54] *Ibid.*, 278; J. Cutler Andrews, "The Antimasonic Movement in Western Pennsylvania," *Western Pennsylvania Historical Magazine*, XVIII (1935), 256.
[55] John N. Boucher (ed.), *A Century and a Half of Pittsburg and Her People*, 4 vols. (New York, 1908), I, 398.
[56] Report of a committee of the Presbyterian Synod at Pittsburgh in 1820, cited in Andrews, "The Antimasonic Movement in Western Pennsylvania," 256.

memorial service.[57] Political Antimasonry thus put into tangible form a widespread, latent hostility.

The transformation of this popular antagonism against Masonry into a political party was facilitated by the fact that the newly formed party lines separating Democrats from National Republicans had not yet hardened, and voters, in contrast to the behavior of more recent generations of Pennsylvanians, did not hesitate to sever their ties with the major parties. Thus, when reports were received from New York in 1828 that Masons had committed murder to prevent the revelation of their secrets, thousands of Pennsylvanians were prepared to accept it as truth, and when the outcry in New York took the nature of a political party, they hastily joined the movement.

The party, as it took shape, lacked effective leadership. The experienced politicians were either National Republicans or Democrats and wary of a party founded upon such an unorthodox principle. For this reason, guidance came from the ranks or from politicians whose ambitions had been thwarted and who, like Thurlow Weed, were prepared to seize Antimasonry as a means of salvaging their political fortunes. Ritner, who had twice failed to gain the gubernatorial nomination and had forfeited his chances of making a third attempt by differing with the Jackson men on the Woolens Bill, obtained a reprieve by entering the party; Amos Ellmaker of Lancaster County, a former Attorney General of the State who had used his office to support a second term for Adams, similarly found new opportunities in the organization. Joseph Lawrence of Washington County and Ner Middleswarth of Union County also were veteran officeholders who found in Antimasonry the means of making a second start; but, by and large, leaders who pushed to the fore were untried in the political game, and leadership was never commensurate with the size of the party.

The organization of the party began in 1828 in scattered localities and spread across the State during the summer of 1829. Its initial State convention in June, 1829, was a slender affair with thirty-five delegates from fourteen widely dispersed counties. The opposition ridiculed the meeting, but the election results the following October revealed that it could not be taken lightly. Wolf defeated Ritner by a safe margin, but the latter polled an astounding 61,000 votes and received majorities in seventeen counties.[58] The returns indicated the regions where Antimasonry would continue to flourish for a decade; the extreme

[57] *Ibid.*, 259.
[58] Wolf, 78,219; Ritner, 61,776. *Hazard's Register*, IV (1829), 394.

Northwest, Washington County in the Southwest, the southern tier of counties, and the Southeast.[59] Ritner's remarkable showing, it should be noted, was due only in part to the growth of Antimasonry; a substantial number of Democrats of the Amalgamation faction cast their ballots for him after having furiously contested the nomination of Wolf.[60]

Reassured by their performance, Antimasons turned to the prosaic task of party-building. They organized a State central committee and encouraged the founding of newspapers. In a short time there were dozens of sheets proclaiming the evils of Masonry. In 1831 State leaders took a prominent part in the Antimasonic National Convention, hailed by later generations of social scientists as the first of its kind in American annals, and secured the nomination of Amos Ellmaker for Vice President as the running mate for William Wirt for President.

Subsequent gains, however, were confined largely to the regions where they had won their first successes, with the result that while some counties returned consistent majorities in State and local contests, others barely commanded a corporal's guard. An important contributing factor in this situation was the growing unpopularity of the Public Works in the counties beyond their orbit. Here Antimasonry became the voice of opposition, particularly after the adoption of a direct tax in 1831 brought home the costliness of the project. Retrenchment continued to be a powerful stimulant to Antimasonry after its pristine vigor had begun to abate.

While Antimasonry was sectional, it gathered its members from no particular racial stock. In western counties, it was supported by the Scotch-Irish, and in Union, Lebanon, and Lancaster counties by citizenry of German stock. Lancaster County polled the largest majorities in the State for Antimasonry, while Berks, also German, remained consistently Democratic. In Union County, the southern townships, predominantly German, were hotbeds of Antimasonry, while the northern townships, with Scotch-Irish antecedents, turned in Democratic majorities. The two sections were isolated, however, and frequently at odds in local affairs.[61] The Antimasons were aware of the clannishness of the "Pennsylvania Dutch" and the magic of a German name at the polls, but in using this device they were merely emulating the older parties.

[59] The latter did not include Philadelphia, city or county. The Antimasonic vote there was only about 5 per cent of the total.
[60] Klein, *Pennsylvania Politics*, 282-286.
[61] The southern half of the county was separated in 1855 to form Snyder County.

The sectional nature of the party handicapped it in competition with the Democrats in a State-wide contest. A coalition of National Republicans or Whigs and Antimasons, however, might give them the control of the State. The result was a recurring tussle between principle and expediency. In counties such as Lancaster where the Antimasons were dominant, they generally opposed any combination with National Republicans. Concessions to Clay men, they insisted, constituted a compromise with Masonry and a sacrifice of principle. In the words of a Lancaster County committeeman, "I would sooner—a thousand times—and so would the Antimasonic party of this county vote for Jackson at once, than be guilty of such a desertion of principle as that proposed by the Clay Masons." He regarded four additional years of Jackson as preferable to eight years of Masonry and Clay.[62] But where Antimasons were weak, a coalition with any or all opponents of the Democrats seemed to be the only means of obtaining an ascendancy.[63] In 1832 the "Exclusives" gained control of the party convention, nominated Ritner for Governor, and completely ignored the claims of the National Republicans. It proved to be sound strategy. The hapless National Republicans, weakened by the inroads of Antimasonry and prepared to take the offensive only in Philadelphia and Pittsburgh, accepted Ritner as the lesser of evils and made no nomination; but this policy offered slight comfort to those laboring to win adherents in Democratic strongholds.

As indicated above, Wolf was re-elected in 1832 after a tight squeeze. The Antimasons, however, received majorities in twenty counties and polled 88,000 votes. They failed to seat Ritner by a bare 3,000 ballots. A slight shift of opinion would place the State in their hands.

With the campaign behind them, Pennsylvania politicians paused to take stock and prepare to launch new offensives. In Philadelphia, National Republican leaders proposed a rapprochement with the Wolf men. Admitting that they had abandoned Wolf, they denied, nonetheless, any hostility to his administration. Their desire to defeat Jackson, they explained, blinded them temporarily; under the circumstances they would have "voted for a post if set up—as soon as Ritner." They now proposed to support Wolf in the legislature in return for the election of John Sergeant to the United States Senate. If the latter proved to be impossible, they would agree to back Samuel McKean,

---

[62] Zephaniah McLenegan to Joseph Wallace, September 13, 1832, Brigadier General William MacPherson Papers, Historical Society of Pennsylvania.

[63] John Borrows to Joseph Wallace, September 7, 1832, *ibid.*

the choice of the Wolf Democrats.[64] John McLean, Associate Justice of the United States Supreme Court, ambitious to unite elements hostile to Van Buren into a party which would promote his candidacy for the Presidency, also urged such a reconciliation.[65] Wolf received this proffer of friendship with ill grace, but McKean toyed with the idea in the hope that it would effect his election to the Senate.[66]

The senatorial election, however, proved to be a stumbling block in the path of the National Republican bid for unity. Neither McKean nor Sergeant would withdraw. Antimasons endorsed a candidate of their own, and the Amalgamation Men cast their votes for Henry A. Muhlenberg, member of Congress from Berks County. The result was a deadlock which remained unbroken despite repeated balloting throughout the session of the legislature. McKean was soon convinced that the National Republicans were insincere and had no intention of making him their choice.[67]

The quarrel continued after the adjournment of the legislature, with the Amalgamation press showing an inclination to support James Buchanan for the post. The latter was identified as an Amalgamator, but he was both conciliatory and available. A Federalist during his early political life, he had been one of the first Pennsylvanians to mount the Jackson bandwagon, and Jackson's friendship was at once a political asset. Involvement in the "bargain and sale" controversy had sidetracked him to a diplomatic post in Russia, but the possibility of an election to the Senate now made him restless to return.[68] He received flattering reports from his friends, one observer declaring that only his arrival in the United States was required to effect it.[69] He at first found Jackson reluctant, but finally obtained his consent by stressing his duty to his aged mother.[70] He reached Pennsylvania two weeks

[64] Joel Jones to George Wolf, January 1, 1833, Secretary of the Commonwealth, Minutes and Papers, Miscellaneous. Jones was reporting a conversation with Horace Binney. James Kay to Henry Buehler, December 31, 1832, *ibid.*

[65] Nicholas Biddle to John McLean, January 30, 1833, John McLean Papers, Library of Congress.

[66] James Kay to Henry Buehler, December 31, 1832, Secretary of the Commonwealth, Minutes and Papers, Miscellaneous; McKean to McLean, January 22, 1833, McLean Papers.

[67] McKean to McLean, January 22, 1833, *ibid.*

[68] Klein, *Pennsylvania Politics*, 177-181.

[69] George Plitt to Buchanan, April 4, 1833, James Buchanan Papers, Historical Society of Pennsylvania; Plitt to Buchanan, July 19, 1833, Buchanan-Johnston Papers, Library of Congress.

[70] Buchanan to Andrew Jackson, May 29, 1833, John Bassett Moore (ed.), *The Works of James Buchanan, Comprising His Speeches, State Papers, and Private Correspondence*, 12 vols. (Philadelphia, 1908-1911), II, 341; Jackson to Buchanan, March 21, 1833, Buchanan Papers.

prior to the opening of the legislature only to be disappointed. The Democratic majority was prepared to agree upon McKean.

The protracted senatorial contest had two significant results. It served to aggravate old enmities among the Democrats which had been shelved temporarily during the gubernatorial campaign. Administration supporters labeled the Muhlenberg group "disorganizers" for their refusal to adhere to the caucus choice. The latter, with little chance of success, urged that the issue be returned to the people and settled at the polls. The stalemate also contributed to the acceptance by the Democrats of the national convention and the nomination of Van Buren with which it was identified. At the outset both Eleventh Hour Men and Amalgamators were reluctant to be associated with Van Buren. However, when his election to the Vice Presidency was assured, the Amalgamators among the presidential electors hastened to announce that although they were instructed to vote for Wilkins they were not opposed to Van Buren. Amalgamation newspapers took a similar position. Their motive was obvious; by falling in line with Jackson's plan for the succession they might claim to be the Jackson party in the State. At the same time, it would emphasize the irregularity of the Wolf administration in general and of McKean in particular, since the latter was an outspoken critic of both the national convention and Van Buren.

Most vindictive of the Amalgamation editors was James Gordon Bennett. As the self-appointed champion of Van Buren and the national convention in Pennsylvania, he fanned the smoldering senatorial issue through the summer and autumn of 1833 in the columns of the *Pennsylvanian*. Calling for union and harmony in one issue, he invited discord in another. McKean, he declared, "hates the Vice President with a most holy and enthusiastic hatred . . . he dreams of Van Buren by night, swears at him by day."[71] He carried on a running battle with the Harrisburg *Reporter*, the acknowledged mouthpiece of the Wolf forces, and eventually crossed swords with the *Globe*, the Jackson organ in Washington.[72] The latter proved to be his undoing.[73] The *Globe* denied Bennett's charge that it opposed McKean. It favored

[71] Philadelphia *Pennsylvanian*, June 21, 1833.
[72] *Ibid.*, July 30, August 1, 12, 1833.
[73] Van Buren would have welcomed McKean's defeat, but he did not consider it advisable to interfere lest he should split the party now strengthened by the election of 1833. John C. Fitzpatrick (ed.), *The Autobiography of Martin Van Buren*, American Historical Association, *Annual Report, 1918*, Vol. II (Washington, 1920), 763.

any Democrat, it insisted, who held the confidence of the party. Turning its sights upon Bennett, it called him a hypocrite in the employ of the Bank of the United States.[74] Bennett gave up the struggle quickly. Cut off from sources of credit by the federal officeholders in Philadelphia, he turned to Nicholas Biddle for funds, apparently without success.[75] Before the close of the year he retired from Pennsylvania and the turmoil of its politics to New York City.[76]

Whatever Bennett's motives may have been, his spirited advocacy of the national convention brought the question into focus and influenced wavering editors in its favor. By the time the legislature convened in December, 1833, a majority of the Democratic papers had given it their approval.

Democrats in the new legislature also revealed a willingness to compromise. Muhlenberg withdrew after the first ballot in the senatorial contest, and McKean was elected on the third ballot.[77] The Wolf men then went into caucus with the Amalgamators and adopted a resolution in favor of the national convention.[78]

The Senator-elect was a power to be reckoned with in the inner circles at Harrisburg. A veteran politician from Bradford County with an active following along the Northern Tier, Secretary of the Commonwealth and confidant of the executive, he was recognized as the political spokesman of the Wolf faction. A bitter partisan, he was frequently in the midst of controversy. His hostility toward Van Buren was of long standing and without qualification. Anxious to allay dissatisfaction in Washington with his election, the Harrisburg *Reporter* quickly offered assurance that McKean was entering the Senate as the friend of all Jackson measures. It hailed his victory as a harbinger of good will.[79] But in less than two weeks McKean dispelled all doubt about his dislike for both Van Buren and the national convention. In a letter to the *American Sentinel* in Philadelphia, he declared, "I am and always have been, decidedly and unequivocally opposed to this singular innovation upon the established usages of the Democratic

[74] Washington *Globe*, September 7, October 29, 1833. The *Globe* did not err in naming Bennett a hypocrite. While editing the *Pennsylvanian* and posing as an ardent supporter of Jackson and Van Buren, he was secretly advising Biddle on ways and means of wearing away Jackson's confidence in Van Buren. See Bennett to Biddle, August 25, 1833, Nicholas Biddle Papers, Library of Congress.
[75] Bennett to Biddle, September 17, 1833, *ibid*.
[76] Washington *Globe*, December 5, 1833.
[77] Philadelphia *Pennsylvanian*, December 9, 1833.
[78] *Ibid*., December 19, 1833.
[79] Reprinted in Philadelphia *Pennsylvanian*, December 13, 1833.

party, and adverse to the consummation of the 'single' and especial object intended to be accomplished by it."[80]

McKean had flung down the gauntlet, but his defiance was not reciprocated by his faction in the legislature. His political star sank rapidly.

[80] Dated December 15, 1833, and reprinted in *Niles' Register*, XLV (December 28, 1833), 295. See also Henry R. Mueller, *The Whig Party in Pennsylvania, Columbia University Studies in History, Economics and Public Law*, CI, No. 2 (New York, 1922), 20.

CHAPTER II

Jackson and the Whigs, 1833-1834

WHILE Pennsylvania Democrats wrangled over the senatorial election, Jackson set the stage for a more devastating internecine struggle. The Bank charter had been initiated by National Republican strategists, Jackson's role being confined to the interposition of his challenging veto. But now he decided to carry the war to his opponents by the removal of the federal deposits in the Bank of the United States. The contest which followed was one of the most spectacular in the political life of the State.

Preferring to face the consequences at once rather than risk the wrath of the Bank in the election year of 1836, Jackson prepared to reduce the Bank to impotence by the gradual reduction of governmental deposits amounting to the sizable sum of ten to twelve million dollars. Biddle retaliated by immediately calling in the Bank's loans, reducing its discounts, and curtailing its activities in general so sharply that he plunged the nation into a Bank-created depression. The policy was deliberately undertaken with the expectation that the ensuing money panic would excite public opinion against the interference of Jackson to such a degree that the latter would be compelled to accept the recharter. The significance of Pennsylvania's position in the contest hardly requires mention. Philadelphia was the home of the Bank; Pennsylvanians had been active in obtaining its charter and zealous in its defense. At the same time the State had returned overwhelming majorities for Jackson in three presidential elections, and was his greatest source of strength in the East.

Curtailment of credits was begun in August, 1833, and continued until the following summer. By September money was scarce; and in November *Niles' Register* observed "a most severe pressure for money."[1] State banknotes were depreciating and interest rates were rising. In December, 1833, laborers were being discharged and extreme gloom pervaded the money market. During the early months of 1834 there were numerous business failures reaching a peak in May.

---

[1] *Niles' Register*, XLV (September 7, 1833), 17. See Ralph C. H. Catterall, *The Second Bank of the United States* (Chicago, 1902), 326.

In July, 1834, when the Bank ceased to restrict its credit, conditions quickly improved, and money was found to be "more plentiful than it was before."[2]

The correspondence between W. McKnight, cashier of the Pittsburgh Branch of the Bank, and Biddle reveals the degree to which the latter's scheme was progressing in Western Pennsylvania. On January 28, 1834, McKnight advised, "Information of curtailment and discontinuance of taking bills on the West by the Branch has spread through the town with the rapidity of lightning, and has produced a wonderful affect and alarm."[3] The Bank was unharmed, he reported, beyond the loss of profits. Three days later he added, "Our policy has produced more pressure and alarm with the large business part of our community than any measure heretofore adopted—and I can assure you it is not as Senator Wilkins has stated in Congress." McKnight was distressed, however, by a letter from Samuel Jaudon of the Washington Branch to a member of the Pittsburgh board of directors which declared that the Bank would have to let the people feel its force by pressing on its customers and thereby compel its charter. McKnight considered it "an unfortunate idea to get out. . . . As yet, the mass of the people are satisfied that the Bank is compelled to make all the curtailments from necessity to protect itself from the vindictive feelings of the government—a contrary opinion would have a bad effect." He assured Biddle that he was endeavoring to hush Jaudon's letter.[4] A day later he observed that the distress was so bad that many businesses were suspending. The Branch, he insisted, would have to protect itself and its friends by extending discounts on personal security. He was encouraged, however, by the general effect.[5] On February 6, 1834, he noted that their town meeting of that day was the largest he had ever seen; Bank supporters outnumbered the Jackson men by three to one, and all of their resolutions were adopted. They also chose a delegation to visit Harrisburg and Washington to present their views and to seek relief.[6] Two weeks later he was able to report that a Pittsburgh member of the State House of Representatives, a Jackson man, had been won over, and that all the Allegheny members would now go for the Bank. He observed that prices were

[2] *Niles' Register*, XLVI (July 19, 1834), 346.
[3] Biddle Papers.
[4] January 31, 1834, *ibid*.
[5] February 1, 1834, *ibid*.
[6] February 6, 1834, *ibid*.

falling. Pig iron, for example, was selling at $26 per ton; only three months before it had been $35. Other prices were declining proportionately.[7]

In Philadelphia also, the panic was used to good effect by the Bank men. They flooded Congress with petitions, dispatched delegations to both Harrisburg and Washington, and organized mass demonstrations. They exerted pressure upon the stockholders of the Girard Bank, a government depository, or "pet bank," to return the government's funds in its vaults and to accept no more deposits. At a meeting of the stockholders on March 17, 1834, hundreds of partisans filled the Girard Bank and the street outside to overflowing. The pressure of the crowd was so intense that the vote of the stockholders was inconclusive, though generally interpreted to give victory to the group favoring the retention of the deposits.[8] A week later the Bank men called a second meeting of the stockholders and gained the decision. The Girard Bank returned its deposits and terminated its contract with the government.[9] Thus, in the East and in the West Pennsylvanians were caught in a gigantic squeeze.

Politicians had little time to prepare to face its implications. Democrats had no heart for the contest. Wolf in his annual message in December, 1832, despite both Jackson's veto of the Bank recharter six months before and his opposition to the Bank during his re-election campaign, urged that the Bank be sustained. He called attention to the resolutions which had been adopted at the previous session, which instructed their Senators and requested their Representatives in Congress to use their exertions to obtain a renewal of the charter of the Bank of the United States. The Bank, he emphasized, provided a medium of circulation in which the people placed their confidence and facilitated the pecuniary transactions of the general government, and should either a too strict interpretation of the Constitution or a too critical analysis of its expediency prevent its renewal, it would be a matter to be deeply regretted.[10] In thus defending the Bank, Wolf was unquestionably echoing the general opinion throughout the State. Even those who disliked Biddle's administration of the Bank

---

[7] February 19, 1834, *ibid.*

[8] Philadelphia *Pennsylvanian*, March 18, 1834. One petition from Philadelphia against the removal of deposits contained 10,259 signers, including 722 manufacturers. See broadside dated February 3, 1834, Historical Society of Pennsylvania.

[9] Philadelphia *Pennsylvanian*, March 27, 1834.

[10] *Pennsylvania Archives*, 4th Series, VI, 53-54.

doubted the wisdom of Jackson's assault. Henry D. Gilpin, government director of the Bank, confided to Edward Livingston that there was much concerning the Bank's management which he disapproved, but that indiscriminate attacks would do more to strengthen than harm it.[11]

As Jackson persevered, however, Democrats began to conform. A bank similar to the Bank of the United States, they argued, might contribute to a stable currency; but the present institution by its mismanagement and political activities had forfeited its claim to public confidence. Few at first advocated the destruction of the Bank without the creation of a substitute. They ignored the panic as long as it was feasible. In January, 1834, Wilkins in the United States Senate insisted that the recession was limited to rumors and exaggerations.[12] But as the panic deepened, they could not evade it. One of Wolf's advisers in Philadelphia who saw through the Bank strategy, yet recognized its potency upon the rank and file, protested.

> Is it right to allow unprincipled men to cut and mangle, maim or squeeze to death the industry of the country, in order to force men into their ranks? They have address enough to mistify the *cause of the evil.* The multitude can not trace it. They feel harm but can not see who does it. It is in vain to reason with them on constitutional questions. You can not get a hearing upon the subject from a man *who is under protest.* He will tell you that *before* the deposits were removed he could meet his engagements—*now* he can not. He looks no further. He cares *much more* about paying his note and saving his credit than he does about the accordance or discordance of the Bank with our institutions. He does not look at its power to convulse the Nation. This is nothing to him. He must pay his note, or he is a ruined man. In this way the U. S. Bank may coerce a perpetual renewal of its charter, . . . by bringing sweeping ruin on thousands of our citizens.[13]

In Harrisburg, Wolf faced the most difficult decision of his four years of office. The controversy posed a problem more immediate than the wisdom or the justice of the removal of deposits or of his support of the national administration. The panic threatened to bring the public improvements to a standstill and to embarrass seriously

---

[11] April 10, 1833, Gilpin Letter Book, XLVII, Gilpin Papers, Historical Society of Pennsylvania.

[12] *Register of Debates in Congress,* 23 Cong., 7 Sess., 375 (January 29, 1834).

[13] Joel Jones to Wolf, March 21, 1834, Wolf Political Correspondence.

the credit of the State. The annual installment upon the State loan would come due on January 22, 1834. Would the installment be paid; could a new loan be floated? If not, what were the alternatives?

Wolf's dilemma was not unobserved by Biddle and his associates, who prepared to use it to their advantage. They began by feeling out his views. After being closeted with the Governor, William H. Keating, Philadelphia Representative and member of the House Ways and Means Committee, reported to Biddle that Wolf did not seem to appreciate the extent of the pressure in Philadelphia and believed that he could rely on the country banks for temporary loans to continue the Public Works. He admitted that

> the removal of deposits was an unwise, uncalled for and to say the least an unjustified measure—whether legal or not he did not wish to say. He spoke of the power of the Bank at this time as showing the dangerous character of an institution possessed of too much influence.

Significant in the light of the Bank's next step in its fight for recharter was Keating's closing advice, "If the installment of the loan is paid nothing can be expected of him; if it is not paid . . . he will be more disposed to meet us in our views."[14] To deflate Wolf's reliance on the country banks, Keating hastened to introduce a resolution in the House calculated to expose their weakness by requiring them to issue reports showing their financial condition during each week of the previous year. He failed to obtain its passage, however, when Democrats, suspecting its purpose, joined to vote it down.

On January 22, 1834, the Bank men heard with genuine satisfaction that the installment had not been paid. They had taken round one; they might inflict a knockout blow by defeating Wolf's efforts to obtain a temporary loan.

All eyes turned to Harrisburg as the twenty-second day of February approached when the State would offer the loan to the public. By the mutual consent of both the friends and foes of the Bank, resolutions in the legislature for and against the recharter and the restoration of deposits were permitted to lie on the table until the disposition of the loan should be determined. "Till then," Keating confided to Biddle, "discussion would be premature. All depends upon the fact of the loan's not being taken."[15] The anticipated day arrived; no offers were received. Wolf was trapped!

[14] January 3, 1834, Biddle Papers.
[15] February 14, 1834, Biddle Papers.

Four days later the Governor in a special message to the legislature made his anxiously awaited decision. To the utter astonishment and consternation of the Bank men, he placed the blame for the financial chaos of the State upon the Bank of the United States rather than upon Jackson. In guarded but firm language, he criticized the Bank's reckless determination to force the recharter and the return of the deposits "by bringing indiscriminate ruin on an unoffending community."[16]

Jackson men were overjoyed; wavering Wolf supporters in the main took their stand behind their leader. In Washington Jackson dashed off a letter of congratulation and offered his thanks

> for the exalted and truly patriotic stand you have taken in the defense of public liberty. . . . It was to have been hoped that our past experience had sufficiently demonstrated the futility of all attempts, however formidable in their character or source, to control the popular will: but there are unfortunately too many amongst us who are not only destitute of knowledge of the people, but who seem wholly incapable of acquiring it.[17]

Among the Jackson press the reaction of the Philadelphia *Pennsylvanian* was typical. It proclaimed in bold type, "Glorious News!! Pennsylvania Erect—The Republic Saved!!"

> The long looked for message of Governor Wolf on the subject of State Loans came to hand last night, overwhelming the Bank faction with confusion, and rousing the spirits of the friends of democracy and equal rights. . . . He agrees with the people that it is better to suffer than to submit to it.[18]

Wolf newspapers which had hitherto avoided a stand on the issue were much more cautious in interpreting his message, but the abuse heaped upon the Governor by the Bank press tended to rally them to his side.[19]

From the Bank forces, Wolf's message elicited a pained surprise. Daniel Webster, who at that moment was sponsoring a recharter bill in the United States Senate, gloomily reported to Biddle, "This is bad business at Harrisburg. We are going here, or were so, till this

---

[16] *Pennsylvania Archives,* 4th Series, VI, 169; *Niles' Register,* XLVI (1834), 26-27. See also Marquis James, *Andrew Jackson: Portrait of a President* (Indianapolis and New York, 1937), 672; Catterall, *Second Bank,* 339.

[17] February [28], 1834, John S. Bassett (ed.), *Correspondence of Andrew Jackson,* 7 vols. (Washington, 1926-1935), V, 243-244.

[18] Philadelphia *Pennsylvanian,* February 28, 1834.

[19] See Philadelphia *American Sentinel,* February 26, March 1, 1834.

Harrisburg blast broke upon us." He believed that relief would only be postponed and not defeated. But for the present he regarded it imprudent to bring forth any measure.[20] John Sergeant, a close friend of Biddle and an indefatigable Bank zealot in the House of Representatives, corroborated Webster's opinion.

> The Governor's extraordinary message [he wrote] has had a bad effect here. . . . I think it will be but temporary. If it had been what a wise or patriotic governor would have said, it would have been conclusive. I am satisfied that things were as I wrote you last. The current was becoming irresistible. It is checked, but I think only for a moment.[21]

Biddle, too, was severely jolted by Wolf's message. Writing to Samuel Breck, a Bank adherent in the Senate, he predicted that the message would only prolong the distress without serving any good object.

> It is melancholy to see a Governor of Pennsylvania thus aiding in the destruction of Pennsylvania interests. What makes it more shocking is, that up to the very moment of sending the message, those who visited him left him under the strongest conviction that he was decidedly friendly to the Bank. In truth he ought to have been, for so far from frustrating his loan, the Bank actually furnished Messrs. Allen the Means of paying the last installment [1833] as the Governor well knew.[22]

Anxious to minimize the effects of Wolf's pronouncement, Bank men made a determined bid to exploit his alleged change of face. Clay charged in the National Senate that Wolf had declared his intention to send a communication to the legislature of a directly opposite character only three days before his message of February 26 and that he had changed his mind overnight. Thomas M. T. McKennan, a National Republican Congressman from Washington County, made a similar accusation in the House. Wilkins and McKean defended Wolf in the Senate, but they avoided any criticism of the Bank.[23] Wolf wrote a denial for the use of his friends in Congress and demanded an explanation from William Leckey, sheriff of Allegheny County and member of a Bank delegation from Pittsburgh

[20] February 28, 1834, Biddle Papers.
[21] Sergeant to Biddle, March 1, 1834, *ibid.*
[22] March 1, 1834, Reginald C. McGrane (ed.), *The Correspondence of Nicholas Biddle Dealing with National Affairs, 1807-1844* (Boston, 1919), 224-225.
[23] For Wilkins' remarks, see *Register of Debates,* 23 Cong., 1 Sess., 1543-44; for McKean's defense, see *ibid.,* 1486.

which had called upon him en route to Washington, whose statement was cited by Bank men to support their contention.[24]

Leckey replied that Wolf had told him that his opinion in regard to the Bank had already been made known in his former messages to the legislature and in the resolutions in favor of the Bank which he had signed; that he did not regard it as his duty to make any expression in relation to the removal of deposits between the general administration and the Bank. The explanation apparently satisfied Wolf, who took no further action.[25] To McKean he confided, "so far at least Mr. Leckey furnishes no proof of Mr. Clay's assertion, and I am very certain that no other individual on earth can do so with truth."[26] It should be noted, however, that Wolf was not denying a sudden or belated change of mind, but only that he had made a statement of his intention to speak out in favor of the Bank charter. It would seem that Wolf continued to believe that the removal of deposits was "ill-timed and unnecessary," and that the management of the Bank, not the Bank *per se,* drew his disapproval.

The drive to discredit Wolf's message failed to mend the damage which it had inflicted. Bank men continued to dispatch petitions and delegations to Washington and to sponsor rallies in hundreds of communities throughout the State. In Philadelphia, a Bank parade and rally in the State House yard attained such tremendous proportions that even its most implacable opponents admitted that it was a colossal spectacle. Among the latter was Roberts Vaux, who could not resist the temptation to view the demonstration at first hand from the shadows. Returning home to describe it to Wolf, he declared,

> It is the last struggle and it is really an imposing death. All the merchants, their apprentices, and clerks are on the ground—Most of the shop keepers—all the tradesmen who have any dependence upon bank favours, no matter how remote, are in attendance—dairymen and carters and laborers whose daily bread depends upon the employment of these people are there—The operatives of all the factories, far and near, the boat men connected with the Schuylkill coal business help to swell the throng, which the Bank presses tomorrow will proclaim in numbers to have been some twenty or thirty thousand souls.[27]

[24] David D. Wagener to Wolf, April 29, 1834, and n.d. [May 1, 1834], Wolf Political Correspondence; Wolf to Leckey, May 2, 1834, *ibid.*

[25] Wolf to Samuel McKean, May 12, 1834, *ibid.*

[26] *Ibid.*

[27] Vaux to Wolf, March 20, 1834, *ibid.*

Bank supporters persevered, also, in attempting to exploit the panic, but they were losing ground; they had overshot their mark. Business people, whose support the financial stringency had been expected to attract, now began to suspect that the panic had been engineered by the Bank. Committees of leading merchants from Boston and New York, including the venerable Albert Gallatin, prepared to repudiate Biddle, and Bank leaders in Congress found a recharter on any terms improbable. Biddle was beaten. The Bank ceased the curtailment, expanded its credits, and the panic ended. Wolf negotiated a loan; the Public Works were resumed.

On the surface, the outcome of this chapter of the Bank controversy appeared to be a sweeping victory for the Democrats. Members of the party in Congress interpreted Wolf's message to mean opposition to the Bank recharter and took their places accordingly. When McKean stepped out of line to cast his vote in favor of Clay's resolution authorizing the restoration of deposits he was roundly denounced; even his old intimates joined in the chorus. Henceforth, he was a "forgotten man." In the General Assembly, Keating's resolution in support of the Bank's recharter was decisively defeated, 51 to 35, and in the Senate, Democrats pushed through resolutions which repudiated the recharter and the restoration of deposits.[28] This armed the Democrats with a campaign issue which evoked a broad, popular appeal. In the hands of Jackson's tacticians, the Bank was identified with corruption, monopoly, and special privilege; the contest, that of the people against the money-changers; or democracy against plutocracy.

But Democratic unity was superficial; under the surface the deposits controversy incited further factional strife. The reluctance with which the Wolf men took a stand has already been noted. The Governor's criticism of the Bank was delivered only after the State loans had gone begging and the public improvements had been jeopardized. Having berated the Bank's policies, Wolf preferred to make no supplementary statement. His message offered no opinion on the withdrawal of the deposits or the possibility of a modified charter. When Van Buren sought to make political capital from Jackson's congratulatory letter to Wolf, he found the latter unwilling to publish it. The Bank press, Wolf explained, would use it to detract and calumniate, and would charge interference from Washington in the

[28] Philadelphia *American Sentinel*, March 22, April 11, 1834.

preparation of his message.[29] Because of this reticence, Wolf made it possible for his opponents within the party during the campaign of 1835 to accuse him of giving merely lip service to Jackson's Bank policy.

Wolf's special message stimulated Bank opposition in the legislature at the expense of party unity. Resolutions in support of the removal of deposits and against the recharter, mentioned above, were unacceptable to a minority of Democrats in the State Senate, and their brethren in the House avoided a test on these issues.[30] A Democratic caucus on March 20 which was called to formulate a plan of attack was poorly attended, thirty of the eighty-nine members including William Patterson, Speaker of the House, finding excuses to remain outside. A resolution against the Bank was adopted, but when a motion was offered that they pledge themselves in writing, but thirty-six signatures could be obtained. When the disaffected began to leave the meeting, the motion was reconsidered and voted down.[31]

A minority of Democrats refused to follow Wolf, preferring to support the Bank regardless of the consequences. McKean's heresy has been observed. It is interesting to note that he gave as his reason for his vote upon the restoration of deposits his desire to abide by the wishes of his constituents, explaining that he had received more memorials calling upon him to support than to oppose it.[32] In Philadelphia, Democrats who joined the ranks of the Bank men took the name of States' Rights Men and Jefferson Society Men.[33] They soon merged with the Whigs. In Northumberland and Lycoming counties, Democrats divided into two factions, both claiming to be the regular party. Both nominated candidates for Congress and the State offices. Whigs and Antimasons, who generally polled a light vote in these counties, threw their weight behind Bank Democrats. They failed to seat their nominees, but carried the larger towns. Henry Frick, editor of the Milton *Miltonian* and chief spokesman for the Bank faction, continued to identify himself with the Democrats. In 1835 he backed Wolf's bid for re-election, but upon his defeat finally attached himself to the Whigs.[34] His experience

[29] James Thompson to Van Buren, March 6, 1834, Martin Van Buren Papers, Library of Congress; Van Buren to Thompson, March 2, 1834, *ibid.*
[30] Philadelphia *American Sentinel*, March 22, 1834.
[31] James Dunlop to Biddle, March 30, 1834, Biddle Papers.
[32] Philadelphia *Pennsylvanian*, June 20, 1834.
[33] Roberts Vaux to George Wolf, March 20, 1834, Wolf Political Correspondence.
[34] Milton *Miltonian*, March, 1834, to December, 1835.

was duplicated by Bank Democrats in many communities throughout the State.

The deposits controversy thus deprived the Democratic party of membership and leadership which it could ill afford to lose. It left many others confused and resentful, committed to a bank policy in which they had little faith and apprehensive of future ventures upon the muddied waters of finance with the irrepressible "Old Hero." Former Governor William Findlay observed prophetically that the friends of Jackson would hang together to sustain the course of his administration, but at its termination "the old Democratic party, already much rent, will I doubt [not] be broken into factions and fragments of factions."[35] He was guilty of an understatement; Democrats did not wait until Jackson left the White House to succumb to factionalism.

The deposits controversy was a breath of life to the expiring National Republicans, who had suffered seriously from the inroads of Jacksonianism and Antimasonry. Heeding the advice of Clay to exploit the economic crisis which followed the withdrawal of federal deposits from the Bank,[36] they called upon all who opposed executive usurpation to rally to their standard, and adopted the name, "Whigs," in accordance with the practice inaugurated in New York.

Leadership came principally from the Philadelphia area where National Republicans had survived the debacle of 1832. In the forefront were John Sergeant, Daniel Groves, Joseph R. Ingersoll, Caleb Cope, and Josiah Randall; members of the Philadelphia Common Councils, including Joshua Lippincott, Joseph B. Smith, and John P. Wetherill; and members of Congress, Francis J. Harper, Horace Binney, and John G. Watmough. They circulated petitions protesting the removal of deposits and sponsored demonstrations in which they cleverly cultivated participation of artisans, mechanics, and shopkeepers. Employers contributed to the movement by closing their establishments during the celebrations. The Select and Common Councils of the city memorialized Congress in support of the Bank recharter and the restoration of deposits, and dispatched a committee

[35] Findlay to Samuel McKean, May 28, 1834, Simon Gratz Correspondence, Gratz Collections, Historical Society of Pennsylvania.
[36] Clay to Biddle, December 21, 1833, McGrane (ed.), *Correspondence of Nicholas Biddle*, 218.

to Washington to interview Jackson, justifying their partisan action upon their responsibility as custodians of the Stephen Girard legacy.[37]

In Pittsburgh, the Whigs staged a giant demonstration, which was said to have been the greatest meeting of the people ever held there, adopted resolutions condemning the removal of deposits, and named a delegation to carry their wishes to Washington.[38] Mass meetings in Chambersburg, York, Easton, Huntingdon, Beaver, Williamsport, Gettysburg, and Chester took similar action.[39]

A Whig victory in the New York City municipal elections in April, 1834, was made the occasion for rallies.[40] In Philadelphia, a delegation of New York Whigs joined in the exercises, bringing with them a model of the frigate *Constitution*, which had been passed through the streets of New York during the election days.[41] Crowds poured into Philadelphia to witness the parade and the miniature frigate, to partake of the feast of "200 great rounds of beef, 400 hams, and as many beeves' tongues, etc., and 15,000 loaves of bread, with crackers, cheese, etc., and equal supplies of wine, beer, and cider," served at Powelton on the Schuylkill, and to hear an address by John Sergeant.[42]

A month later Philadelphia Whigs in conjunction with members of the legislature broadened their activities to encompass a State-wide "Convention of Delegates from the Citizens of Pennsylvania Opposed to Executive Usurpation and Abuse," designed to attract Whigs, Antimasons, and Bank Democrats. Meeting at Harrisburg on May 27, 1834, the assemblage included more than two hundred delegates from forty-four counties. More than one-third of the members were former Jackson men, and thirty had supported him as recently as the election of 1832. The majority of the others had been Shulze adherents and opponents of Jackson. Officers were carefully chosen to give recognition to the diverse elements in attendance: Joseph Lawrence, a prominent Antimason from Washington County and a former member of Congress, was elected as president; Ner Middleswarth, Antimason from Union County and Speaker of the State House

---

[37] *Niles' Register,* XLVI (May 3, 1834), 156.

[38] February 6, 1834. See page 36.

[39] Mueller, *Whig Party,* 13.

[40] Dixon R. Fox, *The Decline of Aristocracy in the Politics of New York,* Columbia University Studies in History, Economics and Public Law, LXXXVI, No. 198 (New York, 1918), 367-368. Whigs elected a majority to the Common Council, but lost the mayoralty contest by a small margin.

[41] Allan Nevins (ed.), *The Diary of Philip Hone* (New York, 1936), 124.

[42] *Ibid.,* 125; *Niles' Register,* XLVI (April 26, 1834), 130.

of Representatives in 1828, and Henry Frick, Milton editor and Bank Democrat, were chosen as vice presidents; and John Sergeant was named chairman of the strategic committee on resolutions.

It was soon discovered that dissidence among the body made any program of co-operation unfeasible. McLean men from the interior found themselves circumvented by Clay partisans from Philadelphia. Bank Democrats were confronted with Whig-inspired resolutions criticizing Wolf's change of face on the Bank. The resolutions were dropped only after the Bank Democrats threatened to withdraw from the convention.[43] Agreement was finally obtained upon a resolution which endorsed "every member of Congress or the Legislature by whatever name he may have been chosen, who in his station has faithfully resisted Executive usurpation and abuse, and firmly maintained the rights of the people."[44] They also addressed a memorial to Washington which denounced Jackson's Bank policy and called upon Congress for relief. The convention failed to effect a permanent organization, but it revealed that Jackson's course on the Bank was breaking down the barriers which separated his opponents and was paving the way for Whig leadership.

Meanwhile, antiremoval activity provided the Whigs with a means of gaining a foothold in the interior, where opposition to Jackson was frequently confined to the Antimasons or to disaffected Democrats. In Bradford County, where Democratic supremacy was virtually uncontested, friends of McKean supported anti-Van Buren men and Bank Democrats as candidates for office.[45] Similarly, in Northumberland County, where the Antimasons furnished only a feeble opposition to the Democrats, Bank men among the latter held a county convention where they adopted resolutions favoring the restoration of deposits and elected delegates to attend the Harrisburg Convention on Executive Usurpation. They also contested the county nominations with the Jackson Democrats. In Milton in that county, 166 citizens signed a restoration petition, including 14 out of 15 storekeepers (the fifteenth was the postmaster), and

> all the wagon and carriage makers, the saddlers, the printers, the plasterers, the potter, the millers, the distillers, the masons. In

[43] James P. Bull to Samuel McKean, May 30, 1834, McLean Papers; *Niles' Register*, XLVI (May 27, 1834), 243; Philadelphia *Inquirer*, June 5, 1834; Milton *Miltonian*, May 24, 31, 1834.
[44] *Niles' Register*, XLVI (May 27, 1834), 243.
[45] David Cash to George Wolf, May 22, 1834, Wolf Political Correspondence; Montrose *Susquehanna Register*, reprinted in Danville *Intelligencer*, October 17, 1834.

sober truth, nearly every tradesman in this good little borough, which contains about 200 voters, has joined in declaring his disapprobation to the present measures of General Jackson.[46]

Milton was soon a center of Whig strength in the county.

In Union County, on the other hand, Antimasons took the lead in calling together the "Democratic Party Opposed to Van Buren and the Removal Policy of Jackson."[47] Antimasons took a similar course in other counties where they were in the ascendancy, and Whig organization in these regions lagged.

During the summer and autumn of 1834 the Whig movement was retarded by the reaction of the public, cultivated by Democratic leaders, against the Bank for its curtailment of credit. "The Jackson men succeeded in some parts of the State in making the question Bank or no Bank, instead of usurpation and Van Buren on the one side, and Democracy and the Constitution on the other."[48]

Hence the Whigs were unable to threaten seriously Democratic hegemony in the State or congressional elections. In Antimasonic districts, Whigs generally supported candidates chosen by the Antimasons. In Pittsburgh, an agreement could not be reached, however, and the two parties offered separate slates. Elsewhere the Whigs endorsed their own nominees in co-operation with Bank Democrats.

The ensuing contest in the fall of 1834 failed to arouse unusual interest except in the Philadelphia area where the Whigs made a determined bid to unseat Joel B. Sutherland in the First Congressional District by nominating James Gowen, an Irish mechanic. It inevitably raised the Irish issue, which was whipped up furiously by the partisan press.[49] The situation became so tense that Biddle took the precaution of removing his family to the country to avoid personal violence.[50]

The election results in 1834 showed no significant trend toward the new party. In fact, the Democrats frequently gained ground, securing seventeen out of twenty-eight seats in Congress, an increase of two

[46] Milton *Miltonian*, March 15, 29, 1834.

[47] *Ibid.*, May 24, 1834.

[48] Harrisburg *Pennsylvania Intelligencer*, October 17, 1834, cited in Mueller, *Whig Party*, 18.

[49] Philadelphia *Inquirer*, September 5, 13, 22, 23, 24, 1834.

[50] Catterall, *Second Bank*, 356.

over 1832. Outside the Philadelphia area the Antimasons were victorious in six districts; the Whigs in none. Sutherland was returned to Congress by a majority of 1,436 votes; and the Democrats increased their majorities in both houses of the legislature and held a margin of forty-one votes on a joint ballot.[51]

The Whigs in defeat, however, had effected an organization and were prepared to use every opportunity to dominate the forces opposed to Jackson.

[51] Philadelphia *Pennsylvanian,* October 15, 17, November 3, 1834.

CHAPTER III

The "Wolves" and the "Muhls," 1834-1835

AS DEMOCRATS assembled at Harrisburg for the opening of the legislature in December, 1834, they came face to face with three challenges to party harmony: the organization of the two houses, the election of a United States Senator to replace William Wilkins, who had succeeded James Buchanan as Minister to Russia, and the gubernatorial nomination. The first two tests were encountered successfully. In the Senate, Jacob Kern of Northampton County, a Democrat with Amalgamation leanings, was re-elected Speaker; and in the House, James Thompson of Venango County, a Wolf Democrat, was named as presiding officer. The latter was achieved, however, only after old enmities had been aired.[1]

The senatorial election, which had been the source of so much bitterness two years before, was won by the Democrats with a minimum of friction. Votes on the first ballot were scattered among numerous candidates, with a majority of the Original Jackson Men voting for Buchanan and a plurality of the Wolf Democrats supporting Dr. Joel B. Sutherland. The latter, a member of Congress and formerly Speaker of the State House of Representatives, was a Philadelphia County "boss" with a large personal following in Southwark. He was weak, however, in the interior of the State. The result was the election of Buchanan on the fourth ballot on December 8, 1834, a decision which was facilitated by his recent two-year absence from the welter of Pennsylvania politics.[2] The strife-torn Democrats had now exhausted their small reserve of conciliation; compromise ceased as they turned to the nomination of a Governor.

The buffeting from two stormy terms of office failed to dull Wolf's zest for the fray. He was ambitious for a third term, the maximum allowed by the Constitution, and a goal no executive had reached since 1814 when Simon Snyder was elected a third time. His second term, as his first, was marked by substantial achievement. Despite the temporary setback occasioned by the failure of the State loan,

[1] Philadelphia *Pennsylvanian,* December 4, 1834.

[2] Philadelphia *Inquirer,* December 9, 1834; Philadelphia *Pennsylvanian,* December 10, 1834.

the public improvements had been extended. The main line was completed to Pittsburgh, and sections of the branches were in operation. A second source of pride was the public education law. A model for other states, it provided for a State-wide system of public education, subject to local option, supported in part by a State educational fund.

It is doubtful, however, whether either of these accomplishments could have been listed as a political asset. In the populous southern counties and in other scattered sections, the improvements were regarded as an extravagance and a tax burden. It was admitted by the most active supporters of the Public Works that the revenues were disappointing; meanwhile, the State debt was mounting by leaps and bounds. The school law was equally controversial. Philadelphia artisans protested because they were deprived of its benefits,[3] whereas voters in up-State counties, especially in Pennsylvania-German centers, rejected the measure.

The school law had been adopted in the spring of 1834 after the groundwork had been prepared by the Pennsylvania Society for the Promotion of Public Schools, committees of correspondence, and workingmen's societies in the 1820's. Worthy of special mention was the work of such zealots as Roberts Vaux, Joseph R. Chandler, Stephen Simpson, and Walter Rogers Johnson. Governor Wolf placed himself squarely behind the movement in his first annual message in 1829, and he returned to the subject in each of his subsequent messages to the legislature. In the State Senate, Samuel Breck of Philadelphia was an indefatigable leader.

The fulfillment of the program began in 1831 when the legislature provided for a common school fund. A year later the House moved to appoint commissioners to prepare a bill, but the Senate did not respond. By 1833-1834, however, there was general agreement in the legislature that a bill should be adopted at once and that the wrinkles might be ironed out in the future.[4] Drawn up under the guidance of Samuel Breck, chairman of the joint committee, the bill created a free, tax-supported, State-wide system of public education, which might be accepted or rejected by local option. The House passed

[3] Philadelphia and Carlisle had systems inaugurated before the passage of the general school law, which rendered them independent of its provisions. See James P. Wickersham (comp.), *Common School Laws of Pennsylvania* (Harrisburg, 1879), 172; Pennsylvania, *Laws, 1833-1834*, p. 178.

[4] Joseph J. McCadden, *Education in Pennsylvania, 1801-1835, and Its Debt to Roberts Vaux* (Philadelphia, 1937), 108-110.

the bill with but one dissenting vote, and the Senate approved it with almost equal unanimity.[5] The bill was signed by Governor Wolf on April 1, 1834.

It was not a party measure; in fact, the movement from its inception had been carried on without reference to party. Among the active spirits of the Society for the Promotion of Public Schools were both Jackson and anti-Jackson men. John Sergeant, George W. Toland, and Benjamin Wood Richards, for example, were National Republicans, while Vaux, Charles J. Ingersoll, and Thomas M. Pettit were Jackson partisans.

The measure quickly gained political significance, however, particularly in the German counties, where the specter of taxation for education raised a storm of protest. Typical of the reaction in many districts was that taken in Union County, where opponents of the law called a meeting of the citizens of the county, regardless of party affiliations, to adopt measures preparatory to repeal the "Aristocratic School Law."[6]

The legislature, when it assembled in December, 1834, was flooded with petitions for repeal. Their volume prompted the House to set up a special committee to study them, and it reported 31,988 signatures for repeal, 2,084 for modification, and 2,575 against repeal.[7] Wolf defended the measure in his annual message,[8] but repeal made rapid progress in the legislature. In fact, it appeared that even the Governor's veto might not be sufficient to save the law. A repeal bill passed the Senate by a substantial margin, but was defeated in the House after an impassioned defense by Thaddeus Stevens, young Antimasonic Representative from Adams County, apparently turned the tide.

An analysis of the votes in the two houses reveals the sectional cleavage. In the Senate, the repeal bill passed the second reading by a vote of 19 to 11. The minority consisted of five members from Philadelphia city and county, two from adjacent districts, and four from districts in the extreme west and north. Members from eastern and southern districts, on the other hand, voted overwhelmingly for

---

[5] In the House, an Antimason, Jesse Grim of Lehigh County, and in the Senate, three Democrats, George McCulloch of Mifflin-Juniata-Huntingdon, John A. Sangston of Fayette-Greene, and Jacob Stoever of Lebanon-Dauphin, voted in the negative. Pennsylvania, *House Journal, 1833-34*, I, 483; Pennsylvania, *Senate Journal, 1833-34*, I, 523-524.

[6] From a handbill quoted in the Milton *Miltonian*, September 20, 1834.

[7] Pennsylvania, *House Journal, 1834-35*, II, 650-653.

[8] *Pennsylvania Archives*, 4th Series, VI, 188-191.

repeal.[9] In the House, thirty-four votes were registered for repeal. Of these, but three were cast by members from districts in the western and northern portions of the State, and none by the Philadelphia group. Fully one-half of the votes for repeal were registered by delegates from the German counties.[10]

A glance at the party alignment reveals that nineteen of the sixty-two Democrats, twelve of the twenty-seven Antimasons, and two of the eleven Whigs in the House voted for repeal, and that fourteen of the twenty-five Democrats and five of the six Antimasons supported it in the Senate. Philadelphia Whigs and Democrats joined with western Democrats to support the school law, while southern and eastern Democrats and Antimasons frequently voted to repeal it.

The principle of public education was thus sustained, and Wolf thereby earned the gratitude of generations unborn. But while he gained friends in the north and west, he lost them in the populous counties in the south and east. Many Democrats in the latter region awaited a call for change.

A doubtful advantage, also, was the patronage of the Governor. Normally an effective means of building up a loyal nucleus of followers in each of the counties, it ran into a snag in the form of the Jacksonian principle of rotation in office. Many in the party had been waiting for two terms for the fruits of office; they were growing impatient. George M. Dallas, now Attorney General of the State, sensed the danger to be anticipated from this source and attempted to impress it upon Wolf. Opposition to a third term, he wrote, was vague and might be allayed by making the proper changes among the officeholders. He sympathized with his hesitancy, but reminded him that

> the current of democratic energy has set in. . . . Our friends exact more now than they have ever before. . . . It may be made a means of permanently securing consolidation and strength for the most elevated and enlarged objects—or it may became a rock on which we shall split into miserable factions, and on which the common enemy will fortify and entrench himself. . . . The first shock can not be resisted without endangering everything. We must go with it to some extent at least, or it will roll over us.

He urged Wolf to place himself at the head rather than resist the movement. As representatives of the popular will, they were "solemnly

[9] The vote on the passage was not recorded. Pennsylvania, *Senate Journal, 1834-35*, I, 387.
[10] Pennsylvania, *House Journal, 1834-35*, I, 887.

54   THE JACKSONIAN HERITAGE

bound to pursue the greatest good for the greatest number." To leave the Governor in no doubt as to details, Dallas appended to his declaration of faith a list of recommendations for office.[11] But to appoint new officials meant the dismissal of old, faithful public servants. Wolf showed little disposition to follow Dallas' timely advice.

His reluctance to play politics to gain the nomination did not deter his partisans from taking steps in his behalf. Their strategy was to forestall opposition by electing and instructing delegates well in advance of the gubernatorial convention. The procedure in Delaware County was typical. There the leadership was taken by Sutherland, who moved into the district from neighboring Philadelphia County after first lining up his own backyard for Wolf. Since Delaware County had been a center of Amalgamation strength, it was expected to be in the van of the opposition. If instead, it were to declare for Wolf, Sutherland reasoned, a second candidate would be at a serious disadvantage and not inclined to risk the contest. He moved quickly, and on December 20 he was able to report complete success, with delegates instructed for Wolf.[12] Similar action followed in other doubtful counties.

The opposition to a third term was not stamped out, however; it was merely retarded. During the closing months of 1834 Original Jackson Men frequently expressed the opinion that Wolf could not be re-elected, whereas a fresh candidate would assure the victory. By mid-December a few newspapers were giving Henry A. Muhlenberg (properly Henry Augustus Philip Muhlenberg) favorable attention, recommending him for the nomination in the event that Wolf declined.[13]

Muhlenberg was an excellent choice as a stop-Wolf candidate. A member of a family with a tradition of leadership among the Pennsylvania Germans,[14] he had built up a large personal following as pastor of the Trinity Lutheran Church of Reading, a position he had

[11] Dallas to Wolf, November 7, 1834, Wolf Political Correspondence.

[12] Sutherland to Wolf, November 8, 1834, *ibid.;* I. N. G. Lescure to Henry Buehler, December 20, 1834, *ibid.*

[13] Philadelphia *Pennsylvanian,* December 13, 1834.

[14] He was a nephew of Frederick A. Muhlenberg, Federalist candidate for Governor in 1793 and 1796; a cousin of John A. Shulze, elected Governor in 1823 and 1826; and a son-in-law of Joseph Hiester, elected Governor in 1820. See Paul A. W. Wallace, *The Muhlenbergs of Pennsylvania* (Philadelphia, 1950); Mueller, *Whig Party,* 21.

filled for twenty-five years. Retiring in 1828 he was immediately supported for Congress by the Jackson men. He gained an easy victory, and was returned in 1832 and 1834. His popularity was an asset to the Democratic party, which consistently polled large majorities in the county. In Congress he supported Jackson measures, including the Bank veto and the removal of deposits. He also endorsed the national convention.[15] He could thus be presented as a consistent Democrat, who would unite the party and assure a victory in the election.

No definite decision to contest the nomination was reached, however, until the meeting of the legislature, when the movement for Muhlenberg quickly took shape.[16] On December 22, 1834, the Philadelphia *Pennsylvanian,* spokesman for the Original Jackson group, heretofore noncommittal, extolled the virtues of the two-term principle in both the national and State governments. It referred to the two-term precedents of Washington, Jefferson, Madison, and Monroe, and reprinted Jackson's recommendation that the presidential term be limited to a single term of four or six years. It sought to nullify the provision of the Pennsylvania Constitution which permitted three terms by showing that the true democrats in the Constitutional Convention of 1790, William Findley and John Smilie, had contended unsuccessfully for the two-term principle. Other papers hastily followed the lead of the *Pennsylvanian,* and "two terms" became the keynote of the Muhlenberg forces. It served a useful function since it based the opposition to Wolf upon democratic doctrine rather than dissatisfaction with his administration or a desire for the spoils. The Wolf faction viewed it as a mere subterfuge to cloak a smoldering enmity and a craving for office. This interpretation was not without justification. The principle of the two terms was seldom mentioned in the correspondence of the Muhlenberg leaders.

After this brief departure into the realm of abstraction, the rival factions came down to earth determined to win the nomination regardless of the consequences to the party. On December 30, 1834, the *Pennsylvanian* deplored the tendency to revert to anger and recriminations, and reminded party members that they were conversing

---

[15] He did not vote on the bill to recharter the Bank. He explained later that he held stock in it and did not wish to participate in the controversy. In January, 1835, however, he declared that he was "opposed to the present or any other National Bank." Letter of January 26, 1835, reprinted in the Harrisburg *Democratic State Journal,* April 11, 1835. See also Mueller, *Whig Party,* 21.

[16] Simon Cameron to Henry Simpson, December 15, 1834, Gratz Correspondence; Henry W. Conrad to Simpson, December 14 and 18, 1834, Roberts Collection, Haverford College.

with friends, with no other point of view than the advancement of the common cause, and were not arrayed against enemies. Two weeks later, however, the same sheet began to bring in personalities. It hinted that Wolf's views upon the Bank of the United States ran counter to the popular will even after Jackson's veto, and that his special message of February 26, 1834, was too guarded to be accepted as a change of mind. A few days prior to the nominating convention in March, 1835, the *Pennsylvanian* charged that Wolf opposed the national convention and, by implication, Van Buren.[17] The Wolf press, meanwhile, ridiculed the possibility of an organized opposition to his renomination. When this was no longer feasible, Wolf sheets minimized the strength of the Muhlenberg faction and stressed the action already taken for Wolf in the counties. But as the contest warmed up, they resorted also to personal attacks. They charged Muhlenberg with inconsistency toward the Bank and with straddling the questions of the Public Works and the school law.

Despite the handicap of a late start, the opposition movement made rapid strides. In counties where delegates had not been chosen, the Muhlenberg men worked feverishly to control the conventions. Where action had been taken for Wolf, they sponsored meetings designed to release delegates from their instructions or to elect new ones. During the closing weeks, both sides resorted to the election of second sets of delegates. It was this misuse of the democratic process which was responsible for the failure of the convention; and it makes an appraisal of the claims of the contestants virtually impossible.

In Philadelphia County, where Sutherland had made certain that delegates favorable to Wolf were named and where Wolf sentiment was undoubtedly in the ascendancy, the Muhlenberg leaders called a last-minute meeting in Spring Garden at a place and time inconvenient to Sutherland's forces centered in Southwark. The rally turned out to be little more than a caucus of Muhlenberg men, who nevertheless proceeded to elect and instruct a delegation to the convention. The Wolf faction made a similar, though unsuccessful, bid for control in Adams County. There the initiative was taken by Henry Buehler, son-in-law and secretary to Wolf, who urged the Wolf partisans to elect a delegation to contest the one previously named by a county convention and known to favor Muhlenberg. He offered to pay the

[17] Philadelphia *Pennsylvanian*, January 12, March 2, 1835.

necessary expenses. "Our arrangements are such," he observed, "that if you keep out the vote of the Adams delegates we are safe."[18]

As the delegates to the gubernatorial convention assembled in the upper room of the courthouse at Harrisburg on March 4, 1835, the issue was in doubt. Contesting sets of delegates from eleven counties and senatorial districts added to the confusion. It meant that the method of organization would be of vital concern; the victory would depend upon which faction could seat the disputed delegations.

The first day was devoted to the question of procedure. The Muhlenberg men sought the admission of uncontested delegates only before taking action upon those which were disputed; they eventually won their point. On the second day the all-important question of the seating of the contested delegations was broached. Muhlenberg leaders proposed that Schuylkill County be voted upon first, since the Wolf delegation there had retired at the last minute in favor of the Muhlenberg group. But the Wolf men had no desire to strengthen the opposition, and insisted that the counties be considered in alphabetical order. Tempers were hot, and the chairman could maintain but a bare semblance of order. In the midst of the clamor the floor began to sink; the convention hurriedly recessed to reassemble in the afternoon on the lower floor. After a protracted debate, the motion to vote upon Schuylkill was defeated by a vote of 48 to 41. Thomas S. Bell of Chester County, a vice president of the convention, speaking for the Muhlenberg forces, thereupon moved that they adjourn and that the entire question be returned to the people. The motion was lost 42 to 47. The Wolf men thus gained the opening round.

On March 6, the third day of the convention, the Wolf faction secured the passage of a motion to vote alphabetically; and Berks County was thus the first on the list. The most rabid Wolf partisans did not seriously doubt that Muhlenberg was the choice of Berks, but it did not deter them from voting to seat their own delegation. Again the Wolf men were successful, this time by the narrow margin of three votes.

[18] Printed in the Philadelphia *Pennsylvanian,* April 15, 1835. The Philadelphia *American Sentinel,* a Wolf sheet, admitted that Buehler's action was "hasty and imprudent," but asked that it be regarded as a youthful indiscretion. The *Pennsylvanian* replied that a man who was thirty-five years of age was almost old enough to assume responsibility. See Philadelphia *American Sentinel,* April 16, 17, 1835; Philadelphia *Pennsylvanian,* April 15, 17, 1835; *Niles' Register,* XLVIII (April 25, 1835), 138.

The events which followed occurred so quickly amid so much confusion that eyewitnesses could scarcely follow them. Bell again moved to adjourn, only to be defeated 41 to 50, with the five Berks delegates voting with the Wolf men. He then presented a written protest against the action taken upon the Berks delegation and the rejection of the Schuylkill members. While Muhlenberg men flocked to affix their signatures, the president attempted to call the roll. But he had barely begun when the members of the Allegheny delegation, which had been voting with the Wolf faction, presented their resignations from the convention. Before they could be acted upon, a motion was made to reconsider adjournment; it was adopted. The Allegheny members thereupon withdrew their resignations and joined the Muhlenberg faction augmented by several Wolf supporters to pass a resolution by a vote of 51 to 41 to dissolve and reassemble at Lewistown. Among the Wolf group to vote for the resolution was James Thompson of Venango County, the president of the convention. Muhlenberg men left the hall rejoicing; but they had not had the last word!

That evening as delegates began to take their departures from Harrisburg, Wolf strategists, including McKean who arrived at the last moment from Washington, Ellis Lewis, President Judge of the Eighth Judicial District and formerly Wolf's Attorney General, and Jesse Burden, a veteran Philadelphia Democrat and member of the State Senate, meeting in a local tavern came to a startling decision. They agreed to ignore the vote of adjournment on the ground that it had not been sanctioned by a majority of all of the delegates, that is, a majority of the 133 who would have been eligible to vote if the full membership had been seated, and to meet on the following day to make a nomination. Accordingly, the Wolf forces in the convention, with the exception of several who demurred, joined by sympathizers, including members of the legislature recruited at the scene, assembled on March 7, 1835, in the Supreme Court chamber of the Capitol and nominated Wolf for a third term. There were two dissenting votes.[19]

The Muhlenberg men denounced the action of the "Wolf Caucus," the "sham convention," and, refusing to acknowledge its authority, went ahead with plans for the Lewistown convention. Thirty-three members of the legislature issued an address to the people of the

[19] Philadelphia *Pennsylvanian,* March 6, 9, 10, 11, 13, 17, 1835; Philadelphia *American Sentinel,* March 6, 9, 10, 11, 13, 14, 1835; *Niles' Register,* XLVIII, (March 28, 1835), 20-21.

State in which they pointed out the irregularity surrounding Wolf's nomination and emphasized that seventeen counties had been entirely without representation. It urged Democrats in all counties to elect delegates to the new convention.[20]

Wolf men, meanwhile, chose to ignore the Lewistown convention and were conspicuous by their absence when it convened on May 6, 1835. Muhlenberg was nominated without opposition. The schism was complete and irrevocable. Both conventions, it might be added, adopted resolutions supporting Van Buren for President, elected delegates to the national convention, and chose presidential electors. Thus, both the Pennsylvania electorate and the national convention were to be called upon to judge the legitimacy of the two candidates.

The chief source of strength of the Muhlenberg party was the dissatisfaction with the Wolf regime. Reasons for discontent were so diverse and so sectional, however, that a State-wide policy was rendered exceedingly difficult. In the Philadelphia area and in the North and West, the school law was popular among potential Muhlenberg supporters, but in the counties where the German element predominated, it was frequently opposed with more feeling than any other measure of the Wolf administration. In the Philadelphia region and along the routes of the public improvements, also, no party could afford to condemn the State Works, but in other sections it was a fruitful point of attack. Constitutional revision, too, was a subject which required extreme caution. In April the legislature provided for a referendum on the question of a constitutional convention. It was adopted without provoking a party issue, but it was dangerously controversial, nevertheless. The result was that while Muhlenberg men seized the offensive they avoided a platform, preferring to exploit local discontent regardless of its character.

In Philadelphia, Muhlenberg men courted the favor of the workingmen. They championed constitutional reform and gave favorable

[20] *Ibid.;* Philadelphia *Pennsylvanian,* March 24, 1835; John Dickey to Muhlenberg, March 9, 1835, Henry A. Muhlenberg Papers, American Philosophical Society. Muhlenberg was apprehensive of a rump convention initiated by his supporters. "My own opinion," he confided to Lloyd Wharton, his spokesman at Harrisburg, "is that unless there be a gross and palpable band, such a one as the people will see *at a glance and therefore resent,* it will be best, directly *after the nomination* has been made to give way. . . . If ruin come to the party let it come from our opponents. They might possibly secede themselves as Sutherland indicated they would if neither the City nor County [Philadelphia] Delegates were admitted. In such a case the blame would rest with them." Muhlenberg to Wharton, February 28, 1835, Mrs. Jesse Wagner Papers, American Philosophical Society.

publicity to the laborer's interests such as the six-to-six workday movement. When the Society of Mechanics and Workingmen in the city and county of Philadelphia addressed questionnaires to the two Democratic nominees, seeking their views upon public education, constitutional reform, penitentiary reform, and the modification of the militia law, Wolf merely referred the society to his record, but Muhlenberg declared his adherence to each. A favorable response was soon forthcoming. The society announced its support of Muhlenberg and listed its reasons for opposing Wolf. The latter, it declared, had showed no interest in constitutional reform, had not clarified his position on the Bank, had recommended prison labor in competition with free mechanics, and had deprived Philadelphia of the benefits of the school law.[21]

In Philadelphia, also, the Muhlenberg party advocated the continuation of the Public Works. But in Berks, they sought to placate hostility to the improvements, yet to avoid embarrassing Muhlenberg in other counties. The result was a resolution, remarkable for its ambiguity:

> Resolved, that however much we may complain of the lavish expenditures and profligate conduct of those persons, connected with the formation of our canals and railroads; causing great irritation of the public mind, and unnecessary taxation, yet we clearly perceive, and fearlessly avow that the improvements, upon which upwards to twenty millions of dollars have been expended, must by judicious system of completion be rendered as available as possible, otherwise the state will suffer a dead loss of millions already appropriated.[22]

In Mercer and Erie counties in the northwestern corner of the State, Muhlenberg leaders capitalized on the failure of the Wolf administration to extend a branch line to connect them with the canal system. In Berks, Union, and other scattered sectors, Muhlenberg backers condemned Wolf for attempting to expose them to the "benefits" of the school law. Muhlenberg men thus offered all things to all people.

[21] Philadelphia *Pennsylvanian*, April 3, 25, June 6, 1835. Muhlenberg's response, however, was not entirely satisfactory. In his reply to the society, he had noted that the public education law was "ill timed," and that the constitution was "upon the whole an admirable one." At the request of William English, writing for the society, he agreed that they might delete these offensive words from the published version of his letter. English to Muhlenberg, March 26 and 28, 1835, Muhlenberg Papers.

[22] Reprinted in the Philadelphia *American Sentinel*, April 10, 1835.

They also sought to strengthen their case by eliciting the magic of Jackson's name. As Original Jackson Men, as vigorous albeit tardy supporters of Van Buren, as the vanguard of the Bank opposition, as spokesmen for the federal officeholders, and as advocates of rotation in office, they rationalized, they were deserving of Jackson's favor. But the latter did not wish to see the party rent by a factional war; least of all at a time when it might upset the plans for Van Buren's succession to the Presidency. Replying to an appeal from Henry Horn, Philadelphia Congressman and Jackson campaign leader, for a word of encouragement to the Muhlenberg forces a short time before the March 4 convention, Jackson declared that he had no intention of interfering in the elections or politics of Pennsylvania and that his letter of congratulation to Wolf for his noble stand against the Bank the year before had no relation to the present gubernatorial contest. At the same time he cautioned Horn against any action which might create disunity in the party and give the enemy an opportunity to divide and conquer.

> In view of such consequences [he concluded] it is my object to guard my friends against the wiles of the enemy, and urge them to postpone such differences as those you allude to, to a period when they could be as well settled as now and without any hazard to the great republican party. . . . I do not pretend to judge to the propriety of the objections you take to the re-election of Wolf; but it can not be doubted that he has stood nobly by his country in the scenes to which I have adverted, and that you should avoid a contest which is not called for by considerations of vital importance to the welfare of the state at this crisis.[23]

Needless to say, Horn reserved this disappointing response for the eyes of trusted Muhlenberg men only. But despite this circumspection, it was to prove embarrassing later in the campaign. Wolf leaders, meanwhile, were satisfied with assurances from Washington that Jackson and Van Buren would be neutral. While the advantages of Jackson's favor could not be discounted, many friends of Wolf were allergic to federal interference in any form.[24]

With the Muhlenberg party thus deprived of the use of Jackson's name and the Wolf men content to accept his neutrality, the question of support from Washington received little attention until it was

[23] January 25, 1835, Bassett (ed.), *Correspondence of Andrew Jackson*, V, 320-322.
[24] Henry D. Gilpin to Van Buren, April 5, 1835, Van Buren Papers; George M. Dallas to Wolf, March 27, 1835, Wolf Political Correspondence.

whipped up by Fourth of July toasts which Jackson upon the request of the rival managers addressed to each group. In both cases, he recited democratic platitudes, but in the toast to Wolf he reiterated his praise of his Bank stand. The Wolf press seized upon it as a token of his favor, and Horn wrote again to Jackson asking him to deny it had any relation to the campaign. Jackson acquiesced, explaining that

> the toast had reference to the past and not the present. . . . If my opinions in regard to Governor Wolf and Mr. Muhlenberg are considered by you of any importance to the public you have them already seriously expressed in my first reply, which you are at liberty to publish if you please.[25]

Horn put this reply into the hands of the press in an attempt to nullify the interpretation which the Wolf papers were giving to Jackson's toast. Whereupon the latter pounced upon Jackson's reference to his previous letter and called upon Horn to release it. He refused; and to his discomfort the Wolf press continued to repeat the request throughout the remainder of the campaign.

Both factions took their cases to the national convention at Baltimore in May, 1835, and sought the admission of their respective delegations as the representatives of the party. The dilemma which they thrust upon that body was succinctly stated by Francis P. Blair, editor of the Washington *Globe*.

> The two sets of delegates from Pennsylvania are bent upon bringing their quarrel before the Convention in some shape, but I trust the attempt will not succeed. Some want a direct issue upon the point of *legitimacy,* where there is no law to decide. Others wish to have a resolution passed in effect to annul the nominations of Electors made by the Wolf convention. I find zealous and devoted friends on each side. . . . They are as furious against each other, as the Montagues and Capulets.

He added that he was trying to get them to leave their dispute for the Pennsylvania voters, but that he was making little progress.[26] Simon Cameron, one of a small minority who had supported Van Buren in 1832, was attending the convention as an observer and declared to Buchanan with a touch of sarcasm that three years before only one-third of a single delegation could be sent to Baltimore in favor of Van Buren, but that now the whole State was fighting for the honor

---

[25] July 21, 1835. Printed in Philadelphia *Pennsylvanian,* July 28, 1835.

[26] Blair to Jackson, May 19, 1835, Bassett (ed.), *Correspondence of Andrew Jackson,* V, 348-349.

of singing his praises.[27] The warring factions were eventually appeased by the admission of both delegations.

The intransigent Democrats made no serious effort to settle their dispute. Buchanan assumed the thankless role of conciliator without success. Anticipating a heated contest at the nominating convention of March 4, he had attempted to commit the party to Van Buren by the adoption of an appropriate resolution by the Democratic members of the legislature. But its introduction by a Muhlenberg supporter had sufficed to prejudice Wolf men against it and thereby to defeat it. The latter lost no time in assuring Buchanan that their opposition implied no hostility toward Van Buren or himself.[28]

After the schism became irreconcilable, Buchanan rejected overtures from both factions. Appealing for his active aid, Muhlenberg inquired, "Will you forsake your friends to go over to your enemies who are only waiting [for an] opportunity to cut your throat?"[29] A Muhlenberg leader in Berks hinted that they might adopt resolutions at their county convention in his favor for the Vice Presidency provided that he would declare himself for their candidate, and Muhlenberg managers in Harrisburg urged him to confer with them. To refuse, they intimated, might jeopardize his political future.[30] Roberts Vaux, meanwhile, explored the possibilities of obtaining his intervention to urge Muhlenberg to retire.[31] But he refused to be drawn into the controversy. He had been elected to the Senate with the backing of leaders of both factions; he wished to antagonize neither. Democrats continued to battle Democrats down to election day, preferring to close their eyes to the increasingly obvious fact that neither candidate could be elected.[32]

[27] May 20, 1835, Buchanan Papers.

[28] James Mitchell to Buchanan, January 15, 1835, *ibid.;* John Dickey to Buchanan, January 9, 1835, *ibid.;* Henry Buehler to Buchanan, January 15, 1835, *ibid.*

[29] March 24, 1835, *ibid.* Buchanan urged Jacob Kern, Speaker of the State Senate, to secure the retirement of both candidates and to call a new convention which might make a nomination acceptable to both factions. But he received little support. Buchanan to Kern, March 19, 1835, Muhlenberg Papers; Buchanan to Muhlenberg, March 29, 1835, *ibid.*

[30] John Hoffman to Buchanan, January 8, 1835, Buchanan Papers; Henry Petriken to Buchanan, March 14, 1835, *ibid.;* Charles B. Penrose to Buchanan, March 30, 1835, *ibid.*

[31] Vaux to Buchanan, March 21, 1835, *ibid.*

[32] Leaders recognized that the schism would result in the election of Ritner as early as the spring of 1835. See Cameron to Buchanan, March 22, 1835, *ibid.;* and Buchanan to Van Buren, May 21, 1835, Van Buren Papers.

64   THE JACKSONIAN HERITAGE

The Wolf-Muhlenberg feud was a godsend to the heterogeneous Antimasons, Whigs, and other anti-Jackson forces in the State. The years between 1832 and 1835 had brought little more than a series of disappointments. Antimasons were in the doldrums scarcely twelve months after their remarkable showing in 1832. The State committee could reach no decision upon the desirability of a convention. A Lancaster County member suggested that their chairman, Joseph Wallace, issue a call without waiting for an agreement, but he made no move, observing

> Our committee is still in power. I wish for my own sake it were not—but I suppose you and myself who have always been willing to work, must tug a little longer at the oar of Antimasonry.
>
> I never begin to tire of this incessant labour, that I do not think of Mr. Adam's watchword . . . "Persevere." So I suppose we ought to hold on.[33]

From Lycoming County, the report of a committeeman was even more pessimistic. Antimasonry was being undermined there, he declared, by the

> canal nobility that have billeted among us. . . . The canal running along the river [Susquehanna] through the most populous part of the county from the lower end nearly to the upper end of it; a great number of those who started out with us and appeared to have some action, are engaged more or less with contracts on it; being closely watched they say they do not like to quarrel with their bread and butter and are in a measure neutralized at this time.[34]

Hence he could make no promises, but could only lie in wait, ready to take advantage of the split which he believed was separating the McKean from the Van Buren Democrats. Reports equally disturbing emanated from Pittsburgh, where National Republicans repudiated their alliance of the previous year with the Antimasons. They charged the latter with "unyielding obstinacy" for their refusal to concur in the election of a National Republican to the State Senate. "Their insidious friendship," they declared, "was more destructive than open hostility."[35]

In the election of 1833, Antimasonic strongholds returned their usual majorities, but elsewhere the party revealed little vitality. Of

---
[33] Zephaniah McLenegan to Wallace, August 7, 1833, William MacPherson Papers.
[34] John Borrows to Wallace, August 18, 1833, *ibid.*
[35] Resolution of a National Republican meeting, reprinted in *Niles' Register*, XLV (November 9, 1833), 166.

significance in the years which followed was the election of Thaddeus Stevens of Adams County to the State House of Representatives. National Republicans showed strength only in Philadelphia. In 1834 the situation was essentially the same. The Bank controversy served temporarily to unite the opponents of Jackson irrespective of party lines. But by election time this advantage had been dissipated by the ineptitude of Biddle's Bank panic. Chastened by defeat, Antimasons turned their backs upon their associates and prepared again to travel the political trail as "Exclusives."

The approach of the gubernatorial election of 1835 found Antimasonry at its lowest point since the original growth of the party. Several members of the State committee doubted the wisdom of undertaking another campaign. When a convention had been agreed upon, few of the members showed a disposition to set the machinery in motion. The call for the convention was delayed a full month while Wallace labored to have a declaration of principles prepared. He was unsuccessful, and the call was finally announced in the columns of the *Sun,* the party organ in Philadelphia, without the declaration.[36]

It proved to be the darkness before the dawn, however. Prospects of Democratic disunity aroused the flagging spirit of Antimasonry, and the convention of March 4, 1835, undertaken with so many misgivings, abounded in harmony and enthusiasm. With but one exception delegates from all districts joined to nominate their perennial favorite, Joseph Ritner, for Governor.[37] In their fervor they went so far as to create a joint Antimasonic-Whig State committee for the management of the campaign.

With the Democrats in two rival camps and victory in sight, however, Antimasons soon regretted their decision to collaborate with the Whigs. Their representatives on the joint committee complained that the Whigs neutralized their exclusive principles; and Wallace warned Ritner of the dangers attending any departure from original and distinctive tenets of Antimasonry. In New York, he observed, the party declined as soon as it compromised with other anti-Jackson groups. Whigs, Wallace maintained, had opposed his candidacy to the day of his nomination; they were not deserving of favors. The

[36] John R. Jones to Wallace, October 17, 1834, William MacPherson Papers; Wallace to Jones, November 4, 1834, *ibid.;* Zephaniah McLenegan to Wallace, November 26, 1834, *ibid.;* Jones to Wallace, November 29, 1834, *ibid.;* McLenegan to Wallace, December 1, 1834, *ibid.*

[37] Delegates from York County voted for Joseph Lawrence and then shifted to Ritner to make it unanimous.

rewards of office should be distributed to tried and true Antimasons who had labored through the years for the cause.[38] The Antimasonic press was equally proscriptive. Original principles were repeated and the Whigs censured for showing but lukewarm support for Ritner's election. When Ritner failed to reply to a questionnaire from a committee of Whigs, the Antimasonic Pittsburgh *Gazette* declared that he could not be bothered to answer every impertinent question.[39]

The Democratic schism served also to revive the Whigs, but unhappy attempts at co-operation with Antimasonry in the past made them wary of a new alliance. In Philadelphia, the *United States Gazette* urged that the party remain noncommittal until the position of the Antimasons could be ascertained. They owed it to themselves, it insisted, to refrain from rushing to the standard of a party whose success would not assure them of the furtherance of Whig principles.[40]

In Beaver County on the Ohio border, the Whigs adopted resolutions in favor of a State convention to nominate a candidate of their own for Governor. In other sections, Whigs supported Ritner's nomination without waiting for promises from the Antimasons. They justified it upon the premise that their primary objective was the defeat of Van Buren and that Ritner's election would go a long way to secure it. In Pittsburgh, Whigs announced their adherence to Ritner's candidacy, but formed a ticket of their own for local offices.[41]

By midsummer, however, Whigs were lining up in all quarters for Ritner, though their lack of enthusiasm was barely disguised. A judicious appeal to Masons by Thaddeus Stevens was circulated widely. "Let no other test be required," he advised, "than a cordial support of our candidates. That will be conclusive proof that they consider their obligations to their country superior to their secret oaths to a foreign power. That is all that Antimasonry requires."[42]

Stevens' soothing words undoubtedly facilitated the coalition, but it did not prevent recurrent bickering. In Dauphin County, for example, the Antimasons adopted a resolution condemning the Bank recharter, a measure close to the hearts of the Whigs. "We consider the question about the United States Bank," it read, "as already dead and settled by the people."[43] The alliance was unquestionably one

---

[38] Zephaniah McLenegan to Wallace, August 8, 1835, William MacPherson Papers; Wallace to Ritner, August 22, 1835, *ibid*.
[39] Reprinted in the Philadelphia *American Sentinel*, July 16, 1835.
[40] March 14, 1835.
[41] Philadelphia *American Sentinel*, July 11, 1835.
[42] Philadelphia *United States Gazette*, August 14, 1835.
[43] Philadelphia *American Sentinel*, August 31, 1835.

of convenience, characterized by mutual distrust. It was the hopeless division of the Democrats, not the strength of the Coalition, which determined the outcome of the election.

Because the schism all but sealed the outcome, the campaign was relatively free from personal abuse. Wolf papers occasionally cast aspersions upon "Parson" Muhlenberg for deserting the pulpit to grovel for the spoils of office. One central Pennsylvania editor declared, "Muhlenberg is a purse proud aristocrat, who has accumulated a fortune by expounding the Gospel."[44] Democratic papers made a few halfhearted efforts to stir up religious prejudice against Ritner by alleging that he was a Catholic and to ridicule his military record in the War of 1812. But such attacks were inconsequential in determining the outcome.

Election returns graphically revealed the effects of the Democratic division. Ritner's victory was decisive. He had a plurality of 28,000 votes over Wolf, who in turn led Muhlenberg by a margin of 25,000. Yet the combined vote of the two Democratic candidates exceeded Ritner's total by more than 12,000. In county after county Ritner's vote varied but slightly from the totals of three years before; his gains seldom exceeding 300 votes. He carried traditional Antimasonic counties and the Whig strongholds of Pittsburgh and Philadelphia. He gained pluralities in strong Democratic sections only when the Democratic votes were almost evenly divided. These pluralities were significant, however, since they enabled the Antimasonic-Whig Coalition to gain a majority of the seats in the House and to increase their strength in the Senate, though holdovers permitted the Democrats to retain control of the latter.[45] Democrats had the hollow satisfaction of seeing their total vote exceed that of their opponents, and they interpreted it to their own satisfaction to indicate that the State would give its electoral vote to Van Buren. But even this ray of optimism was hardly justified; a victory in 1836 would require one Democratic party, not two.

Amidst the excitement of the gubernatorial election little attention was given to the referendum on the holding of a constitutional convention. Supporters of the convention, however, had the satisfaction of seeing the proposal accepted by some eleven thousand votes.[46]

[44] Lewisburg *Democrat,* June 20, 1835.
[45] Pennsylvania, *Senate Journal, 1835-36,* I, 42-43; *Niles' Register,* XLIX (October 17, 1835), 103, 141; Philadelphia *American Sentinel,* October 14, 1835. Results by counties are given in the Appendix, p. 222.
[46] See Chapter VI.

CHAPTER IV

Joseph and His Brethren, 1835-1836

AS THE VICTORS converged upon Harrisburg, three elements were at work seeking to gain an ascendancy: "Exclusive" Antimasons, Whigs, and Moderate Antimasons or Coalitionists, who were willing to sacrifice principle for expediency in order to control the legislature and the patronage.[1] Initiative among the Exclusives was taken by older leaders, men who had waged the battle for eight lean years. They interpreted the victory as an opportunity to expose Masonry and to abolish oaths and secret societies, to restore economy in administration, and to cut taxes. Outstanding among this group were Amos Ellmaker, Antimasonic candidate for the Vice Presidency in 1832, Zephaniah McLenegan, State committeeman from Lancaster, Thomas Elder, State committeeman from Lebanon, Joseph Wallace of Harrisburg, State party chairman, Theophilus Fenn, editor of the Harrisburg *Telegraph,* Neville B. Craig, editor of the Pittsburgh *Gazette,* W. W. Irvin, Allegheny committeeman, and John Richter Jones, Antimasonic printer and editor of the Philadelphia *Sun.* Having constituted the nucleus of the party organization and labored at three elections for Ritner's elevation to the governorship, they were closest to the Governor-elect's ear. They had the satisfaction of seeing a young protégé of Ellmaker, Thomas H. Burrowes of Lancaster County, appointed as Secretary of the Commonwealth, and Joseph Wallace as Deputy Secretary.

They regarded an association with Whigs as a compromise with Masonry, but were willing to hold out the olive branch to the Muhlenberg Democrats. Muhlenberg's candidacy, the leading Antimasonic sheet in Philadelphia declared, was conducted

> in defiance of the lodge. . . . Masonry aided George Wolf against Muhlenberg as well as against Ritner. . . . They have also the additional claim of being a part of that great democratic levy *en masse,* which has just overthrown the demagogues and emancipated the commonwealth. No Muhlenberg Democrat,

[1] The chapter title is taken from Roberts Vaux to George Wolf, November 19, 1835, Wolf Political Correspondence.

who is opposed to secret societies, is excluded [from] office by Antimasonic principles.[2]

The immediate goal to be gained by a union with Muhlenberg Democrats was the control of the Senate, where the Muhlenberg men held the balance of power. Antimasons opened the door for such a rapprochement by supporting and thereby electing Thomas S. Cunningham of the Erie-Crawford-Mercer district, a Muhlenberg Democrat, as Speaker.[3] Muhlenberg men, however, were not inclined to heed the appeal of the Antimasons, preferring to make their peace with the Wolf faction.

The failure of the Exclusives to form a working agreement with the Muhlenberg faction and their unwillingness to grasp the reins of the Antimasonic-Whig Coalition deprived them of the driver's seat which they might have occupied in the Ritner administration, and gave it by default to the Whigs and moderates among the Antimasons.

The Coalitionists regarded the policy of the Exclusives as impractical and obstructive. Though lacking in both organization and leadership, the Coalitionists had several distinct advantages. Many counties owed their majorities for Ritner to the merging of Antimasons and Whigs. They offered the only tangible means of enacting Antimasonic or Whig measures and of defeating Van Buren for the Presidency. In their first test of strength with the Exclusives for the patronage, they salvaged the attorney generalship, James Todd of Fayette County receiving the appointment. With the aid of the Whigs they also selected Ner Middleswarth of Union County as Speaker of the House and Joseph Lawrence as State Treasurer.

Both wings of the party were anxious to use their victory to further the cause of Antimasonry nationally, but they disagreed upon the method. The Exclusives favored the calling of a national convention to nominate candidates for the Presidency and Vice Presidency; Coalitionists opposed it, preferring to find candidates acceptable to the Whigs.[4] The former issued a call for a State convention and approached Daniel Webster and William Henry Harrison to ascertain their positions upon Antimasonry. Both replied in terms which were virtually noncommittal, but Webster's statement was deemed more

[2] Philadelphia *Sun*, reprinted in Philadelphia *American Sentinel*, November 13, 1835. See also the Harrisburg *Telegraph* during the closing weeks of 1835.

[3] Philadelphia *Pennsylvanian*, December 3, 1835.

[4] Amos Ellmaker to Joseph Wallace, October 19, 1835, William MacPherson Papers; John R. Jones to Wallace, October 6, 1835, *ibid*.

satisfactory.[5] More damaging than Harrison's reply was the fact that he was already being taken up by the Whigs; to support him would relegate the Antimasons to a secondary role.

The State convention at Harrisburg on December 14, 1835, found the two factions contesting bitterly for control. Exclusives, led by Thaddeus Stevens, argued for a national convention, while Coalitionists, headed by Todd, opposed it. After a protracted argument the latter group prevailed, putting down a resolution for the convention by a vote of 98 to 36. At that point Stevens and eight others, including Harmar Denny of Allegheny County, the chairman of the convention, presented a protest and stalked out of the hall. Undaunted, the moderate wing reorganized, placed Joseph Lawrence in the chair, and proceeded to make nominations for President and Vice President. They named Harrison for President on the first ballot, giving him 98 votes to 29 for Webster, and chose Francis Granger of New York for Vice President by acclamation.[6] The seceders refused to abide by the majority decision and issued a call for a national convention to meet in Philadelphia on May 4, 1836.

The role of Stevens remains enigmatical. Identified with the Exclusives, who recognized his ability and encouraged him to run for a seat in the Assembly in 1835, he did not hesitate to cut his own path through the maze of party politics.[7] Prior to the election he was conciliatory toward all shades of opinion, professing to exclude only those whose oaths to a secret power were stronger than their patriotism.[8] Later in the legislature he co-ordinated and reconciled divergent Antimasons, Whigs, and Bank Democrats in planning the program. But he did not hesitate to throw all but Exclusives into turmoil by directing an investigation of Masonry. In the State convention he chose to secede rather than remain and accept Harrison's nomination, despite the fact that less than two months earlier he had conceded that Harrison was the only man who could defeat Van Buren.[9] In a letter to John B. Wallace he maintained that by

[5] Harrison to George W. Harris, November 11, 1835, *ibid.;* Harmar Denny to Webster, November 11, 1835, Daniel Webster Papers, Library of Congress; William W. Irvin to Webster, November 27, 1835, *ibid.;* Webster to Irvin, November 30, 1835, *ibid.*

[6] Harrisburg *Antimasonic State Democrat,* December 18, 1835.

[7] Thomas Elder to Joseph Wallace, August 3, 1835, William MacPherson Papers; Stevens to Wallace, August 16, 1835, *ibid.*

[8] See page 66.

[9] Stevens to Wallace, October 24, 1835, John William Wallace Collection, Historical Society of Pennsylvania.

postponing action upon the Presidency they could force a delay in the choice of an opponent for Van Buren, since without the Antimasonic vote no candidate could win. If they should find that Van Buren could not be beaten, they could go their way.

> But if Antimasons are to nominate a man with whom they can not succeed, they will nominate a distinctive Antimason—so as to keep their party inflexibly together, and compel other parties to adopt our principles or endure perpetual defeat. The destruction of Masonry is an object which we shall not lose sight of either in success or defeat.[10]

The Whig element in the Coalition was weak numerically and in a poor position to take the leadership at the outset. They co-operated with the Antimasons in the legislature to give the latter the offices and the printing, and they stood by while Antimasons monopolized the patronage. They were excluded from the Antimasonic State convention and thus had no part in the nomination of Harrison. Meeting in convention on the same date, however, they waited until the Antimasons made their nominations, then adopted the same slate even though numerous Whig leaders preferred Webster. They also accepted the Antimasonic electoral ticket.[11] In all these activities they revealed a conspicuous lack of enthusiasm. A Franklin County leader expressed their dissatisfaction colorfully when he complained, "But what avails our efforts—our masters the Antimasons must settle this matter for us and we will do as we are led, whether they will take up Webster, Harrison, Van Buren or the Devil it is hard to tell."[12] Thus the Whigs cut a small figure. By waiting and playing an opportunistic game, however, they were prepared to take the initiative when the Antimasons faltered.

The focal point of the rivalry within the Coalition was the Governor-elect. Joseph Ritner was richly endowed with qualities calculated to appeal to the age of Jackson. Born in Berks County of poor Pennsylvania German parents, he labored as a weaver until he acquired capital to purchase horses and wagon. He then turned to farming. Attracted by virgin soil in the "West," he joined the stream of pioneers, migrating to Allegheny and thence to Washington County, where he cleared his tract and erected his house. He left his plough in 1821 to take a seat in the lower house of the legislature. He was

---
[10] *Ibid.*

[11] *Niles' Register*, XLIX (December 26, 1835), 293.

[12] James Dunlop to William M. Meredith, December 4, 1835, Meredith Papers, Historical Society of Pennsylvania.

re-elected five times and was Speaker during the 1825-1826 session. He supported Jackson for President in 1824 and 1828, but then plunged into Antimasonry and was nominated for Governor at the first Antimasonic convention in 1829. He was renominated in 1832.

A campaign eulogy in 1835 cast him in heroic mold: "In his person, Joseph Ritner is of middle stature, stout and muscular, and evidently enured to labour. His eyes are dark and piercing, and the cast of his countenance bespeaks firmness and vigour of mind."[13] A second sketch in a similar Arcadian vein declared, "He reaps his own harvest field, eats at the same table with his own hands when the day's work is over."[14] At fifty-five, Ritner's robust frame was yielding to corpulence, and his vigor was abating, but his popularity among Antimasons remained unimpaired.

Ritner's technical equipment for the office was usually passed over lightly by his partisans. He was not trained in the law and had little administrative experience. As Governor he made no serious attempt to shape policy, and leadership thus passed to the legislature, and in particular to Stevens. It should not be assumed, however, that Ritner was a mere rubber stamp. When aroused he could be unyielding. The possibility of his veto could never be discounted by the legislators.

Few meetings of the Pennsylvania legislature have been loaded with more political dynamite than the session of 1835-1836. At the outset, Antimasons in the House secured the appointment of a special committee of five to investigate Masonry. Stevens, its chairman, at once dominated the action. When witnesses refused to appear as they were summoned, he secured the adoption of a resolution which required their attendance. Whigs supported the resolution in order to gain Antimasonic votes for the chartering of the Bank of the United States by the State. Armed with this resolution, the triumphant Stevens compelled some of the highest dignitaries of the State to appear before the committee. The group included former Governor Wolf, George M. Dallas, Robert Christy, Judge Ephraim Pentland of Pittsburgh, Judge Josiah Randall of Philadelphia, and Joseph R. Chandler, editor of the *United States Gazette*. Their testimony created a sensation throughout the State and halted all other business in Harrisburg, as members of the legislature joined the crowd of spectators at the hearing.

---

[13] New Berlin *Antimasonic Star*, August 21, 1835.

[14] York *Republican*, reprinted in New Berlin *Antimasonic Star*, April 17, 1835.

The fireworks came quickly. Chandler, the first witness to be called to the stand, refused to take the oath; and instead read a long prepared statement to justify his position. A second witness, J. B. Freeman, followed the same procedure, but in the midst of his recital he collapsed and had to be carried from the room. When Dallas was called, he answered but refused to come forward. During the resulting battle of wits Judge Pentland, waiting to be called, interrupted to demand that he be committed into the custody of the Sergeant at Arms in order to apply for a writ of habeas corpus to secure his release and return to his court in Pittsburgh. Unable to make itself heard above the ensuing din, the committee adjourned in disorder. Stevens carried the issue to the floor of the House, but the Whigs would have no more of it. Joining with the Democrats, they adopted a resolution to discharge the witnesses. The long-awaited assault upon Masonry was thus a complete fiasco.[15] It undoubtedly hastened the demise of the Antimasonic movement in the State.[16]

Whigs and Antimasons took a mutual interest in measures designed to harass the Democrats. They adopted resolutions instructing McKean and Buchanan in the United States Senate to vote against Thomas Hart Benton's resolution to expunge from the record the vote of censure against Jackson for his removal of the deposits.[17] They also instructed them to vote for Clay's Distribution Bill and against the

[15] *Niles' Register*, XLIX (January 30, 1836), 379. A very interesting description of the hearing is found in a letter from R. Penn Smith, an eyewitness, to William M. Meredith, January 19, 1835 [1836], Meredith Papers. See also George M. Dallas to Mrs. George M. Dallas, January 21, 1836, Dallas Papers, Historical Society of Pennsylvania; Dallas to Henry D. Gilpin, January 18, 20, 21, 1836, *ibid*.

[16] Andrews, "The Antimasonic Movement in Western Pennsylvania," 265, states that with the failure of Stevens' committee, "The life passed out of the Antimasonic movement in Western Pennsylvania." The furor aroused by the investigation of Masonry may be illustrated by an incident which occurred at Lafayette College, Easton, Pennsylvania. Student literary societies invited Stevens to address them on July 4, 1836. But the college president, George Junkin, fearing repercussions, wrote to Stevens urging him to refuse, explaining that he did not wish to draw the institution into the maelstrom of party strife. He pointed out that a number of the trustees, including former Governor Wolf, were political men. Stevens turned down the invitation as requested, but made political capital of it by revealing Junkin's request. The embarrassed president was forced to send a copy of his letter to the literary societies. Junkin to Stevens, March 2, 1836, Edward McPherson Papers, Library of Congress; Junkin to Literary Societies of Lafayette College, March 18, 1836, *ibid.;* Stevens to Literary Societies of Lafayette College, March 19, 1836, *ibid*.

[17] Philadelphia *Pennsylvanian,* March 10, 1836.

Jackson-sponsored substitute which would have expended the federal surplus upon state stocks. Other resolutions condemned federal usurpation and the centralization of authority by the executive.[18]

The Coalition enacted, also, a special election law for the city of Philadelphia, which required an annual registration of voters. Whigs hailed its passage as a curb upon voting frauds in the populous Irish centers of Southwark and Kensington. But Democrats denounced it as a deliberate attempt to deprive the workingman of a vote. They charged that it would operate unequally; that the loss of time and expense would be of little moment to the rich, but oppressive to the laborer.[19]

None of the devices formulated to embarrass the Democrats was more gratifying to Coalition strategists than the apportionment law. Under the guidance of Stevens, districts were juggled so that traditional associations were severed and strangers made to act with strangers. Where solid blocks of Democratic counties seemed to block coalition victories, districts were enlarged, several to elect as many as three senators.

Union and Northumberland counties, for example, once a part of the same county, with a common boundary along the Susquehanna River for twenty-five miles, were separated. Union was joined with Juniata, Mifflin, Perry, and Huntingdon to form a district more than one hundred miles in length and separated by numerous mountain ranges. In this new district, which was allotted two senators, Huntingdon and Union, consistent Antimasonic counties, were expected to outweigh normal Democratic majorities in Juniata, Mifflin, and Perry.[20] Previously, Antimasonic strength in Union County was nullified by Democratic Northumberland. York and Lancaster counties were united to form a district receiving three senators. The predominant Antimasonic vote in Lancaster was counted upon to offset the usual Democratic majorities in York. Traditionally Democratic Montgomery, with a population sufficient to entitle it to one senator, was attached to Chester and Delaware counties to form a district with three senators. Antimasonic strength in Chester and Delaware was expected to more than balance Democratic Montgomery. Franklin

[18] *Niles' Register*, L (June 25, 1836), 291; Philadelphia *Pennsylvanian*, June 20, 1836.

[19] *Ibid.*, May 20, 1836. See the Philadelphia *American Sentinel*, April 23, 1836, for a resolution against the Registry Law adopted at a Democratic rally.

[20] New Berlin *Union Times*, May 21, 1836.

JOSEPH AND HIS BRETHREN

and Adams, Antimasonic centers, were joined with Democratic Cumberland in another two-senator district. Thus, the finished product was a model of gerrymandering.[21]

The Democrats protested that the bill was exceeded in iniquity only by the Bank charter and that the coalition dared not meet the next election manfully.[22] But they were unable to block it. In the passage of this measure, as in the adoption of the Registry Law, eight Democratic Senators who had bolted the party on the Bank bill continued to vote with the Coalition.[23]

The Registry Law, the Apportionment Act, and instructions to the members of the United States Senate, excellent party devices in their own right, were mere side shows to the main event, the chartering of the United States Bank by the State of Pennsylvania.

Just when Nicholas Biddle, president of the Bank, came to a decision to seek a State charter for his expiring institution is a matter of conjecture. The fact that the Bank stock continued to sell at par despite the imminence of its demise under its federal charter has contributed to the assumption that an agreement was reached prior to the election, whereby Antimasons would support the recharter in return for Whig votes for Ritner.[24] The fact that the commitment of Sergeant and other Whig leaders in Philadelphia for Ritner was made only at the last moment, however, would seem to indicate that Biddle's plans materialized after the election, not before it. In any event, Whigs and moderates among the Antimasons were prepared to move for the charter from the first meeting of the legislature. Ner Middleswarth, Speaker of the House, appointed friends of the Bank to the various committees which would normally handle the business of the charter, and went so far as to circulate the list among Bank leaders before it was read in the House. The situation required extreme caution since Antimasons from the interior of the State had little interest in the charter. Furthermore, the Democratic majority in the Senate made it imperative that the Bank gain the support of at least five Democrats in addition to the solid backing of Whigs and Antimasons.

---

[21] Philadelphia *Pennsylvanian*, June 6, 15, 16, 1836; Pennsylvania, *Laws, 1835-1836*, pp. 794-795. A summary of the senatorial apportionments for 1829 and 1836 is given in the Appendix, page 228.

[22] Philadelphia *Pennsylvanian*, May 28, June 4, 6, 20, 1836.

[23] See page 79.

[24] See Thomas F. Woodley, *Thaddeus Stevens* (Harrisburg, 1934), 173.

Since the charter could not surmount such an obstacle, Biddle and his strategists struck upon a plan to combine in a single bill the charter, appropriations for public improvements, and the repeal of the State tax. The cohesive element was a bonus to be paid by the Bank in return for the charter. It would finance the improvements and make tax repeal feasible. The repeal of the tax alone was deemed insufficient to entice doubtful votes. One of Biddle's confidants explained, "Every one here . . . knows that the temptation of a turnpike, or a few miles of canal and railroad as a beginning on a favorite route is nearly irresistible."[25] The drafting of this "Omnibus Bill" was entrusted to Stevens, chairman of the House Inland Navigation and Internal Improvement Committee.

Sitting behind closed doors, Stevens and his committee scattered the improvements over the State, giving extra favors to doubtful members and especial consideration to Democrats in the Senate who would have to be detached from the opposition. Stevens, meanwhile, did not overlook his own favorite project, the Gettysburg Railroad, or as his adversaries termed it later, the "Tapeworm."

While Stevens prepared the bill, Biddle did the spadework among the Senators and toiled to insure the co-operation of the Governor. In his drive to perpetuate his institution, he overlooked no detail and spared no cost. From his office in Philadelphia flowed a steady stream of directives: a "model" charter to the chairmen of the Committee of Ways and Means and the Committee on Banks in the House; concessions which would be agreeable; modifications which would be unacceptable; loans which the Bank would offer for the improvements; subscriptions to turnpike companies; the amount and disposition of the bonus; cash or credit to bring key personnel to Harrisburg; advice on procedure to prevent the impression that it was a Philadelphia measure.[26] The correspondence was carried back and forth from Harrisburg by trusted confederates and was sometimes delivered by third parties in order to avoid the prying eyes of Democratic postmasters.[27]

---

[25] William B. Reed to Biddle, December 12, 1835, McGrane (ed.), *Correspondence of Nicholas Biddle*, 258. He added that the commencement of the work was required only upon new lines, "just to be able to go home to boast of having made a beginning."

[26] Biddle Papers.

[27] Joseph McIlvaine to Biddle, January 10, 1836, *ibid*. This letter is filed under date of January 16.

Biddle sent forth an efficient body of lobbyists or "borers," made up of volunteers and mercenaries, or as he termed them, "militia" and "regulars."[28] The former included James Todd, Ritner's Attorney General, who kept Biddle abreast of the Governor's impressions of the bill. His interpretation was frequently at variance with the judgment of Stevens and the "regulars," however, and the latter soon regretted his presence.[29] Another of the "militia" was Peter Ritner, brother of the Governor, whose reports, in contrast to Todd's, minimized the executive's doubts.[30] Biddle welcomed the aid of the volunteers as long as it was useful, but he placed responsibility for the passage upon the "regulars." "The 'militia,' " he declared, are prompt "to promise and flourish, but the regulars alone are to be relied on."[31]

The core of the regulars was made up of John B. Wallace, a Crawford County Whig and formerly a member of the House, Joseph McIlvaine, a Philadelphia Whig and veteran lobbyist,[32] and William Robinson, a Muhlenberg Democrat from Pittsburgh, a former member of the House and more recently a delegate to the gubernatorial convention, where he had been instrumental in effecting its unprecedented adjournment without making a nomination. The correspondence of McIlvaine and Wallace furnishes a day-by-day account of the progress of the Bank bill and of their multifarious activities behind the scenes. They show concern lest amendments should render the completed bill unacceptable to Ritner, or possibly to Biddle, but they indicate no lack of confidence on its passage through the legislature. The necessary Democratic votes in the Senate were virtually assured at the outset by the use of liberal appropriations for local improvements.[33]

[28] Biddle to McIlvaine, January 13, 1836, *ibid.*

[29] John B. Wallace to Biddle, February 6, 7, 8, 1836, *ibid.*

[30] Joseph McIlvaine to Biddle, n. d. [January 25-28, 1836], *ibid.* This is catalogued under December, 1836.

[31] Biddle to McIlvaine, January 13, 1836, *ibid.*

[32] A year later McIlvaine was elected to the House, where he led the Bank forces against Democratic attempts to rescind the charter.

[33] In fact, Wallace reported their names to Biddle a full week before the bill was introduced in the Senate. He advised that the votes of John Dickey, Charles B. Penrose, Thomas S. Cunningham, and Henry H. Fore were safe, and those of Alexander Irvin, Uzal Hopkins, and David Middlecoff almost safe. Of the eight Democrats who finally supported the charter, only Jesse Burden's position was still in doubt. Wallace to Biddle, February 3, 1836, Biddle Papers.

The case of Alexander Irvin illustrates the efficacy of this device. To a fellow Democrat in Clearfield in his home district he confided,

> I must confess that I do not like the bill but . . . I must go for the bill or loose [sic] my appropriations. I will be much abused I know, but it can not be helped. . . . The Ritner men will swear at me if I don't go for the bill and loose [sic] there [sic] appropriations which in Lycoming county are heavy and I promised them to go for the Elmira Railroad. . . . As the Bill now stands we get $20,000 to our turnpikes—I do not like the bill and I can not tell you its fate. It will pass—if old Joe does not place his veto upon it.[34]

John Dickey, another Democrat to receive costly improvements, was promised a branch bank at Beaver in his home district as an additional concession when he showed signs of wavering,[35] and Charles B. Penrose of the Cumberland-Perry district, who was worried about his subsequent treatment by the Democratic press, was reconciled by Biddle's purchase of the Harrisburg *Chronicle*, an antibank paper, at the cost of $3,500.[36]

Three amendments were inserted in the bill by the Senate in order to reassure Ritner. The first gave the State the authority to repeal the charter; the second required the payment of an additional bonus to the school fund; the third, which Biddle accepted with considerable reluctance, prohibited the issuance of banknotes under ten dollars.[37]

One cannot read the Biddle correspondence without coming to the conclusion that the strategy was planned and executed with rare skill. Biddle doubtless believed that his payment of $25,000 each to the three regulars among the "borers" and his total outlay of $130,000 to obtain the charter was a sound investment.[38]

On January 19, 1836, with plans well laid, Stevens introduced the bill in the House, using the innocuous title, "An Act to Repeal the State Tax and to Continue the Improvement of the State by Railroads

---

[34] Irvin to William Bigler, January [February] 9, 1836, William Bigler Papers, Historical Society of Pennsylvania.

[35] Biddle to McIlvaine, January 31, 1836, Biddle Papers.

[36] McIlvaine to Biddle, February 8, 1836, *ibid.*

[37] James Todd to Biddle, February 3, 1836, *ibid.;* John B. Wallace to Biddle, January 26, 1836, *ibid.*

[38] McIlvaine to Biddle, June 13, 1836, *ibid.;* Wallace to Elihu Chauncey, March 1, 1836, *ibid.* See also the report of the investigating committee appointed by the Pennsylvania General Assembly in 1840, printed in Pennsylvania, *House Journal, 1842,* II, Appendix, 172-531.

and Canals, and for Other Purposes."[39] The Improvements Committee approved it, pausing only long enough to rename it, "An Act to Repeal the State Tax on Real and Personal Property and to Continue and Extend the Improvements of the State by Railroads and Canals, and to Charter a State Bank to be Called the United States Bank." In three days Stevens pushed it through the lower house by a party vote, while the Democratic press, taken by surprise, hastily voiced its opposition. In the Senate, too, where it was introduced on February 10, the bill moved swiftly despite intensive pressure by the press to hold Democrats in line.

On February 1 the Philadelphia *Pennsylvanian* pointed to the solidarity of Democrats in the House and challenged the allegation that five Democrats in the Senate were ready to vote for the measure. But on February 11 it asked, "What is the matter with Charles B. Penrose?" Two years before, it observed, he had occupied the greater part of three days in the Senate delivering a philippic upon the Bank. Dickey, it continued, had been even more violent in his opposition. Opponents of the charter received a temporary reprieve when Jacob Krebs, Democrat from the Schuylkill district, charged that he had been offered a bribe to support the bill. A brief investigation revealed, however, that the "offer" had been a hoax, perpetrated in a local tavern by a Democrat, Henry W. Conrad, member of the House from Schuylkill County, an opponent of the charter.[40] Having overcome the bribery charge, the supporters of the bill speedily whipped it into shape. It passed the Senate on February 16 by a vote of 19 to 12, eight Democrats joining the Bank men. Thus, there were votes to spare, and at least one Democrat committed to the bill voted with the minority when his aid was not required.[41] Two days later the signature of Governor Ritner made it a law. The State of Pennsylvania thus suspended the death sentence which Jackson had imposed upon the "Monster."

[39] The Tax Law of 1831 was the measure involved.

[40] Wallace to Biddle, February 10, 1836, Biddle Papers; Philadelphia *American Sentinel*, February 12, 1836; *Niles' Register*, XLIX (February 20, 1836), 434; L (March 19, 1836), 46.

[41] The eight Democrats were Jesse R. Burden of Philadelphia County, John Dickey of Beaver County, Henry H. Fore of Bedford County, Uzal Hopkins of Columbia County, David Middlecoff of Adams County, Charles B. Penrose of Cumberland County, Thomas S. Cunningham of Mercer County, and Alexander Irvin of Clearfield County. George N. Baker of Philadelphia County voted in the negative when his support was not needed. Baker to Biddle, February 5, 1836, Biddle Papers.

Experience was to demonstrate that the charter was costly to the Bank and the State alike. By its terms the former was obliged to pay a cash bonus of $4,500,000 and make a loan to the State of $1,000,000 at 4 per cent for a period not to exceed one year. It was required to invest $6,000,000 in Pennsylvania stocks and subscribe $675,000 to railroad and turnpike stocks. In addition, there was the sum expended upon the "borers." The Bank thus made a large initial outlay for privileges which it expected to enjoy for thirty years. But Biddle's hopes were never realized. Panic and mismanagement joined to bring an untimely end to the "Marble Palace" on Chestnut Street, Philadelphia, before six years had elapsed. As for the State, the bonus permitted the extension of the Public Works upon a vast and costly pattern, but the repeal of the State tax cut off the revenue required for its sustenance. The Panic of 1837 found the State without cash or income. It was soon in serious financial straits.[42]

But these unfortunate results were not apparent in 1836. The Whig and Antimasonic papers were lavish in their praise of the legislature. One Whig sheet boasted that no session in years had been so fruitful.

> They found the state under a system of taxation, her public works unfinished, her treasury empty; and absolute necessity, if some new course was not adopted, of increasing the public debt, of continuing and increasing the taxes, or stopping the completion of the public works. What has been done? Let this question be asked by every Pennsylvanian and he will find an answer in the repeal of the tax laws, in the progress of the public works without an increase of the public debt, and a full treasury. Is this not worthy of commendation? Let the same policy be continued, and we shall soon have our improvements completed, the trade of the west secured to Pennsylvania, a sinking fund established for the extinction of the public debt, and a tide of prosperity.[43]

Another paper pointed with pride to the repeal of the State tax, and appropriations to the common schools, which would "raise the veil of ignorance and elevate the poor man's child to the same advantages of the rich, for a sound and practical education."[44]

Not emphasized in the press was the fact that the session of the legislature marked the ascendancy of the Whigs in the Coalition and

[42] Reginald C. McGrane, *Foreign Bondholders and American State Debts* (New York, 1935), 64-65; *Hunt's Merchants' Magazine*, XX (1849), 256-269; Pennsylvania, *House Journal, 1840*, II, Pt. 2, 254-255.

[43] Harrisburg *Intelligencer*, reprinted in *Niles' Register*, L (April 9, 1836), 91.

[44] Harrisburg *Telegraph*, March 26, 1836.

the decline of "Exclusive" Antimasonry. Leadership had been taken by the Whigs in the nomination of Harrison, in the adoption of the Registry Law, in instructing Democratic Senators in Washington, and, most conspicuously, in the passage of the Bank charter.

The depths to which "Exclusive" Antimasonry had fallen was revealed by the failure of their national convention. Early in April the party executive committee issued a call to the Antimasons of the nation to assemble in Philadelphia on May 4, 1836. In the address, they charged that the State convention of the previous December had been controlled by Whigs and Masons. To rectify this situation, they announced that the State would be represented by a full and unpledged delegation. They urged Antimasons in other states to take similar action. "The distracted condition of the Antimasonic Party throughout the Union, caused by the fatal proceedings of the Pennsylvania State Convention," the address concluded, "requires this step as the only thing to save it from utter prostration."[45]

The response to the call, however, was disheartening. Among the Antimasonic papers in Pennsylvania, only the Gettysburg *Star,* closely identified with Stevens, and the Pittsburgh *Times* seem to have supported it. The convention proved to be a slender affair. Stevens seized the opportunity to condemn Harrison's nomination at Harrisburg and the role of the Whigs in effecting it.[46] But it was of little consequence. The convention adjourned without taking any action. Time was running out upon Antimasonry.

[45] Philadelphia *American Sentinel,* April 2, 1836. The address was signed by Thaddeus Stevens, Samuel Parke, and William W. Irvin. See Charles McCarthy, "The Antimasonic Party: A Study of Political Antimasonry in the United States, 1827-1840," American Historical Association, *Annual Report, 1902* (Washington, 1903), I, 365-574.

[46] Philadelphia *American Sentinel,* May 6, 1836.

CHAPTER V

Nourishment for the "Monster," 1836-1837

THE election of 1835 left the Democrats in two hostile camps; their watchword, vindication, not conciliation. Wolf leaders bombarded Jackson with requests for an honorable office for their chief, and at Harrisburg Muhlenberg members of the legislature refused to go into caucus with the Wolf men, preferring to bargain with the Coalition for the offices and the printing rather than accept a minority role in the party.[1] The latter, Wolf supporters contended, destroyed all hopes of a pacification. "A union with such men is impossible," a Lancaster County leader warned, "the Ex-Reverend and his immediate followers must and will be shook [sic] off."[2]

The proscription, however, was not echoed by the rank and file of the party. In counties where one faction was definitely predominant, the majority showed a disposition to offer the olive branch to the minority; and union and harmony meetings were held in increasing numbers throughout the State.[3] In Philadelphia, the presence of Van Buren was made the occasion for an informal gathering of both factions, and Van Buren contributed a union toast to the cause. The press, with occasional relapses, also showed a willingness to forgive and forget. Rival Democratic editors in Harrisburg issued a joint call for peace, and the Philadelphia *Pennsylvanian* proposed the maxim, "Concession and Compromise—everything for the cause and nothing for men."[4] Wolf papers, following the lead of the Philadelphia *Sentinel,* conceded that the two-term principle had been accepted by the Democrats with respect to both State and federal offices.[5] And of more significance than platitudes for an immediate

---

[1] See page 69. The Senate was made up of thirteen Whigs and Antimasons, twelve Wolf Democrats, and eight Muhlenberg Democrats.

[2] Reah Frazer to Buchanan, January 1, 1836, Buchanan Papers. For a justification of the action of the Muhlenberg partisans, see Lloyd Wharton to Muhlenberg, December 1, 1835, Muhlenberg Papers.

[3] Peter Wager to Buchanan, October 30, 1835, Buchanan Papers.

[4] November 2, 1835.

[5] October 19, 1835.

reconciliation, Muhlenberg sheets in the interior urged the acceptance of the electoral ticket endorsed by the Wolf men.[6]

The latter concession led the Wolf men in January, 1836, to participate in a Muhlenberg-sponsored Jackson Day convention in Harrisburg, a meeting which they had earlier rejected in favor of a March 4 convention of their own. It proved to be a boon to conciliation. In an atmosphere of cordiality, the Muhlenberg men officially endorsed the electoral ticket of their rivals, and in return, the Wolf members agreed to a resolution which declared that the proceedings of the March 7, 1835, convention had been unauthorized and without precedent in Democratic usages. In so doing, they conceded that the nomination of Wolf was irregular. A central party committee was named to replace the rival State organizations; and behind the scenes an agreement was reached whereby the two Democratic papers in Harrisburg, the *Reporter* and the *State Journal,* were combined, with the editors of each joining into partnership.[7]

The Jackson Day convention restored the party organization, but the disposition of Wolf remained a bothersome problem during the months which followed. Wolf spokesmen set their hats for the collectorship of the port of Philadelphia with its extensive patronage, but Jackson wisely refrained from removing the incumbent in a stronghold of the Muhlenberg faction.[8] In March, 1836, Jackson offered to make Wolf the Comptroller of Treasury, a newly created office, or an auditor in the Treasury Department, but Wolf refused them as unworthy of his previous station.[9] Four months later, however, Wolf reconsidered and accepted the comptrollership. Muhlenberg men then called for compensation; and Jackson, en route to Tennessee, interrupted his homeward journey to give his assurance that he would appoint Jesse Miller, a Muhlenberg leader in Congress, as auditor.[10] He thereby removed another barrier to unity.

The superficial healing of the wounds was augmented tremendously by the revival of the Bank controversy. It permitted Democrats to live 1834 over again, to take the sword from Jackson's hands, and, presumably, to slay the "Monster" a second time.

[6] See Philadelphia *American Sentinel,* November 2, 3, 6, 9, 1835.

[7] Philadelphia *Pennsylvanian,* January 11, 13, 14, 18, 1836.

[8] Roberts Vaux to Wolf, October 26, 30, November 24, 1835, Wolf Political Correspondence; Daniel M. Brodhead to Wolf, October 30, 1835, *ibid.*

[9] Buchanan to Brodhead, March 15, 1836, Daniel M. Brodhead Papers, Library of Congress.

[10] Buchanan to Jackson, July 8, 1836, Moore (ed.), *Works of James Buchanan,* III, 125; Jackson to Buchanan, July 11, 1836, Buchanan Papers.

As rumors circulated that the Bank of the United States would seek a Pennsylvania charter, Democratic papers in a chorus denounced the scheme and called upon the Senate to destroy it.

> Is there no hope—refuge—sanctuary left? [the Philadelphia *Pennsylvanian* inquired] Yes—we trust there is. We look to the Senate of the state for safety in this dangerous extremity. Every Democrat then, who values his reputation for consistency—who respects the voice of the party . . . will record his vote against this new attempt upon the liberties of the people.[11]

Democrats in their convention on January 8, 1836, adopted a resolution against the charter which branded the Bank an "unconstitutional, moneyed monopoly."[12] The passage of the charter in the Assembly stepped up the tempo.

> If we had cause to fear here [Henry D. Gilpin observed in Philadelphia], it is now at an end. The madness of our opponents has done for us all that the greatest sagacity could not have accomplished. You would really believe here that the feud of last summer had never existed. The public meeting last Monday was the largest, the most harmonious and the most resolute I almost ever saw. The truth is we now rest on fundamental principles.[13]

When a minority of Democrats in the Senate began to vote with the Coalition, Democratic papers turned their bitterest invective upon them. They gave no quarter to the "inglorious eight" who voted for its final passage; likening them to Benedict Arnold, they called upon them to resign from their seats in the Senate. In Washington, Van Buren added his voice to the expression. In reply to an invitation to attend a mass meeting in Hamilton County, Ohio, held to celebrate "the relief of the County from the thraldom of the Bank," Van Buren declared that the same power had again entered the field and had gained a victory over the popular will; that instead of commercial distress this time it had taken a noiseless approach to legislative power and had secured its respite through the "inexcusable improvidence of the state legislature."[14]

---

[11] January 6, 1836.

[12] Philadelphia *Pennsylvanian*, January 14, 1836.

[13] Gilpin to Buchanan, February 2, 1836, Buchanan Papers.

[14] Van Buren to Hamilton County Committee, February 22, 1836, reprinted in *Niles' Register*, L (April 23, 1836), 135-136. Muhlenberg was alarmed lest he should be identified with his "friends" in their support of the Bank charter in the Senate. He wrote to them, "entreating and warning," but to no avail. Muhlenberg to Rebecca Muhlenberg, January 30, February 7, 1836, Muhlenberg Papers. See also Lloyd Wharton to Muhlenberg, January 11,'1836, *ibid*.

Biddle's newly purchased Harrisburg *Chronicle,* posing as a Democratic paper, strove vainly to vindicate the Bank Democrats in the Senate; to dissociate the Bank as a State institution from its merits as a national bank, and to remove the question from politics; but it seemed to have little effect. As a political device, the paper was a bad investment![15]

The degree to which the charter issue revitalized the party was indicated by the subsequent course of the eight Bank Democrats in the Senate. Repudiated on the platform and in the press, they abandoned all hopes of reinstatement. After a brief and abortive attempt to rally Bank Democrats under the banner of "The States' Rights Party of Pennsylvania," they attached themselves to the Coalition.[16]

The Bank issue continued to serve as a unifying force for the Democratic party during the campaign of 1836. Yet there was little agreement upon a course of action.

Hard-Money Men or Locofocos, whom contemporaries commonly termed the radicals, urged the repeal of the charter by the legislature; and men of a more conservative mold such as Buchanan and George M. Dallas advocated its repeal through constitutional amendment. But both of these expedients were repugnant to friends of banking and paper money who feared that an assault upon the charter might precipitate an all-out attack upon banking *per se* and threaten the sanctity of contract. A Young Men's Democratic Convention meeting at Harrisburg on July 4, 1836, narrowly averted an open rupture when a radical Bank resolution was offered. Harmony was restored only after it had been rendered completely innocuous.[17] The Democratic press, due to this disagreement, avoided constructive proposals, and was content to hurl invectives upon the Bank and its creators.

The Coalition press, meanwhile, underscored the Democratic weakness upon the Bank issue and maintained that the opposition to the charter was dictated by the New York Democratic clique and was destructive to the genuine interests of the State. By identifying it with Van Buren they hoped to capitalize upon his unpopularity.[18] But

[15] The *Chronicle* began its defense of the charter on May 30, 1836.
[16] Philadelphia *Pennsylvanian,* March 8, 1836; Mueller, *Whig Party,* 27.
[17] Philadelphia *Pennsylvanian,* July 11, 1836.
[18] Harrisburg *Chronicle,* June 22, 1836; Philadelphia *National Gazette,* August 16, 1836.

their efforts were unproductive. The State election returns in October, 1836, revealed a sweeping Democratic victory despite the handicap of the elaborate gerrymandering of the Coalition. Democrats increased their membership in the House from thirty-one to seventy-two and filled each of the eight vacancies in the Senate. Thaddeus Stevens and Ner Middleswarth were among the casualties of the Democratic surge, despite the fact that they stood for office in traditionally Antimasonic counties.[19] In Philadelphia County, Joel B. Sutherland, whose political organization had been the envy of politicians for more than a decade, was rejected by his constituents, who elected Lemuel Paynter, a mechanic, to his seat in Congress. Sutherland had made the mistake of defending Jesse R. Burden, one of the "inglorious eight."[20] In the Huntingdon-Perry-Mifflin-Juniata-Union senatorial district, one of the most gerrymandered in the State, the Democratic nominee, David R. Porter, was a surprise victor. It gave him Statewide publicity and made him a strong candidate for Governor.[21]

The November, 1836, election for President was a much closer affair. The Bank magic was not as effective as it had been in October. Yet it undoubtedly secured votes for the colorless Van Buren, who carried the State by about 2,500 votes. In defeat, the Coalition Men had one consolation. They had been instrumental in the legislature in selecting November rather than October for the election of delegates to the constitutional convention and had thereby augmented their representation in that body.[22]

By exploiting the Bank charter, Democrats achieved a political landslide. But eighteen members of the 1835-1836 House of Representatives were returned to office. Of the seventy-two Democrats in the 1836-1837 House, sixty-three were taking seats in that body for the first time, and most of them were barely known beyond their own localities. As a result, the legislature, and the House in particular, was an enigma to the most astute observers of the political scene.

The first indication of its potentialities was furnished by a senatorial election. Buchanan, seeking re-election, had straddled the fence during the gubernatorial contest and had lost friends on both sides. The choice was thus between the unenthusiastic support of Buchanan

---

[19] Stevens in Adams County and Middleswarth in Union County.
[20] Philadelphia *Pennsylvanian,* October 7, 10, 11, 12, 1836; Philadelphia *American Sentinel,* October 4, 8, 11, 1836.
[21] New Berlin *Union Times,* October 22, 1836.
[22] See Chapter VI.

in the interest of harmony and the advocacy of rival Muhlenberg and Wolf adherents with the likelihood of a renewal of the feud. Muhlenberg, ambitious for political preferment, was willing to risk the latter. A show of strength by his friends, he argued, even though they should eventually throw their strength to Buchanan, would serve to show the latter his dependence upon their favor and be of value in the future.[23] Muhlenberg's organ in Reading, the *Democratic Press*, promoted his candidacy at the expense of Buchanan. A favorite theme was the consistency of Berks County's Democratic majorities in contrast with Lancaster County, where, it emphasized, the Bank party reigned supreme.[24]

Buchanan, it might be added, complained to Van Buren of the Muhlenberg activity and enclosed an offensive article from the *Democratic Press*. Their opposition, he declared, had succeeded in keeping the Harrisburg *Keystone*, the Philadelphia *Pennsylvanian*, and other papers silent. "I believe Muhlenberg to be your true friend; and I consider him the dupe now as he was upon a former occasion. The object is to make him the means of dividing the Democratic Party."[25] Muhlenberg's candidacy came to nought, however, when the Democrats went into caucus and named Buchanan as the nominee of the party.

Due to the large Democratic majority on a joint ballot of the two houses, Buchanan's election now appeared a certainty. But the Coalition used Fabian tactics in the hope of dividing its opponents. Resorting to a technicality, the Senate postponed a joint session from day to day, after first placing Muhlenberg's name among the list of nominees.[26] The strategy boomeranged, however, when Muhlenberg rejected Coalition support[27] and Governor Ritner agreed to sign a special election bill which would have required an immediate election.[28] When the two houses finally went into joint session, Buchanan

[23] Muhlenberg to Henry Simpson, October 30, 1836, Gratz Correspondence; Lloyd Wharton to Muhlenberg, December 8, 1836, Wagner Papers.

[24] Reading *Democratic Press*, November 15, 1836.

[25] Buchanan to Van Buren, November 18, 1836, Moore (ed.), *Works of James Buchanan*, III, 128-129. The clipping is in the Van Buren Papers.

[26] Hamilton Alrick to Buchanan, December 12, 1836, Buchanan Papers; Samuel D. Patterson to Buchanan, December 12, 1836, *ibid*.

[27] Muhlenberg to John Miller, printed in the Harrisburg *Keystone*, December 10, 1836.

[28] George Plitt to Buchanan, December 9, 1836, Buchanan Papers; Samuel C. Stambaugh to Buchanan, December 13, 1836, *ibid.;* John Hassard to Buchanan, December 14, 1836, *ibid.;* Reah Frazer to Buchanan, December 19, 1836, *ibid*.

was quickly elected by a party vote. Democrats thus emerged from their first contest unscathed.

The incongruous Democrats thereupon ran into a problem far more distracting than the election of a United States Senator: What course should they follow in relation to the Bank? With their opponents in command in the Senate and the gubernatorial office, a repeal of the charter was impractical, and action was limited to such devices as an investigation of its passage or possibly mild regulatory measures which might elicit the approval of the Senate and the Governor. But even such halfway contrivances as these were beset with difficulties. Conservative Democrats, working behind the scenes, were fully as zealous as the Whigs in their defense of the Bank and banking in general. A brief sketch of the activities of several among this group will serve to bring their position into focus.

Robert Patterson, prominent Philadelphia politician and chairman of the presidential electors of the State, made the meeting of the electors in Harrisburg the occasion to propagate the Bank's case. To Biddle, he confided, that he had been "at the proper places at the proper times," endeavoring to produce the right feeling among the electors and the legislators. He reported that he had stressed the impolicy of interfering with existing institutions and had urged resistance to dictation from any quarter. Pennsylvania, he emphasized, "had played second fiddle long enough, and must set up for herself." In short, he had impressed them with "Pennsylvania interests, Pennsylvania measures, carried out by Pennsylvanians."[29] Patterson expressed a similar opinion to Van Buren, omitting, of course, any reference to his labors in the Electoral College. He urged the rescinding of the Specie Circular as a means of restoring public faith, and elaborated upon the virtues of the Bank as a check upon local banks.[30]

Lewis Dewart of Northumberland County, Speaker of the House, former Federalist, one-time member of Congress, businessman, and railroad speculator, accepted the hospitality of Bank lobbyists in Harrisburg and minimized their fears of an investigation. Should one be voted, it would be perfunctory in character, he advised. The committee would not go to Philadelphia, but would merely send for those persons who would be willing to straggle to Harrisburg.[31] Dewart subsequently found occasions to serve the Bank from the Speaker's chair.

[29] Patterson to Biddle, December 3, 1836, Biddle Papers.
[30] Patterson to Van Buren, April 27, 1837, Van Buren Papers.
[31] Cheyney Hickman to Biddle, January 15, 1837, Biddle Papers.

Simon Cameron, a rising young Democratic politician and Middletown bank president, commuting to Harrisburg during the session of the legislature where he was lobbying for a bill favorable to the York and Baltimore railroad, took time from his special interest to cultivate the "proper" attitude on the Bank issue. Reporting to Biddle, he declared, "The intelligent members of the party are tired of the continued war upon the Bank and are willing to get out of it. I go to Washington tomorrow morning to see if I cannot get some influence to operate from that quarter upon the main violent ones at Harrisburg."[32]

Muhlenberg, while supporting Jackson and Van Buren measures in Congress, permitted the use of his name in Harrisburg to restrain his followers from taking a course unfriendly to the Bank. Lloyd Wharton and George Keim, the latter a Congressman-elect of Berks County and a recognized Muhlenberg spokesman, joined the march upon Harrisburg to put pressure upon the Berks County delegation, and Wharton made a hurried round trip to Washington, returning with Muhlenberg's proposal for a compromise, a device which would permit Bank opponents to adopt legislation purporting to be harmful, but which in reality would serve only "to gull the multitude."[33] Muhlenberg also addressed a statement to Speaker Dewart.

The sentiments of these Democrats were echoed by a substantial element of the party, particularly men who were impressed with the need for paper money and bank credit to finance the public improvements and facilitate corporate enterprise. While they could not afford to support the Bank charter openly, they were willing neither to lose the appropriations provided in the bonus nor to overlook the possibility of additional investments by the Bank in the future. They were determined to shield the Bank from harm.

Hard-Money Men, on the other hand, took a position completely antithetical to that of their paper-money brethren. Adherents of the metallic currency maxims of Jefferson, John Taylor, and, more recently, William M. Gouge,[34] and responsive to the leadership of Jackson, Taney, Kendall, and Benton, they sought to limit the control of banks over currency. They believed this would eliminate periodic

---

[32] Cameron to Biddle, January 31, 1837, *ibid.*

[33] Joseph McIlvaine to Biddle, January 19, 1837, filed under 1836, *ibid.;* McIlvaine to Biddle, February 1, 1837, filed under 1836, *ibid.;* Lloyd Wharton to Biddle, February 21, 1837, March 4, 1837, *ibid.*

[34] Arthur M. Schlesinger, Jr., *The Age of Jackson* (Boston, 1945), 117.

orgies of speculation, destroy monopoly, restore the money power to the people, and remove the tendency of banks

> to make the world dishonest and profligate—to increase crime and licentiousness; to make industry tributary to idleness and give vice a supremacy over virtue . . . [and to] increase too to a vast extent the tendency in society to the extremes of wealth and poverty.[35]

On the national scene, they endorsed the Bank veto, the removal of deposits, the Specie Circular, the resumption of minting gold coins, and the restriction upon small notes. In the State, they supported the elimination of banknotes of smaller denominations, the defeat of bank charters in the legislature, and the repeal of the charter of the United States Bank by the legislature or the constitutional convention. It is difficult to estimate the strength of this group, since party members frequently paid lip service to these principles during political campaigns, then reverted to a do-nothing policy.

In Philadelphia, many of the rank and file of the party were converts of hard money. Leadership was furnished to a considerable degree by the intellectual fringe. It included Charles J. Ingersoll, author, one-time member of Congress and Bank adherent, but now a vigorous opponent of banking and corporate privilege, "who looks upon common people through gold specs and ornaments his fingers with costly diamonds";[36] and Thomas Earle, affluent lawyer, journalist, humanitarian, and champion of constitutional revision. They were counseled also by Henry D. Gilpin and Henry Horn, veteran Jackson campaigners. In the city where the Whigs predominated, Hard-Money Men had few opportunities to demonstrate their talents, but the county frequently furnished spokesmen in the legislature.

In Luzerne County, Democrats split into two hostile camps, the one faction committed to Locofoco doctrine, the other to a more conservative position. They competed bitterly for the offices, and their party conventions were replete with strife. Both controlled newspapers and used them to carry their quarrel to the public. The Coalition, which was weak in the county, adopted the policy of making no nominations and supporting the conservative faction. In 1835 the radicals sent Benjamin Bidlack to the State House of Representatives, where he waged a losing battle against the Bank charter. A year later each faction elected a delegate to the constitutional convention; and in 1837 in a special election to fill a vacancy in the

[35] Wilkes-Barre *Republican Farmer and Democratic Journal,* July 5, 1837.
[36] Harrisburg *Pennsylvania Telegraph,* June 1, 1837.

convention the conservatives defeated Bidlack, the candidate of the Hard-Money Men, by a narrow margin.[37] Elsewhere in the State Locofocoism was thinly scattered and lacking in organization.

The diversity of opinion among the Democrats, the irreconcilability of the two extremes, the inexperience of the members of the legislature, and the well-planned strategy of the Bank's forces precluded effective action against the Bank.

Biddle's procedure in safeguarding his institution from the machinations of the Democrats created a pattern which he followed each year thereafter until the Bank finally closed its doors. In many respects it resembled his drive for a charter during the previous session. Now, however, he was fighting a defensive engagement. His first objective was to prevent criticism or hostile action from coming into the open. "Our true policy is delay, delay, delay," he declared. It was not a question of what the result would be. "Nothing can be proved but much will be alleged—nothing found but much asserted. A much greater triumph than any acquittal is not to be tried." In Europe, he observed, the owners of American property had no way of knowing the character of the members of the House and thinking them decent people might believe that the Bank was under a sort of trial.[38]

Accordingly, when the supposedly radical Democrat, John Hill of Westmoreland County, introduced a resolution in the State House of Representatives on December 23, 1836, calling for an inquiry into the manner and means of the passage of the charter and the conduct of the Bank and its agents since that date,[39] Biddle unleashed his professional lobbyists, Joseph McIlvaine, John B. Wallace, and William Robinson, abetted by special agents for specific tasks, Bank directors, and volunteers, with orders to keep the resolution buried. McIlvaine was now a member of the House and more than ever the key figure in the Bank's strategy. He not only gained the confidence of Speaker Dewart, but received from him the chairmanship of the Internal Improvement Committee over the protests of the radicals. He also cultivated the chairman of the Ways and Means Committee, William F. Johnston, a future Governor of the State, "a pretty clever sort of lawyer from Armstrong," a valuable ally in the weeks which followed.[40] Aided by the Speaker, the resolution was delayed, but

[37] Wilkes-Barre *Republican Farmer and Democratic Journal*, October 18, 1837.
[38] Biddle to McIlvaine, January 17, 1837, Biddle Papers.
[39] Philadelphia *Pennsylvanian*, December 24, 1836.
[40] McIlvaine to Biddle, December 13, 1836, Biddle Papers.

not killed.[41] Hill eventually got the floor and brought it to a vote. Democrats of all shades and a minority of the Coalition, unable to justify opposition to an investigation, joined to adopt it by an overwhelming vote.[42]

Anticipating the above action, McIlvaine and his aides set up their second line of defense, which was to turn the investigation into a Bank victory. They secured a committee which was lacking both in experience and legal talent. Of the seven named by Speaker Dewart, three were identified as radicals, but none of the three was a lawyer and none was acceptable to Democratic leaders. Of the other four, three were regarded as friends of the Bank, and the fourth was so obscure that his views could not be immediately ascertained.[43] After the personnel of the committee had been determined, the Bank lobbyists scrutinized each member and applied the persuasion deemed to be most efficacious.

Possibly the most potent lever in their hands was the Improvement Bill. McIlvaine used his committee post to strengthen doubtful members with attractive appropriations. He used this technique with telling effect upon Chairman Hill, who feared that a whitewash report would arouse the wrath of his constituents, who were shouting for the Bank's blood. The committee was subsequently enlarged to eleven; and when it appeared that William F. Johnston, an improvement-minded Democrat, would exert a good influence upon others on the committee, McIlvaine induced a "less manageable" member to resign to make room for him.[44] By these devices the investigation was limited to the testimony of a handful of witnesses, made up for the most part of members of the previous session who had participated actively in the contest and were "willing to struggle" to Harrisburg.[45]

Of those heard, Thaddeus Stevens received the major attention; and he was seldom in better form. Instead of apologizing for the Bank, he maintained that the State had scored a notable victory. Cleverly emphasizing his own role, he insisted that he had first determined the sum which the Bank would offer as a bonus and had then doubled it, despite protests from the Bank's agents, and that when it appeared doubtful that the Bank would accept his terms he had inquired to ascertain whether the Girard Bank, also seeking a

[41] McIlvaine to Biddle, January 19, 1837, *ibid.*
[42] Philadelphia *Pennsylvanian*, January 25, 1837. The vote was 82 to 11.
[43] McIlvaine to Biddle, n. d. [January 21, 1837], Biddle Papers.
[44] McIlvaine to Biddle, February 1, [1837], *ibid.*
[45] Cheyney Hickman to Biddle, January 15, [1837], *ibid.*

charter, would take them. In the face of this situation, the Bank had been forced to accept this offer. The Bank men applauded Stevens' testimony in spite of his contention that they had come out second best. William B. Reed, a special agent of the Bank, gleefully informed Biddle that Stevens had emphasized the impositions levied upon the Bank so effectively that

> before he was half through instead of being corrupted by you he put himself and the Governor and the Senate before the Committee as your most rapacious oppressors for the good of the state. The majority of the Committee would barely let him finish and the moment he said he had concluded he was discharged.[46]

The investigation muddled along for a few days, then adjourned to prepare a report.

The Bank men now girded themselves for the final assault. The investigation had uncovered nothing significant, and Biddle had little to fear from the majority report. But he was apprehensive lest the radicals, because of their dislike for the Bank or their desire to manufacture political capital, would issue a minority report condemning Bank practices in general terms. The situation was further complicated following the adjournment of Congress by the influx of Democratic Congressmen and other officeholders, who attempted to strengthen the radicals on the committee. McIlvaine reported a decided change in Hill's views caused in part by the uncertainty of the Improvement Bill, "but chiefly by a gang of scoundrels who are swarming here, including Buchanan and Jesse Miller."[47] But McIlvaine and his group persevered and brought Hill into line by saving his local appropriations from being stricken from the Improvement Bill and by exerting the pressure of the friends of the improvements upon him. The majority report, though mildly critical in several instances, was essentially the work of the Bank lobby.[48] Immediately upon its completion, a Whig member rushed a copy to William B. Reed, who worked through the night preparing a counterreport, a complete vindication of the Bank. In the morning it was signed by three members as the minority report.[49]

[46] February 27, 1837, *ibid.*
[47] McIlvaine to Biddle, n. d. [March 20, 1837], *ibid.*
[48] McIlvaine to Biddle, March 23, [1837], *ibid.* Biddle received a preliminary draft drawn up by his lobbyists. He made several minor alterations and returned it. Biddle to McIlvaine, March 7, 1837, *ibid.*
[49] Reed to Biddle, March 24, 1837, *ibid.;* McIlvaine to Biddle, March 24, [1837], *ibid.;* William B. Fling to Biddle, March 26, 1837, *ibid.*

A last bit of drama remained to be unfolded. After the majority report had been presented and a motion made to lay it upon the table, George R. Espy, a radical from Venango County, offered an amendment which instructed the Judiciary Committee to bring in a bill repealing the charter of the Bank.[50] His move came as a complete surprise to the Bank's friends and foes. McIlvaine declared that he had never seen such a breathless moment in any legislature. "Nobody spoke except some three of four Jackson men who ran to beg him to withdraw it as out of place."[51] Bank men remained silent rather than run the risk of making it a party test.[52] Espy would not be diverted and forced the reluctant House to a vote. It was lost 31 to 60.[53] The results were gratifying to the Bank group, "though the experiment was a dangerous one."[54] The amendment, having been disposed, the report was accepted unanimously and the committee discharged. The Bank thus resisted the challenge of its foes and revealed the Democrats in their true colors, that is, as hopelessly split on the Bank.

Just prior to adjournment twenty Democrats who had joined with Bank men to defeat Espy's amendment, seeking to refute criticism and to appease their constituents, issued a statement in explanation of their votes. They declared that an acceptance of Espy's amendment would have confused the issue, since the action would have appeared to originate with the committee. They denied that they were friendly toward the Bank and insisted that it was inimical to the welfare of society, whether the charter had been obtained fairly or not. They maintained that they favored the repeal of the charter, but released their statement after it was too late to test their sincerity.[55] When word leaked out that the above action was contemplated, McIlvaine hastened to reassure his employer. It would not be signed by a majority of the House, he observed accurately, and in all events would be merely something for the journal. And so it was![56]

Hard-Money Men were naturally displeased with the outcome. William English, a Philadelphia County radical and member of the committee, explained lamely that he had agreed to sign the majority report in deference to Hill's wishes and had discovered too late "that

[50] Philadelphia *United States Gazette,* March 27, 1837; Reed to Biddle, March 24, 1837, Biddle Papers.
[51] McIlvaine to Biddle, March 24, 1837, *ibid.*
[52] Reed to Biddle, March 24, 1837, *ibid.*
[53] Philadelphia *American Sentinel,* March 27, 1837.
[54] McIlvaine to Biddle, March 24, 1837, Biddle Papers.
[55] Philadelphia *Americal Sentinel,* April 18, 1837.
[56] [March 29, 1837], filed at close of 1837, Biddle Papers.

Hill, Gilmore and Johnston had been enlisted in favor of the Bank; their compensation the Improvement bill."[57] Benjamin Mifflin, editor of the Philadelphia *Pennsylvanian,* staunch Jackson-Van Buren sheet in Philadelphia, declared that a great indifference was being manifested about the party and its operations thereafter.[58] Buchanan gloomily forecast a division in the ranks of the party which might endure for years to come.[59] Cameron, glad to see the efforts of the Hard-Money Men come to nought, observed shrewdly that every movement in the legislature added to the permanent strength of the Bank.[60]

During the closing weeks of the legislature, McIlvaine had carefully nurtured the Improvement Bill so as to keep its progress parallel with that of the investigation. The intense competition for appropriations and the plethora of amendments offered made the task extremely difficult. In order to insure its passage, he had found it necessary to increase both the number and size of the grants until it had reached the unprecedented sum of $3,031,943[61] and had aroused the misgivings of the Governor. It finally passed both houses a few hours before the Investigating Committee made its report. But it got no further; Ritner vetoed the bill, and the House failed to pass it over his head. It had served its immediate purpose for McIlvaine, but was injurious to his long-range strategy, since it destroyed "the fulcrum of all operations."[62] McIlvaine delivered a tirade upon the veto from the floor of the House, but this afforded little consolation to Democratic members.[63] They were forced to return to their homes empty-handed, with neither Biddle's scalp nor improvements to appease their irate constituents.

[57] John J. McCahen to Buchanan, April 7, 1837, Buchanan Papers. Samuel A. Gilmore, an Improvement Democrat from Butler County, worked with McIlvaine to wear down Hill's opposition to a favorable report. McIlvaine to Biddle, [March 22, 1837], filed at close of 1837, Biddle Papers.
[58] Mifflin to Buchanan, April 18, 1837, Buchanan Papers.
[59] Buchanan to McCahen, April 1, 1837, *ibid.*
[60] Cameron to Buchanan, February 14, 1837, *ibid.*
[61] *Niles' Register,* LII (April 15, 1837), 104.
[62] McIlvaine to Biddle, April 1, 1837, Biddle Papers.
[63] Philadelphia *United States Gazette,* April 5, 6, 1837.

CHAPTER VI

The Constitution of 1838

ARDENT Jeffersonians in Pennsylvania were never fully reconciled to the Constitution of 1790 and continued to revere the names of John Smilie of Fayette County and William Findley of Westmoreland, who had fought a losing battle against the forces of conservatism in the convention. They were most dissatisfied with the excessive patronage of the Governor, life terms for judges, three consecutive terms for the executive, and the restrictions upon the amending power. They also objected to the power of the legislature to charter corporations and to authorize banks to issue notes.

Action to remedy these grievances, however, encountered the determined resistance of vested interests. The most formidable opposition frequently came from the executive and his officeholders, who had no desire to sacrifice the patronage by a revision of the constitution. Hence, whether a Federalist or Republican, Democrat, Antimason, or Whig occupied the gubernatorial chair, he could be counted upon to obstruct a revision. Allied with the administration, regardless of party lines, were certain conservative elements which preferred to perpetuate the old order, whatever its faults, rather than risk the hazards of a constitutional convention. Included in this catgory were the Germans, a conservative force since the Colonial era; business and commercial groups; and large property holders. The issue transcended party lines, yet Federalists, National Republicans, and Whigs in chronological succession rallied to the defense of the constitution. Jeffersonians and Democrats, on the other hand, supplied the motivation for change. Antimasons were divided along sectional lines. Counties in the western and northern portions, only partially organized in 1790, championed reform from the outset; and by the third and fourth decades of the nineteenth century urban workingmen were adding their voices to the cause.

The reform movement was stimulated in 1824 by Jackson's victory in the State. A bill providing for a referendum was pushed through the legislature, but the voters decisively rejected a convention by a margin of more than 15,000. The conservative East overwhelmed the radical North and West. Yet the referendum revealed a strong minority opinion in favor of modification, and the flood tide of democracy which swept Jackson into the Presidency in 1828 renewed and strengthened the demand for reform. Jackson contributed to the movement in his vibrant veto of the Bank recharter in which he castigated the monied aristocracy for its perversion of government to serve its private purposes; and by the winter of 1832-1833 the movement for constitutional revision was again in full swing. Numerous petitions for a convention were presented to the legislature; and in Philadelphia the Association for the Abolition of Offices for Life carried on an active program.

This organization was composed for the most part of mechanics and artisans and was headed by a fringe group of intellectuals. Its leading spirit, Thomas Earle, braved the wrath of the Philadelphia bar to pursue the issue. The association called for the further democratization of government by the reduction of the Governor's term to two years and of his eligibility to four years out of any eight; the appointment of judges by the Governor, subject to confirmation by the Senate, for five-year terms; election by the people of justices of the peace, prothonotaries, and court clerks; the amendment of the constitution by popular vote; the guarantee of more certain and equal suffrage. It also advocated certain social and economic controls, including an extensive and liberal system of public education, and restrictions upon the granting of perpetual charters of incorporation.[1] The association distributed petitions, carried on an extensive correspondence, sponsored public rallies, and gave publicity to reform in the press; for example, it published letters from public officials in New York, Rhode Island, Ohio, and Indiana, where judges were limited to definite terms, testifying to the advantages and popularity of the system. In the autumn of 1833 it attempted to secure the nomination of men to the legislature who were pledged to constitutional reform. When the regular parties refused to give reform a forthright endorsement, it made its own nominations. But voters clung to their traditional loyalties, and reform candidates polled a bare 150 votes.

Meanwhile, on August 26, 1833, reformers held a convention at Harrisburg to give their movement a State-wide organization. But it advertised the weakness rather than the strength of the cause. Only

[1] Philadelphia *Pennsylvanian,* January 23, March 15, 1833.

sixteen delegates from five or six counties made an appearance.[2] Five of the members came as representatives of the Philadelphia Association. The convention elected George Kremer as its chairman and drew up a set of resolutions which it addressed to the legislature. Kremer's choice was unfortunate. A former member of Congress from Union County, he owed his escape from a political grave solely to his sensational, but unconfirmed, charge of "Bargain and Sale" in Congress in 1825 against Adams and Clay following Adams' choice for President over Jackson in the House of Representatives. Kremer's life during the eight years intervening had been filled with stump speeches in which he never failed to reiterate his accusation. His prominence in the convention enabled its critics to ridicule it without directly facing the issue of reform. Typical were the comments of the Milton *Miltonian:*

> The Reformists with the celebrated George Kremer at their head, held a *State Convention* at Harrisburg last week to alter the constitution of Pennsylvania. *Sixteen* delegates only were in attendance !!! and yet it is called a S T A T E convention. Mr. Kremer for the 4th time delivered himself of a speech concocted for the occasion, first at home, then at Danville, next at Wilkesbarre, and lastly in the celebrated assemblage of a few choice spirits at a STATE convention. How the mighty have fallen.[3]

It was merely a temporary setback, however. A second reform convention which met at Harrisburg on January 8, 1834, attracted more than thirty delegates and numerous observers.[4] Reformers again received a hearing in the legislature. The House adopted a bill which provided for a referendum, but it died in the Senate.[5]

To this point the question of constitutional reform was avoided by the politicians since it cut across party lines. But in the autumn of 1834 it was injected into the political scene by the Muhlenberg Democrats, who were anxious to base their campaign upon the democratic principle of two terms rather than simply a dislike for Wolf or a desire for office. In Philadelphia, partisans of Muhlenberg flocked to a rally of the Reform Association in an effort to push through a two-term resolution, but they were resisted by Wolf's supporters. Earle and the other officers were forced to stand aside while the two

[2] Counties included were Philadelphia, Union, Dauphin, Luzerne, and Columbia. Lewisburg *Journal*, September 4, 1833; Philadelphia *Pennsylvanian*, September 6, 1833.
[3] September 7, 1833.
[4] Philadelphia *Pennsylvanian*, January 13, 17, 1834.
[5] *Ibid.*, April 8, 1834.

Democratic factions vied for control. After a noisy session, the Wolf men found themselves outnumbered and withdrew.[6] Encouraged by this success, Muhlenberg adherents were soon sponsoring meetings called in the interest of reform. The Muhlenberg press in Philadelphia called for two terms, Muhlenberg, and reform. Papers in the interior followed their example, and on January 9, 1835, the Philadelphia *Pennsylvanian* claimed that thirty-six Democratic presses were advocating reform.

Meanwhile, the Wolf administration became more specifically identified with the opposition to constitutional revision. Wolf praised the constitution in his annual message in December, 1834, referring to it as "a matchless instrument";[7] and the Harrisburg *Reporter*, administration mouthpiece, disparaged the activities of the reformers and minimized the strength of their movement. In the legislature, however, the administration made no move to block a referendum bill. It thereby passed, and the issue was turned over to the electorate to be voted upon at the October election.

It is difficult to evaluate the effects of the gubernatorial election of 1835 upon the referendum. During the campaign it received scant attention. The Philadelphia *American Sentinel* interpreted Fourth of July toasts to indicate a total indifference on the part of all parties toward the proposed convention. According to its survey of newspapers from nineteen counties, but two regular and fifteen volunteer toasts were offered, and of these, twelve were made in defense of the existing document.[8] The popular vote tended to confirm this report of apathy. More than 38,000 voters who cast ballots for Governor registered no vote upon the question of the convention. Apparently, there was more indifference among those who opposed than those who adhered to reform. By a vote of 86,570 to 73,166, the people of the State gave their sanction to the convention.[9] Of the four parties participating in the three-cornered contest for Governor, only the Muhlenberg men openly championed it, and even they were divided. In fact, three of the five counties carried by

[6] *Ibid.*, November 20, 1834.
[7] *Pennsylvania Archives*, 4th Series, VI, 346-347.
[8] July 18, 1835.
[9] Berks, Northumberland, and Schuylkill. Election results are printed in Pennsylvania, *Proceedings and Debates of the Convention of the Commonwealth of Pennsylvania, to Propose Amendments to the Constitution, Commenced and Held at Harrisburg, on the Second Day of May, 1837*, 14 vols. (Harrisburg, 1837-1839), I, iv.

Muhlenberg gave majorities against the convention. Wolf Democrats frequently voted for it despite the convictions of their leader. Of the seventeen counties which fell into his column, thirteen returned majorities in its favor. The Antimasons made no commitments upon the subject, and the election results demonstrated the wisdom of their silence, since counties which returned pluralities for Ritner were almost evenly divided upon the question of the convention.[10] Philadelphia City with the strongest Whig concentration in the State voted decisively against it. Thus, with the exception of the Whigs, the results suggest that party lines were of little significance.

Geographical cleavages, on the other hand, were meaningful. In the West, only Somerset and Bedford cast majorities against the convention, and in the North every county favored it. By contrast, the counties in the Southeast, with a single exception, voted in the negative. It was the voice of the rank and file, not the political leaders, which called for a more democratic government.

It remained for the politicians, however, to implement the call for reform. With Ritner now in the driver's seat, Whigs and Antimasons became the defenders of the old constitution, and the Wolf leaders, the advocates of change. The Democratic majority in the Senate promptly agreed upon a bill providing for the immediate election of delegates. They hoped to complete the convention in time to submit the amendments to the voters at the October, 1836, elections.[11] In the House, however, where the Coalition held the upper hand, the Senate bill was amended by the crafty Stevens so as to put off the choice of delegates to the convention until the presidential election in November. This would serve two purposes; it would delay the convention a full year, and it would link the election of delegates to the presidential campaign. The latter was expected to strengthen the Coalition in the convention because of the unpopularity of Van Buren among Wolf Democrats. After numerous postponements, the House finally agreed to Stevens' amendment, and just prior to adjournment the Senate yielded also.[12] In the meantime, the Coalition adopted its apportionment bill and thereby further enhanced its power in the convention.

Having determined the date for the election of delegates, the Coalition press labored to create the impression that the Democrats

[10] In fourteen counties there were majorities against it; in sixteen, majorities favored it. In the Southeast, only Cumberland voted favorably.

[11] Philadelphia *Pennsylvanian*, January 29, 1836.

[12] Philadelphia *American Sentinel*, February 8, 9, 10, 1836; Philadelphia *Pennsylvanian*, March 8, 24, 25, 1836.

contemplated a radical rewriting of the constitution which would destroy the sanctity of property, depress the commercial community, and institute mob rule. They seized upon scattered statements by Democrats which emphasized the authority of the convention to make extensive changes and circulated them over the State. One of these written by George M. Dallas to a committee of correspondence of Smithfield, Bradford County, was repeated almost daily in Coalition papers. Dallas suggested no extreme modifications, but pointed out that, "When ours shall assemble, it will possess within the territory of Pennsylvania, every attribute of absolute sovereignty, except such as may have been yielded and are embodied in the Constitution of the United States."[13] Despite the fact that Dallas had taken no conspicuous part in the reform movement, the Coalition press exploited his statement to the full. They excoriated his radicalism and identified it with the Democrats generally. In the House, William B. Reed, Philadelphia Whig and henchman of Biddle, referring to Dallas, declared that the Democrats were following a "degraded authority . . . a wandering Jacobin, whose gray hairs should have taught him better."[14]

The attempt of Coalition papers to press their advantage may be illustrated by citing briefly an editorial in the Harrisburg *Chronicle*, the paper which Biddle purchased during the Bank controversy. The election, it declared, posed a question as important as any issue since the Declaration of Independence. Men were seeking power who had threatened the ruin of free and liberal institutions; men who would seek to vacate titles and deeds to property and who might go so far as to institute agrarianism, which would require the division of goods and compel the frugal to share their earnings with the idler, the spendthrift, and the drunkard. "They are not democratic," it concluded, "the Anti Bank party is revolutionary in every feature."[15] In Philadelphia County, Whigs circulated last-minute handbills directed in particular against Thomas Earle and Pierce Butler, nominees to the convention, which charged them with being aristocrats, enemies of the people and of popular institutions, and devotees of European radicalism.[16]

Democrats charged the Coalition with misrepresentation and argued that the members of the convention were merely agents of the people

[13] *Ibid.*, September 13, 1836.
[14] Harrisburg *Telegraph*, reprinted in Philadelphia *American Sentinel*, February 10, 1836.
[15] November 2, 1836.
[16] Philadelphia *Pennsylvanian*, November 4, 1836.

and that their amendments would have no sanction unless and until ratified by a vote of the electorate. They insisted that the Coalition in reality wanted no reforms. They were unable, however, to mend the damage already sustained.

The election on November 8, 1836, resulted in the choice of sixty-seven Democrats and sixty-six Whigs and Antimasons. It was a setback to the Democrats, who only three weeks previously had elected seventy-two members to the House, while the Coalition could salvage but twenty-eight. Democrats were further discomfited when a special election in the Union-Juniata-Mifflin district, required by the death of a Democratic member, resulted in the triumph of an Antimason. The balance was thus reversed.[17]

A majority of the delegates to the convention, whether they were Whigs, Antimasons, or Democrats, were either farmers or lawyers. Other occupations represented included physicians, merchants, manufacturers, surveyors, and artisans. The Philadelphia *United States Gazette* tabulated the membership as follows:[18]

	Democrats	Opposition
Farmers	27	29
Lawyers	16	24
Physicians	6	4
Merchants	4	5
Manufacturers	3	3
Surveyors	4	0
Artisans	5	1
Editors	0	1
Gentlemen	1	0
Total	66	67

Leadership within the Coalition, it might be noted, was assumed by Thaddeus Stevens and a small body of Whigs from Philadelphia, who in terms of education, wealth, social background, and experience deviated from the pattern of their Antimasonic associates and their Democratic opponents from the interior of the State. The Philadelphia Whigs without exception were prominent in the professions or in business. The delegation consisted of John Sergeant, Charles Chauncey, Matthias W. Baldwin, Joseph Hopkinson, Thomas P. Cope, William M. Meredith, John M. Scott, James C. Biddle, and Joseph R. Chandler.

[17] *Ibid.*, November 18, 1836; Philadelphia *American Sentinel*, May 23, 29, 1837.
[18] Cited in **Mueller,** *Whig Party,* **34, and Hartz,** *Economic Policy,* **24.**

The Coalition used its slight advantage to dominate the organization of the convention when it assembled at Harrisburg on May 2, 1837. They elected John Sergeant as president and secured control of the strategic committees.[19] They were further strengthened by the tendency of conservatives among the Democrats to vote with them on controversial issues.

It should not be assumed, however, that the Coalition was spared the conflict of interests which characterized its activities in the legislature. The convention was less than a week old when Stevens, who was elected to the convention after being defeated a month before for the House, dropped a bombshell into the lap of the Coalition by moving that a special committee be appointed to investigate secret societies. A Democratic delegate with a sense of humor moved to strike out the words "secret societies" and substitute "Antimasonry." But the Whigs, preferring to placate Stevens rather than risk the loss of Antimasonic support, co-operated to create the committee.

Three weeks later Stevens again shattered the equanimity of the Coalition when he urged that the membership of Philadelphia city and county, or any other county, in the House of Representatives be limited to six, and that the smallest counties have at least one. In defense of his recommendation, he delivered a philippic against Philadelphia, "a great and grievous ulcer on the body politic."[20]

To the delight of the Democrats, William M. Meredith, a Philadelphia Whig, took up the challenge. In the words of one witness, Meredith

> poured forth for two hours the most poignant strain of personal invective against Mr. Stevens I ever heard—to which the latter in the main attempted—completely prostrated as he was—no reply but a few words of very tame defence. Whether this dissolves the Coalition remains to be seen.[21]

The Antimasonic Harrisburg *Telegraph* charged that Meredith's assault had been secretly plotted by the Masons in the convention in retaliation against Stevens for his efforts to amend the constitution so

---

[19] For details of the convention, see Roy H. Akagi, "The Pennsylvania Constitution of 1838," *Pennsylvania Magazine of History and Biography*, XLVIII (1924), 301-333; and Pennsylvania, *Proceedings and Debates of the Convention.*

[20] James Donagan to Buchanan, June 6, 1837, Buchanan Papers. The city and county of Philadelphia had a total of fourteen representatives in the House; no other county had as many as six.

[21] Charles J. Ingersoll to Buchanan, June 6, 1837, *ibid.;* Woodley, *Thaddeus Stevens,* 101.

as to make secret societies and extrajudicial oaths illegal.[22] The Coalition survived this shock, but the explanation lay in the dissensions of the Democrats, not in the unity of the Whigs and Antimasons.

During the early weeks of the convention two issues in particular tended to bring out basic disagreements—currency and banking, and the tenure of judges. The majority report of the Committee on Currency, Banking, and Corporations recommended that no changes be made, but Charles J. Ingersoll presented a minority report, signed by four of the nine members of the committee, which condemned the current banking system and urged the establishment of a hard-money currency. The question of printing Ingersoll's report indicated the Democratic dissidence. A majority of them gave it their support, but a minority refrained from voting rather than risk its passage. Thomas Earle opposed it, not because he favored the present system, but for the reason that he preferred a general banking law and not the elimination of the banking privilege. He obtained little support from his colleagues. The motion to print the minority report was lost by a vote of 57 to 67.[23] Democrats divided again a short time later upon Earle's motion to limit the Governor's tenure to a single three-year term and to elect judges by popular vote.[24] The combination of conservative Democrats with the Coalition continued to block the efforts of the reformers with the result that little was accomplished when the convention recessed, after ten weeks of labor, on July 14, 1837, to avoid the discomforts of Harrisburg in midsummer.

In reviewing the work to that point, newspapers generally found evidence to confirm their predilections. *Niles' Register,* after pointing out the inconsequential nature of the changes, remarked, "What a commentary upon the clamor which raised upon the necessity of a reform in that instrument, and how fortunate the members of the convention were so divided as to prevent its perversion for the purposes of party."[25] The Philadelphia *American Sentinel* observed that the recess would postpone the submission of the amendments until the following year and doubted the wisdom of continuing the convention.

> The proceedings of the convention have latterly received little attention from the people; they saw clearly that no beneficial

---

[22] June 8, 1837.
[23] Philadelphia *American Sentinel,* May 26, 1837.
[24] *Ibid.,* June 14, 1837; Philadelphia *Pennsylvanian,* July 3, 1837.
[25] LII (July 15, 1837), 305.

results were likely to follow from the labors of a body so equally divided between the antagonist parties, and its failure to effect anything has therefore excited no surprise. We believe the people would be entirely satisfied if it were never to meet again.[26]

The analysis of the Philadelphia *Pennsylvanian,* by contrast, was optimistic. The convention, it noted, had been organized and dominated by Coalition leaders who sought no changes. Whigs and Antimasons had at first swung into line, but dissensions and the growing realization that they opposed all reforms had produced dissatisfaction. The reformers, it concluded, were gaining ground.[27]

The convention reassembled in Harrisburg on October 17, 1837, holding sessions in the State Capitol until November 23, when the approaching session of the General Assembly led it to adjourn to Philadelphia and resume its deliberations in the Music Fund Hall there on November 28. The work of the convention after its summer recess confirmed the predictions of the *Pennsylvanian.* Delegates paid less attention to party lines. Antimasons sometimes voted with the reform element of the Democrats to permit the acceptance of moderate alterations. Generally speaking, the modifications tended to enlarge the powers of the electorate at the expense of the executive. Local officials such as justices of the peace and clerks of the courts were made elective; judges were made appointive for definite terms, subject to confirmation by the Senate; the Governor's tenure was reduced from three to two consecutive terms; terms of Senators were cut from four to three years. Perhaps the most significant of the changes was the tenth article, which provided that future amendments might be added by their passage in two successive legislatures and their ratification by the people at large without the need of a constitutional convention. One modification, on the other hand, erected a barrier in the path of social and political democracy. It restricted the franchise to "white freemen."[28] The growing force of anti-Negro prejudice in the State was clearly revealed by the overwhelming backing which was given to this amendment; the final vote being 88 to 32. No other alteration cut so completely across party lines or received such decisive support.[29]

[26] July 12, 1837.
[27] July 25, 1837.
[28] Article III, Section 1. The constitution is printed in *Pennsylvania Archives,* 4th Series, VI, 499-525. Supreme Court Justices were to be appointed for fifteen-year terms; other judges for ten-year terms, except associate judges of the courts of common pleas who were to serve five-year terms.
[29] Philadelphia *Pennsylvanian,* January 24, 1838. See Edward R. Turner, *The Negro in Pennsylvania* (Washington, 1911).

The dire warnings of the conservatives that the convention would be a hotbed of radicalism were not substantiated. The only threat against the Bank of the United States was a resolution calling for the appointment of a committee to consider whether the people of the State could repeal or modify the charter either by legislative enactment or a constitutional amendment and, if decided in the affirmative, to consider whether it would not be expedient to take action for repeal or alteration.[30] It was postponed indefinitely by a vote of 68 to 49.[31] Steeled by this victory, conservatives secured the adoption of two resolutions which testified to their profound respect for the sanctity of contract. The first, approved by a vote of 66 to 7, declared that contracts made on the faith of the Commonwealth were inviolable; the second, passed by a vote of 59 to 41, affirmed that a charter to a bank or other corporation was a contract and unless it were misused or unduly granted, a matter to be determined by the courts, could not be voided.[32] Both were superfluous since the courts consistently accepted this position.

Just prior to adjournment a belated attempt was made by anticharter men to circumscribe further the awarding of bank charters. As introduced, the proposal required a notice of application for six months, limited the term of a charter to twenty years, and reserved to the legislature the privilege of withdrawing a charter if it became injurious to the State. Several amendments more radical in nature were offered. One, for example, required the passage of bank charters by majorities of two-thirds or by two successive legislatures and permitted the repeal of charters by a similar procedure. The amendments were voted down by the usual combination of conservative Democrats with the Coalition. The original proposition was then adopted after the clause which authorized the withdrawal of the charter if injurious was rendered innocuous by the addition of the words, "in such a manner, however, that no injustice shall be done the corporations."[33] The latter, it was presumed, would forestall hostile action by removing the matter to the courts. The anticharter men also secured a prohibition upon the inclusion of charters in

[30] *Niles' Register*, LIII (December 2, 1837), 209.
[31] *Ibid.* Biddle had urged a test vote upon the repeal of the charter of the Bank of the United States, but his aides opposed it.
[32] *Ibid.*
[33] Philadelphia *Pennsylvanian*, January 15, 1838; Philadelphia *American Sentinel*, January 11, 12, 1838. See Article I, Section 25.

"omnibus" bills.[34] There could be no replica of Stevens' strategy in the chartering of the Bank of the United States, and "logrolling" would henceforth require more minute planning.

Since the amendments were effected largely by the union of Democrats with a minority of Antimasons, it was only natural that the former should look upon them as their own and that the Whigs should take the lead in opposing them. As the convention adjourned on February 22, 1838, sixty-two of the sixty-four Democrats then in attendance signed an address to the people of the State which urged that the amendments be accepted.[35] The Democratic press responded favorably. A typical editorial argued that the amendments were salutary and more democratic than the corresponding provisions of the old constitution and that they removed many of its aristocratic and monarchical principles and gave greater powers to the people. Opponents of the amendments, it declared, should show that the appointment of judges for life was more democratic than terms, and the appointment of aldermen more democratic than election.[36] A few Democratic sheets, on the other hand, advocated their rejection; the *Lycoming Gazette,* for example, referred to the amendments as "a medley of incongruities and blunders."[37]

The keynote of the Whig opposition was sounded by John Sergeant in his valedictory address before the convention, and the Whig press echoed his sentiments. Objections were voiced against the contents of the amendments and the Democratic leadership which shaped them. "Who believed then, or who believes now," the Philadelphia *National Gazette* asked, "that such men are, or ever will be fit social and political guides?"[38] Prominent Whigs lent their talents to the preparation of editorials and pamphlets in both English and German. Chief Justice John B. Gibson of the State Supreme Court, whose life tenure was jeopardized by the amendments, took up his pen to protect himself from the uncertainties of a fixed term. In a letter to a Whig editor, he glowingly observed.

> I have seen but two of your numbers; but Judge R. [Randall][39] who has read them all, thinks they will be effective. Ah, sir, could

---

[34] Article I, Section 25.
[35] Philadelphia *Pennsylvanian,* February 23, 1838. The two Democrats who did not sign the address were David M. Farrelly of Crawford County and James M. Porter of Northampton County, brother of David R. Porter.
[36] *Ibid.,* February 26, 1838.
[37] Reprinted in Philadelphia *American Sentinel,* March 19, 1838.
[38] February 24, 1838.
[39] Archibald Randall, Associate Judge of Common Pleas, Philadelphia.

you but read my pamphlet on the subject! It is written in choice high dutch—pure Saxon I assure you. . . . It has already begun to stagger the enemy.[40]

Former Governor Shulze returned to the political stage after more than a decade in retirement to defend the old constitution. In a letter to a Whig editor which was circulated widely in the press he declared,

> I have confidence that the work of the good men of the Revolution will not be laid aside, to take up and adopt the piece of patchwork which was put together by the late generally condemned convention. The Germans of Pennsylvania will hold fast to what they know to be good.[41]

The Antimasons, meanwhile, found themselves on the horns of a dilemma. The Ritner leaders had cause for opposing the amendments but even better reasons for avoiding any commitments. Most important among the latter was the fact that the vote on the constitution took place on October 9, 1838, the day of the gubernatorial election. Re-election was of more immediate significance to them than the outcome of the constitution. The Antimasonic press reflected this confusion and was generally evasive. The perplexity of the Antimasons may be suggested by the experience of James Merrill, a prominent member of the convention from the interior of the State. Upon the adjournment of the convention in Philadelphia, Merrill began his homeward journey uncertain whether he would support or reject the amendments. Arriving in Harrisburg, he sought to confer with party leaders, but without success. In his own words, "I tried to talk with Ritner and called several times at his room; but he was always beset by others. . . . Stevens seemed steeped in business and Fenn was absent."[42]

After reaching his home in New Berlin, Union County, he put his ear to the ground, only to become more uncertain.

> One of my old oracles here says the amendments are exactly what they ought to be. He has read the whole and says he is perfectly satisfied. . . . Some of our Democrats speak with strong disapprobation of the provisions for future amendments but will not say they will oppose the adoption of the new constitution. . . . I do not think by what I can hear, that either party

[40] Gibson to Thomas J. Wharton, July 22, 1838, W. W. Porter Papers, Historical Society of Pennsylvania.
[41] Reprinted in the Philadelphia *American Sentinel,* September 22, 1838.
[42] Stevens was now a Canal Commissioner and chief tactician of Ritner's re-election campaign. Theophilus Fenn was the editor of the Harrisburg *Telegraph.*

will act decisively on the subject. . . . I feel a good deal of anxiety to see the effect of spreading our work fully before the people—I have strong fears, that there are too many popularity traps to allow the objections to get a fair hearing.[43]

As the date of the referendum approached Merrill and other Antimasons in Union County worked quietly for the rejection of the amendments, but they hesitated to bring their activities into the open lest Democrats should rally to the defense. They refrained, therefore, from agitating the subject until the last moment, and then, with the Democrats off guard, flooded the county with handbills—printed in Philadelphia.[44]

During the summer and autumn of 1838 the constitutional issue, for a third time in four years, was made subordinate to an exciting political contest. The gubernatorial election of 1838 was one of the bitterest in the history of the State, and it crowded the constitution into the background. The Whig presses continued to appeal to "Let well alone," and Democratic papers contributed occasional editorials in favor of the changes. The public remained apathetic. The amendments were too moderate to alarm conservatives or to arouse the admiration of radicals. On election day, October 9, 1838, there were 113,971 voters who registered approval of the new constitution and 112,759 who indicated their disapproval. The amendments were thus incorporated into the organic law of the State by the very narrow margin of 1,212 votes.[45]

Since the constitutional convention met amidst the first turbulent scenes of the Panic of 1837 and had to compete for public attention with such dramatic events as the suspension of specie payments, the controversy over the Independent Treasury, and the attempt to repeal the State charter of the Bank of the United States, it received only a small fraction of the interest which it might have attracted during quieter times. Few of the papers considered the proceedings of sufficient moment to require the services of special correspondents. They sometimes reprinted excerpts from the Harrisburg journals, but such

[43] Merrill to William M. Meredith, March 5, 1838, Meredith Papers.

[44] Merrill to Meredith, September 20, 1838, *ibid.* For a sketch of Merrill's work in the convention, see Philadelphia *Pennsylvanian,* January 1, 1838. Whigs and Antimasons should have been familiar with the amendments since the Secretary of the Commonwealth consistently advertised them in the Coalition papers while avoiding the Democratic sheets. See *ibid.,* June 18, 1838.

[45] Sectional cleavages were similar to the referendum of 1835. Pittsburgh *Daily Advocate and Advertiser,* October 16, 1838; Pennsylvania, *Proceedings and Debates of the Convention,* XIII, 260-61.

summaries were usually brief and they were seldom accompanied by editorial comment. This tended to discourage flights of oratory designed to impress fellow members, the gallery, or home constituents. Once the new constitution was accepted the debates were quickly forgotten.[46]

The Constitution of 1838 marked no sharp break with the past. There was neither a rush to add further amendments by the use of Article X nor a noticeable deterioration in the prestige of the courts resulting from changes in tenure. The gloomy forecast of the Harrisburg *Telegraph* that there would be a constitutional convention every five years was not borne out.[47]

The most important political consequence was the curbing of the Governor's patronage. Executives were soon hard pressed to reward their followers. Such was certainly the experience of Governor Francis R. Shunk following his inaugural in 1845. In a letter to President-elect Polk, he asked to be excused for writing numerous letters of recommendation for Pennsylvanians who were seeking federal posts. He explained:

> I have to regret that I am compelled to write so frequently, but I know you will find an apology for me when you reflect upon the position I occupy. By our new Constitution the patronage of the Executive is so limited and the competition is so great, that its exercise tends rather to destroy than to increase his influence. Having little to give, to withdraw from his friends who are going to Washington, a letter to the President, would be regarded as most ungracious.[48]

[46] One exception was the record of George W. Woodward of Wilkes-Barre. Woodward had been elected to the convention on the Democratic ticket despite a factional dispute which rent the party in Luzerne County. He entered actively into the debates, usually aligning himself with the reform wing of the party. He supported Ingersoll's hard-money scheme and championed the appointment of judges for terms. On the question of immigration and citizenship for foreign-born, however, he took issue with his party and advocated that the privileges of voting and officeholding be denied to foreigners who should henceforth enter the State. His words were recalled eight years later by his political opponents, including judges of the State Supreme Court, and were used to block his election to the United States Senate and a short time later his confirmation as Associate Justice of the Supreme Court of the United States—defeats which rocked the Democratic party in the State. See Philadelphia *Pennsylvanian,* February 21, 1838; Wilkes-Barre *Republican Farmer,* November 29, 1837; January 10, 1838; Charles J. Ingersoll to Henry D. Gilpin, January 1, 1838, reprinted in William M. Meigs, *The Life of Charles Jared Ingersoll* (Philadelphia, 1897), 204-206. See also pages 189, 192-193.

[47] September 26, 1838.

[48] Shunk to Polk, February 24, 1845, James K. Polk Papers, Library of Congress.

Observed at long range, the constitution appears to have been an opening wedge for the effecting of additional gains in the elective principle. In 1843, for example, the legislature provided for the election of Canal Commissioners by popular vote. Eight years later an amendment making State judges elective was approved.

Thus, Pennsylvania responded to the democratic spirit of the era. Henceforth, Governors would find their patronage sharply curtailed and their tenure shortened. Senators would go before the voters every three years instead of four; and in recognition of the Jacksonian principle of rotation in office, judges would serve for definite terms rather than for life. Finally, politicians would cope with an electorate augmented by the addition of new voters and strengthened by the assumption of increased responsibilities.

CHAPTER VII

The Depression, Banking, and the Buckshot War 1837-1838

AS LEGISLATORS returned to their homes at the close of the 1836-1837 session, they came face to face with new problems arising from the Panic of 1837. Signs of distress were apparent during April, and people were talking of a "spring recession" brought on by excessive speculation and inflated values. Then on May 9 Pennsylvanians were shocked at the news that New York banks had suspended. "Runs" followed upon Pennsylvania banks and in less than forty-eight hours most of them had also suspended. Issues of the recent legislative session were crowded into the background as the panic monopolized the public mind. "Your proceedings at Harrisburg," where the constitutional convention was in session, "do not command much attention beyond the friends of the members," one Philadelphian observed, "the whole community is too deeply absorbed in the excitement of the money affairs."[1]

DEPRESSION POLITICS

Explanations and panaceas for the crisis were legion. Whigs and Bank Democrats traced its origins to the untimely war upon the Bank of the United States and the Specie Circular. Ritner, in a proclamation issued to justify his refusal to call a special session of the legislature, declared that the cause of the embarrassment did not originate in Pennsylvania, but stemmed from the "unnecessary and unauthorized interference of the general government with the currency and monied transactions of the country."[2] The Antimasonic press agreed that a special session offered no solution. An honest legislature, one paper insisted, could do little, but this one "wouldn't hesitate to apply a bellows to the blast until everything was prostrated."[3] Another observed that "little could be hoped for from the deliberations of a body in which a majority was so factious and so entirely destitute of

[1] John R. Latimer to William M. Meredith, May 9, 1837, Meredith Papers.
[2] Philadelphia *Pennsylvanian*, May 23, 1837.
[3] Harrisburg *Pennsylvania Telegraph*, May 23, 1837.

talent."[4] Democrats attributed the depression to "over trading, over banking and speculation and extravagancies."[5] Radical Democrats saw a solution in the hard-money doctrine.

Philadelphia, which was at once the greatest concentration of bank strength in the State, with one-third of the banks and approximately 85 per cent of the banking capital, and the center of Democratic radicalism, was a sounding board for the conflicting expressions of opinion.[6] Four days after the suspension, the radicals held a mass meeting in Independence Square. It was projected and carried out entirely by the working classes without consultation with Democratic leaders and was said to have been the largest ever assembled there. The crowd, estimated at 20,000, was orderly; speeches were temperate, but feeling was strong. The banks were charged with the responsibility for the recession, and the suspension was declared to be a malicious scheme to force the national administration to repeal the treasury circular and compel the people to submit to a national bank. Resolutions included a criticism of small banknotes and monopolies and a recommendation that hard money be made the only legal currency. A committee was appointed to inquire of the banks in Philadelphia how far they would go toward redeeming their five-dollar and ten-dollar notes in specie.[7]

Reassembling a week later, they adopted resolutions which censured the existing system of banks, corporations, and monopolies in the State, and called upon the constitutional convention to limit the authority of the legislature to create them. Though they denied any connection with parties they sustained the federal government's policy on the currency. The climax came with the reading of the replies from the banks. With one exception, they were identical refusals to make any promises regarding resumption. Rebuffed, the meeting adjourned amidst an obvious lack of good will.[8] Democratic papers printed the proceedings, but took the precaution to dissociate themselves from the opinions expressed there. The conservative Philadelphia *American Sentinel* went so far as to deprecate the tone

[4] Pittsburgh *Gazette*, reprinted in Philadelphia *American Sentinel*, May 30, 1837.
[5] Philadelphia *Pennsylvanian*, May 23, 1837.
[6] There were seventeen banks in Philadelphia with $51,000,000 capital; in the remainder of the State there were fifty-two banks with a capital of $8,000,000. See *McElroy's Directory* (Philadelphia, 1837).
[7] Henry D. Gilpin to Van Buren, May 15, 1837, Van Buren Papers; Philadelphia *American Sentinel*, May 18, 1837.
[8] Henry D. Gilpin to Martin Van Buren, May 22, 1837, Van Buren Papers; Philadelphia *American Sentinel*, May 27, 1837.

and language, which it termed "ill advised and calculated to produce injury."[9] The Whig press, of course, severely criticized this outburst of radicalism.[10]

A month later the voters of Philadelphia County had an opportunity to register a collective expression upon the currency and banking issue. A special election to fill a vacancy in the House of Representatives pitted Charles J. Ingersoll against Charles Naylor, the Whig nominee. The former was in the thick of the struggle in the constitutional convention to curb banking and corporate privileges and was recognized as a champion of the hard-money doctrine. The Whig press initiated a vigorous campaign to discredit Ingersoll among conservative Democrats. They emphasized his radicalism and insisted that his election would signify an approval of the errors of the administration and give permanency to the ruinous position into which the nation had plunged. The furor surrounding Ingersoll left Naylor almost completely ignored.[11] The strategy was effective; Bank Democrats remained away from the polls, and Naylor was elected by 231 votes in a district normally Democratic.[12]

The continued absorption of the public in the panic was reflected in the fall elections. With no national offices to be filled, interest was confined to the election of the legislature. The Whig press attempted to tag the Democrats with Locofocoism; a Democratic legislature, it maintained, would seek the forfeiture of the charters of all banks in the State.[13] The Antimasonic Harrisburg *Telegraph* emphasized the extravagance of the previous legislature and called upon party members to save themselves from an increase in the State debt and taxation.[14] Democratic papers frequently advocated the regulation of banking.

> The question to be decided is whether the Banks shall rule the Government, or the Government rule the Banks [a radical Union County paper declared]. If the Democrats are defeated the banks will hail it as a verdict in favor of the suspension of specie payments as they did in the case of Mr. Ingersoll's defeat,

[9] May 18, 1837.
[10] Philadelphia *Pennsylvanian*, May 26, 1837.
[11] Philadelphia *United States Gazette,* June 14, 16, 26, 1837; Philadelphia *Pennsylvanian*, June 8, 9, 15, 16, 21 1837.
[12] Philadelphia *American Sentinel,* June 30, 1837.
[13] Philadelphia *Inquirer,* reprinted in Philadelphia *Pennsylvanian,* August 18, 1837; *ibid.,* September 21, 1837.
[14] August 16 and October 2, 1837.

and the suspension will be legalized by the Legislature. On the other hand, if the Democrats are successful the banks will be compelled to redeem their notes or else wind up their affairs. The three Democratic candidates for the House in the Union-Mifflin-Juniata district pledged themselves to oppose an increase in bank capital, support the repeal of the charter of the United States Bank, and adhere to the Independent Treasury.[15] Democrats in the main, however, were cautious and noncommittal. They could not afford to be identified too closely with Locofocoism. In Luzerne, for example, Democrats failed to place the radical Benjamin A. Bidlack in the constitutional convention despite the fact that they sustained their nominees for other offices by about three hundred votes.

The election on October 10, 1837, resulted in the choice of fifty-six Democrats and forty-four Whigs and Antimasons to the lower house. While the Democratic majority in the State exceeded by several thousands that received the previous November in the presidential election, the gerrymandering again reduced the number of Democrats elected to the Senate and gave the Coalition a majority of five.[16] The legislature thus lacked a working majority for the third consecutive year.

The lawmakers who gathered in Harrisburg in December, 1837, were in an unenviable position. The panic pressed upon them. Work upon the State improvements as well as numerous private railroad projects was suspended as a result of the failure of the appropriation bill. Banks remained unable to resume specie payments, and voters in all sections of the State were demanding regulatory legislation. The Independent Treasury plan presented an additional issue to discordant Democrats. Finally, the impending gubernatorial election intensified the political activities of all factions.

The session was but a few hours old when Democrats aired their dissensions. On the vote for the printer of the House journal, eight Democrats bolted the caucus choice, the editor of the Harrisburg *Reporter,* and joined with the Coalition to elect the editors of the Harrisburg *Keystone.* Their motives were obvious. The *Reporter* championed the Van Buren administration, including the Specie Circular and the Independent Treasury, whereas the *Keystone* voiced the opinions of the paper-money or Improvement Men. Upon the election of the *Keystone,* the two journals plunged into a battle of

[15] New Berlin *Union Times,* October 6, 1837.
[16] Danville *Intelligencer,* October 30, 1837; Buchanan to Jackson, October 26, 1837, Andrew Jackson Papers, Library of Congress.

words, and persisted in their quarrel despite the fact that forty-one Democrats in the House signed a statement which condemned the conduct of both parties.[17]

In reality, two of the editors of the *Keystone*, Orville Barrett and Ovid F. Johnson, the latter a Harrisburg lawyer and soon to be Governor Porter's Attorney General, had made a secret agreement with Biddle's "borers." They undertook to use their influence to prevent the passage of any hasty, radical measures against the banks, to soften prejudice on the subject and set public opinion right, to get a moderate, rational Democratic nominee for Governor, and to set in motion the nomination of Commodore Charles Stewart for the Presidency. Six months later when Barrett and Johnson were trying to collect the sum of $20,000 which they alleged had been promised, they insisted, "Our part of the agreement has been *more* than fulfilled."[18] The editors may have exaggerated their contributions, certainly Biddle held that opinion, but there is no doubt that the *Keystone* strengthened Bank Democrats through the legislative session.

The furor over the printing was but a prelude to a more serious disagreement upon the Independent Treasury. Democratic leaders would have preferred to avoid the Independent Treasury, but the initiative was taken from their hands by Biddle and the Whigs who hoped to defeat the bill in the United States Senate, where its fate was in doubt, by instructing Buchanan to vote against it. Confident of success in the face of the Democratic majority in the House, Biddle set to work with his characteristic energy to push the desired resolution through the legislature. Meanwhile, he called upon Clay to delay the measure and await the anticipated action in Harrisburg.[19]

On February 3, 1838, William F. Johnston, who had worked efficiently behind the scenes during the previous session to render the investigation of the United States Bank innocuous, introduced a resolution in the House which requested the members of the national House of Representatives and instructed the United States Senators to use their influence for a postponement of the Independent Treasury

---

[17] Harrisburg *Reporter*, December 8, 12, 1837; Harrisburg *Keystone*, December 9, 1837.

[18] Ovid F. Johnson to Orville Barrett, June 28, 1838, Biddle Papers. See also Johnson to William Robinson, July 9, 1838, *ibid.;* Robinson to Biddle, August 6, 1838, *ibid.;* Johnson to Robinson, August 22, 1838, *ibid.;* Robinson to Biddle, n. d. [August, 1838], *ibid.*

[19] Biddle to Clay, February 3, 1838; Clay to Biddle, February 5, 6, 1838; Charles S. Baker to Biddle, February 7, 9, 1838, McGrane (ed.), *Correspondence of Nicholas Biddle*, 299-303.

bill until the next session of Congress.[20] A Van Buren man countered by offering a resolution in support of the Independent Treasury. Thus, the issue was joined. The *Reporter* denounced Johnston's action and suggested that he avoid deception by modifying his resolution to read, "A Resolution to continue the embarrassment under which the people are now suffering, and prepare the way FOR A NATIONAL BANK." Ovid F. Johnson replied in the *Keystone*, charging Samuel D. Patterson, United States Marshal of the Eastern District of Pennsylvania and until four months before the editor of the *Reporter*, with unwarranted interference. "As official editor of the officers of the general government," Johnson declared, he was "attempting to drill the Legislature."[21] Patterson's denial followed in the columns of the *Reporter*.[22]

David R. Porter, member of the Senate and soon to be Governor of the State, urged Buchanan to intercede. He placed the blame upon Patterson, who, he maintained, had promised to withdraw completely from the *Reporter,* but had now returned. "I have had an interview with the gentlemen of the *Keystone,*" he continued, "and I think I have been instrumental in allaying the exasperated state of their feelings until something be done. The *Keystone* has all the talent, and has got decidedly the lead." If Patterson could be removed from Harrisburg and a friend of the *Keystone* be appointed marshal of the Western District at once, Porter pointed out, he would give his pledge that the *Keystone* would "come out for the sub-Treasury at once and manfully sustain the administration." But if Patterson were not removed, he concluded, he could not "be held accountable for the course that may be taken by my friends."[23] With two of these friends in the *Keystone* secretly promoting the interests of Biddle, Porter was promising more than he could have realized. Buchanan wrote at once to Patterson, who in turn denied that he had written the offensive articles and insisted that he had been linked with them solely because of his presence in Harrisburg.[24]

When Johnston's resolution came up for debate a sufficient number of Democrats joined with the Coalition to give them the advantage. Friends of the Independent Treasury had no recourse but to resort to amendments and delays. One of Biddle's lobbyists who witnessed the scene reported to him, "The Van Buren men called the Yeas

[20] Harrisburg *Reporter*, February 6, 1838.
[21] Philadelphia *American Sentinel*, February 8, 1838.
[22] Harrisburg *Reporter*, February 9, 1838.
[23] Porter to Buchanan, February 8, 1838, Buchanan Papers.
[24] Patterson to Buchanan, February 20, 1838, *ibid.*

and Nays on us 17 different times on the vote to adjourn—every man stood firm but we had to submit to an adjournment on account of our friends it being nearly half past 3 o'clock."[25] Three desertions from the ranks of the Coalition required a brief delay, but three days later with several recent absentees back in their seats the foes of the Independent Treasury carried their resolution to a successful conclusion. It was adopted by a vote of 51 to 49, seven Bank Democrats voting with the majority.[26] Two additional resolutions were adopted to ease the path of the seven Democrats, one expressing confidence in Van Buren and a second recommending that the federal funds be handled so as to separate as far as possible the banks from the government. "This is of course humbug," Biddle was quickly assured.[27] The resolutions were hastily agreed upon by the Coalition-controlled Senate and sped to Clay. He had waited less than two weeks for the consummation of the project.[28]

The Whigs and Improvement Democrats were overjoyed at their decisive, though narrow, victory. Simon Cameron, who had been doubtful whether the resolution could be squeezed through the House, confided to a fellow banker in Philadelphia that its passage was "a great and glorious victory." It would go a long way to prevent any hostile action in relation to the banks.[29] The Harrisburg *Keystone* expressed a preference for the separation of banks from the government, but it did not consider it a test of a man's Democracy. Hence the seven Democrats could not be charged with irregularity. It called Johnston's resolution a "strange medley" which would permit the Senators in Washington to interpret it as they desired.[30] The conservative Philadelphia *American Sentinel* regretted that resolutions favorable to the Independent Treasury were being adopted at ward meetings, since the best Democrats in the State were opposed to it. "No truer or more sincere Democrat is to be found," it declared, "than W. F. Johnston of Armstrong County."[31] The Harrisburg *Reporter,* on the other hand, referred to Johnston as "the chief

---

[25] Charles S. Baker to Biddle, February 8, 1838, McGrane (ed.), *Correspondence of Nicholas Biddle,* 302.

[26] Harrisburg *Reporter,* February 13, 1838.

[27] Baker to Biddle, February 16, 1838, Biddle Papers.

[28] Philadelphia *American Sentinel,* February 19, 1838. Clay was ultimately unsuccessful in blocking the Independent Treasury bill in the Senate despite Buchanan's vote; it was later defeated in the House of Representatives.

[29] Cameron to Simon Gratz, February 12, 1838, Gratz Correspondence.

[30] February 17, 1838.

[31] August 17, 1838.

conspirator against the harmony and integrity of the Democratic party."[32] Van Buren Democrats denounced the resolution but urged Buchanan to obey it rather than resign. The latter, they argued, would precipitate a scramble for his office, split the party, and possibly result in the election of Johnston or one of his group by a combination of Improvement Democrats with the Coalition.[33]

The struggle over the Independent Treasury in the legislature had its repercussions in all parts of the State. Opinion among the members of the Democratic gubernatorial convention on March 4, 1838, was found to be too divergent to permit any pronouncement. Democratic rallies were sponsored by its friends and foes, frequently in the same localities. The over-all picture was one of uncertainty and disunity.[34]

BANK POLITICS

While politicians matched wits upon the Independent Treasury, they did not lose sight of the all-absorbing issue, the banking and the currency. After two years of controversy centering upon the charter of the United States Bank, the question had broadened to encompass the relationship of the State with all the banks within its borders. Legislators agreed, in the main, that their constituents desired a banking bill. But there was little agreement upon its principles and scope. Whigs found it difficult to ascertain whether Antimasons sought bank reform or preferred merely to toy with it to exploit its political potentialities. Democrats represented positions as irreconcilable as those held by the radicals, who supported a hard-money system, on the one extreme, and the conservatives such as Johnston and Cameron, who were as zealous as Biddle in their defense of banking, on the other. Cameron, for example, remained in Harrisburg throughout the session of the legislature so that he might be on hand to prevent the passage of legislation which might injure his bank. When he found the financial burden excessive he called upon Philadelphia bankers for aid. "It is but fair," he explained, "that the banks in the city should incur some of the expenses necessary to their safety. I should not, under other circumstances accept anything from them.

[32] February 13, 1838.
[33] Henry Myers to Buchanan, February 19, 1838, Buchanan Papers; Alexander M. Peltz to Buchanan, February 20, 1838, *ibid.;* John M. Read to Buchanan, March 3, 1838, *ibid.*
[34] The seven Democrats who voted for Johnston's resolution undoubtedly injured their political standing. None was returned to the legislature. Read to Buchanan, October 21, 1838, *ibid.*

But you know a man can not live at Harrisburg on the winds."[35] They quickly complied.

Legislation in any form was opposed by the Bank forces. Biddle had his customary band of agents on the scene, though McIlvaine's sudden death at Harrisburg on January 16, 1838, deprived him of his most valuable tactician and his closest contact with the Improvement Democrats. Both Cameron and Ovid F. Johnson addressed brief eulogies to Biddle, and the latter called on him in person to learn his views, "which the death of our lamented friend Mr. McIlvaine has rendered it impossible to do."[36] The Philadelphia banks agreed in conference to send a committee to "represent the true interests" of the banks of the city, and the Bank of North America dispatched a director, George Handy, to Harrisburg on its own account.[37]

Such was the setting at Harrisburg for the universally anticipated bank bill, which was introduced in the House on January 15, 1838, by Samuel Stevenson of Philadelphia County, chairman of the Banking Committee. It provided for a general regulation of banking and included a prohibition upon the issuance of notes under ten dollars, the elimination of bonuses from bank charters, and requirements that banks issue annual reports, sell their stock at auction, yield excess profits to the State, and make specie payments. It also made stockholders personally liable for obligations of the banks. It was a radical bill and unacceptable to bank supporters of all parties. Stevenson moved to take up the bill out of order, but failed to obtain the necessary two-thirds vote when eight Bank Democrats joined Whigs and Antimasons to block it. Yet it received a majority vote, and supporters of the bill seized upon it as a test of strength; while opponents worked unsparingly to block it or render it harmless.[38]

The enigma was Thaddeus Stevens. Back in the House after having been retired for a year by the voters of Adams County, he was more than ever the central figure in the Ritner administration. When the bill came up for discussion, he advocated bank reform, and proceeded to offer amendments to it. His action was alarming to both Improvement Democrats and Whigs. The former hesitated to oppose Stevens lest they should jeopardize appropriations for their improvements

[35] Simon Cameron to Simon Gratz, February 12, 1838, Gratz Correspondence. See also his letter of February 9, 1838, *ibid*.

[36] Johnson to Biddle, February 12, 1838, Biddle Papers; Cameron to Biddle, January 20, 1838, *ibid*.

[37] "Descriptive Catalogue of the Records of the Bank of North America Deposited with the Historical Society of Pennsylvania," 59.

[38] Philadelphia *Pennsylvanian*, February 1, 1838.

and give the administration credit for its passage. By going along with Stevens "responsibility for ultra measures would be presented to the world as the property of Governor Ritner. This would lead the Whigs to flee from Ritner for gambling with their interests. The Democrats could then put up a conservative candidate and the Whigs would go for him."[39]

Whigs struck back at Stevens by threatening to kill the improvement bill, which included an appropriation for his pet, the Gettysburg Railroad. Improvement-minded Antimasons, in turn, refused to postpone the bank bill unless Whigs voted for their appropriations. One of the bankers in Harrisburg summarized the situation succinctly, when he declared that the administration sought to pass a bank bill in order to re-elect their Governor, then discard it, "that is, knock our brains out, and then repeal it and reanimate the extinguished spirit." He added that all parties were in a dilemma; none would back out.[40] In the end, it was Stevens and the Antimasons who weakened. Faced with the alternative of accepting a radical bill or no measure at all, they chose the latter. When the bill came up for a final vote in the House it passed, with a few exceptions, by a party vote, with Whigs and Antimasons voting against it. Two Democrats, William F. Johnston of Armstrong and Samuel F. Reed of Philadelphia County, voted with the opposition.[41] In the Senate, the Stevenson bill was hastily rejected. The outcome was a political setback for the Ritner administration. Democrats had supported a popular cause and had been able to place the responsibility for its defeat upon the Antimasons. Whigs were content to escape with the banks and currency untouched.

The Election of 1838 and the Buckshot War

The faltering steps of the Democrats on the road to reunion following their disastrous parting of the ways in 1835 have been observed. The Bank charter, the campaigns of 1836 and 1837, and the federal patronage made contributions to amity. There were also sharp clashes of opinion. The constitutional convention, the Independent Treasury,

[39] Charles S. Baker to William D. Lewis, February 8, 1838, Biddle Papers.
[40] William D. Lewis to William M. Meredith, February 11, 1838, Meredith Papers.
[41] Philadelphia *Pennsylvanian*, February 16, 19, 22, 23, 26, 27, 1838. The vote in the House was 56-40. Johnston's vote coming only a few weeks after his resolution against the Independent Treasury virtually ended his connection with the Democratic party. He was defeated for re-election, and he was a Whig when he was later elected to the Senate.

banking and currency revealed underlying disagreement. But cleavages upon these matters tended to cut new lines and obliterate the old. Thus Democrats as they approached the gubernatorial election of 1838 were able to avoid the pitfalls of 1835.

The Democratic press began to speculate upon the nomination as early as August, 1837. Old Wolf partisans led off, urging the nomination of a new candidate. "He must be a new man heretofore *untried*, and fresh from the ranks of the people."[42] The reason for this course was obvious. Two terms was now an accepted party principle and would soon be written into the constitution of the State. Wolf was not given serious consideration, whereas Muhlenberg was a potential candidate. Editors who had supported him in 1835 denied that the proscription of candidates would contribute to harmony. The delegates should be free to choose "a new or old man" without partiality or prejudice.[43] Friends of Muhlenberg in Berks County were chosen as delegates to the nominating convention, and there were frequent expressions in his favor. Wolf interjected himself into the contest to decline the use of his name. In a statement more indicative of a spirit of petulance than tolerance, he declared that the passions of 1835 had not subsided, and if an unsuccessful candidate of that day should undertake a second trial he would be overwhelmed by popular indignation.[44]

The Antimasonic Harrisburg *Telegraph* noted that it was a "singular, first instance of a man declining a nomination, arrogating to himself the right of instructing others to follow his example—aye, his patriotic sacrifice." Wolf, it declared, was "only a man of straw— to shoot down the parson with."[45] Muhlenberg did not withdraw, but he was removed from the running by the timely intervention of Van Buren, who hustled him off to Europe to become the nation's first Minister to Austria. He accepted his "banishment" with reluctance.[46] It solved one problem and created another, when Wolf resigned in a huff from his post in the Treasury Department and remained adamant notwithstanding an urgent appeal from Buchanan to reconsider. Failing in this, Buchanan urged Van Buren to name Wolf as Collector of the Port of Philadelphia in place of James N.

[42] Harrisburg *Reporter*, August 22, 1837.
[43] Philadelphia *Pennsylvanian*, August 24, 1837.
[44] Wolf to the Philadelphia *American Sentinel*, printed in the issue of October 26, 1837.
[45] November 9, 1837.
[46] Muhlenberg to Henry D. Gilpin, December 12, 1837, Gilpin Papers.

Barker, the incumbent, who in turn could be given Wolf's position.[47] Barker, a Jackson holdover, would have little choice but to agree. Van Buren grasped the proposal and handed Wolf the most coveted plum in Pennsylvania over the protests of party leaders in Philadelphia.[48]

With Wolf and Muhlenberg temporarily pacified, Democrats gave their attention to the nomination. To be "available," a candidate had to fit into a rather narrow mold. First, he could not have participated too actively in the campaign of 1835 in behalf of either Muhlenberg or Wolf. In the second place, he dared not be identified as a radical on the one hand or a conservative, who had offended by being irregular on party issues, on the other. The situation called for a nonentity or a man who had only recently scaled the political ladder.

As the convention on March 4, 1838, approached, David R. Porter was mentioned frequently. A resident of Huntingdon County, he had vaulted upon the political stage in 1836 as a result of his election to the State Senate in a district which the Coalition considered a model in gerrymandering. His business and political experience was varied. He studied law, but was never admitted to the bar. A venture into ironmaking ended in bankruptcy during the Panic of 1819, but he was a successful farm owner and a noted breeder of horses and cattle. He held numerous local offices and served two terms in the House during the early 1820's. In the election of 1835 he voted for Wolf but took no active part in the campaign.[49] During his two years in the Senate he was identified as an Improvement Man, but he supported party measures including the Independent Treasury. Bank men regarded him as safe. Their opinion was strengthened by his vote against a resolution to make stockholders personally liable for the obligations of defaulting banks.[50] He was a close friend of William F. Packer and Ovid F. Johnson of the Harrisburg *Keystone,* who contributed substantially in the press and behind the scenes to effect his nomination.

[47] Buchanan to Van Buren, February [8], 1838, Van Buren Papers; Harrisburg *Telegraph,* February 12, 1838.
[48] Henry Horn to Van Buren, February 19, 1838, Van Buren Papers; Charles J. Ingersoll to Buchanan, February 16, 19, 1838, Buchanan Papers; York *Republican,* February 21, 28, 1838.
[49] David R. Porter to Henry Simpson, February 13, 1838, Roberts Collection.
[50] Philadelphia *Pennsylvanian,* March 6, 1838; Charles S. Baker to Biddle, March 5, 1838, Biddle Papers.

Among the others mentioned for the nomination, only two, Daniel Sturgeon and Calvin Blythe, entered the convention with an active following. Sturgeon, a resident of Fayette County, a former Speaker of the State Senate, Auditor General during the Wolf regime, and now State Treasurer, had the support of delegates from Fayette and other counties along the Southern Tier; while Blythe, Secretary of the Commonwealth under Shulze and a friend of Wolf and McKean, had the backing of a nucleus of old Wolf men. However, their combined vote on the first ballot did not equal the strength of Porter, and the latter was nominated on the second ballot.[51] By avoiding the Independent Treasury the convention, in contrast to that of 1835, adjourned harmoniously.[52] Having won the nomination, Porter made a hurried exit from Harrisburg in order to visit a sick member of his family, it was said, and to avoid the pitfalls of the Senate, "a very unsafe spot for a politician."[53]

The renomination of Ritner was a foregone conclusion. It was made without opposition on March 5, 1838, but with little enthusiasm. The convention adopted the usual Antimasonic platitudes, which Antimasons repeated mechanically and Whigs disregarded. It was generally recognized that Antimasonry neither in principle nor in practice after three years in office would attract the required support. Hence, Antimasonic tacticians mapped an intensive campaign which overlooked few political devices at their disposal.

Most important of these was the handling of the improvements. A costly improvement bill similar to the one which Ritner had vetoed a year before was pushed through the legislature with the aid of the Improvement Democrats. It revived improvements which had languished for the lack of funds and inaugurated numerous others. To head it up, Ritner appointed Stevens to the Canal Commission and reshuffled that body a second time in five months to give him the right kind of assistance.[54] The commission immediately made Stevens its chairman and set to work to transform the improvements into a gigantic political machine for the cause of Antimasonry.

[51] Harrisburg *Reporter,* March 6, 1838.

[52] George G. Leiper to Van Buren, March 18, 1838, Van Buren Papers; Muhlenberg to Van Buren, March 12, 1838, *ibid.*

[53] Simon Cameron to Buchanan, March 22, 1838, Buchanan Papers. Porter returned to the Senate prior to adjournment. On April 4 he voted with the Democrats against taking a loan from the United States Bank to finance the improvements. Charles S. Baker to Biddle, April 4, 1838, Biddle Papers.

[54] The Commission as named in May, 1838, consisted of Elijah F. Pennypacker, John Dickey, and Stevens.

DEPRESSION, BANKING, AND THE BUCKSHOT WAR

According to his [Stevens'] opponents the "moral character or religious principles" of bidders for contracts on the public works were investigated before the bid was considered. A "missionary fund" was collected from the successful bidders "for the purpose of diffusing useful knowledge among the people." Colonization along the extensions of the public works, more thorough than anything previously attempted, was resorted to in order to carry doubtful districts in the coming election.[55]

The activities of the commission may be pieced together from the correspondence of William C. McPherson, a young medical doctor and secretary of the commission, to his father, J. B. McPherson, a Gettysburg businessman and railroad director. Two days after Stevens' appointment he reported a grand tour over the Public Works to be pursued at a slow pace and to require several months to complete. "They intend going to work in earnest. The appointment of Mr. Stevens has thrown the Loco Focos into consternation here. They say it is a *gun powder plot* to blow them up."[56] The commissioners went first to Bristol and "had a delightful trip up the Delaware" to Easton where the State Works made a junction with the Lehigh Navigation system and the Morris Canal, which linked the Delaware to Jersey City. They returned to Philadelphia by stage.

> Dickey . . . took occasion to introduce politics with other matters and always with management. The face of things in that region wears a pleasing aspect. We rode the canal in an open skiff and stopped often. Pennypacker acted as steersman, I as bowsman. The folks thought us the real democrats.[57]

Returning to Harrisburg, they continued their journey on the main line of the canal. A Democrat who watched their progress northward along the Susquehanna below Harrisburg observed critically,

> They were in our town [Marietta] a few days ago stopping at every tavern, electioneering and offering to bet money that his Black Majesty [Ritner] would be reelected, promising a railroad to the Marietta folk merely for an electioneering purpose. When they got to Bainbridge, they got *Stevens, Dickey* and *Pennypacker,* in a small skiff in the canal, and was [sic] towed along by a horse, and they stopped at every tavern and lock house along the

---

[55] Mueller, *Whig Party*, 45. See also Pennsylvania, *House Journal, 1838-1839*, II, Pt. 2, p. 1 ff., 372 ff., *ibid., 1840*, II, 225 ff.

[56] William C. McPherson to John B. McPherson, May 16, 1838, Edward McPherson Papers.

[57] William C. McPherson to John B. McPherson, May 30, 1838, *ibid.*

canal . . . promising every person a bridge across the canal or anything they would ask for.[58]

They proceeded northward to the Juniata and thence along its banks to Huntingdon, where Stevens decided to remain for a few weeks in Porter's "back yard." Conditions seemed so favorable there that Stevens promised "a majority for the old farmer of 12 or 1500 *at least.*" They had uncovered, McPherson reported, developments concerning Porter sufficient

> to *damn* any man. . . . We will be able before a month to prove that Mr. Porter is guilty of *perjury.* We will prove by a respectable member of the Society of Methodists that he [Porter] transferred to him $6,000 of property . . . before he took the benefit and had them retransferred after he went through the mill. This old man is now conscientious and anxious *to die in peace.*[59]

A disastrous flood, which tore out numerous dams and locks between Hollidaysburg and Huntingdon, occurred while the commissioners were in that region and temporarily diverted their attention to the more prosaic task of canal repairs. Stevens at once proved himself equal to the challenge. A hurried note to Biddle, in which he pointed out that canal funds were exhausted, that a special session of the legislature was inadvisable, and that the United States Bank by a timely loan had an opportunity to show its patriotism and crush the hostility of the "rascals" to banking institutions, brought a quick and a favorable response.[60]

"You are a magician greater than Van Buren, and with all your professions against Masonry, you are an absolute right worshipful Grand Master," Biddle jocularly replied. "Today I write the letter to the Governor of which I annex a copy. This is worth to you a dozen resumptions."[61] Stevens' reply, dispatched from Tunkhannock on the North Branch of the Susquehanna, brimmed with confidence. "As usual you did the thing handsomely. If we do not beat the rascals now, why I will resign."[62]

[58] Jacob Glatz to Buchanan, June 25, 1838, Buchanan Papers. For an explanation of this reference to Ritner as his "Black Majesty," see page 130.

[59] William C. McPherson to John B. McPherson, June 5, 1838, Edward McPherson Papers. He is accusing Porter of transferring assets before undergoing bankruptcy and then of having the property retransferred to him later.

[60] Stevens to Biddle, June 27, 1838, Biddle Papers.

[61] Biddle to Stevens, July 3, 1838, McGrane (ed.), *Correspondence of Nicholas Biddle,* 315.

[62] Stevens to Biddle, August 1, 1838, Biddle Papers.

DEPRESSION, BANKING, AND THE BUCKSHOT WAR 127

McPherson's secretarial duties, which included a campaign biography of Porter with the Huntingdon "revelations," took him back to Harrisburg, but communications from the commissioners enabled him to follow their political pilgrimage into the western sector and along the branches. On June 20 he reported that Dickey had informed him that "the missionaries in their journeys by land and water do not forget the *main* object, and that all things look well."[63]

Antimasonic leaders also sought to obtain political capital from the resumption of specie payments. After a year of waiting, resumption in the midst of the campaign would be hailed by business and could not fail to elicit a warm response from the rank and file. As early as April Ritner, through Secretary of the Commonwealth Burrowes, urged Biddle to offer to resume specie payments provided the federal administration would rescind the Specie Circular.[64] Biddle was not prepared to act, having previously insisted that the government must first remove its distinction between specie and notes.[65] The repeal of the Specie Circular on May 30, 1838, however, turned Biddle and other bankers to a consideration of resumption.[66] Representatives of the Philadelphia banks discussed the matter on June 1 and appointed a committee to investigate the situation and correspond with banks in neighboring states.[67]

At this point the Antimasonic board of strategy went into action. On June 4 Stevens asked Biddle when specie payments could be resumed; "Not that I expect an answer, but perhaps some mandatory proclamation by the 'Farmer' might be turned to good account if we knew the exact time."[68] On June 28 McPherson revealed to his father that Stevens' plan was awaiting the proper moment for consummation.

> The banks of Philadelphia you know are friendly to the Governor, and are anxious to help him and his cause. They are quietly fixing a day for the resumption of specie payments, and as soon as they determine it the Governor will be informed, when he will come out with a *tearing proclamation* commanding

[63] William C. McPherson to John B. McPherson, June 28, 1838, Edward McPherson Papers.
[64] Ritner to Burrowes, April 20, 1838, Gratz Correspondence.
[65] Biddle to Samuel Jaudon, May 31, 1838, McGrane (ed.), *Correspondence of Nicholas Biddle*, 311.
[66] Biddle to John Quincy Adams, printed in *Niles' Register*, LIV (June 9, 1838), 226.
[67] Mueller, *Whig Party*, 47; Harrisburg *Reporter*, June 8, 1838; Philadelphia *United States Gazette*, June 2, 1838.
[68] June 4, 1838, Biddle Papers.

them to resume by such a day. . . . This we conceive a bold *stroke*, and one which must make us votes. You see through the object no doubt. Mr. B. [Burrowes] told me last night that the day could not be beyond *1st of August*. I wanted you to have this information so as to be ready. In politics there is not too much honesty, I find, but the enemy must be fought with their own clubs. . . . With the *big project* mentioned above, what can defeat us?"[69]

With the Independent Treasury defeated in Congress, the time seemed propitious, and on July 13 Ritner released a proclamation to the press. It required the resumption of specie payments on August 13. His action was received enthusiastically by the Whig and Antimasonic press which had previously condemned efforts of Democrats in the legislature to set a date for resumption, and was denounced as "humbug" and "an insult to the intelligence of the people," by Democratic papers. The latter maintained, but offered no evidence to support it, that the proclamation was issued only after the banks had agreed secretly to resume.[70] The bankers acted promptly. Meeting in Philadelphia on July 23 with bank representatives from Massachusetts, Rhode Island, Connecticut, Maryland, Delaware, Virginia, and Kentucky, they secured an agreement to resume specie payments on August 13 as the Governor had directed.[71]

Ritner was overjoyed at the outcome and referred to his own part in the resumption as "an act of high and gratifying duty to the state." He praised both the citizens of the State for their "firmness and forbearance" and the banks for their "judicious conduct."[72] When the long-awaited day arrived, Whigs and Antimasons made it an occasion for celebration. At Harrisburg at nine o'clock, the hour at which the banks opened and

> shelled out the white and yellow boys, the mountains and valleys of the Susquehanna resounded with the roar of cannon. The chop-fallen Loco Focos quaked and trembled as the deafening peals broke upon their ears. . . . *The Promise of Joseph Ritner Was Redeemed; the People were not deceived.*[73]

[69] Edward McPherson Papers.
[70] Harrisburg *Reporter*, July 11, 1838 [extra edition], July 13, 1838; Philadelphia *American Sentinel*, July 14, 1838; Philadelphia *Pennsylvanian*, July 14, 16, 27, 1838.
[71] Mueller, *Whig Party*, 47; Philadelphia *National Gazette*, July 26, 1838.
[72] Ritner to Biddle, August 1, 1838, Etting Collection, Historical Society of Pennsylvania.
[73] Harrisburg *Telegraph*, August 15, 1838.

DEPRESSION, BANKING, AND THE BUCKSHOT WAR 129

It is impossible to say how many were deceived by Ritner's proclamation and the resumption which followed. It provided the Coalition, however, with a timely and dramatic achievement. They lost no opportunity to feature it during the closing weeks of the campaign.

It was inevitable that a contest launched with such intensity would be bitterly contested. Stevens and his touring escorts unearthed rumors that Porter had not only taken advantage of the bankruptcy law but had defrauded his creditors as well; and that he had lived in sin with a notorious prostitute, Peggy Beatty, and was the father of several illegitimate children. The latter charge circulated through Coalition papers in the form of a letter signed by one John Porter of Mifflin County, who claimed to be Porter's natural son. The contest as portrayed by the Coalition press was one between the honest German farmer and a fourth-rate country lawyer, notorious for his extravagance and dishonesty, "an old rake, accustomed to high life—to do as he pleases, to tyrannize over the poor wood-chopper and laborer."[74] The same theme was emphasized by the Harrisburg *Telegraph* in the following German couplets:

> Joseph Ritner ist der Mann
> Der den Staat regieren Kann,
> David Porter ist der Mann
> Der die benefit nehmen Kann.[75]

Ritner's treatment by the Democrats was equally scurrilous. A campaign "Biography of Ritner," profusely illustrated and overflowing with buffoonery, was widely circulated and reprinted in the press. It gave especial attention to the Governor's personal appearance.

> He is about five feet ten inches in height, broad shoulders, with an ample development of the ABDOMINAL region and a corresponding COUNTERPOISE on the other side. He bears little resemblance to Edward I, King of England surnamed "Long Shanks," but a much more striking similitude to Charles the Fat, whose ample shoulders, round cheeks, and PARENTHETICAL LEGS are well known in history.

Elsewhere it read, "at three different points, across the shoulders, hips, and knees he is precisely of the same diameter." The cartoons revealed the portly Executive being instructed in dancing by a French master; stuffing himself with food on a "fast day"; and having

---

[74] See page 126; Harrisburg *Telegraph*, June 6, August 8, 1838. A suit for libel in Lehigh County after the election vindicated Porter. Mueller, *Whig Party*, 48; Harrisburg *Reporter*, May 10, 1839.
[75] Harrisburg *Telegraph*, June 21, 1838.

a nightmare in which the murderers of Morgan were making an attempt upon his life.[76]

The Democratic press charged Ritner with abolitionism, basing their accusation upon a brief passage in his annual message to the legislature in December, 1836, in which he criticized the "gag rule" in Congress. They also seized upon occasional indications among Antimasons and Whigs in the legislature and in the press of a willingness to tolerate abolitionism and to support jury trials for fugitive slaves. The evidence was weak, and the charge was vigorously denied in Coalition papers. Nevertheless, Democrats continued to repeat the allegation, seeking thereby to exploit the unpopularity of abolitionism in the State.[77]

The Democrats reserved their most eloquent invective for the Gettysburg Railroad or "tapeworm," as they preferred to label it because of its undeniably circuitous course, and its sponsor, Stevens, who nourished it with liberal appropriations from the legislature. Acknowledged to be of doubtful utility and a means of colonizing Antimasonic voters, it was extremely vulnerable to attack. Sketched without showing the terrain it seemed grotesque and appeared to warrant the charge that it started nowhere and ended nowhere. Democratic editors reprinted illustrations of the railroad week after week and castigated Stevens unsparingly. Before the close of the campaign the "tapeworm" was a household expression throughout the State.

A campaign characterized by such an emphasis upon personalities undoubtedly served to cloak the bankruptcy of Antimasonry on the one hand and merge incongruous Democratic factions on the other. It failed, however, to remove long-standing dissensions, which had plagued the Coalition from its inception. Ritner made a bid for harmony by appointing William B. Reed of Philadelphia, a Whig and Mason, as Attorney General of the State.[78] But it was too little and too late. Whigs declared their support of Ritner in county conventions and in the press, but the two parties continued to work at cross purposes in making preparations for the election of 1840 and in organization of slates for State and local offices. In Chester County,

[76] *Ibid.*, August 8, 15, 1838. The biography was attributed to Ovid F. Johnson of the Harrisburg *Keystone*. The Antimasonic Harrisburg *Telegraph* reprinted it, hoping that it would fill its readers with indignation.

[77] Philadelphia *United States Gazette*, February 3, 1837; *Niles' Register*, LII (March 18, 1837), 34. In January, 1838, the House refused the use of its hall for a State antislavery convention. *Ibid.*, LIII (February 3, 1838), 353.

[78] Philadelphia *United States Gazette*, March 30, 1838.

for example, the two parties supported rival candidates and drew up resolutions defending their positions; and in the Adams-Franklin district they were in complete disagreement over a candidate for Congress.[79]

The contest also engendered a will to win at any price, and encouraged a spirit of intolerance which threatened for a time to disrupt the democratic processes. As the returns from the election on October 9, 1838, were tabulated, it was apparent that Porter was victorious, but that the control of the House and the balance of power in a joint session of the two houses were in doubt.[80] Two sets of returns from Philadelphia County prolonged the uncertainty and produced a deadlock which defied a solution. A charge of fraud in the incorporated Northern Liberties in the county led the Democratic election judges, who constituted a majority of the board, to reject and destroy the returns from that district, although fraud was alleged in but one ward. Whig election judges refused to accept the majority decision and drew up a second set of returns in which they included the wards in the Northern Liberties which contributed Whig majorities. The Democratic version indicated the election of Democrats to the State Senate and House; the Whig returns, the election of Whigs. The party which made its interpretation the official one would control both the House of Representatives and a joint vote of the houses. Attention was focused upon Harrisburg to observe the position of the Ritner administration and to follow the procedure of the Senate. The latter would be controlled by the Coalition regardless of the outcome.[81]

Ritner's attitude was quickly revealed in a statement released by Burrowes, who had added the chairmanship of Ritner's campaign to his duties as Secretary of the Commonwealth. Addressed to "The Friends of Joseph Ritner," it called for an immediate investigation of the irregularities, and proposed that during the interim that they "treat the election of the ninth inst. as if we had not been defeated and in that attitude abide the result."[82] Democrats were at once outraged and belligerent. Burrowes' interpretation, if accepted, would

[79] Mueller, *Whig Party*, 44-45; Philadelphia *United States Gazette*, March 21, June 27, 1838; Thomas Bell to Buchanan, September 5, 1838, Buchanan Papers; James Dunlop to William M. Meredith, September 10, 1838, Meredith Papers.

[80] Porter defeated Ritner by 127,821 votes to 122,325. Pennsylvania, *Senate Journal, 1838-1839*, I, 42-43. See Appendix, page 223.

[81] *Niles' Register*, LV (October 27, 1838), 129.

[82] *Ibid.*, LV (November 24, 1838), 205; Pennsylvania, *Senate Journal, 1838-1839*, II, 975-976.

involve not only the seats in the legislature, but would bring into question the election of Porter and the acceptance of the constitution which had been conceded by Coalition leaders.[83]

It appeared to many Democrats that the Ritner administration was trying to set aside the election and thereby deprive them of victory. As legislators assembled in Harrisburg, both parties revealed a reckless determination to seat the disputed delegations. A Whig member of the House from Philadelphia who urged a new election in the Northern Liberties as the fairest means to settle the issue found no echo to his views "from a single member of the party now at Harrisburg." Whigs were resolved to admit their claimants "regardless of the means." He found Democrats with whom he talked also unfavorable to his proposal.[84] Three days later his doubts were overcome. "I am however now in the boat and will stay there, blow wind come luck."[85]

By the time the legislature convened on December 4, 1838, Harrisburg was crowded with spectators, many of whom had converged upon the capital by rail and canal from points as distant as Philadelphia. The atmosphere was charged. When the House met in the morning, it at once split into two bodies, commonly referred to by the names of their respective chairmen; the Hopkins House made up of fifty-six Democrats, including the eight disputed members from Philadelphia County; and the Cunningham House composed of fifty-two Whigs and Antimasons, including the eight Whig claimants from Philadelphia County. Excluding the disputed members, both bodies lacked a majority of the total membership of the House. The advantage lay with the Cunningham House, however, since the Coalition-dominated Senate was expected to recognize it as the legal body.

When the Senate convened that afternoon the hall was jammed to capacity. The business had scarcely begun when the crowd interrupted and forced an adjournment. Speaker Charles B. Penrose, Secretary Burrowes, and Stevens, fearing bodily harm from the irate demonstrators, made a hasty retreat through a rear window and

---

[83] William C. McPherson declared in a letter to his father on October 14 that "It is about time to acknowledge ourselves 'licked' [in the gubernatorial election] .... I never saw Mr. Stevens so determined to go at anything in earnest as he is this investigation. He says he will give Mr. Porter plenty to do *anyhow*." Edward McPherson Papers.

[84] Henry L. Spackman to William M. Meredith, December 1, 1838, Meredith Papers.

[85] Spackman to Meredith, December 4, 1838, *ibid.*

reported the situation to the Governor.[86] The latter, after first being rebuffed by the commanding officer of federal troops at Carlisle, called out the State militia. Major General Robert Patterson, in ordering the troops to assemble, required that they provide themselves "with thirteen rounds of buckshot cartridges." In so doing, he inadvertently gave the entire episode the rather misleading title, "The Buckshot War."[87]

From December 5 to December 7, while the militia was en route from Philadelphia, crowds milled about the capital, keeping Whigs and Antimasons in a state of anxiety. "There is no protection or law here," McPherson observed. "Two thirds of the citizens sanction it—they surrounded the arsenal this morning but did not gain admittance." The Senate attempted no meeting on the day following its untimely adjournment, and when the Cunningham House assembled it ran into difficulty. "As soon as the Speaker pro tem took the seat he was surrounded and carried out though not hurt." The Speaker was allowed sufficient time to depute another member to adjourn the House![88] Two days later on December 7, the throng had quieted; some were leaving town. The Senate assembled in a hall in the town without interference. On the day following, the Senate invited Whig claimants to take their seats in that body. They appeared, but asked to be excused until their status had been determined by an investigation.[89] On December 9 the militia arrived. Their presence was sufficient to remove further threats of violence.

The pacification of the mob and the restoration of the Senate to its chamber in the Capitol, however, did not mean smooth sailing for the Coalition. Resolutions to investigate the election in Philadelphia County were postponed by the combined votes of Democrats and a minority of Whigs and Antimasons.[90] For a week the deadlock continued unchanged; then the bottom fell out of the Coalition

[86] For Burrowes' role, see Robert L. Mohr, *Thomas Henry Burrowes, 1805-1871* (Philadelphia, 1946), 16-36. Two Philadelphia radicals, John McCahen and Charles S. Brown led the demonstration. See Henry L. Spackman to William M. Meredith, December 4, 1838, Meredith Papers.
[87] *Niles' Register*, LV (January 5, 1839), 295-297; *ibid.*, LV (December 8, 1838), 240; Mueller, *Whig Party*, 51-52; Pennsylvania, *House Journal, 1838-1839*, II, Pt. 2, 245 ff.
[88] William C. McPherson to John B. McPherson, December 5, 1838, Edward McPherson Papers.
[89] James Hanna to William B. Reed, December 8, 1838, Meredith Papers.
[90] William C. McPherson to John B. McPherson, December 10, 1838, Edward McPherson Papers.

strategy. Three of their members withdrew from the Cunningham House and took seats in the Hopkins House. It gave the latter a total of fifty-one, not counting contested delegates, which was a majority of the total House membership.[91] For another week, however, the Coalition ignored the advantage now held by the Hopkins House, while Democrats threatened to call a convention to take the measures required to reorganize the Senate.[92] But such an extraordinary device was not necessary. The Coalition could no longer keep its members in line. On Christmas five Whigs and Antimasons joined with twelve Democrats in the Senate to recognize the Hopkins House by the narrow margin of 17 to 16.[93]

It was a bitter blow to the Coalition. The crestfallen McPherson declared,

> Mob rule has prevailed. The boasted supremacy of the laws has been trampled upon. The vote of five men professing to act with us as a political party sanctioned the recognition of the Hopkins house. . . .
>
> Either one could have saved us. Now our friends feel disgraced, so much so that many of them will go home—Mr. Stevens among that number.
>
> The Senate sat until 4 o'clock and on this holy day, rendered so by the birth of our religion, prostituted the *only safeguard* which can be thrown around our institutions.
>
> The subject is humiliating, our disgrace as a party is acknowledged. What security do we have that future houses will not be organized by such a horde of bandetti?[94]

His words were prophetic. Antimasonry never recovered from its loss of face, and the disgusted Stevens, refusing to enter the Hopkins House, returned to his home in Gettysburg.[95]

A Philadelphia Democrat who had witnessed the stirring scenes at Harrisburg exulted, "Whiggery is I presume an inmate of the tomb

---

[91] They were Chester Butler and John Sturdevant of Luzerne and John Montelius of Union. The Lewisburg *Standard* on December 27, 1838, printed Montelius' explanation of his action. See also Harrisburg *Telegraph*, December 18, 1838.

[92] George W. Barton to Buchanan, December 18, 1838, Buchanan Papers.

[93] The five were John Strohm, Lancaster; Abraham Miller, Philadelphia; James McConkey, York; David Fullerton, Franklin; Peter Michler, Lehigh-Northampton; and Elihu Case, Bradford-Susquehanna.

[94] William C. McPherson to John B. McPherson, December 25, 1838, Edward McPherson Papers.

[95] Stevens' address to the people of Adams County in defense of his course was printed in the Harrisburg *Telegraph,* January 18, 1839.

of the Capulets from this time forward in Pennsylvania. It has become *ridiculous* and a worse epithet for a party even than *wicked*, for men are more cheerfully accounted knaves than fools."[96]

The triumphant Democrats showed no disposition to spare the vanquished. The committee arrangements for the inauguration of Porter denied Ritner the customary place of the retiring Governor in the procession to the Capitol. Porter marched to the inaugural ceremony alone, while Ritner waited in the chamber of the House of Representatives with a few friends who had remained to witness this "mortification."[97]

[96] John K. Kane to Lewis S. Coryell, December 27, 1838, Lewis S. Coryell Correspondence, Historical Society of Pennsylvania.

[97] William C. McPherson to John B. McPherson, January 15, 1839. A few days later the defeat was brought home in another manner. In a special election of a State Senator in the Franklin-Cumberland-Adams district, General Thomas C. Miller, a member of the Harrisburg Committee of Safety and one of the most conspicuous leaders of the Democratic host during the Buckshot War, was victorious over his Coalition opponent. The district had been regarded as a pillar of Coalition strength as recently as three months before. Miller's election reversed the results in October by 1,300 votes. McPherson to McPherson, January 17, 23, 1839, *ibid.;* Philadelphia *Pennsylvanian,* January 21, 1839. For the report of the committee appointed to investigate the Buckshot War, see Pennsylvania, *Senate Journal, 1838-1839,* II, 820 ff.

CHAPTER VIII

Porter at the Helm, 1839-1840

WHILE the Buckshot War absorbed the attention of the public, politicians were contesting behind the scenes for the ear of the Governor-elect. Wolf and Muhlenberg partisans, Van Buren men, Improvement Democrats, and Bank men journeyed to Huntingdon to press their claims. They found Porter cordial but evasive.[1] He revealed a determination to make his own decisions without deference to individuals or groups, and, except for a possible understanding with the editors of the *Keystone,* he seems to have been uncommitted. He was careful, however, to balance Wolf with Muhlenberg men in distributing the patronage.[2]

After considering Samuel D. Ingham and Edward B. Hubley, a relative of Muhlenberg and a member of Congress from Schuylkill, active supporters of Wolf and Muhlenberg respectively, for Secretary of the Commonwealth, he offered the office at the last moment to Francis R. Shunk, Clerk of the House and Democratic strategist during the Buckshot War, who was popular among both Muhlenberg and Wolf men.[3] For Attorney General he chose Ovid F. Johnson, lawyer, journalist, member of the *Keystone* clique, and agent of the United States Bank.[4] He named William F. Packer, a publisher of the *Keystone,* Edward B. Hubley, and James Clarke to the Canal Commission. Packer had been a Muhlenberg supporter and Clarke an adherent of Wolf.[5]

---

[1] Buchanan in particular prepared to place Porter under his tutelage. But he waited in vain for an invitation to Huntingdon. See Buchanan to Porter, October 22, November 1, 1838, W. W. Porter Papers, Historical Society of Pennsylvania; Porter to Buchanan, October 26, 1838, Buchanan Papers; Buchanan to John Sterigere, November 2, 1838, *ibid.;* George W. Barton to Buchanan, December 18, 1838, *ibid.* Reports from early visitors to Porter may be found in the following letters: Lewis S. Coryell to Biddle, October 15, 1838, Biddle Papers; Lloyd Wharton to Biddle, October 21, November 22, 1838, *ibid.;* George W. Barton to Buchanan, November 11, 1838, Buchanan Papers.

[2] Buchanan to J. Randolph Clay, April 18, 1839, Presidents of the United States, Dreer Collection, Historical Society of Pennsylvania.

[3] George W. Barton to Buchanan, December 18, 1838, Buchanan Papers.

[4] See page 116.

[5] Philadelphia *United States Gazette,* February 2, 4, 1839.

136

By steering a middle course between the Wolf and Muhlenberg factions, Porter contributed to the solidarity of the party; but he offset this advantage by identifying himself in Harrisburg with the *Keystone* and thereby alienating the editors of the *Reporter;* and in Pittsburgh and Philadelphia by rewarding personal friends with offices rather than depending upon the party organizations for recommendations. In so doing, he helped to foster disaffection in each of these areas.

With the key offices filled, Porter was at once confronted with uncompleted improvements, an income inadequate to meet running costs, an interest payment of $600,000 due, and an empty treasury. He secured an authorization for an emergency loan from the legislature, but received no offers from the banks, now paying specie for their notes but still bogged in the quicksands of the panic. In meeting the crisis, Porter showed qualities which characterized his two terms of office: a resourcefulness to meet the staggering financial obligations of the State; and a determination to protect the banks from regulations which appeared injurious to their welfare, despite the objections of the Hard-Money Men.

He led off by dispatching Shunk to Philadelphia to sound out the bankers, and when he failed, he sent Johnson on a similar mission. The latter had the advantage of being acquainted personally with Biddle and other bankers, but he too found them unreceptive. Porter at length obtained a temporary loan, but received no offers for a larger sum required to put the State Works into shape for the spring season. In a special message to the legislature he reported that the banks had rejected the proposed loan of $1,200,000 despite their concession that money was not scarce, and he intimated that their refusal resulted from a predetermined agreement to defeat the loan.[6] He did not permit his criticism of the banks, however, to interfere with his negotiations. Engaging a former bank lobbyist, Daniel M. Brodhead, as an agent and go-between, an employment which the latter found to be "honorable, profitable and pleasant,"[7] he found that he could bargain for the loans. The United States Bank, he learned through Brodhead, would not only take the $1,200,000 loan, but would finance new improvements, provided that it would not be called upon to lend additional sums under the

---

[6] Philadelphia *United States Gazette,* March 11, 1839; Philadelphia *Pennsylvanian,* March 12, 1839.
[7] Brodhead to Joel R. Poinsett, May 11, 1839, Joel Roberts Poinsett Papers, Historical Society of Pennsylvania.

provisions of its charter.[8] Porter promptly assured Brodhead "that if those two loans be taken and authority be given by law at the present session to sell the Bank stock now held by the state, they will not be called upon during the present year for any advances under their charter."[9] He thereby avoided a showdown. The legislature adopted an improvement bill during a special session in June, 1839, and in September the United States Bank took the State loan of $2,000,000. It enabled Porter to maintain the credit of the State through the first year of his office. The United States Bank in return received the privilege of issuing five-dollar notes in the amount of the loan—a concession which Biddle had sought since the adoption of the charter three years before.[10]

By financing the interest upon the debt, current expenses, and improvements with borrowed money, Porter like Ritner was merely postponing the inevitable day of reckoning. It was not long delayed. The revival of business accompanying the resumption of specie payments in 1838 was not sustained, and a sharp recession occurred in the fall of 1839.[11] On October 9 the banks of Philadelphia again suspended; banks in the interior quickly followed them. A few days after the suspension Porter released a letter devoted to the subject of the emergency. He urged that the banks be treated with "forbearance and moderation" and declared that he had no intention of shaking the confidence of the public in the ability of the banks "to meet all their obligations."[12]

His action was at once a source of controversy, and posed deep-rooted problems for the party. The new legislature unlike its predecessor would find the Democrats in control in both houses. Porter would thus face a resurgent Democratic party and the likelihood of an assault upon the banks. Could the executive and the legislature find a common ground for action, or would they disagree and thereby place another block upon the path of Democratic harmony?

When the legislature convened in January, 1840, the Democrats lost no time in registering their disregard for the wishes of Porter. They gave the printing of the House journal to the editors of the

[8] Brodhead to Porter, March 16, 1839, Biddle Papers.
[9] Porter to Brodhead, March 18, 1839, *ibid.*
[10] *Niles' Register*, LVII (September 28, 1839), 65.
[11] Reginald C. McGrane, *The Panic of 1837* (Chicago, 1924), 110, 205-206.
[12] Harrisburg *Telegraph*, October 17, 1839.

State Capital Gazette, a rebuke to the *Keystone* clique, and elected Daniel Sturgeon to the United States Senate, defeating James Clarke, the choice of the Porter men in the legislature.[13] A few weeks later Democrats in the House by a party vote passed a bill requiring the immediate resumption of specie payments by the banks of the State. Improvement Democrats voted for the bill in order to avoid an open break with the majority. Several members, including the Speaker, denounced it upon the floor, then voted for it.[14] At this point Porter intervened with a special message in which he declared, "if a too rigorous system of measures be adopted to coerce the payment of the liabilities of the banks immediately, the credit of the state must and will be seriously and disastrously affected." He urged resumption "within a reasonable time," but insisted that the existing pressure and cumbrous public debt made it imperative that the State show indulgence.[15]

His message, in effect, a veto in advance, elicited an immediate outcry from Van Buren men. In the State Senate Charles S. Brown, a Philadelphia County radical, denounced it as a compromise of principle; and in Philadelphia Democrats expressed their indignation at a public rally. Buchanan wrote to Porter in alarm, "You have perhaps never witnessed anything like the exaltation either felt or affected, of the Whigs here when the first news of your special message arrived." No harm might result, he advised, "provided the Legislature should fix an early day for the resumption of the Banks. Should they adjourn without doing this, the integrity of the party will be in great danger."[16] From the Hermitage, the aging Jackson observed sorrowfully what he interpreted to be the baneful effects of the banks upon the Governor and the legislature.

> I am afraid that there are some apostates in the Pennsylvania Legislature, some Penroses[17] whose principles bent before the money power—of this we will see, and I also fear that Governor Porter made a bad move on the political chess board under other influence [than] that of real Democratic and republican principles. If he had not sent his hasty message, a *trumph card* in favor of

[13] Benjamin Parke to Buchanan, December 13, 1839, Buchanan Papers.
[14] Harrisburg *Telegraph,* February 7, 11, 1840; Philadelphia *Pennsylvanian,* February 1, 1840.
[15] Harrisburg *Telegraph,* February 4, 1840; Harrisburg *Keystone,* February 3, 1840.
[16] Buchanan to Porter, February 24, 1840, W. W. Porter Papers.
[17] See pages 77-78.

140   THE JACKSONIAN HERITAGE

Bankism all things would went [sic] on well in the Legislature of Pennsylvania.[18]

The *Keystone* hurriedly explained that a "reasonable time" for resumption meant April 1, May 1, or June 1, but Porter offered no interpretation.[19] Two days after his plea for forbearance the Philadelphia banks, prodded by the managers of the United States Bank who argued that it was important to the State and its institutions that the interest on the State loans be paid promptly, came forward with an offer to take the loan. They also presented a memorial to the legislature in which they maintained that they could not resume specie payments until February 1, 1841.[20]

To the radicals it appeared that Porter's message and the prompt action of the banks in taking the loan and seeking to delay resumption until the following session of the legislature added up to a bargain: an indulgence in the form of a suspension for a year in return for quantities of "irredeemable and depreciated paper." Poverty, not the will of the people, it was declared, was relied on to gain the consent. If resumption could be delayed until 1841, why could not the same argument be used when that date arrived to postpone it indefinitely?[21]

The fate of the movement for an early resumption served to confirm this suspicion. The Senate passed a bill which required immediate resumption but which differed from the House bill in minor details. The two houses could find no satisfactory compromise, and the deadlock was broken only after the Senate sidestepped a comprehensive bill and adopted instead a resolution setting the resumption date on January 15, 1841, barely two weeks earlier than the date requested by the banks. Six Improvement Democrats voted with the Coalition to accomplish its adoption. In the House more than twenty Democrats who had earlier supported immediate resumption similarly joined with the Coalition to permit a concurrence with the Senate.[22] In a sense the resolution legalized suspension by requiring banks which were not paying specie to subscribe up to $3,000,000 in

[18] Jackson to Francis P. Blair, April 9, 1840, Bassett (ed.), *Correspondence of Andrew Jackson*, VI, 56-57.
[19] Harrisburg *Keystone*, February 6, 1840.
[20] Philadelphia *Public Ledger*, February 19, 1840; "Descriptive Catalogue of the Records of the Bank of North America Deposited with the Historical Society of Pennsylvania," 62-63.
[21] Philadelphia *Pennsylvanian*, February 17, April 1, 1840.
[22] *Ibid.*, April 1, 2, 1840.

State loans according to the value of their capital stock.[23] Porter thus met the interest on the debt and financed the improvements, and the banks secured a year's grace from their obligations.

The legislature on June 14, 1840, in a special session took a significant step on the long road toward the financial rehabilitation of the State when it adopted a tax bill which included levies upon real and personal property. The bill cut across party lines in both houses.[24] After a four-year holiday, Pennsylvania's taxpayers would again pay for a part of the costs of government.

Porter's conciliatory policy toward the banks sustained both the State and the banks through another panic year. But in so doing he deepened the wedge between the conservative fringe which supported him and the Van Buren–Hard-Money Men who vehemently denounced his course. Thus while the Van Buren administration freed the federal government from a dependence upon banks by the adoption of the Independent Treasury, the Porter administration strengthened the thongs which bound the State to its banking institutions. This divergence between the party at Washington and the party at Harrisburg was all the more ominous since it occurred in a presidential election year.

The campaign of 1840 began early in Pennsylvania. The year 1838 was but a few weeks old when Antimasons, seeking to get the jump on their political bedfellows, the Whigs, inaugurated a movement for William Henry Harrison. It was brought into the open at their gubernatorial convention on March 5, 1838, where they adopted a resolution by a unanimous vote in support of his candidacy.[25] Eight months later on November 13, 1838, Pennsylvania's delegates took a leading role in the nomination of Harrison and Daniel Webster at the Antimasonic National Convention in Philadelphia.[26] The disastrous defeat of Ritner in October, 1838, followed by the humiliation of the Buckshot War tied the fortunes of the party even more closely to the presidential campaign. "Harrison is now the rallying cry," a party member reported as the dejected Antimasonic officeholders prepared to leave Harrisburg.[27]

Whigs, meanwhile, prepared to strike out for themselves and make their own presidential nomination regardless of the wishes of the

[23] *Ibid.*, April 2, 1840.
[24] *Ibid.*, June 12, 1840; Philadelphia *American Sentinel,* June 15, 1840.
[25] Harrisburg *Telegraph,* March 9, 1838.
[26] *Ibid.*, November 14, 1838.
[27] William C. McPherson to John B. McPherson, January 10, 1839, Edward McPherson Papers.

Antimasons. In January, 1839, the Philadelphia *United States Gazette* came out for Clay, and thereby provoked a spirited controversy with the supporters of Harrison.[28] Whigs from twenty-five counties met at Chambersburg on June 13, 1839, to reach a decision upon a nominee. After a heated contest between the partisans of Clay and Harrison, the victory went to the former by a margin of two to one. They kept the door open, however, by expressing a willingness to accept the verdict of the national convention.[29] The concession failed to reconcile the Harrison men, headed by Charles B. Penrose and John Dickey, former Bank Democrats, who entered a protest and withdrew from the convention.[30] In the end it was the Clay men, however, who yielded in the interest of expediency. In shifting to Harrison, they again turned over the leadership to the Antimasons, who dominated the State convention at Harrisburg on September 4, 1839, which named the delegates to the Whig national convention.[31]

The national nominating convention of the Whig party assembled at Harrisburg on December 2, 1839, in the recently completed Lutheran Church. Clay and Harrison were the principal rivals for the presidential nomination, and General Winfield Scott had considerable support among the several delegations.

The Harrison faction from Pennsylvania had the satisfaction of seeing former Governor John A. Shulze seated as a vice president and Charles B. Penrose elected secretary. But they were unable to deter Clay partisans from three districts from appearing and seeking recognition as delegates. A showdown was averted by admitting both Clay and Harrison claimants, a maneuver which left the Pennsylvania delegation safely in the Harrison column.[32]

When an informal poll of the convention indicated that Clay was in the lead, Harrison men from Pennsylvania, Ohio, and Indiana worked with Thurlow Weed, the New York "boss," in his role as President-maker. At his bidding, they endorsed the unit rule, designed to offset scattered support for Clay from many sections. The proposal was introduced by Penrose and carried as an amendment to the

[28] Philadelphia *Pennsylvanian*, January 21, 1839.
[29] Nathan Sargent, *Public Men and Events* . . . , 2 vols. (Philadelphia, 1875), II, 75.
[30] Philadelphia *American Sentinel*, June 18, 1839; *Niles' Register*, LVI (June 22, 1839), 259.
[31] *Ibid.*, LVII (September 14, 1839), 46-47.
[32] *Ibid.*, LVII (December 14, 1839), 248-252; Freeman Cleaves, *Old Tippecanoe: William Henry Harrison and His Time* (New York, 1939), 314-315.

motion to poll the states. Under this unit rule, the initial ballot showed 103 votes for Clay, 91 for Harrison, and 57 for Scott.[33]

Having already established Harrison as the second choice of several of the states voting for Scott, Weed was now prepared to deliver the nomination to the former. The plan was executed after recessing for twenty-four hours so that the Harrison men could try to conciliate the Clay partisans. When the ballot was taken, Scott delegations from New York, Michigan, and Vermont shifted to Harrison to give him the majority necessary for nomination. After failing to induce a Clay stalwart to accept the Vice Presidency, the nomination was given to John Tyler of Virginia.[34] The convention closed amidst a flurry of oratory in which Pennsylvania partisans of both Webster and Clay participated.

Having secured the nomination of Harrison, Antimasons discarded Webster, who had been nominated at Philadelphia for the Vice Presidency, and accepted Tyler.[35] The Coalition thus had a common slate. It should be pointed out, however, that the Antimasons had no intention of losing their identity by being drawn into the Whig party. They co-operated to name a Harrison State Committee, but they retained their own party organization and directed their own campaign.[36]

Democrats faced the election of 1840 without much enthusiasm. Gone was the magic of Jackson; in his place was the colorless Van Buren embarrassed by a prolonged financial dislocation. Throughout the State Van Buren and Porter men contested to control the party organization and to monopolize the spoils. They were discordant and proscriptive.

The first Democratic bid for 1840 came in 1838 when elements opposed to Van Buren's re-election organized a movement in support of Commodore Charles Stewart, a naval hero of the War of 1812, commanding officer of the *Constitution* and currently in charge of the Navy Yard at Philadelphia. An appropriate biography was published and subsequently reprinted in the press.[37] The editors of the

[33] *Ibid.*, 317; Harriet A. Weed (ed.), *Life of Thurlow Weed, Including His Autobiography and a Memoir*, 2 vols. (Boston, 1884), I, 480-482; Oliver P. Chitwood, *John Tyler, Champion of the Old South* (Philadelphia, 1939), 166.

[34] Weed (ed.), *Life of Thurlow Weed*, I, 482.

[35] Harmar Denny to Webster, January 31, 1840, Webster Papers.

[36] Thomas H. Burrowes to Joseph Wallace, February 28, July 18, 1840, Edward McPherson Papers.

[37] *Biographical Sketch, and Services of Commodore Charles Stewart of the Navy of the United States* (Philadelphia, 1838).

Harrisburg *Keystone* in particular cultivated the movement, insisting later that the costs incurred were underwritten by Biddle.[38] The Stewart boom culminated in a mass demonstration at Harrisburg on July 4, 1838, where the "old commodore" as honored guest accepted the plaudits of the crowd and presented the citizenry with a cannon.[39] It was a colorful spectacle, but unproductive politically. The politicians preferred to bide their time. By the close of the year Stewart's name had receded into the background.

Interest in the nomination quickened in 1839. Van Buren's renomination was now a foregone conclusion, but the vice-presidential candidate remained an intriguing uncertainty. Richard M. Johnson, the incumbent, had been elected by the Senate in 1836 after failing to receive a majority in the Electoral College. It was believed that this would deter him from making a second attempt. It did not, but while the issue remained in doubt Democrats vied to promote the claims of Senator William R. King of Alabama, John Forsyth, Van Buren's Secretary of State, and Thomas Hart Benton, Missouri's flamboyant defender of metallic currency in the United States Senate. The movement for King was fostered by Buchanan and was closely interwoven with his own ambitions for the Presidency. King, if successful, would not become a candidate for President in 1844, but would use his influence to bring about Buchanan's nomination. This would strengthen the latter in the Deep South and be a boon to his candidacy. King's nomination thus offered the possibility of a Pennsylvania President in 1844. Buchanan received a flattering response from up-State politicians, and numerous editors promptly came out for King.

In Philadelphia, however, he made little headway. There Van Buren leaders were active in behalf of Forsyth, and Hard-Money Men were leaning toward Benton. In seeking to promote their respective candidates each group looked to Van Buren for a token of his favor, but the cautious executive held aloof. When Felix Grundy of Tennessee resigned as Attorney General, spokesmen for each faction flocked to Washington to present their claims. Van Buren first offered the post to Buchanan. He turned it down but immediately launched a vigorous movement in favor of James M. Porter, a brother of the Governor.[40] Success would solidify Buchanan with the administration

---

[38] See page 116.

[39] William C. McPherson to John B. McPherson, June 28, 1838, Edward McPherson Papers; Simon Cameron to Lewis S. Coryell, June 2, 1838, Coryell Correspondence.

[40] Buchanan to David R. Porter, December 3, 9, 28, 1839, W. W. Porter Papers.

of the State and be indicative of Van Buren's blessing. The latter, however, next offered the appointment to George M. Dallas, who had recently returned from a diplomatic mission to Russia, and when Dallas declined he appointed Henry D. Gilpin of Philadelphia. It was a deep disappointment to Buchanan, who complained to Governor Porter, "The President's disposition towards myself is proclaimed upon the house-top."[41]

The vice-presidential controversy terminated suddenly when Johnson announced his intention to run for a second term. By the time Democrats met in convention at Harrisburg on March 4, 1840, his endorsement was generally conceded. Only the Lancaster County delegation, composed of ardent Buchanan men, insisted upon a test of strength, refusing to withdraw King until after a vote had been taken. The result was a decisive victory for Johnson who received 107 votes to 22 for King. The latter was then withdrawn and Johnson made the unanimous choice of the convention.[42]

A more serious threat than the vice-presidential rivalry in the campaign of 1840 was the cleavage between the Van Buren and Porter men. The dissatisfaction with Porter's appointments in Philadelphia and Pittsburgh, his reliance upon the *Keystone* clique and the Improvement Men, and the opposition of the hard-money group to his bank policy have been indicated. At the March 4 convention rival delegations from Luzerne, Lycoming, Schuylkill, and Philadelphia counties presented themselves for admission. In each case, one group was identified with Van Buren, the other with Porter. The convention eased itself out of this dilemma by admitting both delegations from Luzerne, Lycoming, and Schuylkill, and excluding both groups from Philadelphia County. In order to give the latter a voice in the convention, members of the legislature from that county were finally given seats.[43] With the Philadelphia Van Buren men thus eliminated, the convention adopted a resolution for Porter by a unanimous vote: "Resolved: that the democracy of Pennsylvania have just reason to be proud of her Chief Magistrate, Governor Porter, and that they have, not only an undiminished, but an increased confidence in his worth, integrity and merits."[44] By avoiding any mention of Porter's measures, the convention adjourned without airing the Van Buren-Porter

[41] Buchanan to David R. Porter, January 8, 1840, *ibid.*
[42] John W. Forney to Buchanan, March 5, 1840, Buchanan Papers; Philadelphia *United States Gazette,* March 6, 1840; Harrisburg *Telegraph,* March 6, 1840.
[43] Philadelphia *Pennsylvanian,* March 6, 7, 20, 1840.
[44] Harrisburg *Telegraph,* March 5, 1840.

factionalism. Even such an innocuous platitude was unacceptable, however, among Van Buren men, who relegated it to the status of a "snap judgment."[45]

During the weeks following the convention, dissatisfaction over the patronage in Philadelphia continued to agitate the Van Buren men there. To fill vacancies on the bench of the newly created criminal court in Philadelphia, Porter appointed George W. Barton, an active Buchanan partisan, Robert T. Conrad, a holdover from the abolished Court of Criminal Sessions, and Joseph M. Doran.[46] Of the three, Barton and Conrad were completely unacceptable to the Van Buren organizations in the city and county.[47] The death of former Governor Wolf, Collector of the Port of Philadelphia, a few days later precipitated a scramble for that post. Democrats from the interior in Congress recommended the appointment of a man from that section on the ground that they had been neglected in the patronage, a charge vehemently denied by the Philadelphia group. When word reached Philadelphia that a man from the interior was to be appointed, Democrats could barely be restrained. George M. Dallas observed to Henry D. Gilpin,

> The City and County Democrats are at this moment so much exasperated at the conduct of a clique who surround and manage the Governor . . . that I have to entreat incessantly for forebearance, moderation and silence. They consider themselves put under the ban, and not without reason. Their principles have been denounced, their delegates rejected, and judges are foisted over them whom they detest. If in addition to their present load of suffering, they are to receive a blow from Washington, what's to be done?[48]

The rumor was not unfounded. A few days later the appointment of Calvin Blythe of Dauphin County was announced.[49] Feeling against Porter, who was credited with the action, was so bitter in Philadelphia that a rally called by his friends was invaded by Van Buren men and forced to disband.[50]

[45] George M. Dallas to Henry D. Gilpin, March 17, 1840, Gilpin Papers.
[46] The Democrats abolished the Court of Criminal Sessions established by the Coalition in 1838 in order to remove Coalition judges. They replaced it with the Court of General Sessions. See J. Thomas Scharf and Thompson Westcott, *History of Philadelphia, 1609-1884*, 3 vols. (Philadelphia, 1884), II, 1573.
[47] James Page to Buchanan, June 11, 1840, Buchanan Papers; George M. Dallas to Henry D. Gilpin, March 17, 1840, Gilpin Papers; Philadelphia *United States Gazette*, March 11, 1840.
[48] Dallas to Gilpin, March 17, 1840, Gilpin Papers.
[49] Philadelphia *Pennsylvanian*, March 12, 19, 1840.
[50] Dallas to Gilpin, April 17, 1840, Gilpin Papers.

The hostility of the Porter and Van Buren men was reflected in the press. In Philadelphia, for example, the *Spirit of the Times,* mouthpiece of the Hard-Money Men, engaged in a drawn-out controversy with the *American Sentinel,* spokesman for the Porter faction. The former charged the latter with indifference toward Van Buren and the Democratic nominees for the legislature; the latter retaliated by reprinting abusive references to Porter from the columns of the *Spirit of the Times* following his resumption message.[51] Papers in the interior took the *American Sentinel* to task. "Every opportunity is embraced [by the *Sentinel*] with a significant avidity to do the party harm," John W. Forney affirmed in the columns of the Lancaster *Intelligencer.*[52] Dissensions such as these offered a poor antidote to the coonskin campaign of the Coalition.

The Democrats had a dearth of peacemakers. Buchanan, who attempted this role, found the road arduous and lightly traveled. In May, 1840, he conferred with Porter in Lancaster where he impressed upon him "the absolute necessity of union and harmony between the state and national administrations."[53] A week later he carried a similar message to Van Buren in Washington. The latter, he assured Porter, expressed a

> great regard for you, and said he had given conclusive evidence of it by the appointment of Judge Blythe . . . to gratify your wishes. . . . We spoke freely [about] certain politicians in Philadelphia and I have no doubt from what he said that he will exert his influence in some manner to prevent them from any longer treating you unfairly.[54]

Meanwhile, Buchanan urged that the legislature adopt a bank regulatory act as a means of promoting conciliation.[55] When he was invited to Reading to participate in a celebration of the Fourth of July with Vice President Johnson, he refused to accept until the committee reversed its decision to omit Porter from the list of guests.[56] He gained his point; the Vice President and the Governor appeared on the same platform.

Buchanan carried on a voluminous correspondence with politicians in all parts of the State; in Philadelphia and Pittsburgh, for example,

---

[51] Philadelphia *American Sentinel,* August 24, September 8, 1840; Philadelphia *Spirit of the Times,* September 4, 1840.
[52] Reprinted in the Philadelphia *American Sentinel,* October 16, 1840.
[53] Porter to Buchanan, May 20, 1840, Buchanan Papers.
[54] Buchanan to Porter, May 30, 1840, W. W. Porter Papers.
[55] *Ibid.*
[56] Robert M. Barr to Buchanan, June 19, 27, 28, 1840, Buchanan Papers.

he worked to prevent Van Buren men from airing their grievances against Porter, and in Lancaster he rebuked Forney for abusing the *American Sentinel* in the *Intelligencer*.[57] In September he stumped the western counties. At Pittsburgh, his presence facilitated the participation of Van Buren and Porter partisans in a common demonstration.[58] He returned to his home with his voice broken, but with his spirits high. The West, he reported, would do better for Van Buren than it had done in 1836.[59] Buchanan's optimism proved to be unwarranted, however. There were too few fellow travelers.

The campaign of 1840 in Pennsylvania was similar in most respects to that waged throughout the nation. Coonskin caps and hard cider, "Tip and Tyler," "Harrison the poor man's friend," mass demonstrations, all combined to make Harrison the folk hero and the champion of the people, a role which Jackson had filled so well a bare four years before. Whigs and Antimasons, however, did not hesitate to add issues peculiar to the State. They placed the responsibility for the State debt, increased by more than six million dollars in less than two years by the Porter administration, upon the Democrats. Reckless expenditures, they insisted, had jeopardized the credit of the State and brought back the unpopular State taxes which the Coalition had repealed.

They charged repeatedly from the platform and in the press that a Democratic victory would lower the wages of American labor, basing their claim upon a speech of Buchanan, delivered in the Senate in support of the Independent Treasury, in which he had urged the adoption of a hard-money currency in the ordinary transactions of business and in the payment of wages of labor. "Reduce our nominal to the real standard of prices throughout the world," he had declared, "and you will cover our country with blessings and benefits." The Coalition press removed his reference to wages from its context, made it appear to be a movement to reduce wage levels, and circulated it widely. They hailed Harrison as the champion of the workingman and denounced Van Buren as his oppressor. Buchanan, they insisted, would reduce the laborer to prevailing levels in Germany, France, and England and other hard-money countries. To the usual "Tippecanoe

---

[57] Forney to Buchanan, December 21, 1840, *ibid.;* James Page to Buchanan, June 2, 1840, *ibid.*

[58] John B. Butler to Buchanan, September 21, 1840, *ibid.*

[59] Buchanan to Van Buren, September 25, 1840, Van Buren Papers.

and Tyler too," Coalition rallies added, "No reducing of wages" and "a fair price for labor."[60]

Buchanan spared neither time nor effort in an attempt to refute the charge. In Lancaster, his supporters challenged Antimasons to publish jointly Buchanan's speech and the reply of Senator John Davis of Massachusetts. Antimasons would have no part of it, but continued to repeat the low-wage allegation.[61] Buchanan's defense served only to spur his opponents, and his friends were soon suggesting that further agitation would only make matters worse.[62] It proved to be just another irrational issue in an irrational campaign.

Having failed to harmonize their differences and having lost the initiative to the Coalition, Democratic leaders concluded the campaign under a cloud of pessimism.[63] At Parkesburg in Chester County, one politician reported hopefully to Buchanan that the hard cider campaign was alienating the Quakers, who would remain away from the polls rather than vote for Harrison.[64] But in Centreville nearby, another observer noted that Quakers showed no pang of conscience in supporting a man who had nothing but his military record.[65] In Bellefonte, Centre County, Democrats drank their toasts on the Fourth of July with lemonade in order to register their disgust for the excesses of the Whigs, but they were compelled to admit that their attendance "Was not quite as large as the hard ciderites as they had all their force out to a man even all the old Quakers that never before witnessed such a scene."[66]

The October elections showed unmistakably the apathy of the Democrats. Their majorities in the legislature were erased, and the Coalition assumed control of both houses simultaneously for the first time. In the congressional elections Democrats fared better, electing fifteen of a total of twenty-eight members. In the Third District in Philadelphia County, where disputed returns in 1838 had produced the spark which touched off the Buckshot War, the radical Charles J. Ingersoll overwhelmed his Whig opponent, Morton McMichael, by

[60] Buchanan delivered this message on March 3, 1840. See Harrisburg *Telegraph*, March 10, May 1, 1840; New Berlin *Union Star*, September 18, 1840.
[61] Forney to Buchanan, April 16, 1840, Buchanan Papers.
[62] Henry Petriken to Buchanan, May 7, 1840, *ibid.*
[63] *Ibid.*
[64] James Boon to Buchanan, June 4, 1840, *ibid.*
[65] James M. Watson to Buchanan, June 5, 1840, *ibid.*
[66] J. S. Proudfoot to Buchanan, July 9, 1840, *ibid.*

1,200 votes.[67] But this was an exception. The closeness of the results kept the presidential issue in doubt to the end of the campaign. The election returns revealed a victory for Harrison and Tyler by the narrow margin of 343 votes. The Democrats, the Philadelphia *Pennsylvanian* observed, were defeated not by arguments or policies of the Coalition, but by an appeal to the emotions and "by the creation of an impression that new men and measures might in some unknown way be beneficial."[68] In fairness, it might have added that the Democrats lost by default; like the hare in the fable, they failed to run the race.

[67] Philadelphia *Pennsylvanian,* October 15, 1840.

[68] *Ibid.,* November 11, 1840. Harrison electors polled 144,018 votes to 143,675 for Van Buren electors. *Niles' Register,* LIX (November 14, 1840), 165. See Appendix, page 223.

GEORGE WOLF
Governor, 1829-1835

Copy by James R. Lambdin from the original by Joseph Kyle. Courtesy of the Historical Society of Pennsylvania and the Pennsylvania Department of Commerce.

JOSEPH RITNER
Governor, 1835-1839

Copy by James R. Lambdin from the original by Jacob Eichholtz. Courtesy of the Historical Society of Pennsylvania and the Pennsylvania Department of Commerce.

DAVID RITTENHOUSE PORTER
Governor, 1839-1845

Portrait by Edward D. Marchant. Courtesy of the Historical Society of Pennsylvania and the Pennsylvania Department of Commerce.

FRANCIS RAWN SHUNK
Governor, 1845-1848

Portrait by James R. Lambdin. Courtesy of the Historical Society of Pennsylvania and the Pennsylvania Department of Commerce.

WILLIAM FREAME JOHNSTON
Governor, 1848-1852

Portrait by J. Augustus Beck. Courtesy of the Historical Society of Pennsylvania and the Pennsylvania Department of Commerce.

GEORGE MIFFLIN DALLAS
Vice President of the
United States, 1845-1849

Engraved by W. T. Bather. Courtesy of the Historical Society of Pennsylvania.

JAMES BUCHANAN
Minister to Russia, 1830-1834
United States Senator, 1834-1845
Secretary of State, 1845-1849

Engraved by J. Sartain from painting by Jacob Eichholtz. Courtesy of the Historical Society of Pennsylvania.

NICHOLAS BIDDLE
President of the
Bank of the United States

Engraved by J. Sartain from painting by Jacob Eichholtz. Courtesy of the Historical Society of Pennsylvania.

THADDEUS STEVENS

After a portrait by J. L. Williams. Courtesy of the Historical Society of Pennsylvania

HENRY AUGUSTUS PHILIP
MUHLENBERG
U. S. Congressman, 1829-1838
Minister to Austria, 1838-1840

Drawn from life on stone by A. C. Smith. Courtesy of the Historical Society of Pennsylvania.

SIMON CAMERON
United States Senator, 1845-1849

Detail from full-length painting by unidentified artist. Courtesy of the Historical Society of Dauphin County.

DAVID WILMOT
Congressman, 1845-1851

From [David Craft], History of Bradford County, Pennsylvania, page 407.

CHAPTER IX

The Redemption of Credit and the Repudiation of Porter, 1840-1843

AMIDST the rejoicing over Harrison's victory, the Whigs competed to capitalize on their long-awaited opportunity to garner the spoils. Cleavages along traditional lines were at once apparent, with former Antimasonic wheelhorses from the interior in opposition to Clay leaders of the Philadelphia area. The former gained an initial advantage when the delegation to the Electoral College recommended Stevens for Postmaster General and designated former Governor Ritner to carry the election returns to Washington.[1] Philadelphia Whigs, meanwhile, groomed John Sergeant for the same cabinet post; both groups buttonholed Whig legislators as they arrived in Harrisburg to enlist them for their respective candidates; and both Stevens and Sergeant hastened to Washington to press their claims.[2] Spokesmen for Stevens represented him as an "original" Harrison man, despite his obvious preference for Webster in 1836.[3] Sergeant's support of Clay was unquestioned, but his backers were hopeful that Harrison would reward Clay men for their aid in the election. The result was foreseen by Whigs and Democrats alike; Harrison found it more expedient to look elsewhere for his cabinet than to antagonize either faction.[4]

In the competition for lesser posts, the Philadelphia faction bested the up-State group and had the satisfaction of seeing their friends in the key posts in the customs and the Philadelphia post office. In the legislature, also, the Antimasonic faction found victory disappointing. They organized the Senate according to plan, but in the House, a combination of Democrats with Philadelphia Whigs defeated Ner Middleswarth, their caucus choice for Speaker, and elected

---

[1] George W. Barton to Buchanan, December 12, 1840, Buchanan Papers.
[2] Samuel Park to Joseph Wallace, December 25, 1840, William MacPherson Papers.
[3] Joseph Wallace to William Henry Harrison, January [n. d.], *ibid.*
[4] William Ayres to A. P. Reading, January 3, 1841, Biddle Papers; Charles F. Adams (ed.), *Memoirs of John Quincy Adams, Comprising Portions of His Diary from 1795 to 1848,* 12 vols. (Philadelphia, 1874-1877), X, 388, January 2, 1841.

William Crabb of Philadelphia. It advertised their weakness in the party.[5]

With the veto power hanging over them, the Whigs could expect to carry out no program beyond the adoption of resolutions and the passage of bills which Porter would find bothersome whether he signed or rejected them. Accordingly, they instructed Buchanan and Sturgeon in the United States Senate to vote for the repeal of the Independent Treasury with the remote possibility that they might resign rather than obey instructions.[6] They obeyed. They also passed a bill which provided for the election of Canal Commissioners. Porter vetoed it, as expected, but he thereby opened himself to the criticism that he opposed a democratic reform.[7]

Most damaging to Whig ambitions was the death of Harrison and the succession of Tyler to the Presidency. While the former had not rewarded Pennsylvania with a cabinet appointment, his popularity remained untarnished; in fact, Whigs frequently referred to themselves as the Harrison party. They never called themselves Tyler men! During the five months prior to his repudiation by the Whigs, Tyler was already using the patronage to strengthen his position among former Antimasons and Democrats. He appointed Ritner as Treasurer of the Mint at Philadelphia in the face of Whig opposition, and instructed Jonathan Roberts, Collector of the Port of Philadelphia, to distribute his patronage among "The different associations of men who supported us" and to consult among others, Joel Sutherland, former Democratic boss in Southwark.[8] How successful he would have been in molding a personal following is a matter of conjecture since his veto of the bill to create a third Bank of the United States brought his career as a Whig to a dramatic close and made him a President without a party. It was a damaging blow to Pennsylvania Whigs and presaged disaster in the gubernatorial election several months later.

Democrats had little time to lick their wounds following the defeat of Van Buren. The retention of the Governorship hinged upon a rapprochement between the Porter and Van Buren elements. Prospects of such a reunion were far from bright. The State's fiscal policy, the banks, and the improvements presented problems no nearer solution in 1841 than in 1840. One ray of light penetrated the gloom of

[5] William C. McPherson to John B. McPherson, January 7, 1841, Edward McPherson Papers.
[6] Philadelphia *Pennsylvanian*, February 1, April 19, 1841.
[7] Philadelphia *United States Gazette*, March 1, May 3, 1841.
[8] Thomas Ewing to Jonathan Roberts, April 21, 1841, Gratz Correspondence.

defeat; with the Jackson dynasty removed from the scene, Pennsylvania Democrats were freed from the necessity of conforming to causes emanating from Washington. Banks might be sustained and even the privilege of issuing small notes granted without the risk of executive displeasure.

Porter made a bid for the support of the radicals in his annual message to the legislature in January, 1841. Anticipating the resumption of specie payments on schedule on January 15 as provided by the legislature in 1840, he called for a thorough reform of the banking system, urged that legislation be enacted to make any future suspensions of specie payments by a bank *ipso facto* a forfeiture of its charter, and recommended that for the present no additional banking capital be created.[9]

He soon had cause to regret his seemingly harmless concession to hard-moneyism. Twenty days after resumption had been effected, a run upon the United States Bank forced it to close its doors; within seventy-two hours the banks of the State had suspended. The crisis spread to Maryland and Virginia, but the New York banks weathered the storm. The third bank crash in less than four years, coming almost without warning, again threw the State into turmoil. There was this significant difference in the reaction of the public mind. Whereas, heretofore, banks and banking generally had been condemned, now criticism was centered upon the United States Bank. At a rally in Philadelphia the Bank was declared to be lost "past redemption."[10] In Philadelphia also, Philip Hone observed on February 15,

> The Bank of the United States seems to be in worse "smell" . . . here than in New York. Dreadful stories are told of peculation and robbery. This unhappy concern would appear to have been an immense sock, into which everyone put his hand and took as much as he wanted, from Mr. Biddle to the lowest employee. . . . Is it to be wondered at that the people of this country should rail against banks?[11]

From Washington, Buchanan hastened to impress Porter with the justification of the Bank's liquidation and to steel him for the final contest. "As long as it shall continue to exist, it will continue to

[9] Philadelphia *American Sentinel*, January 8, 1841; *Pennsylvania Archives*, 4th Series, VI, 704-726.
[10] Philadelphia *Pennsylvanian*, February 12, 1841.
[11] Allan Nevins (ed.), *The Diary of Philip Hone, 1828-1851*, 2 vols. (New York, 1927), II, 521.

derange the business of the country and produce again and again those revulsions to which we have been subjected."[12] He added

> If I were capable of envying any man I should envy the position in which you are now placed. The eyes of the Democracy of the whole Union are now directed towards you with intense anxiety. . . . To put down the Bank of the United States will be a measure of the greatest relief to the State.[13]

The Bank had apologists who maintained that the legislature erred in requiring resumption too quickly and who insisted that its immense resources guaranteed the ultimate redemption of its notes.[14] But the prestige of the Bank was unquestionably damaged, and a critical report of its management by a committee of the stockholders depressed it to a new low.[15]

On the other hand, a spirit of forbearance for other banks was evidenced from the start. The Philadelphia *American Sentinel,* for example, placed the blame for hard times upon the people of the State, not the banks. The distress of the latter, it maintained, resulted from public and private extravagance. "We have goaded them into their present crippled and unfortunate condition." Because they yielded in part and have become embarrassed, "we raise a wonderful hue and cry against them."[16] Hard-Money Men who saw in the suspension an opportunity to eliminate banks and paper currency by merely applying the Banking Act of 1840 found little support in the press.

The implications for Porter were similar to those faced by Governor Wolf in 1833. The payment of interest on the State debt and the continuation of the improvements depended upon the negotiation of a loan; and the banks, despite their inability to pay specie, appeared to be the only possible source of credit. Under the circumstances he could not afford to invoke the penalties for suspension or support even more exacting regulations which he had proposed in his message. And temporarily, at least, he found the control of the legislature by the Whigs a blessing in disguise. He remained noncommittal and forced the Whigs to take the initiative. The latter prepared a bank bill and guided it through the legislature. It removed the penalties placed upon suspension by the Act of 1840,

---

[12] Buchanan to Porter, February 17, 1841, W. W. Porter Papers.
[13] *Ibid.*
[14] Philadelphia *United States Gazette,* February 5, 1841.
[15] Hugh R. Fraser, *Democracy in the Making: The Jackson-Tyler Era* (Indianapolis and New York, 1938), 98-99.
[16] March 2, 1841.

permitted the United States Bank to reduce its capital and relieved it of its obligations for further loans under its charter, and allowed the banks to issue small notes and to pay dividends up to 5 per cent for the duration of the suspension. Democrats in both houses voted against it, and it reached Porter as a Whig measure. He vetoed it on April 8, 1841, and the Whigs failed to pass it over his head. Democrats thus met their first test without division.[17] Their unanimity was quickly shattered, however, by the Whig maneuver which followed.

In a revenue bill drawn up by William F. Johnston, who was back in the legislature as a Whig, aid for the banks was ingeniously linked to the procurement of funds for the empty treasury. It included a tax upon real estate, luxuries, and licenses, suspended indefinitely the penalties upon defaulting banks, and invited the latter to participate in a loan of $3,000,000 in return for which they might issue notes in denominations of one, two, and five dollars equal to the sum of their subscriptions. Holders of these notes in the amount of one hundred dollars or more could demand their redemption in State stock. The "Relief Bill," as it was called, thus safeguarded the banks, including the United States Bank, and provided the State with funds to pay the interest on the debt and continue the improvements by the issuance of "bills of credit." It had three serious flaws: first, the notes, redeemable only in State bonds, would certainly depreciate in value; second, the constitutionality of the procedure was doubtful; and third, the tax was inadequate to the needs of the State.[18]

These objections, however, were overlooked by the Whigs, who pushed the bill through both houses on April 30, 1841, less than four weeks after the loss of the previous bank bill.[19] Porter vetoed this bill, also; but with very different results. Improvement Democrats, including ardent Porter men who saw in the bill the continuation of their Public Works, could no longer be held in line. In the Senate, five Democrats absented themselves from the vote to override the veto, and it thereby passed by the necessary two-thirds vote.[20] Two days

[17] Philadelphia *Pennsylvanian*, March 29, April 5, 9, 1841; Philadelphia *United States Gazette*, March 29, April 1, 1841.

[18] McGrane, *Foreign Bondholders and American State Debts*, 68-69; Philadelphia *United States Gazette*, April 19, 28, May 3, 1841.

[19] *Ibid.*, May 3, 1841.

[20] The vote on the bill was 17-14; the vote to override the veto, 17-8. Democrats not voting were John Gibbons, Northampton-Lehigh; Samuel Headley, Columbia-Schuylkill; Ebenezer Kingsbury, Luzerne-Monroe-Pike-Wayne; Robert Fleming, Lycoming-Northumberland-Clearfield-Clinton; and Thomas C. Miller, Franklin-Cumberland-Adams. *Ibid.*

later on May 3 the Democrats in the House, after first meeting in caucus to keep wavering members from joining the Whigs, voted against the bill and sustained the veto.

The Whigs immediately countered by rushing through both houses a similar bill, which differed from the original only in that it excluded the United States Bank from its benefits. It had barely left the legislative halls, however, when the Improvement Democrats in the House bolted. In a tense atmosphere, the vote to override the veto of the original bill was reconsidered. Four Democrats severally announced their intentions to forego party principle for necessity, while Edward Penniman of Philadelphia County attempted to crack the party whip to hold others in line.[21] Their defection, however, was decisive. The veto was overridden by a vote of 62 to 28, twelve Democrats voting with the majority.[22] Thus the controversial Relief Bill was adopted over Porter's veto; and the Democrats again broke ranks on the currency and banking issue. Their division gave the United States Bank a new lease on life and enabled the banks to issue small notes after repeated earlier failures to obtain this privilege.

On the surface, it was a stinging rebuff to Porter and a blow to Democratic harmony. But observed in the light of the gubernatorial election of 1841 which followed, it is apparent that it strengthened the party. The Porter administration was hard pressed for money and credit. To have defaulted upon the interest on the bonds or to have abandoned work upon the improvements would have been disastrous to its prestige. Yet no other means of meeting these obligations was offered. The passage of the Relief Bill over Porter's veto permitted him to have his cake and eat it too; he could officially oppose concessions to the banks, yet use the revenue to sustain his administration.

Alexander K. McClure declared in his reminiscences that Porter vetoed the bill "with full knowledge that it would be passed over his veto in both branches and was quite willing that it should be done, as there was no other possible way of providing means for the

[21] The four Democrats were Joseph Douglas, Crawford County; Alexander Holeman, Venango-Clarion; Hendrick B. Wright, Luzerne; and John A. Gamble, Lycoming. Philadelphia *Inquirer,* May 3, 1841.

[22] The twelve Improvement Democrats were: George Boale, Centre County; Gaylord Church and Joseph Douglas, Crawford; James L. Gillis, Warren-Jefferson-McKean; Alexander Holeman, Venango-Clarion; Jesse C. Horton, Northumberland; Franklin Lusk, Susquehanna; John May, York; John Weaver, Schuylkill; Andrew Cortwright and Hendrick B. Wright, Luzerne; and John A. Gamble, Lycoming. Philadelphia *United States Gazette,* May 6, 1841.

payment of state interest and the indebtedness for public improvements."[23] He thus implied that Porter had reached an understanding with the Improvement Men or at least that he was aware of their intention to bolt before he imposed his veto. Pennsylvania historians have accepted this interpretation.[24] There appears to be no evidence of collusion, however. At the same time, there is reason to believe that he was gratified at the turn of events. Identified as an Improvement Man, he could not afford, on the one hand, to risk the wrath of the Hard-Money Men by signing the bill. "No man of sense in this commonwealth no matter to what party he belongs," Buchanan had advised, "can expect you to approve a bill indefinitely suspending all existing penalties against the banks."[25] On the other hand, he had no intention of seeing his friends martyred because of their last-minute change of front. He and his advisers, including Ovid F. Johnson, the central committee of the party at Harrisburg, and the editors of the Harrisburg *Keystone,* labored to restrain the press from assailing the "twelve" and to justify the course of the latter on the ground that they were expressing the wishes of the electorate in the improvement districts.[26]

They were not entirely successful. The radical Philadelphia *Spirit of the Times* fulminated,

> These are the traitors! These are the men who could forget everything in their thirst for gold! . . . People of Pennsylvania, look to them! Put on them the seal of reprobation! Let them be scouted from decent society. Brand them with the mark of blackest infamy, and teach your children to mention them as you would mention with execration the traitor Arnold, the traitor Burr, or the traitor Hull.[27]

After registering hasty and intemperate denunciations, most Democratic papers, however, showed a willingness to take a conciliatory course and the controversy faded rapidly from the press.

[23] Alexander K. McClure, *Old Time Notes of Pennsylvania,* 2 vols. (Philadelphia, 1905), I, 62-63.

[24] Wayland F. Dunaway in *A History of Pennsylvania* (New York, 1935), 467, for example, declares "he vetoed it with the full knowledge that it would be passed over his veto and was doubtless glad that this would be done since there seemed to be no other way of coping with the situation."

[25] Buchanan to Porter, April 19, 1841, W. W. Porter Papers.

[26] Ovid F. Johnson to Hendrick B. Wright, May 15, 1841, Hendrick B. Wright Papers, Wyoming Historical and Geological Society, Wilkes-Barre; Edwin W. Hutter to Wright, May 14, 1841, *ibid.;* Anson V. Parsons to Wright, May 26, 1841, *ibid.;* James Peacock to Wright, May 28, 1841, *ibid.*

[27] Reprinted in Philadelphia *Inquirer,* May 7, 1841.

The rank and file were not so easily mollified. Hendrick B. Wright, one of the "twelve" found a hostile demonstration awaiting him in Wilkes-Barre.[28] Only three of the group were returned the following year to the legislature.[29] And at least two of them were defeated by Democratic opponents who made the Relief Bill their campaign issue.[30] It was not made a test of party regularity, however, and they were not driven from the party. This permitted hard-money advocates and Improvement Men to act in concert in the gubernatorial campaign and to postpone their intestine strife until the next session of the legislature.

The campaign of 1841 in contrast to those of 1835 and 1838 was spiritless and devoid of emotionalism. Possibly the fervor of 1840 had exhausted the Whigs; obviously the advent of Tyler added nothing to their enthusiasm. Another contributing factor was the money panic. With the attention of the public occupied with problems arising from the bank suspension and the dislocation of business, there was an apathy toward politics. Finally, the renomination of Porter, conceded by all factions, was unpopular among the radicals. Their support was perfunctory.

Three men had preconvention backing for the Whig nomination for Governor: General Joseph Markle of Venango County, an Indian fighter under Harrison, who was heralded as a second "Tippecanoe" and favored by the western element; Ner Middleswarth of Union County, perennial candidate of the Antimasonic faction; and John Banks, a Berks County judge, the choice of the eastern Whigs. When it was found that the latter was in the lead among the delegates in the convention at Harrisburg on March 10, 1841, Markle and Middleswarth withdrew, and Banks was nominated without opposition.[31]

Porter's renomination was not seriously contested. A few papers identified as Van Buren sheets advocated the nomination of a new man upon whom all Democrats could agree.[32] But they did not take their opposition to the convention, meeting in Harrisburg on March 4, 1841, and Porter was named by acclamation.

[28] George B. Espy to Hendrick B. Wright, May 24, 1841, Wright Papers.
[29] Andrew Cortwright and Hendrick B. Wright of Luzerne and John A. Gamble of Lycoming.
[30] Jesse C. Horton of Northumberland and Franklin Lusk of Susquehanna. See Stephen Wilson to Hendrick B. Wright, November 6, 1841, Wright Papers; Lusk to Wright, February 15, 1843, *ibid.*
[31] Philadelphia *Inquirer*, March 10, 11, 12, 1841.
[32] Reading *Democratic Press*, reprinted in the Philadelphia *Inquirer*, February 4, 1841.

The Whigs recognized that victory hinged upon the factional strife among the Democrats and directed their activities so as to cultivate it. They interpreted Porter's veto of the Relief Bill as a surrender to the radicals. This was questionable strategy since Porter was assured of the votes of the Improvement Men and weakest among the hard-money group. They also enlarged upon reports of feuds and intrigues over the Presidency, Vice Presidency, and gubernatorial succession in 1844 among the partisans of Buchanan, Richard M. Johnson, Commodore Stewart, and Porter. They made little headway.[33] Having survived the strife attending the Relief Bill, the Democrats refused to be diverted from their adherence to Porter, and they returned him to office on October 12, 1841, with a margin of 23,000 votes. Democrats regained control of both houses of the legislature, the Senate by a single vote, the House by forty-four votes.[34]

With their numbers augmented, Democratic factions prepared to test their strength in the new legislature. The Improvement Men seized the offensive to support Hendrick B. Wright, who had voted for the Relief Bill, for Speaker of the House. Success would demonstrate their power and be a personal vindication for Wright. The correspondence of the latter provides an excellent insight into the operations of the Improvement Men. The center of their power lay in Harrisburg in the *Keystone* clique and among the advisers of Porter.[35] They could count upon support from Central and Northern Pennsylvania and from one faction in the Pittsburgh area.[36] They were able to bargain for votes for Wright in Bedford by agreeing to back Jacob Mann of that county for State Treasurer.[37] Porter, Simon Cameron, and Henry A. Muhlenberg gave Wright their support in confidence, as did John W. Forney, recognized as the unofficial spokesman for Buchanan in Harrisburg.[38] The Improvement Men were weakest in the Philadelphia area and in counties along the southern and western tiers.

[33] *Ibid.*, June 1, 1841.
[34] Mueller, *Whig Party,* 74. The official returns showed 136,504 votes for Porter and 113,473 for Banks. A discrepancy of twenty votes exists between the sum of Bank's vote by counties and the published total. Pennsylvania, *Senate Journal, 1842,* I, 113-114. See Appendix, page 224.
[35] William F. Packer to Hendrick B. Wright, October 24, 1841, Wright Papers; Anson V. Parsons to Wright, October 30, 1841, *ibid.;* Isaac G. McKinley to Wright, December 4, 1841, *ibid.*
[36] James K. Moorhead to Wright, November 3, 1841, *ibid.*
[37] George W. Bowman to Wright, November 8, 1841, *ibid.*
[38] David R. Porter to Wright, December 1, 1841, *ibid.;* Cameron to Wright, November 1, 1841, *ibid.;* Muhlenberg to Wright, November 22, 1841, *ibid.;* Forney to Wright, November 7, 1841, *ibid.*

The Van Buren group supported J. Ross Snowden for Speaker. He had been a consistent advocate of banking reform in the House and had led the Democratic minority against the Relief Bill. The latter was a vital factor in the outcome, since it emphasized Wright's irregularity. The rival factions agreed upon a caucus where Snowden emerged the victor. He was thereupon elected as Speaker by a party vote. He rewarded the Improvement Men for their support of the caucus by making Wright the chairman of the Internal Improvements Committee and Gamble of Lycoming County, another of the "twelve," the chairman of the Ways and Means Committee.[39]

The Improvement Men again found themselves in the minority a few days later in a caucus for Treasurer. This time they ignored the decision of the majority to support William B. Anderson, a former member of the House with a radical record, and threw their votes to Mann. The Whigs, hopelessly outnumbered, switched to Mann on the second ballot and secured his election. They explained that his election was the lesser of two evils.[40]

Having aired their factionalism, the Democrats were hardly prepared to face the acid test of their unity, their old nemesis, the currency, banking, and the deficit. The financial crisis appeared to be more serious in January, 1842, than at any time since the beginning of the panic five years before. The suspension continued, and bankers predicted that disastrous results would accompany any attempts at coercion. Resumption, they argued, would have to wait until the currency appreciated to the value of gold and silver, and until a prompt and efficient means had been found to pay the interest on the State debt. The Bank of North America demonstrated its pessimism by offering to sell its State bonds at a discount of 50 per cent.[41] The Relief Bill had not provided the revenue anticipated, and the notes which were issued had depreciated rapidly. There were no funds in sight for interest payments or for improvements. Public morale was low; there was growing conviction that the improvements had been a bad investment and that further expenditures upon them should be suspended.

On December 30, 1841, a Democratic rally in Philadelphia, called to discuss the State debt, brought home the gravity of the crisis. The meeting was organized by party leaders: George M. Dallas delivered

---

[39] Philadelphia *United States Gazette,* January 10, 1842.
[40] *Ibid.,* January 19, 1842; Philadelphia *Spirit of the Times,* January 19, 21, 1842.
[41] Bank of North America to J. H. Deford, January 20, 1842, cited in "Descriptive Catalogue of the Records of the Bank of North America Deposited with the Historical Society of Pennsylvania," 69.

the address and Henry D. Gilpin presented the resolutions. The latter included a statement in praise of Porter's pre-election pledge to pay the State debt and a recommendation that the legislature require resumption at an early date. After the adjournment, a body of dissidents who had been unable to obtain a hearing held a rump session. Led by Andrew Miller, an outspoken radical, they adopted a resolution which declared that the debt was unconstitutional, that the faith of the State was illegally pledged, and that the people were under "no moral, legal or political obligation to bear any burden of taxation or make any sacrifice of personal comfort to keep it unbroken." It urged the sale of the improvements and the payment of the creditors in proportion to their claims. The unpaid balance, which would have run into millions, would be defaulted.[42]

It is impossible to ascertain how many people approved this resolution. Pennsylvania historians have sometimes assumed that the State was on the verge of bankruptcy and repudiation. McClure wrote of the "general popular clamor for open repudiation,"[43] and Dunaway declared that a "widespread demand arose for the repudiation of the debt."[44] They appear to have unduly emphasized the danger of repudiation. The press, almost without exception, hastened to denounce the sentiments of the resolution. Even the Philadelphia *Spirit of the Times,* frequently cited as evidence of the pressure for repudiation, insisted that the State would meet its obligations. It confined its defense of the rump to a criticism of the leaders of the original meeting for refusing to hear the minority opinion.[45]

A few days later Porter in his annual message reaffirmed his determination to pay the debt and declared his opposition to the sale or rental of the State Works.[46] Both houses by unanimous votes promptly adopted resolutions against repudiation, and committees of both bodies issued reports which denounced the doctrine. The press, the executive, and the legislature thus yielded no quarter to repudiation.[47]

[42] McGrane, *Foreign Bondholders and American State Debts,* 69; Philadelphia *Pennsylvanian,* January 1, 1842.
[43] McClure, *Old Time Notes,* I, 58.
[44] Dunaway, *History of Pennsylvania,* 466.
[45] Philadelphia *Spirit of the Times,* January 1, 1842.
[46] Philadelphia *Pennsylvanian,* January 7, 1842.
[47] Philadelphia *United States Gazette,* January 12, 1842; Pennsylvania, *House Journal, 1842,* II, 44-48; McGrane, *Foreign Bondholders and American State Debts,* 70.

The fact that repudiation had been voiced, however, was sufficient to stir the legislature into action. Democratic factions temporarily acted as a unit, and Whigs frequently disregarded party lines. There was a general agreement that an adequate tax program would have to be formulated and that the suspension must cease even though it might result in the failure of some institutions.

While committees of the legislature wrestled with the problem, public confidence took a turn for the worse. During the last week of January, 1842, there were numerous runs upon the banks. On the twenty-eighth the Girard Bank in Philadelphia failed to open.[48] Two days later the Bank of Pennsylvania was beset by withdrawals, and on the day following Porter closed it with a court injunction to protect State funds deposited there.[49] Runs occurred almost simultaneously upon all the banks in the Philadelphia area; and the directors in emergency session agreed to resume specie payments on August 1, 1842, and to receive each other's notes during the interim.[50]

The proposal did not go far enough to divert legislative action. In the House, a bill requiring immediate resumption was speedily adopted by a party vote.[51] The Senate bill, however, provided for a system of gradual resumption spread over a period of five years. The latter was at once denounced on the platform and in the Democratic press, and petitions of protest poured into Harrisburg. One was said to have contained a "countless" number of signatures and to have stretched fifteen feet in length.[52] The bill was discarded, and another similar to the House bill was passed in its place, with a minority of Whigs joining the Democrats.[53] It was accepted by the House and signed by the Governor.

There was little agreement upon its potentialities. The *United States Gazette* declared it to be "utterly impossible for the banks," while the *Pennsylvanian* argued that the community had nothing to lose and everything to hope for thereby. The public, it insisted, would tolerate no further delay. It was prepared to see the banks which could not resume pass into liquidation.[54] The *Spirit of the*

---

[48] Philadelphia *Pennsylvanian*, January 28, 1842.
[49] *Ibid.*, January 31, 1842; Philadelphia *United States Gazette*, February 1, 1842.
[50] Philadelphia *Spirit of the Times*, January 31, 1842.
[51] Philadelphia *Pennsylvanian*, February 8, 1842.
[52] Philadelphia *Spirit of the Times*, February 18, 1842.
[53] Philadelphia *Pennsylvanian*, March 9, 1842.
[54] Philadelphia *United States Gazette*, March 14, 1842; Philadelphia *Pennsylvanian*, March 4, 1842.

CREDIT REDEMPTION, REPUDIATION OF PORTER

Times exulted, "Let them break! And we shall so much the sooner be put in possession of a sound currency."[55]

The banks appeared to be stunned by the law for immediate resumption. For several days they ignored it, while heavy withdrawals forced the weakest institutions to close their doors. The stronger banks after a few days of uncertainty, however, proceeded to resume specie payments. Confidence was quickly restored. The cautious Philadelphia *United States Gazette* was willing to admit that the panic had quieted and that conditions looked brighter.[56] Hidden from both the friends and foes of resumption was the fact that the economic cycle was turning; prosperity was just around the corner.

The banking act, followed almost immediately by the resumption of specie payments, was a turning point in the history of the Democratic party. The controversy attending the chartering of the Bank of the United States by the federal then the State government, the problem of harmonizing the position of the party in relation to banking and currency with that of the administration in Washington, and the regulation of banking through the prolonged economic depression had combined for a decade to split the party into warring factions. But it had at length resisted the temptation to divide. A year later economic recovery and the adoption of a realistic tax program relieved Democrats from the ordeal of further tests upon these issues.

A by-product of the controversy over banking and currency was the decline of Porter's political fortunes. Re-elected in 1841 by the largest plurality in a gubernatorial contest between 1826 and 1854, his future appeared bright. With a wide-open contest taking shape for the Presidency, he seemed to be in a splendid position to bargain for the Vice Presidency or a cabinet post. These possibilities were never realized; long before 1844 Porter had been relegated to political oblivion.

His descent of the political ladder began almost immediately after the advent of his second term. It took the form of a misunderstanding among his official family which resulted in the resignations of Secretary of the Commonwealth Francis R. Shunk, of Henry Petriken, the Deputy Secretary, and of the members of the Canal Commission. Shunk's loss was especially serious since he was one of the most

[55] Philadelphia *Spirit of the Times,* March 18, 1842.
[56] March 21, 1842. The United States Bank did not survive to enjoy the return of prosperity. It had closed its doors finally on **February 4, 1841.**

popular politicians in Harrisburg and a likely nominee for Governor in 1844. It identified Porter more than ever with the Improvement Men, an impression which he strengthened further by naming Anson V. Parsons of Lycoming County as Shunk's successor.

While the rival ambitions of Porter and Shunk made a break inevitable, the immediate issue was the disposition of the printing. The party was plagued by a multiplicity of papers in the capital, each depending upon a share of the patronage for survival. Porter insisted upon rewarding the *Keystone,* mouthpiece of the Improvement Men and advocate at that time of the candidacy of Richard M. Johnson for President, and upon withholding financial aid from the *Reporter.* The publisher of the latter, Samuel D. Patterson, had long been a thorn in Porter's flesh. He was now promoting Buchanan for the Presidency. Failing to strike a compromise and refusing to tie his future to Johnson and Porter, Shunk dissociated himself from the administration and moved to Pittsburgh. It undoubtedly enhanced his prospects for 1844, especially in the western counties.[57]

A month later Porter became involved in another issue which injured him politically. Flushed by the prospects of success in their drive for immediate resumption, Democrats in the legislature created a joint committee to investigate the activity of the banks in relation to the legislature since 1836.[58] The Committee summoned George Handy, a professional lobbyist in the employ of the United States Bank. He appeared, promised sensational revelations, but refused to testify unless protected from prosecution in the courts. In a matter of hours the legislature adopted a joint resolution directing the Attorney General to issue a *nolle prosequi* in the event that Handy should be subsequently indicted for his part in the matter. It was signed by the Governor.

Handy's extravagant promises riveted the attention of the State upon his testimony. He and his associates, he revealed, had spent more than $130,000 "boring" for the United States Bank in 1840 through an intermediary, Daniel M. Brodhead. He produced letters,

[57] John W. Forney to Buchanan, January 24, February 7, 1842, Buchanan Papers; Porter to Buchanan, February 20, 1842, *ibid.;* Harrisburg *Keystone,* January 22, 29, 1842.
[58] Philadelphia *Pennsylvanian,* February 11, 12, 1842. The committee consisted of two Whigs, George Sharswood of Philadelphia City and John Ewing of Washington County; two Improvement Democrats, Morrow B. Lowry of Crawford County and J. H. Deford of Fayette County; and one Van Buren Democrat, Edward Penniman of Philadelphia County.

CREDIT REDEMPTION, REPUDIATION OF PORTER 165

alleged to be Brodhead's which described the expenditure of funds for the purchase of "lumber" from members of the legislature, J. M. Porter, and even the Governor.[59]

At this point Porter produced a sensation of his own. In a special message to the legislature he charged that the letters presented by Handy contained

> unjust, unwarrantable, and false references to the Executive, of a nature so gross and wicked, as to call for an immediate and rigorous prosecution of all parties concerned, so that if the charges or insinuations be true, the Executive may be duly punished, or if false, that those who have made, or insinuated them, may be exposed to the judgment of the law and to public condemnation.[60]

The message lent itself to two interpretations. Was it the act of a courageous Governor who would shield no one from the consequences of his acts, or was it a means of silencing the witness? The issue took the form of a duel between Porter and the committee. The former, through Attorney General Ovid F. Johnson, brought Handy to trial in the Court of General Sessions of Philadelphia, but George Sharswood, chairman of the committee, refused to yield the materials in his hands, arguing that they had not completed their work and that the trial would interfere with it.[61] The deadlock was broken when Judge George W. Barton ruled that the court could not compel the committee to give up the letters and released Handy for lack of evidence.[62]

The committee thereupon renewed its investigation, but subsequent testimony was unproductive. Brodhead found the occasion propitious for an extended visit to New York State, where he was beyond the jurisdiction of the committee. Deprived of this key witness, the investigation languished, while rival factions attempted to make capital of it. The Harrisburg *Keystone* charged Speaker Snowden with conspiring to connect the Governor with the transactions of the United States Bank in 1840. He appointed the committee, it alleged, after consulting Porter's enemies in the legislature. Snowden replied with such "insulting and ungentlemanly epithets" that the *Keystone* refused to print it. The Harrisburg *Reporter* and

[59] Philadelphia *Spirit of the Times*, April 9, 1842; William Ayres to Biddle, April 2, 1842, Biddle Papers.
[60] *Pennsylvania Archives*, 4th Series, VI, 900; Philadelphia *Pennsylvanian*, April 6, 1842.
[61] *Ibid.*, April 29, 1842.
[62] *Ibid.*, May 4, 1842; Philadelphia *Inquirer*, May 10, 1842.

the Harrisburg *State Capital Gazette* showed no such delicacy.[63] When Handy declared subsequently that he and the other "borers" had kept the money and duped the Bank, the *Keystone* seized his statement as a vindication of the Governor and the Improvement Democrats.[64]

The committee revealed its political complexion when it rejected the motion of a Porter man to call upon the executive to give testimony before it. The vote was three to two with the two Whig members and Edward Penniman, a Van Buren Democrat, making up the majority, and the two Improvement Men, the minority.[65] The committee then concluded its hearings and proceeded to disagree upon a report. The majority, consisting as before of the two Whigs and Penniman, reported that they had found no evidence of corruption on the part of the Governor or the members of the legislature. The minority report emphasized the total failure of the Whigs, Antimasons, and Bank men to pin anything upon the Governor or the legislature.[66] Porter and the Improvement Men were thus officially exonerated, but the investigation left many unconvinced and the administration under a cloud.

Most damaging to Porter were the inept attempts of the Improvement Men to control the party in the presidential campaign of 1844. They had nothing to gain from a renomination of Van Buren; the Buchanan bandwagon was already rolling, and the Porter men could expect to find no room on the driver's seat. Hence, they were prepared to attach themselves to any incipient boom which promised to give them the leadership.

Early in 1842 they made a bid to swing the party to the support of Richard M. Johnson, who had recently been endorsed by the Kentucky legislature. The Harrisburg *Keystone* began to give him favorable mention as a warrior and statesman; and Improvement Men promoted a rally in Harrisburg on February 12, 1842, ostensibly in the name of Irish independence, but actually to inaugurate a Johnson movement. A recent oration by Johnson in support of the Irish was read, and resolutions lauding his services were adopted.

[63] Harrisburg *Keystone,* June 8, 1842.
[64] Philadelphia *Pennsylvanian,* June 22, 25, 1842.
[65] Harrisburg *Keystone,* July 13, 1842.
[66] Philadelphia *Pennsylvanian,* July 14, 18, 1842; "Report of the Joint Committee of Investigation Appointed by the Legislature of Pennsylvania, to Investigate Whether Corrupt Means Had Been Used to Procure Legislation Favorable to the Banks from 1836-1841," Pennsylvania, *Senate Journal, 1842,* II.

A month later they officially launched the Johnson campaign at a mass meeting in Harrisburg. Prospects appeared to be bright. Johnson welcomed their support, and while he regretted that he could contribute no funds to the cause, he assured them that if success crowned their efforts he would remember them and serve them.[67] He also fell in with their proposal that he tour the State and participate in a celebration of the Battle of the Thames to be held at Danville upon its anniversary on October 5.[68]

Through the summer Johnson was extolled from the stump at dozens of local rallies in Central and Northern Pennsylvania. But the movement failed to penetrate the other sectors, and by autumn it was definitely on the wane. Nonetheless, his visitation was a continuous ovation from one border of the State to the other. No Democrat in the nation except Jackson elicited the popular response accorded the "Hero of the Thames," and the "Slayer of Tecumseh." A Buchanan man graphically described his progress eastward to Hollidaysburg as follows:

> Col. R. M. Johnson arrived here yesterday—his march has been one of subjugation and triumph ever since he entered Pennsylvania. Wreaths and chaplets, triumphal cars, the pomp and circumstances of glorious war, the paraphernalia of civic processions and military escort and raised arches and patriotic and heralding inscriptions have been presented at every place. He is gracious and the people are grateful. I am pleased that as a guest our state has thus honored him.[69]

Johnson proceeded eastward upon the canal to Harrisburg; thence northward along the Susquehanna River with Governor Porter as an escort to Danville.[70] After celebrating the Battle of the Thames he continued up the river to the Wyoming Valley, and from thence to Williamsport on the West Branch of the Susquehanna for another military parade. It is interesting to note that Buchanan refrained from joining the procession, preferring not to compete with the venerable hero for the plaudits of the crowd. When it was reported that he was considering an appearance at the Williamsport parade, one of his closest advisers hurriedly interposed his objections.

> Suffer the Hero of the Thames to play his part. Permit him who by his personal prowess slew Tecumseh to pass away before

[67] Johnson to Hendrick B. Wright, March 14, 1842, Wright Papers; Harrisburg *Keystone*, February 9, 16, March 9, 16, 1842.
[68] *Ibid.*, March 23, 1842.
[69] John B. Butler to Hendrick B. Wright, September 30, 1842, Wright Papers.
[70] Harrisburg *Keystone*, October 13, 1842.

you introduce one who by his intellectual strength has wrestled with giants and mastered them.

Might it not be as well to suffer old Tecumseh with his pet Indian and his Excellency David Rittenhouse Porter, Generalissimo of the Pennsylvania line and future Vice President of the United States . . . to share the glory of a parade in Williamsport undisturbed.[71]

Finding that the Johnson movement was bogging down elsewhere despite his unquestioned popularity in the State, Improvement Men decided to give Lewis Cass a trial. They launched the campaign at Harrisburg in November, 1842, following the issuance of a call for a Cass convention in Indiana and in anticipation of his arrival in Boston from France.[72] In January, 1843, they feted Cass in Harrisburg with apppropriate ceremonies including a reception given in his honor by the Governor. The citizenry turned out in force to pay tribute to this erstwhile warrior, statesman, and diplomat, but the "cheers all had the chills," and when Cass resumed his journey to Michigan he left little semblance of an organization.[73] Cass's failure was due in part to his weakness in other states and in part to the inability of the Improvement Men to reach an agreement upon the presidential succession; some continuing to adhere to Johnson and others, including Porter, gravitating toward Tyler.

Governor Porter seems to have taken no active part during 1841 and 1842 in the councils of the Improvement Men as they mapped their strategy on the Presidency.[74] His correspondence with Buchanan reveals a friendly interest in the latter's pretensions. When Buchanan emphasized the seriousness of Democratic dissensions, Porter belittled both the Johnson and Stewart factions and urged that they be treated kindly. "I would as soon attempt to control the winds as to manage some of those people," he declared. The real danger, he insisted, came from Buchanan's indiscreet friends who encouraged factionalism by their proscription of the Improvement Men.[75]

[71] James X. McLanahan to Buchanan, October 11, 1842, Buchanan Papers.
[72] John Davis to Van Buren, November 16, 1842, Van Buren Papers.
[73] John W. Forney to Buchanan, January 25, 1843, Buchanan Papers; Albert C. Ramsey to Buchanan, February 8, 1843, Buchanan-Johnston Papers; Andrew C. McLaughlin, *Lewis Cass* (Boston and New York, 1899), 196-199.
[74] Oscar D. Lambert indicates in his *Presidential Politics in the United States, 1841-1844* (Durham, 1936), 111-114, that Porter led the Cass movement in the State. He overemphasizes his role, though some of his advisers were among its leaders.
[75] Porter to Buchanan, February 20, 1842, Buchanan Papers. See also Buchanan to Porter, February 13, 22, April 7, 1842, W. W. Porter Papers.

By the beginning of 1843, however, Porter was prepared to pin his hopes for the Vice Presidency upon the candidacy of Tyler. It offered only a slender chance of success; but all other avenues of preferment were closed. The Democrats in Pennsylvania, whom Tyler attracted by the magnet of his patronage, had little standing in the party. Some, such as Joel B. Sutherland, his Naval Officer at Philadelphia, had been cast out of party councils for their irregularities; others, such as Calvin Blythe, his Collector of the Port in Philadelphia, were veteran officeholders who were anxious to hang on to the payroll even though it carried them to a political graveyard.

The manifestation of the Tyler-Porter alliance was the appointment of James M. Porter, brother of the Governor, as Secretary of War.[76] In Harrisburg, the *Signal,* hitherto a supporter of Johnson, shifted to Tyler, catching many Johnson men by surprise.[77] Simultaneously, the *Keystone,* for more than four years the unwavering spokesman for Porter men and measures, became Porter's bitter opponent. In explanation, the editors declared that he had presented communications to them designed to give the party to Tyler and that when they refused to print them, the Tyler-Porter men ceased supporting them for the printing and backed a printer whom they could control.[78] Several weeks later Porter dismissed Seth Salisbury, a founder and leading spirit of the Johnson movement, from his sinecure as State Librarian, presumably because he refused to abandon Johnson for Tyler.[79] Porter's shift was emphasized further by the resignation of Deputy Secretary of the Commonwealth Edwin W. Hutter, a Buchanan man whose presence in the Porter administration had become anachronistic.[80]

By allying himself with Tyler, Porter wrote the death sentence to his political career. Politicians deserted the sinking ship with alacrity. After a tour of the western counties, Buchanan declared that he had not heard a kindly word spoken of Porter. "His fall has been more sudden that that of any other public man I have ever known."[81] In Franklin County, James X. McLanahan insisted that he knew not

[76] Philadelphia *Pennsylvanian,* March 13, 1843.
[77] *Ibid.,* March 14, 1843.
[78] Harrisburg *Keystone,* April 1, 1843.
[79] *Ibid.,* April 26, 1843.
[80] Edwin W. Hutter to Hendrick B. Wright, May 30, 1843, Wright Papers; Philadelphia *Pennsylvanian,* May 11, 1843; Harrisburg *Keystone,* May 10, 1843.
[81] Buchanan to George Leiper, July 22, 1843, Buchanan Papers. See also Buchanan to J. Randolph Clay, July 21, 1843, Dreer Collection.

a single Porter man, "no not one."[82] In Bradford County, William B. Foster, Jr., Democratic nominee for Canal Commissioner, feared that his election was jeopardized because he was being confused with another William B. Foster in Western Pennsylvania who was known to be friendly toward Porter.[83] Only a handful of papers continued to support Porter, and a majority of these were owned or controlled by officeholders.[84] The press generally condemned Tyler's appointment of "Brother Jim" and urged his rejection by the United States Senate.

Porter was defeated in his efforts to control the organization of the legislature and the election of printers in 1843. He was overwhelmed when he attempted to block the popular election of Canal Commissioners, the bill finally passing the House by a vote of 85 to 1.[85] It was injurious to both his patronage and his prestige. He was denounced for the appointment of his son as "Juvenile" sheriff of Philadelphia. The office of Deputy Secretary of the Commonwealth went a'begging with no takers. In January, 1844, James M. Porter's appointment was rejected by the United States Senate by a one-sided vote, with both Buchanan and Sturgeon voting against his confirmation. Whigs were determined to thwart Tyler's bid to ally himself with Porter Democrats. Democrats were equally resolved to have no part in furthering Tyler's ambitions.[86] Thus the Tyler-Porter coalition came to nought. Porter had gambled and lost. Few mourned his downfall.

[82] McLanahan to Buchanan, July 21, 1843, Buchanan Papers.
[83] Foster to Buchanan, October 2, 1843, *ibid*.
[84] Harrisburg *Keystone,* April 5, 1843; Philadelphia *Pennsylvanian,* May 4, 12, 1843.
[85] *Ibid.*, April 6, 1843.
[86] Chitwood, *John Tyler,* 284; Philadelphia *Pennsylvanian,* February 1, 12, 1844.

CHAPTER X

The Campaign of 1844

THE PRESIDENTIAL campaign of 1844 began early in Pennsylvania. Van Buren's defeat freed the Democrats from dictation from Washington and turned them to their own devices. They wasted little time in getting into action. Less than two weeks after Harrison's inauguration supporters of Commodore Charles Stewart issued a lengthy address to the people of the State in the columns of the Philadelphia *Spirit of the Times* upon the propriety of his nomination.[1] The movement began and ended, however, "in the aspirations of a few young men to gain a little notoriety aided by one or two hangers on."[2] Among the former were the editors of the *Spirit of the Times* and Richard Vaux, son of Roberts Vaux. The latter included Richard Rush, who had turned his party coat with each change in the political breeze, and William English, a champion of constitutional reform in Philadelphia in the 1830's. They organized an "Old Ironsides Club," sponsored rallies, wrote articles for the press, and encouraged the movement in the interior. Numerous papers printed Stewart news, but few endorsed him for the Presidency.[3] In fact, the Stewart boom would have suffered an early demise had not Buchanan's alarm given it more consequence "by his sensitive opposition, than it would otherwise obtained."[4]

Buchanan entered the campaign confident that his chances for the nomination were bright provided that he had "the moral influence of Pennsylvania" in his favor throughout the nation. "If it were everywhere believed that at the proper time she would press me, this would be half the battle."[5] The Stewart movement, of course, dispelled this impression, and Buchanan decided to make a bid for the nomination at the risk of being premature.[6] His Lancaster ally,

[1] Reprinted in the Philadelphia *United States Gazette,* March 16, 1841.
[2] Henry D. Gilpin to Van Buren, June 18, 1841, Van Buren Papers.
[3] Richard Rush to Richard Vaux, May 19, 1841, Miscellaneous Collection, Library Company of Philadelphia; Philadelphia *Pennsylvanian,* May 11, 1841.
[4] Henry D. Gilpin to Van Buren, June 18, 1841, Van Buren Papers.
[5] Buchanan to David R. Porter, December 10, 1841, W. W. Porter Papers.
[6] Buchanan to George G. Leiper, May 22, 1842, Buchanan Papers.

John W. Forney, joined him in passing the word to politicians across the State. Both Buchanan and Forney, for example, dispatched letters to Hendrick B. Wright on the same day; Buchanan to justify his determination to begin at once, and Forney to obtain Wright's aid in bringing the Wilkes-Barre *Farmer* into line and in preparing a Buchanan rally in Harrisburg after the opening of the legislature.[7] Response from the press was generally favorable, and politicians responded to the call.[8] In the Philadelphia area, however, Van Buren leaders remained aloof; in Berks, Muhlenberg with his eye on the gubernatorial nomination in 1844 was unwilling to jeopardize the aid of the Van Buren men by an early advocacy of Buchanan; and in Harrisburg, Improvement Men were exploring Richard M. Johnson's potentialities for the Presidency.[9]

Forney went to Harrisburg to investigate the Johnson activity and came away with the impression that it was of little consequence.[10] Buchanan men, nonetheless, held a demonstration in Harrisburg on March 23, 1842, to offset a similar Johnson rally. Results were gratifying. Strong resolutions endorsing Buchanan were adopted, and a central committee was charged with the responsibility of doing the spadework upon a State convention to nominate the "Pennsylvania Candidate." The resolutions treated Porter kindly, an undisguised attempt to woo him from the Johnson men.[11] The central committee issued an address to the Democrats of the State in July, 1842, which set forth the arguments for Buchanan's nomination and announced that the convention would meet on January 8, 1843. The date was no accident. It would fill the capital with Buchanan men at the very moment that the newly convened legislature would be acting upon his re-election to the Senate. It was also Jackson Day.[12] The decision was not reached, however, without misgivings. There was apprehension lest zealots should attempt to go too far. To nominate delegates to the national convention, for example, would only

[7] Forney to Wright, December 15, 1841, Wright Papers; Buchanan to Wright, December 15, 1841, *ibid.*

[8] Henry Petriken to Buchanan, December 22, 1841, Buchanan Papers.

[9] Robert M. Barr to Buchanan, December 19, 1841, *ibid.*; George Plitt to Buchanan, December 14, 1841, *ibid.* For the Johnson movement see pages 166-168.

[10] Forney to Buchanan, March 4, 1842, Buchanan Papers.

[11] James X. McLanahan to Buchanan, March 23, 1842, *ibid.*; Philadelphia *United States Gazette*, April 18, 1842; Philadelphia *Pennsylvanian*, March 25, 1842. The central committee consisted of Samuel D. Patterson of the Harrisburg *Reporter*, Henry Buehler, Jacob Seiler, Edwin W. Hutter, and J. McAllister. Philadelphia *Pennsylvanian*, July 29, 1842.

[12] *Ibid.*

invite similar action by the Johnson, Cass, and Van Buren men. It was essential that they be conciliatory and harmonious and that they base their case upon the claims of the State for the nomination.[13] The committee wavered upon a postponement as late as November, 1842, but finally agreed to proceed as planned.[14]

Preparations for the convention served to strengthen Buchanan in districts where he had lacked support heretofore. His friends seized the initiative along the Northern Tier, in Pittsburgh, and in Philadelphia, old centers of Van Buren strength. John B. Butler in Pittsburgh and Forney and George Plitt in Philadelphia worked tirelessly to secure active Buchanan organizations.[15]

The convention was a triumph for Buchanan, made possible in a large measure by the skillful strategy of his leaders—Forney, Reah Frazer, Benjamin Champneys, James X. McLanahan, Butler, and Simon Cameron. It should not be inferred, however, that they worked as a team. Forney, Champneys, and Frazer were distrustful of Cameron and Butler because they attempted to serve Porter and Buchanan simultaneously, and Forney was critical of Frazer's opposition to Porter in the convention. But it did not prevent the achievement of their objective.[16] Their plan, in brief, was to be amenable in the organization of the two houses of the legislature in both of which the Democrats held substantial majorities, to caucus prior to the senatorial election in order to commit doubtful members, and to postpone the official business of the convention until the election had been consummated. In Cameron's words, they would be "as harmless as doves and as cunning as serpents."[17]

Accordingly, McLanahan and Champneys withdrew from the contest for Speaker of the Senate, and Buchanan men voted with Porter men in the House upon the printing.[18] Sixty-six Democrats supported Buchanan in caucus. Conspicuous among the absentees were Porter men, who were reluctant to enhance Buchanan's chances for the Presidency by re-electing him to the Senate.[19] Buchanan leaders retaliated by forcing a postponement of the confirmation of Judge

[13] John B. Butler to Buchanan, December 6, 1842, Buchanan Papers.
[14] Butler to Henry Buehler, November 14, 1842, Miscellaneous Papers, Division of Public Records, Pennsylvania Historical and Museum Commission.
[15] Plitt to Buchanan, November 23, December 8, 14, 1842; Forney to Buchanan, December 5, 1842, Buchanan Papers.
[16] Forney to Buchanan, January 1, 1843, *ibid.*
[17] Cameron to Buchanan, January 4, 1843, *ibid.*
[18] Champneys to Buchanan, January 11, 1843, *ibid.*
[19] J. Porter Brawley to Buchanan, January 9, 1843, *ibid.*

Ellis Lewis, a favorite among the Porter men, as judge of the Lancaster district, while they observed their action upon the senatorial contest. They adjourned the convention from day to day awaiting the outcome of the election. The vote on January 10, 1843, after narrowly avoiding a postponement engineered by a combination of Whigs and Porter men, resulted in Buchanan's election. He received seventy-four of the seventy-six Democratic votes thereby defeating his Whig opponent, John Banks, by a wide margin.[20]

Having overcome the crisis of the senatorial election, Buchanan men turned to the work of the convention and gave their enthusiastic endorsement to the "Pennsylvania Candidate." They issued an address to the nation setting forth Pennsylvania's claims, and adopted resolutions lauding Buchanan, her favorite son.[21] One incident marred the unanimity of the gathering. David Lynch, a Pittsburgh member, objected to a resolution which paid a slight compliment to Porter and moved that it be stricken out.[22] It touched off the explosion which Buchanan strategists had endeavored to avoid throughout the week, and before they could regain control, one delegate after another rose to heap abuse upon the Governor. Forney appealed for moderation and attempted to have the resolutions adopted collectively but to no effect. The Porter resolution was finally adopted with fifteen irreconcilables dissenting.[23] With the Porter issue behind it, the convention adjourned upon a note of optimism.

The convention pushed Buchanan into the lead in the State in the presidential contest. Dozens of Democratic papers placed his name at their mastheads, and even his opponents were compelled to acknowledge his strength.[24] One step remained, the election of delegates to the national convention instructed for Buchanan, but it was not taken. The endorsement of Buchanan by the Pennsylvania Democrats failed to evoke a favorable response elsewhere, and time worked to the advantage of Van Buren.

The Van Buren men made little headway in the face of the Buchanan movement until the summer of 1843, when Van Buren's candidacy in other states developed such proportions that his nomination appeared probable. Then, with his old officeholders as nuclei,

[20] Brawley to Buchanan, January 10, 1843, *ibid.*; Cameron to Buchanan, January 10, 1843, *ibid.*; Forney to Buchanan, January 10, 1843, *ibid.*
[21] Forney to Buchanan, January 10, 13, 1843, *ibid.*
[22] Lynch to Buchanan, January 13, 1843, *ibid.*
[23] John B. Butler to Buchanan, January 10, 1843, *ibid.*; Cameron to Buchanan, January 13, 1843, *ibid.*
[24] Henry D. Gilpin to Van Buren, February 14, May 5, 1843, Van Buren Papers.

they made rapid progress. The initiative was taken by the Van Buren element in Philadelphia, where his leadership had not been seriously challenged. Henry D. Gilpin, George M. Dallas, Henry Horn, John K. Kane, and others sponsored a Jefferson Day meeting in Van Buren's honor on April 13, 1843, and reactivated the Hickory Club.[25] While they were too weak in the interior to retrieve the State from Buchanan, they were nonetheless in a strong position. They could afford to await the movement of the waters.

Buchanan clung to the possibility that Van Buren and Calhoun might split the convention and open the door for a compromise candidate. When this hope vanished, he withdrew from the contest on December 14, 1843.[26] His decision had expediency to recommend it; by retiring five months prior to the convention he would place the ultimate winner under obligation to him. However, it was unpopular with many of his followers, since they had little opportunity to start again and could only stand by while Van Buren men assumed the leadership.[27]

Democrats in the interior refused to accept Van Buren, however, without a struggle. They gave a last-minute reprieve to the Johnson campaign by instructing their members to the State convention for him. Between January 10 and February 28, 1844, the *Democratic Union* of Harrisburg listed ten county and senatorial districts where such action was taken, and only the lack of time seems to have prevented Democrats in other districts from taking a similar course. In the convention on March 5, 1844, Johnson received 36 votes from delegates representing nineteen counties and ten senatorial districts to 97 votes given to Van Buren.[28] It was a commendable showing and attested unmistakably to an extensive opposition to Van Buren. Of the twenty-five delegates elected to the national convention at Baltimore, barely one-half were identified as Van Buren men, a weakness which quickly came to light in Baltimore, where twelve of the delegation did not hesitate to violate the spirit of their instructions.

[25] Henry Simpson to Van Buren, April 15, 1843, *ibid.*

[26] Buchanan released his statement in the Lancaster *Intelligencer*. It was reprinted in the Philadelphia *Pennsylvanian*, December 27, 1843. See also Buchanan to J. Randolph Clay, July 21, 1843, Dreer Collection; Buchanan to J. Glancy Jones, January 2, 1844, J. Glancy Jones Papers, Historical Society of Pennsylvania.

[27] Cameron to Buchanan, December 27, 1843, Buchanan-Johnston Papers; Henry A. Muhlenberg to Buchanan, December 24, 1843, Buchanan Papers; Jesse Miller to Buchanan, December 13, 1843, *ibid.*; John B. Butler to Buchanan, January 15, 1844, *ibid.*; O. H. Browne to Van Buren, January 1, 1844, Van Buren Papers.

[28] Harrisburg *Democratic Union*, March 7, 1844.

Van Buren's ill-timed letter urging the postponement of the annexation of Texas was a breath of life to his opponents. Annexation was popular among Pennsylvania Democrats and was supported by the members of Congress and by Sturgeon and Buchanan in the Senate. It was also approved by the Democratic press. One up-State paper issued a call for a county meeting to release the delegates to the convention from their instructions for Van Buren.[29] Several Buchanan leaders, including Cameron and John M. Read, went so far as to announce a last-minute meeting of the central committee for this purpose.[30] Van Buren men on the committee in Philadelphia learned of it less than forty-eight hours prior to the time of the meeting, and Henry D. Gilpin rushed to Harrisburg to head it off. Their fears were not realized; the lack of a quorum prevented official action.[31] Buchanan's friends, including two delegates to the national convention, called upon him seeking his permission to present his name, but he refused. He would accede to it, he advised, only after Van Buren had been given a fair trial and had been withdrawn.[32]

Leaders hostile to Van Buren flocked into Baltimore sensing an upset. Gilpin observed to Van Buren that

> All the Governor's, Buchanan's and Cass's forces are on the ground—the Governor is here in person—and they have persuaded some of our delegates—I hope not more than four or five that they do not violate their instructions by merely voting for this two thirds rule, if they afterwards vote in obedience to their instructions on the nomination.[33]

He proved to be unduly optimistic. By a vote of 13 to 10, the Pennsylvania delegation postponed a resolution which declared that support of the two-thirds rule violated their instructions. They reached no further agreement.[34] On the following day twelve of the twenty-five delegates, including Hendrick B. Wright, who had been chosen president of the convention, voted for the two-thirds rule. Their defection was a serious blow to Van Buren's prospects and virtually assured the adoption of the rule.[35] Having destroyed Van Buren, these delegates proceeded to vote for him. They shifted subsequently

---

[29] New Berlin *Union Times,* May 17, 1844.
[30] Henry D. Gilpin to Van Buren, May 23, 1844, Van Buren Papers.
[31] *Ibid.*
[32] Henry Welsh to Buchanan, May 20, 1844, Buchanan Papers; Buchanan to Henry D. Foster and Benjamin H. Brewster, May 25, 1844, *ibid.*
[33] Gilpin to Van Buren, May 26, 1844, Van Buren Papers.
[34] John L. O'Sullivan to Van Buren, May 27, 1844, *ibid.*
[35] Philadelphia *Pennsylvanian,* May 30, 1844.

to Buchanan, then joined the stampede to Polk.[36] In defeat, however, the Van Buren men in Pennsylvania received an unexpected boon in the form of the Vice Presidency. After it had been declined by Van Buren's ally in New York, Silas Wright, it was offered to George M. Dallas. He accepted, to the discomfiture of the Buchanan men.

For the Whigs, there were lean years following their repudiation of Tyler in the summer of 1841 and the loss of the gubernatorial election the same year. Without patronage from Washington or Harrisburg, there were few crumbs. Jonathan Roberts continued for a time as Collector of the Port of Philadelphia, but he disagreed repeatedly with Tyler and the Tyler men. In the spring of 1842 Tyler asked for his resignation, and when he refused, he dismissed him and appointed a successor whom the Whig-controlled Senate refused to confirm.[37] Tyler and Roberts carried their quarrel to the press, where it dragged along to the delight of the Democrats and to the credit of neither party.[38]

Lacking loaves and fishes and the fervor of 1840 to sustain them, the Whigs fared badly in the elections of 1842 and 1843.[39] The latter had a special significance in that Canal Commissioners were elected by the people for the first time. Whigs had advocated the removal of the Canal Commissioners from the Governor's patronage during the first four years of the Porter regime, but the Democrats abetted by Porter's vetoes had blocked it. However, by 1843 Democrats were no longer desirous of protecting Porter's patronage, and they joined with the Whigs to overwhelm the executive's opposition.[40] The law

[36] John L. O'Sullivan to Van Buren, May 28, 29, 1844, Van Buren Papers. See the Harrisburg *Democratic Union,* June 12, 13, 1844, for the defenses of Benjamin H. Brewster and Reah Frazer.

[37] Walter Forward to Jonathan Roberts, December 10, 1841, Gratz Correspondence; Roberts to Forward, April 30, 1842, *ibid.;* Chitwood, *John Tyler,* 371; Philadelphia *United States Gazette,* May 11, 1842; Philadelphia *Spirit of the Times,* May 7, 1842.

[38] Henry D. Gilpin to Van Buren, September 15, 1842, Van Buren Papers; Roberts to the Public, May 3, 1842, Gratz Correspondence; Forward to Roberts, September 10, 1842, *ibid.;* Philadelphia *United States Gazette,* September 22, 1842. See also Philip S. Klein (ed.), "Memoirs of a Senator from Pennsylvania: Jonathan Roberts, 1771-1854," *Pennsylvania Magazine of History and Biography,* LXII (October, 1938), 513-527.

[39] In 1842 there were nineteen Democrats and fourteen Whigs in the Senate and sixty-two Democrats and thirty-eight Whigs in the House; in 1843 there were twenty-two Democrats in the Senate and eleven Whigs, and fifty-eight Democrats in the Assembly and forty-two Whigs. Philadelphia *Spirit of the Times,* October 17, 1842; Harrisburg *Democratic Union,* October 25, 1843.

[40] *Pennsylvania Archives,* 4th Series, VI, 979; Pennsylvania, *Laws, 1843,* p. 337; Philadelphia *Pennsylvanian,* April 6, 20, 1843.

provided for the election of three members of the board for terms of one, two, and three years, respectively, with one member to be elected annually thereafter for a term of three years.[41] Successful in stripping Porter of his most valued patronage, the Whigs remained unable to seize it for themselves, since the Democrats carried their candidates by the safe margin of 14,000 votes.

Among the factors contributing to the Whig defeat was their failure to reconcile the old Antimasonic faction in Lancaster, now headed by Thaddeus Stevens. The latter established a paper, the Lancaster *Union,* nominated an Exclusive ticket for county offices, and sent a delegation to the State convention held at Harrisburg on September 6, 1843, to nominate candidates for Canal Commissioners.[42] They were refused admission.[43] They would not admit defeat, however, and nominated a slate of candidates of their own for the Canal Commission. On election day they polled about two hundred votes and doubtless kept a larger number of sympathizers from voting. In addition to injuring the Whigs in the State contest, they contributed to the election of a Democrat, Benjamin Champneys, to the State Senate, a rare political phenomenon in Lancaster County.

The Lancaster Antimasonic faction also took an active part in a movement to foist General Winfield Scott upon the Whigs of the State. They endorsed Scott as early as October, 1841, solicited the support of former Antimasonic leaders, and organized a Scott central committee.[44] For a time the campaign gained headway, and his name appeared at the mastheads of numerous newspapers. Scott eagerly fell in with the plan and made a brief trip to Pennsylvania in May, 1842, to encourage it. He believed that Clay's health would not permit the rigors of another contest, and he prepared to take his place.[45] The movement showed promise through the spring of 1842, then came to a halt due to its failure to attract Clay men.

Its weakness was graphically revealed in July at Harrisburg, where the Scott faction assembled in what they had heralded as a State convention. In all, eleven counties, almost without exception old Antimasonic strongholds, were represented, and the list of officers read like a page from the files of Antimasonry, with the Lancaster

---

[41] *Ibid.* April 6, 1843.
[42] Harrisburg *Democratic Union,* June 21, 1843.
[43] Philadelphia *United States Gazette,* September 8, 1843.
[44] Stevens to Winfield Scott, October 20, 1841, Thaddeus Stevens Papers, Library of Congress; Scott to Stevens, November 1, 1841, *ibid.*
[45] Scott to Stevens, May 5, 1842, *ibid.;* George R. Poage, *Henry Clay and the Whig Party* (Chapel Hill, 1936), 108.

group monopolizing the committees. The delegates lauded the services of Scott and recommended the calling of a national convention to meet at Harrisburg in December, 1843.[46] Their enthusiasm, however, failed to compensate for empty seats. The convention was a failure. The Scott campaign and the ambitions of the Antimasonic faction to restore their political fortunes were buried in a common grave.[47]

From this time until Clay's eventual nomination, there was little doubt of the outcome. The Whig press lined up behind Clay and disagreed only upon the vice-presidential and gubernatorial nominations.

As in 1841 the Whigs were lacking in leadership in the contest for Governor. John Banks, the nominee in 1841, Joseph Markle, and James Irvin, an ironmaster and member of Congress from Centre County, were the preconvention favorites. The latter was endorsed by the press in the central portions; Markle was the choice of the West, and Banks of the East. None had a close-knit organization to promote his candidacy in the convention, but each had a band of loyal and determined delegates. As a result, the convention meeting in Harrisburg on March 4, 1844, divided three ways; and ballot after ballot was taken without reaching a decision. On the twenty-first, however, Bank's supporters began to shift to Markle, and on the following ballot he received the nomination.[48]

In pinning their hopes upon him, the Whigs gambled that Markle's military renown would exude sufficient glamor to offset his unfamiliarity in the central and eastern sectors of the State. Markle had raised a company in 1812 despite pressing financial burdens, had joined Harrison in the Northwest Territory, and had fought British and Indians. After the war he had taken up farming in Westmoreland County. Whigs discovered him there in 1841. His previous ventures into politics as a candidate for the State House of Representatives and for Congress had ended in defeats. But they had not dulled his "availability." As a warrior-farmer in the mold of Harrison, his political experience, or the lack of it, was of little moment.

Among the Democrats, meanwhile, the decline of Porter left the field open to aspirants for the gubernatorial nomination. Senator Sturgeon, Judge Nathaniel B. Eldred of Warren County, Thomas S.

[46] Philadelphia *Pennsylvanian,* July 30, 1842; Chambersburg *Repository and Whig,* June 16, August 4, 1842.
[47] Philadelphia *North American,* January 5, February 5, 1844.
[48] *Ibid.,* March 6, 1844.

Bell of Chester County, and Francis R. Shunk had active supporters. The leading candidate, however, was Henry A. Muhlenberg, who hoped to take advantage of his first opportunity to vindicate himself after the fiasco of 1835. In 1838 the schism was too recent to permit his candidacy, and he had been removed from the scene by an appointment as Minister to Austria. In 1841 the renomination of Porter kept the door closed, but 1844 offered a second opportunity. Old animosities had cooled, and Wolf, who had refused to forget their quarrel, was dead. Muhlenberg had placed Buchanan's friends under obligation to him by refusing to oppose the latter for the Senate in 1837 and 1843. He had the support of the Van Buren party in the Philadelphia area and in Allegheny and Erie counties in the West where the names of Van Buren and Muhlenberg were frequently linked. He also had the backing of many of the Improvement Men in Central Pennsylvania, including those who adhered to Porter after his split with Shunk. The aid of the latter was particularly valuable, since opinion in this region was almost evenly divided. His popularity in the German counties remained undiminished. By the autumn of 1843 it was obvious that he was far in the lead for the nomination.

As the convention date approached, however, his opponents joined forces to promote the candidacy of Shunk. Born in Montgomery County, he was a familiar figure in Harrisburg, having served as Clerk of the House of Representatives and as secretary to the Canal Commissioners for more than twenty years. Congenial, with a facility for retaining the friendships of all factions, he excelled as a peacemaker rather than a leader. In 1838 his active participation in the "Buckshot War" sent his political stock soaring, and Porter made him Secretary of the Commonwealth. Shunk's relations with Porter never seem to have been cordial, however, and he had little influence in the inner circles of the administration.[49] Following his resignation from the cabinet he practiced law in Pittsburgh. His withdrawal from Harrisburg at once freed him from the stigma of Porterism and made him the logical opponent of Muhlenberg in the region where the latter was weakest.

The Shunk bandwagon gathered momentum rapidly as one western district after another instructed its delegates for him. In the central portions of the State in York, Lancaster, Dauphin, Mifflin, Union,

[49] A Democratic politician noted at a later date that he "never knew him [Shunk] to declare an opinion about any exciting matter, but the 'Buckshot War.'" John B. Sterigere to Buchanan, February 3, 1848, Buchanan Papers.

and Lycoming counties, however, the outcome was in doubt until the last moment. In Lancaster County, Muhlenberg's lead seemed for a time to preclude serious opposition; and Buchanan, who preferred to avoid an agitation of the issue among his partisans while engaging in his candidacy for the Presidency, assured Muhlenberg that the county would sustain him if he were permitted to handle it in his own way. But in December, 1843, Muhlenberg wrote in alarm that Lancaster County now appeared to be in doubt.[50] Buchanan explained rather lamely that the failure of Berks County to instruct its delegates to the January 8, 1843, convention for him and the tendency of Muhlenberg men to associate themselves with Van Buren had mortified his friends and turned them from Muhlenberg. He agreed that the Shunk movement had made progress and admitted that he was no longer certain of the outcome.[51]

When Buchanan arrived in Lancaster for the Christmas recess, he found that his name had been joined with Shunk's and that his most active friends there, including Champneys and Frazer, were at the head of the Shunk faction. He moved at once to dissociate himself. To have become a partisan of either faction with both groups friendly to him, he declared, would have invited political suicide.[52] Muhlenberg's fears were confirmed; Lancaster instructed its delegates for Shunk. Muhlenberg and Buchanan expressed the mutual hope that they might remain personal friends, but the former made no secret of his dissatisfaction with the Buchanan leaders. "Knowing something of the County as well as of the influence of these Gentlemen," he retorted, "I am not to be told that the County was opposed and could not be managed."[53]

As the convention assembled at Harrisburg on March 4, 1844, the partisans of both Muhlenberg and Shunk anticipated victory.[54] There was slight evidence of a spirit of compromise as they jockeyed for position. The party appeared to be on the brink of disaster, with Muhlenberg again the center of controversy. Both factions attempted to control the organization of the convention, and, amidst a turmoil

---

[50] Muhlenberg to Buchanan, December 10, 1843, *ibid.*
[51] Buchanan to Muhlenberg, December 13, 1843, *ibid.*
[52] Buchanan to Muhlenberg, December 29, 1843, *ibid.*
[53] Muhlenberg to Buchanan, December 24, 1843, *ibid.*
[54] Shunk to John LaPorte, February 17, 1844, Society Autograph Collection, Historical Society of Pennsylvania; Cameron to Buchanan, January 21, 1844, Buchanan Papers; Forney to Buchanan, February 25, 1844, *ibid.;* Philadelphia *Pennsylvanian,* February 10, 1844; Cameron to Muhlenberg, March 5, 1844, Wagner Papers.

which defied for a time all attempts to proceed, each insisted that it had elected its nominee as the chairman. They finally agreed to permit the rival claimants for the chair to name a chairman.[55] Having surmounted this obstacle, they promptly disagreed upon the procedure for seating the disputed delegations. After a lengthy argument, the Muhlenberg group prevailed by the narrow margin of two votes. Spurred on by this initial advantage, they seated their friends and secured the nomination on the first ballot.[56]

Shunk acknowledged defeat; the schism of 1835 was not repeated. It proved to be a wise decision for Shunk since it made him available as Muhlenberg's successor upon the latter's death in August.

The campaign of 1844 was spirited from beginning to end. The nomination of Polk was a stimulant to the Democrats after they had reconciled themselves to the apparent inevitability of Van Buren's success. The enthusiasm, however, stemmed from their release from Van Buren rather than from their confidence in Polk. Pennsylvania Democrats were not alarmed at the prospects of the annexation of Texas as were their brethren in New York and New England, but they feared that Polk would advocate free trade and thereby hand the election to Clay by default. During the weeks immediately following the Baltimore Convention, Democrats flooded Polk with entreaties that he be cautious upon the tariff. "A dignified reserve on this topic such as characterized the language of General Jackson when a candidate," he was assured, was all that was required to rally the party to his support.[57]

The well-nigh universal apprehension of the Democrats upon the tariff reflected a significant shift of opinion in the State. Following the adoption of the Tariff of 1833 interest in the tariff subsided, and, except for brief flurries after the beginning of the Panic of 1837, it continued to attract little attention until 1840. Then the cumulative effect of the panic, heavy importation of foreign goods, the

[55] They chose James C. Marshall, an Eldred man. Philadelphia *United States Gazette*, March 6, 1844.

[56] The vote was Muhlenberg 69, Shunk 53, Sturgeon 5, Bell 3, and Bigler 1. It was not as close as those taken during the organization, since the supporters of Sturgeon, Bigler, and Bell now voted for their own candidates. *Ibid.*; Harrisburg *Democratic Union*, March 5, 1844.

[57] John K. Kane to Polk, May 30, 1844, Polk Papers. See also Jesse Miller to Polk, May 31, 1844, *ibid.*; Robert J. Walker to Polk, May 31, 1844, *ibid.*, written after a hurried trip to Philadelphia to obtain Dallas' acceptance of the vice-presidential nomination; James M. Porter to Polk, June 3, 1844, *ibid.*; Henry A. Muhlenberg to Polk, June 3, 1844, *ibid.*; Hendrick B. Wright to Polk, June 12, 1844, *ibid.*

increased use of anthracite coal in the production of pig iron, and the approach of drastic tariff reductions as provided by the Act of 1833 combined to revive the case for protection, with the anthracite producers in the vanguard. In the campaign of 1840 Whigs attempted to capitalize upon the tariff, while Democrats sought to subordinate it to the currency and the Independent Treasury.[58] The hard cider frenzy relegated it to a secondary status, but by 1842 the principle of protection was supported by Democrats as well as Whigs. When the tariff bill of that year was passed by the House, ten Democrats and ten Whigs among the Pennsylvania delegation voted for it, none voted against it, and three Whigs and five Democrats refrained from voting. In the Senate, both Buchanan and Sturgeon voted favorably in accordance with a resolution of the Pennsylvania legislature.

The long-awaited economic recovery which followed in 1842 and 1843 was inevitably associated with the tariff, and Democrats embraced it as their own. In 1844 the McKay Bill which provided for a general reduction of rates was rejected by resolutions of the legislature with but one dissenting vote; and Pennsylvania Whigs and Democrats opposed it in Congress.[59]

The tariff was thus a vital issue to Democrats in the campaign of 1844; an unguarded word by their nominee would bring disaster. Their misgivings were dispelled, however, by Polk's famous Kane letter. "In adjusting the details of a revenue tariff," he wrote, "I have heretofore sanctioned such moderate discriminating duties as would produce the amount of revenue needed, and at the same time afford reasonable incidental protection to our home industry."[60] It was received with rejoicing by the Democrats and permitted them to make the claim that Polk was as good a tariff man as Clay.[61]

When Whigs pointed to free-trade passages from Polk's speeches in Congress and in Tennessee, Democrats countered with quotations from Clay's proposals for concessions to the South in the debate upon the Compromise Tariff of 1833. It is doubtful whether they convinced many voters that Polk was a friend of protection, but

[58] Malcolm R. Eiselen, *The Rise of Pennsylvania Protectionism* (Philadelphia, 1932), 124-138. The distortion of Buchanan's remarks by the Whigs when he attempted to differentiate between inflated and real wages in that campaign has been indicated on pages 148-149.

[59] *Ibid.*, 148-150.

[60] Polk to John K. Kane, June 19, 1844, reprinted in Philadelphia *North American*, July 2, 1844.

[61] George M. Dallas to Polk, July 7, 1844, Polk Papers; John K. Kane to Polk, July 2, 1844, *ibid.*; Sargent, *Public Men and Events*, II, 235.

they neutralized the Whig advantage sufficiently to divert the public mind to other issues. While Whigs paraded the tariff, Democrats displayed "Clay the Duelist" and "The Bane and the Antidote," that is, Clay and Frelinghuysen; and during the closing weeks of the campaign Buchanan rescued the issue of the United States Bank from desuetude and evoked an enthusiastic response from Democratic gatherings along the Northern Tier.[62] The Democrats also attempted to exploit the traditional hostility of the Antimasonic faction for Clay, but this backfired when Ritner declared that he considered Clay to be the lesser of two evils.[63]

During the early weeks of the campaign the gubernatorial contest was subordinated to the presidential election. Then the pace quickened. On August 11, 1844, Muhlenberg died suddenly, and Democrats were faced with the difficult task of naming and supporting a new candidate less than two months before the election. They acted with remarkable unanimity. The central committee and the *Democratic Union* at the capital simultaneously came out for Shunk. It was the signal to Democratic leaders and the press throughout the State. Buchanan, meanwhile, worked effectively to pacify Muhlenberg partisans. He obtained a reluctant promise from Simon Cameron to get into line and encouraged Shunk to be conciliatory. The latter promptly assured the Muhlenberg men that he would not discriminate against them in the patronage.[64] Shunk was nominated without opposition by a special convention held at Harrisburg on September 2, but not before he had become involved in a controversy with the Native Americans which seriously jeopardized his election.

A succession of riots involving Native Americans and Irish in Kensington in Philadelphia County during May and July, 1844, served to make nativism a potent force in the campaign in that area. Political organization began with a rally in Independence Square on June 7. Mass delegations from Kensington, Southwark, and Spring Garden arrived to the tune of "Hail Columbia," and the crowd became so large that platforms were erected in different parts of the square, with four meetings being conducted at the same time.[65] Interest was sustained by the Philadelphia *North American*, which

[62] Buchanan to George Plitt, September 19, 1844, Buchanan Papers; Plitt to Buchanan, September 22, 1844, *ibid.*
[63] Philadelphia *United States Gazette*, August 2, 1844.
[64] George M. Dallas to Polk, August 11, 1844, Polk Papers; Buchanan to Shunk, August 14, 15, 30, 1844, Buchanan Papers; Shunk to Buchanan, August 17, 1844, *ibid.;* Cameron to Buchanan, September 5, 1844, *ibid.*
[65] Philadelphia *North American*, June 8, 1844.

assailed the Irish for their clannishness and their retention of Irish loyalties, accused them of fraudulent registrations and irregularities at the polls, and called upon Congress for stringent naturalization laws.[66]

While the excitement was at its height, Native Americans learned that Shunk had participated with Catholics in Pittsburgh in the laying of a cornerstone. They also uncovered a statement attributed to him which indicated that he supported the Catholic contention that the Bible should be removed from the public schools. The *North American* at once charged that Shunk was a Catholic, and Whig sheets by the score repeated the accusation. In fact, they raised such a din that Shunk, after considerable hesitation, answered the charges. He denied that he was a Catholic, but agreed that the Bible might be removed from the schools where public opinion was divided upon the subject.[67] His statement failed to pacify his accusers. They continued to belabor him for his alleged duplicity until the election.

The inability of the Native Americans to make headway in the interior deterred them from attempting a State-wide contest, but they used their strength in the normally Democratic Philadelphia County to drive a bargain with the Whigs. In return for the support of the latter for their candidates for the legislature, they agreed to back Clay and Markle. Democrats looked on helplessly, hoping that the vote in the interior would offset their losses in Philadelphia.[68]

One departure from tradition occurred during the campaign when Markle made a lengthy tour of the State in his own behalf. From Westmoreland he proceeded northward through Allegheny and Butler, thence eastward by way of Somerset, Bedford, and Huntingdon counties to Harrisburg. He then moved on to Berks and Philadelphia. The pilgrimage was climaxed at the latter place by his appearance on the platform with Daniel Webster.[69] Heretofore, candidates had remained on the side lines while their friends took the stump. It is true that Markle said nothing, since the strategy of the Whigs was to exploit his military career by parades and demonstrations where he appeared handsomely mounted. For those who wished to learn something of the man in addition to his bearing, manner,

[66] *Ibid.*, June 4, 10, 1844.
[67] Pittsburgh *Post*, September 14, 1844; Harrisburg *Democratic Union*, September 11, 1844; Shunk to Reuben Hale, September 16, 1844, Roberts Collection.
[68] John K. Kane to Polk, October 1, 9, 1844, Polk Papers; George M. Dallas to Polk, October 8, 9, 1844, *ibid.*
[69] Philadelphia *North American*, October 1, 2, 3, 1844; Harrisburg *Democratic Union*, October 2, 1844.

countenance, and republican dignity, the *United State Gazette* offered the assurance that "Those who have had an opportunity of conversing with him find him well informed upon important questions of national and state policy, well read in history, possessing a discriminating judgment and a cultivated taste."[70]

Markle's break with precedent was not unobserved by the press. One Democratic sheet declared that he had degraded himself to the level of a "common traveling electioneer" by huckstering to gain votes.[71] The Whig strategy was unproductive. Nevertheless, it was a significant change. Future gubernatorial candidates were freed to take the stump whenever the device seemed favorable. Shunk, for example, made several speeches in the campaign of 1847.

The gubernatorial election in October, 1844, resulted in a triumph for the Democrats by a narrow margin; and Democrats also retained control of both houses of the legislature. Native Americans carried Philadelphia County and thereby sent eight men to the House and one to the Senate.[72] Only their failure to get a foothold in other counties saved Shunk from defeat.

Both the Whigs and Democrats interpreted the election returns to indicate success in November. The former pointed out that Shunk was much better known to the voters than Markle and unlike Polk was not vulnerable upon the tariff. Democrats, on the other hand, predicted that Polk would receive the support of many who had been lured by the Native Americans into the Markle camp. The election returns revealed that the optimism of both was unwarranted. Polk received a majority of approximately 6,000 votes, but the coalition of Native Americans and Whigs retained its advantage in Philadelphia County.[73]

Democrats thus survived their most serious challenge since 1840. By subscribing to Polk's definition of "reasonable incidental protection," however, they mortgaged their future. A word from Polk could bring foreclosure.

[70] October 3, 1844.
[71] Harrisburg *Democratic Union*, October 3, 1844.
[72] Shunk's margin was approximately 4,300 votes. In Philadelphia County, a Democratic majority of 3,114 of the previous year was transformed into a deficit of 1,938. The Democratic vote in the city was cut by 1,237 votes from the previous election. Philadelphia *North American*, October 10, 1844. Official returns gave Shunk 160,322 and Markle 156,040 votes. Pennsylvania, *Senate Journal, 1845*, I, 68-69. See Appendix, page 224.
[73] Harrisburg *Democratic Union*, November 13, 1844. Polk electors received 167,245 votes to 160,863 for the Clay electors. *Niles' Register*, LXVII (November 23, 1844), 181, with corrections from Philadelphia *Public Ledger*, November 14, 1844. See Appendix, page 225.

CHAPTER XI

Pennsylvania Interests and the Walker Tariff 1845-1847

POLK'S triumph coming upon the heels of Shunk's election unloosed a flurry of activity among Democratic politicians seldom equaled in the history of the State. Both emerged as surprise victors: Polk, the original, though by no means obscure, "dark horse," and Shunk, after failing as a "stop Muhlenberg" candidate, an unexpected nominee in the closing weeks of the campaign. Thus at the outset there was neither a Polk nor a Shunk party, and Democrats of all factions competed for the spoils. Buchanan, the favorite son, took a commanding lead in the contest when the State's delegation to the Electoral College, with a single dissenting voice, recommended his appointment as Secretary of State. Active also were Dallas, the Vice President-elect, who was ambitious to be the spokesman for Polk in the State; Henry Horn, perennial chairman of the Jackson Hickory Club in Philadelphia, who pressed his claims as leader of the Van Buren men; and Tyler's officeholders, who pointed to their support of Polk in the campaign to justify the retention of their posts. Equally vigorous in the scramble for the spoils were Hendrick B. Wright and the others of the Pennsylvania delegation to the Baltimore convention who had supported the two-thirds rule, politicians who had known Polk when he was a member of Congress, and Governor Shunk, who found his own patronage inadequate to satisfy the demands of his friends.[1] It created a situation conducive to dissension and factionalism.

Enter Cameron

Shunk's appointments revealed a greater penchant for rewarding his partisans than pacifying the Muhlenberg faction. Secretary of the Commonwealth Jesse Miller, Attorney General John K. Kane, and Surveyor General John LaPorte were intimate friends of Shunk and therefore unacceptable to the Muhlenberg men. The latter viewed

[1] The Polk Papers contain many letters from Pennsylvania politicians seeking offices and offering advice.

Kane's appointment with particular disfavor since they claimed the second ranking office in the cabinet in return for their last-minute agreement to support Shunk.[2] Their failure to obtain a share of the patronage left them restive and prepared to bargain with the Whigs in the senatorial election. The latter encouraged such a combination since they could hardly expect to elect a Whig. Let them support a Democrat, it was argued, who would stand by the interests of the State. If they could agree upon such a man, a sufficient number of "virtuous" Democrats might be found to join with them to elect him.[3]

The Whig strategy proved to be abortive in its first trial. Democrats met in caucus on January 13, 1845, reached a decision and proceeded to re-elect the incumbent, Daniel Sturgeon, by a party vote. They did so, however, only after they had revealed an almost complete lack of organization. In caucus, Sturgeon, who was identified with neither the Shunk nor the Muhlenberg factions, could muster but eleven votes on the first ballot. The remainder were scattered among twenty-eight nominees. Northern men made a bid to name a candidate from that section, but they divided their strength, the Shunk men endorsing Judge George W. Woodward and Muhlenberg's partisans supporting Judge Nathaniel B. Eldred. The division ultimately made Sturgeon a compromise choice.[4]

A few days later the Democrats again acted harmoniously in caucus, agreeing to support James R. Snowden for State Treasurer. It was a victory for the Shunk men and was secured despite grumbling from the Muhlenberg faction. He was then elected by a party vote on January 20, 1845. The caucus was a turning point in the Shunk administration. It convinced the Muhlenberg men that they could expect no favors by acting in concert with the Shunk group. Only the defeat of Shunk in 1847 seemed to promise the restoration of their fortunes. Meanwhile, they prepared to resist further attempts of the administration to reward its favorites with offices.[5]

The appointment of Buchanan to the State Department on February 17, 1845, forced the discordant Democrats to face their second senatorial contest in less than two months. The Muhlenberg

[2] John M. Read to Buchanan, December 10, 1844, Buchanan Papers; Buchanan to Shunk, December 18, 1844, *ibid.*

[3] Philadelphia *United States Gazette,* December 7, 1844; Philadelphia *Pennsylvanian,* November 27, December 27, 1844.

[4] Harrisburg *Democratic Union,* January 15, 18, 1845; Philadelphia *North American,* January 15, 1845. Sturgeon was elected over James Cooper, a Whig of Adams County, by a vote of 72 to 49 on January 14, 1845.

[5] Simon Cameron to Buchanan, January 20, 1845, Buchanan-Johnston Papers.

men refused to go into caucus, and the forty-eight who were finally induced to join it found an agreement extremely difficult. After numerous ballots the administration forces mustered twenty-five votes, a bare majority, for Judge Woodward, and he was declared to be the party nominee. It was believed by the Shunk tacticians that Woodward, a resident of Luzerne County, would attract the northern members of the party, including a sufficient number of the Improvement Men to carry the election.[6]

They erred. Woodward wore the Shunk label despite the fact that he was a Porter appointee. Damaging also to his election prospects was the bitter factionalism in Luzerne, where Democrats had been divided into two hostile camps for more than a decade.[7] His nomination by the caucus stirred his Luzerne opponents, headed by Hendrick B. Wright and William S. Ross of the State Senate, into feverish activity. They dispatched lobbyists to Harrisburg, brought to light a long-forgotten nativist speech of Woodward's which he had delivered in the Constitutional Convention of 1837, and circulated the report that he was a free trader.[8] Strengthened by this opposition to Woodward from his own county, the Improvement Men remained adamant. Eleven cast their votes for Simon Cameron, and four others joined them on the second ballot. They thereby blocked Woodward's election and made possible the surprising triumph of Cameron.

In his first contest for the Senate, Cameron revealed himself to be an astute and opportunistic politician, characteristics which he exemplified throughout his long and controversial career. There is reason to believe that he planned his strategy well in advance of the election. An active partisan of Muhlenberg, he could expect nothing from the Shunk administration; to wait patiently for the next gubernatorial election was hardly in keeping with his restless temperament. Cameron observed to Buchanan in December, 1844, that he was being mentioned for the Senate to replace Sturgeon by several men "whose notice flatters me very much."[9] On February 8, in anticipation of Buchanan's resignation from the Senate, he reported

[6] Oliver Watson to Hendrick B. Wright, March 14, 1845, Wright Papers; Pittsburgh *Gazette*, March 15, 1845.
[7] See page 90.
[8] Ross to Wright, March 11, 26, 30, 1845, Wright Papers; O. Watson to Wright, March 14, 1845, *ibid.*; George P. Steele to Wright, March 16, 1845, *ibid.*; Jefferson K. Heckman to Polk, March 14, 1845, Polk Papers; Jesse Miller to Polk, March 12, 1845, *ibid.*
[9] December 7, 1844, Buchanan Papers.

that he would tell him in confidence when he saw him in Washington who would succeed him;[10] and on February 26 he expressed a desire to know the exact date of the election.[11] Meanwhile on February 17 a member of the State House of Representatives informed Buchanan that "General Cameron is making a bold push to keep enough men out of caucus with the Whigs to elect himself."[12]

Cameron cleverly kept his intentions under cover and thereby avoided unfavorable publicity from the Democratic press, which was emphasizing the obligation to the caucus and criticizing Porter and other Democrats who were suspected of bargaining with the Whigs. The first ballot taken on March 13, 1845, revealed, however, that Cameron was the logical choice to defeat the Democratic caucus nominee, and Whigs and Native Americans took steps to support him. A committee of the former requested his opinions upon the tariff and the distribution of the proceeds from the sale of public lands. His reply was completely satisfactory and revealed the gulf which separated him from the traditional Democratic position. He declared his unqualified adherence to the Tariff of 1842 and pledged to sustain it without change. He also promised to support distribution to the states.[13] The Native Americans also addressed Cameron seeking to ascertain his views upon the naturalization laws. He avoided a forthright endorsement of nativism but kept the door open, declaring that increased immigration would require an extension of the term of probation prior to the granting of citizenship.[14]

The effects of these commitments were immediately apparent. On the second ballot on March 14 he received the votes of fifteen Democrats and nine Whigs; on the third, seventeen additional Whigs and two Native Americans cast their votes for him; and on the fourth, the votes of twelve more Whigs increased his total to fifty-five. At this point, Caucus Democrats moved to adjourn, but without success, and Cameron was elected on the following ballot, receiving the votes of sixteen Democrats, forty-four Whigs, and seven Native Americans.[15]

Alexander K. McClure recalled that Cameron enlisted the aid of certain Presbyterian ministers in Harrisburg, who were sympathetic

[10] Buchanan Papers.
[11] *Ibid.*
[12] John Y. James to Buchanan, February 17, 1845, *ibid.*
[13] Cameron to Messrs. Cooper, Kunkle, Brady, Sanderson, and others, March 13, 1845, Simon Cameron Papers, Library of Congress.
[14] Cameron to Native Americans, March 12, 1845, *ibid.*
[15] Edwin W. Hutter to Buchanan, March 12, 1845, Buchanan Papers; Philadelphia *United States Gazette*, March 15, 1845; Pittsburgh *Gazette*, March 17, 1845.

toward his candidacy because of his liberal benevolence. At an opportune moment, they interceded to obtain the votes of several Whigs, who had refused to join the swing to Cameron. They were successful; the most obdurate, Jasper E. Brady of Franklin, a veteran legislator of Scotch-Irish stock, capitulating "finally with tears streaming down his cheeks."[16]

The forty-six-year-old Senator-elect had thrived upon controversy since his emergence as a politician twenty years before. Printer, banker, construction contractor upon State and federal works, and railroad promoter, Cameron did not permit political orthodoxy to interfere with what he interpreted to be the welfare of business and industry. While Democrats advocated restrictions upon bank charters and corporate organization, Cameron frequented the legislative halls at Harrisburg "boring" for his own projects—as well as those of his friends. His success in business and politics combined with his political insurgency gained for him warm friends and implacable enemies. Aggressive, indefatigable, and a master of intrigue, he might be disliked but not ignored.

Cameron's election precipitated a furor within the Democratic ranks. Caucus leaders bitterly assailed the conduct of the Improvement Men, and the press handled them roughly. Unsatisfied with these expressions, administration leaders, headed by Jesse Miller, Benjamin Champneys, and Reah Frazer, moved to place an official stamp of opprobrium upon them. Acting before passions had cooled, they prepared an address which extolled the virtues of the caucus and denounced those who refused to abide by it. They also asked Vice President Dallas and Secretary Buchanan to append statements. The former, in a blistering attack declared that

> it is scarcely possible to use language too decisive in condemnation of those, who, professing attachment to the political party . . . suddenly disclaim the usages, principles and candidates of that party, and form, in order to oppose and defeat it, a coalition with its avowed adversaries.[17]

Buchanan, on the other hand, carefully avoided any criticism of the legislature "for electing whom they pleased to the Senate of the United States."[18] Possibly the receipt of a letter from Cameron, in which he declared that he relied upon his friendship, contributed

[16] McClure, *Old Time Notes*, I, 98.
[17] Reprinted in the Harrisburg *Democratic Union*, June 25, 1845. The original dated March 24, 1845, is in the Dallas Papers.
[18] Buchanan to Democratic Members of the Legislature, March 31, 1845, Buchanan Papers.

to his moderation, though he appears to have opposed the course of the Caucus Democrats from the start.[19]

The Improvement Men, meanwhile, were hard pressed to justify their action. In the Senate, William S. Ross attributed his vote to Woodward's free-trade doctrines. But when Caucus Men called for evidence, he failed to produce it despite a hurried appeal to his friends in Luzerne for aid.[20] Alexander Power, a member of the House from Crawford County, drew up an elaborate defense of his vote for his constituents in which he repeated the free-trade and nativist charges against Woodward.[21] His arguments, too, were challenged by the Caucus leaders, who published a letter of Woodward's written just prior to the election in which he declared his adherence to the Tariff of 1842 and his opposition to Native Americanism.[22]

Time, however, favored Cameron and the Improvement Men. The conviction took root, particularly among Caucus Democrats in the interior, that the proscription of Cameron and his supporters would serve only to weaken the party in the October election. The press also adopted a more conciliatory tone. When the Caucus leaders prepared to release their philippic, they could obtain few signatures. It was finally published without them.[23]

If the campaign to discredit the Improvement Men performed no other function, it advertised the want of confidence of the Shunk administration in Cameron and placed him at a disadvantage in the competition for the federal patronage.[24] Unable to reward his friends, Cameron found that he could thwart his enemies and embarrass Polk by blocking his appointments. When Polk attempted to right "the wrong" which Woodward had received at the hand of the Improvement Men by naming him to the United States Supreme Court on December 23, 1845, a decision which he reached despite the fact that Woodward was not the choice of Buchanan, Dallas, or

---

[19] Cameron to Buchanan, March 25, 1845, Buchanan-Johnston Papers; John W. Forney to Buchanan, April 2, 1845, *ibid.*; Forney to Buchanan, March 24, 1845, Buchanan Papers.

[20] Ross to Hendrick B. Wright, March 17, 24, 30, 1845, Wright Papers.

[21] Reprinted in Philadelphia *Pennsylvanian*, June 14, 1845.

[22] Woodward to William Hollinshead, reprinted, *ibid.*, April 8, 1845.

[23] *Ibid.*, June 21, 1845; Harrisburg *Democratic Union*, June 25, 1845; York *Democratic Press*, July 16, 1845. Cameron reported to Buchanan that the sixteen Improvement Democrats who voted for him called upon Shunk, who gave them his assurance that he had taken no part in the movement of the Caucus leaders to discredit them. Cameron to Buchanan, March 27, 1845, Buchanan-Johnston Papers.

[24] Cameron to Hendrick B. Wright, May 22, 1845, Wright Papers; Cameron to Buchanan, October 20, 1845, Buchanan-Johnston Papers.

PENNSYLVANIA INTERESTS AND THE TARIFF 193

other leaders, Cameron secured the support of the Whigs and a handful of Democrats in the Senate to defeat his confirmation.[25]

A short time later Cameron secured the same backing to reject Polk's appointment of Henry Horn as Collector of the Port of Philadelphia. His action was popular among politicians outside of the Philadelphia area who coveted the office and its patronage, and damaging to the prestige of the Van Buren party in Philadelphia. It was extremely irksome, also, to Polk, who resolved to await an opportune moment and submit Horn's name a second time. He did so on June 24, 1846, but with the same result; Cameron refused to reconsider despite a humiliating personal plea by Horn.[26] Polk finally named James Page, a former postmaster of Philadelphia during the Jackson-Van Buren administrations. Page was no more popular among politicians in the interior than Horn, but unlike the latter, who had entered politics as a Federalist, he had a consistent political record. Cameron did not contest his confirmation.

Polk's rebuff to Cameron and the campaign of the Caucus Democrats to demoralize the Improvement Men fell short of driving them from the party and into the arms of the Whigs. Tradition proved to be a stronger bond than the pull of economic interests which drew the Improvement Men to the Whigs. Each new iron furnace which lighted the skies over the State, however, weakened the former and strengthened the latter.

Tariff Chills

The year 1845 was marked by a temporary lull in politics. Democrats expended their energies contending for offices, Whigs looked on from the side lines empty-handed. The election of a Canal Commissioner barely stirred them from their lethargy. The Democratic nomination made at Harrisburg on September 4, 1845, turned upon the question of a franchise for the Baltimore and Ohio Railroad to

[25] The six Democrats were Cameron, Thomas Hart Benton of Missouri, Ambrose H. Sevier and Chester Ashley of Arkansas, and David L. Yulee and James D. Wescott of Florida. Milo M. Quaife (ed.), *The Dairy of James K. Polk During His Presidency, 1845-1849*, 4 vols. (Chicago, 1910), I, 153. See also William R. King to Buchanan, January 27, 1846, Buchanan Papers; George M. Dallas to Hendrick B. Wright, January [n. d.], 1846, Wright Papers. Polk expressed the belief that Buchanan gave countenance to Cameron's opposition. David Wilmot, whom Polk consulted on the appointment, held a similar opinion. See Quaife (ed.), *Diary of James K. Polk*, I, 153, 183, 190. Buchanan called the rumor, however, "such stuff as dreams are made of." Buchanan to C. E. Lester, January 30, 1846, Gratz Correspondence.

[26] Quaife (ed.), *Diary of James K. Polk*, I, 218-219, 264, 426, 433, 437, 468, 469, 485-487; Henry Horn to Polk, June 14, 1846, Polk Papers.

extend its main line westward from Cumberland, Maryland, through the southwestern corner of the State. The western element in the convention endorsed a candidate committed to the franchise, whereas delegates from the eastern and central portions, fearful of the competition of the Baltimore and Ohio with the State Works or a future railroad along a central route and apprehensive of the development of Baltimore at the expense of Philadelphia, supported a man identified with their position. Victory went to the latter group on the second ballot.[27] The failure of the Whigs and Native Americans, meanwhile, to agree upon a candidate virtually eliminated them from the contest; and James Burns of Mifflin County, the Democratic nominee, was elected on October 14, 1845, by a margin of about 30,000 votes, and Democrats returned majorities to both houses of the legislature.[28]

In reality the calm was a prelude to storm. Politicians were marking time—awaiting Polk's action on the tariff. Whigs placed themselves squarely behind the Tariff of 1842 and prepared to resist modification. However, they were not averse to opening the tariff issue in order to exploit dissensions among their opponents. Democrats, on the other hand, viewed it with foreboding. Few, whatever their personal predilections reciprocated David Wilmot's determination to support tariff revision even "if I am to stand entirely alone on that question."[29] Polk observed with satisfaction that Pennsylvania leaders reacted favorably to his tariff message, but he could scarcely have overlooked the note of caution which pervaded these expressions, that Pennsylvania's peculiar interests must be safeguarded.[30] Democrats called for protection in the press and from the platform; and some went so far as to join with Whigs in public demonstrations. Most conspicuous among the latter was a State tariff convention at Hollidaysburg on November 12, 1845, presided over by former Governor Porter. Democrats and Whigs in attendance disagreed upon details, but took

[27] Israel Painter of Westmoreland County was the choice of the West; James Burns of Mifflin County of the East. Philadelphia *Pennsylvanian*, September 11, 1845. The Baltimore and Ohio franchise had been debated at length during March and April in the legislature, and it had finally been postponed. *Ibid.*, March 17, April 15, 17, 1845.

[28] The vote was as follows, James Burns (Democrat), 119,510; Samuel D. Karns (Whig), 89,118; and Robert H. Morton (Native American), 22,938. *Ibid.*, October 31, 1845.

[29] Wilmot to John LaPorte, December 13, 1845, Society Autograph Collection, Historical Society of Pennsylvania.

[30] Quaife (ed.), *Diary of James K. Polk*, II, 55; Eiselen, *Rise of Pennsylvania Protectionism*, 186.

a common stand in support of the Tariff of 1842.[31] Democratic leaders, however, generally shunned such combinations with their rivals.

The introduction of the McKay Tariff Bill in Congress intensified the controversy. Whigs insisted that the Democrats were guilty of fraud in the election of 1844 or were gulled by Polk; they were "rogues or fools."[32] Democrats denied the allegation, but they were admittedly confused and embarrassed. Legislators at Harrisburg made the tariff the first order of business in January, 1846. The State Senate adopted a resolution in support of the Tariff of 1842 without opposition, but in the House Democrats added amendments which endorsed the Independent Treasury and rejected a national bank and distribution. Whigs then refused to vote, and the resolution with the amendments was carried by the Democrats with four dissenting votes. Democrats in the Senate thereupon secured the adoption of the resolution with the amendments relating to the Independent Treasury and the national bank, but divided upon the third, dealing with distribution, and it was lost. This attempt to mitigate their irregularity by mixing the bitter with the sweet, that is, the tariff with the Independent Treasury, the bank, and distribution, apparently convinced no one. Whigs continued to press for protection and the Tariff of 1842 as the position of the Democrats became more and more untenable.

In Washington, meanwhile, Whigs and Democrats in the House, with one exception, David Wilmot of Bradford County, lined up with the opposition to the bill. In the Senate, Cameron and Sturgeon bent their efforts toward a similar goal. Their attempts to defeat it came to nought, however, when Vice President Dallas broke a tie which sent the bill to a third reading and eventual passage. He held his obligation "to the Country, to the whole of the American People," he explained, above that to the, so-called, Pennsylvania doctrines.[33]

The passage of the tariff raised a storm of protest from the Whigs and left the Democrats temporarily demoralized.[34] Cameron called

[31] *Ibid.*, 183; *Niles' Register*, LXIX (November 22, 1845), 181; Harrisburg *Democratic Union*, November 5, 1845.

[32] Philadelphia *Pennsylvanian*, January 3, 1846.

[33] Dallas to Henry M. Phillips, July 3, 1846, Dreer Collection. See also Dallas to Phillips, July 28, 1846, *ibid.*

[34] The Tariff of 1846 or Walker Tariff. John W. Forney reflected the Democratic bewilderment when he wrote to Buchanan: "It is a terrible question. You can not conceive how it worries us. We do not like Mr. M'Kay's bill, and yet it will not do to attack Mr. Polk." Letter of July 30, 1846, Buchanan Papers.

for repeal, and found many Democrats in the improvement counties receptive to his proposal. But he neither owed anything nor expected anything from the Polk administration. Few leaders could afford such independence.

Buchanan, after a brief reflection, decided that the keystone of the Democratic tariff policy should be modification, not repeal. Conceding in private that he preferred the Act of 1842 to that of 1846, he urged that the former be regarded as dead and that the latter be modified to give more adequate protection to home industries. He elaborated his views in a series of letters to Forney, who printed them in the editorial columns of the Philadelphia *Pennsylvanian*,[35] though not without certain misgivings. It was one thing to advocate modification, Forney observed, but a very different thing to promise it in so many words, since little could be expected from a President or a Congress devoted to free trade.[36]

In rural areas where industrialization lagged, the tariff was handled with less embarrassment. Along the Northern Tier, Wilmot made his support of the tariff act the campaign issue, and the Democratic press there fell into line.[37] And in York and Adams counties, Democrats accepted the Act of 1846 with little discord. In the former, resolutions in favor of the Act of 1842 were defeated in a county convention.[38]

But the over-all picture was one of uncertainty. The effects were clearly indicated by the elections which followed. Whigs made the tariff the sole campaign issue despite the efforts of the Democrats to minimize it. They emphasized the duplicity of the Democrats in electioneering for Polk as a friend of protection, scored their tardy

[35] Philadelphia *Pennsylvanian*, August 4, 5, 8, 10, 1846; Moore (ed.), *Works of James Buchanan*, VII, 46-47.

[36] Forney to Buchanan, August 23, 1846, Buchanan Papers.

[37] Charles B. Going, *David Wilmot, Free-Soiler: A Biography of the Great Advocate of the Wilmot Proviso* (New York, 1924), 145, 148. Elsewhere, Wilmot continued to be a target for criticism in the press, and his introduction of the Wilmot Proviso in the House of Representatives has been ascribed to his desire to find an issue which would restore his popularity. See Richard R. Stenberg, "The Motivation of the Wilmot Proviso," *Mississippi Valley Historical Review*, XVIII (1932), 535-541.

[38] The convention met August 11, 1846. Albert C. Ramsey to Buchanan, September 23, 1846, Buchanan Papers. On August 25, 1846, the York *Democratic Press* in an editorial, "The Privileged Class," attempted to correct what it regarded as a false impression that iron and coal interests should be held paramount to all others. Why, it asked, should not the interests of the farmer and the blacksmith be considered? It referred to Wilmot in its issue of September 15, 1846, as "This great champion of the interests of the **farmers of Pennsylvania**."

abandonment of the Tariff of 1842, and took special delight in publicizing their dissensions. A favorite device of the Whig press was to divide Democratic candidates into two categories, those clinging to the Tariff of 1842 and those who had swallowed the Tariff of 1846, and to append the query, "Which is the Democratic party, both can not be."[39] The Whig press was replete with statistics purporting to demonstrate the growth of coal mining, iron production, and domestic trade resulting from the Tariff of 1842. Coal production in the Schuylkill area, the *Miners' Journal* pointed out, had doubled between 1842 and 1845 after remaining stationary from 1837 to 1842. The Tariff of 1846, it predicted, would curtail the coal industry and reduce wages of miners as much as twenty to thirty cents per day.[40]

Democrats found no effective means of combatting the Whig offensive and on election day, October 13, 1846, went down to defeat. In the vote for Canal Commissioners, the only State-wide contest, the Whig nominee, James M. Power of Mercer County, triumphed over William B. Foster, Jr., of Bradford County, the Democratic incumbent, by approximately 9,000 votes. The latter was especially vulnerable because of his residence in a stronghold of free trade and his political association with Wilmot. Improvement Men made no secret of their preference for Power.[41] A year before Democrats had carried the same office by more than 30,000 votes. Whigs elected seventeen out of twenty-four Congressmen and gained control of both houses of the legislature, holding sixty-one seats in the House and eighteen in the Senate.[42] Wilmot was re-elected to Congress by a narrow margin, though opposed by tariff Democrats in his district. It added up to the most decisive Whig victory since the election of Ritner in 1835 and gave them control over the legislature for the first time since 1840. Democrats took refuge in the fact that the voting was light and that bad weather undoubtedly cut their strength in rural areas. But few questioned the potency of the tariff in their

[39] Pottsville *Miners' Journal,* October 3, 1846.
[40] *Ibid.,* July 11, 1846. It published the following statistics on May 16, 1846:

1837	540,000 tons
1842	572,000 tons
1845	1,132,000 tons

[41] Harrisburg *Argus,* September 2, 1846.
[42] Eiselen, *Rise of Pennsylvania Protectionism,* 206-207; Mueller, *Whig Party,* 133.

downfall, and some went so far as to predict that it would give the State permanently to the Whigs.[43]

Yet time favored their recovery. Chastened by defeat, they generally accepted the Buchanan formula, the Tariff of 1846 with modifications. Democrats in the House demonstrated their solidarity by unanimously rejecting a Whig-sponsored resolution calling for the restoration of the Tariff Act of 1842.[44] Polk's vigorous foreign policy in Oregon and the war with Mexico elicited their enthusiastic response. Most important of all, the business recovery which had accompanied the adoption of the Tariff of 1842 continued uninterrupted after the passage of the Act of 1846, and a poor harvest in Europe stimulated the grain market.[45] Democrats were reluctant at first to identify prosperity with the tariff lest the former should not be sustained.[46] But by the spring of 1847 their doubts were largely dispelled, and they were defending the Act of 1846.

A Second Term for Shunk

Democratic acceptance of the Walker Tariff permitted them to enter the gubernatorial campaign of 1847 with renewed vigor, but it did not heal the cleavages within the party. A faction among the Improvement Men, headed by former Muhlenberg leaders, persisted in their opposition to the Shunk administration. Prodded by Buchanan, Shunk made a bid for their favor in June, 1846, when he appointed John M. Read as Attorney General in the place of Kane, who had accepted an appointment to the bench of the United States District Court of Eastern Pennsylvania.[47] The elevation of Read, a prominent Philadelphia attorney and a former Muhlenberg partisan,

[43] Buchanan to Henry D. Foster, November 19, 1846, Buchanan Papers; Jesse Miller to Buchanan, November 9, 1846, *ibid.*; John W. Forney to Buchanan, October 29, 1846, *ibid.*; Cameron to Buchanan, October 20, 1846, Buchanan-Johnston Papers; James Thompson to Polk, November 8, 1846, Polk Papers.

[44] Philadelphia *Pennsylvanian*, January 14, 1847.

[45] A resident of Mercer County reported to Buchanan that four or five new iron furnaces were erected in that county during the six months following the adoption of the Walker Tariff, "most of them by men who have long been practiced in the business. . . . This does not look as if they thought the change was going to ruin them." He added: "The County abounds with ore and coal, there are now I believe 12 or 15 furnaces in operation. . . . You can on a dark night stand on the roof of our court house and see the light of 7 or 8 furnaces in full operation." John Findley to Buchanan, December 8, 1846, Buchanan Papers.

[46] Buchanan to Henry D. Foster, November 19, 1846, *ibid.*; Jesse Miller to Buchanan, November 9, 1846, *ibid.*

[47] Shunk to John LaPorte, June 25, 1846, Society Autograph Collection, Historical Society of Pennsylvania; Quaife (ed.), *Diary of James K. Polk*, I, 463-464.

appeared to answer Shunk's critics. But unfortunately for Democratic unanimity, Read was soon at odds with his associates and resigned in five months.[48] Shunk replaced him with a close friend, Benjamin Champneys, and offered no further concessions to the Muhlenberg group.[49]

The Democratic element opposed to the renomination of Shunk began operations more than a year before the election. They advocated the choice of a new man, using the one-term principle for justification.[50] A Dauphin County convention in September, 1846, adopted a resolution calling for an adherence to a single term and recommended Judge Nathaniel B. Eldred for the nomination.[51] The disastrous Democratic defeat in the election of 1846 supplied more grist for their mill. They now charged that Shunk should be rejected because he could not be re-elected. His election in 1844 by a bare 4,000 votes with the party undivided, they argued, pointed to his inevitable defeat. Only a new man could reunite the party.[52] As the date of the nomination approached conventions in Warren, Dauphin, Union, Lebanon, McKean, Wayne, Pike, Erie, and Luzerne counties adopted resolutions favoring the one-term principle.[53] Cameron, who encouraged the activity from Washington, estimated that only the addition of the Philadelphia delegation was required to defeat Shunk's renomination.[54]

The hopes of the anti-Shunk forces, however, were quickly dissipated in the nominating convention held at Harrisburg on March 4, 1847. Finding themselves in the minority, they were unable to seat their claimants from disputed districts. They thereupon attempted to block Shunk's nomination by the adoption of the two-thirds rule, but they failed by a vote of 93 to 30. As a last resort, they moved to adjourn only to find themselves again in the minority. Shunk was then nominated on the first ballot with but twenty-four dissenting

[48] George Plitt to Buchanan, December 14, 1846, Buchanan Papers; Read to Hendrick B. Wright, June 27, 1846, Wright Papers.
[49] Champneys had been a close associate of Buchanan, but they became estranged when Buchanan refused to denounce the election of Cameron to the Senate. See Hendrick B. Wright Papers.
[50] Charles D. Eldred to Hendrick B. Wright, May 2, 1846, Wright Papers. Eldred was editor of the Williamsport *Lycoming Gazette.*
[51] Harrisburg *Argus,* September 9, 1846.
[52] *Ibid.,* December 9, 16, 23, 1846; January 13, 1847; Williamsport *Lycoming Gazette,* reprinted in Philadelphia *Pennsylvanian,* November 28, 1846.
[53] Wilkes-Barre *Luzerne Democrat,* January 6, 1847; Harrisburg *Argus,* January 20, 1847; Philadelphia *Pennsylvanian,* January 23, 25, 1847.
[54] Cameron to Henry Simpson, January 11, 1847, **Gratz Correspondence.**

votes.[55] Having sustained Shunk, the convention united upon Morris Longstreth, a former Muhlenberg leader from Montgomery County, for Canal Commissioner. It helped to mollify the Improvement Men and to unify the party for the election.[56]

The Whig nomination was contested by supporters of James Irvin, a candidate for the nomination in 1844, and of James Cooper, a protégé of Thaddeus Stevens. Cooper had served in Congress and in the legislature and had been elected as Speaker of the House following the Whig triumph in 1846. He was popular in the interior, particularly along the Southern Tier and in old Antimasonic strongholds.[57] Irvin was available for two reasons. He voted for the Tariff of 1842 in the House of Representatives, and he was an ironmaster, an attractive combination among an electorate stirred to a consciousness of Pennsylvania's special interests. Irvin was the favorite in Philadelphia and Pittsburgh and in industrial centers in the interior.[58] By the opening of the convention on March 4, 1847, the Irvin forces were in the ascendancy, and they nominated their candidate on the first ballot.[59] To impress the voter further with the tariff issue, the convention then nominated another ironmaster, Joseph H. Patton, for Canal Commissioner.[60]

The Whigs entered the campaign determined to accentuate again the weakness of the Democrats on the tariff and to demonstrate that they had abandoned Pennsylvania's true interests by subscribing to the southern leadership in Washington. The Shunk administration, they insisted, "can not be permitted to shuffle off its responsibilities for all the madness, depravity and disgrace of the government at Washington."[61] It would have to share the blame for an endless war, increased taxation, an expanding national debt, and an extension of slavery.[62] In pursuing this policy, however, the Whigs failed to gauge the shifting temper of the electorate. They might argue that

[55] Harrisburg *Argus*, March 6, 1847; Wilkes-Barre *Luzerne Democrat*, March 10, 1847.

[56] J. Glancy Jones to Buchanan, July 21, 1847, Buchanan Papers; Philadelphia *Pennsylvanian*, March 6, 1847.

[57] Richard Peters to John McLean, February 6, 1847, McLean Papers.

[58] Philadelphia *Pennsylvanian*, July 6, October 23, 1846; Philadelphia *North American*, October 22, 1846; Pottsville *Miners' Journal*, December 5, 1846; Philadelphia *United States Gazette*, November 25, December 9, 1846.

[59] Irvin received 89 votes, and Cooper received 36. Philadelphia *North American*, March 12, 1847.

[60] Philadelphia *Pennsylvanian*, March 12, 1847.

[61] Philadelphia *North American*, March 30, 1847.

[62] *Ibid.*, July 3, 1847.

the high prices of grain resulted from "a visitation of God"[63] and not the Tariff of 1846, but they were not persuasive. The calamity which they had forecast failed to materialize; also, the war with Mexico was popular despite the problem of slavery in the territories which might ultimately accrue to the United States.

The Wilmot Proviso, it is true, was supported initially by members of both parties in Congress and in the legislature.[64] But unlike the Democrats of New York, who divided into two hostile camps, Pennsylvania Democrats gradually retreated to occupy middle ground. When the Proviso was introduced a second time in the national House of Representatives as an amendment to a $3,000,000 appropriation bill in February, 1847, Democratic members from Pennsylvania opposed it in committee,[65] and five of them voted against it on its final passage; one member, Richard Brodhead, delivering a principal address for the opposition.[66] The change was reflected in the press. Nature having excluded slavery from the Southwest, it was argued, the Proviso would serve no purpose except to arouse the worst feelings of the southerners.[67]

Democrats found their path smoothed by the attitude of the Whigs toward the Proviso. While they continued to charge that the Polk administration plotted to extend slavery into the Southwest, they no longer embraced the Wilmot Proviso as their own brainchild. Instead, they portrayed it as a scheme concocted by a friend of Polk to restrain northern Democrats from bolting the party.[68] The Whigs thereby dealt a blow to the prestige of the Proviso in the State, toppling it from the crest of nonpartisanship into the trough of party politics. Democrats no longer hesitated to attack the Proviso, and in August, 1847, Buchanan paved the way for its virtual abandonment at this time.

In a letter to the Berks County Democratic Harvest Home Committee he called for an adherence, first, to the Constitution, which relegated the legality of slavery to the states, and second, to the

[63] The Irish Famine.

[64] Resolutions endorsing the Wilmot Proviso were adopted in both houses of the legislature. Three Democrats voted in the negative in the Senate. Philadelphia *North American,* January 23, 28, 1847.

[65] James Thompson to Polk, February 15, 1847, Polk Papers.

[66] Philadelphia *Pennsylvanian,* March 16, 1847; Philadelphia *North American,* February 19, 1847; *Niles' Register,* LXXII (March 6, 1847), 18.

[67] Philadelphia *Pennsylvanian,* February 17, 1847.

[68] Philadelphia *North American and United States Gazette,* August 13, September 3, 1847; Philadelphia *Pennsylvanian,* September 2, 1847.

Missouri Compromise for guidance in the West. He declared that the issue was unnecessary since climatic conditions made slavery impractical in the Mexican territory. Abolition, by fomenting sectionalism, was a threat to the Union.[69] Buchanan's position was echoed in the press and from the platform. By October it was accepted widely by the Democrats of the State.[70]

The Whigs thus failed to capitalize on both the tariff and the Wilmot Proviso. Upon other issues such as the rivalry of the Baltimore and Ohio and the Pennsylvania Railroads for franchises and the disposition of the Public Works, they were equally indecisive, since these matters were sectional and tended to cut across party lines.

Three weeks before the close of the campaign the Whigs sprang a surprise calculated to arouse the latent discord between the Shunk and Muhlenberg factions. On September 23, 1847, the *North American and United States Gazette* in Philadelphia published a letter which accused high-ranking members of the Shunk administration, including Jesse Miller and Henry Petriken, of writing articles abusive of Muhlenberg and his aides in the Harrisburg *Champion* following Shunk's defeat by Muhlenberg in the convention of 1844. The articles bore such unflattering captions as "The Blooded Parson,"[71] "Treasury Robbed,"[72] and "The Money Power."[73]

The author of the letter, Seth Salisbury, was an obscure but zealous politician from Bradford County. He had been United States Marshal of the Northern District during Van Buren's administration and State Librarian under Porter, but had failed to obtain an appointment from Shunk or Polk. Cameron had urged Buchanan to

[69] Buchanan to Berks County Committee, August 25, 1847, Buchanan Papers; Philadelphia *Pennsylvanian*, August 30, 1847.

[70] Not to be outdone by his rival, Dallas speaking at Pittsburgh also rejected the Proviso. He urged that the status of slavery in the West be determined by popular sovereignty. See John W. Forney to Buchanan, September 8, 20, 1847, Buchanan Papers; Wilson McCandless to Buchanan, September 15, 1847, *ibid.*; George M. Dallas to Ellis Lewis, October 16, 1847, Ellis Lewis Papers, Historical Society of Pennsylvania.

[71] This refers to Muhlenberg, of course, who had both wealth and an illustrious ancestry. See Philadelphia *North American and United States Gazette*, September 24, 1847.

[72] This article charged a Muhlenberg supporter with responsibility for a defalcation of public funds. One passage read, "Muhlenberg will do for pap-suckers, bank aristocrats, anti school, or rather anti equal rights party." Philadelphia *North American and United States Gazette*, September 23, 1847.

[73] It alleged that Muhlenberg was wealthy enough to buy out all the other leading candidates, but insisted that his money was insufficient to secure his election. Reprinted, *ibid.*

find a place for him, explaining in language at once colorful and prophetic:

> He is as poor as a rat and as enterprising as a monkey. If you don't give him bread, his facility for scribbling and his acquaintance with the printers, together with his persevering industry will keep the whole state in a ferment. He is now dubbed an editor of the Harrisburg Argus and there is no tire in him. I say make him watchman [at the capitol]. This will feed him, and a man with a full belly is not half as troublesome as a hungry one.[74]

Receiving no office, Salisbury more than justified Cameron's prediction. His letter and articles from the *Champion* were reprinted in the Whig press. Democratic editors rushed to the defense, and the press was filled with charges and countercharges.[75] Temporarily, the issue overshadowed the Proviso and the tariff. It had scarcely begun to subside by election day on October 12. It is difficult to estimate the effects of the controversy, but it fell short of dividing the Democrats at the polls.

The outcome was a Democratic victory. Shunk was re-elected by a margin of 18,000 votes, and Longstreth was chosen Canal Commissioner by a similar vote. Democrats returned a substantial majority to the House, but holdovers gave the Whigs an advantage in the Senate. The results for Governor would have been less decisive, however, if the Native Americans had not persevered in supporting their own candidate, since the combined Whig and Native American returns were but 7,000 less than the Democratic vote.[76]

The Democrats thus bounced back from their reversal in 1846 despite the tariff and the Proviso, but the results clearly indicated that a slight shift of the political axis would be sufficient to change the balance of power again.

[74] Cameron to Buchanan, April 11, 1847, Buchanan-Johnston Papers.

[75] The truth of the accusation remains shrouded in a mass of conflicting testimony. The Philadelphia *North American* later conceded that Jesse Miller was innocent of any participation in the articles. See the issue of November 15, 1847. Forney dismissed Salisbury's "revelation" with the remark, "He [Salisbury] is bodily purchased, and is now said to be drunk in Harrisburg, in the very clothes bought for him by Irvin." Forney to Buchanan, September 24, 1847, Buchanan Papers.

[76] In the Senate there were fourteen Democrats and nineteen Whigs; in the House, sixty-five Democrats and thirty-five Whigs. The official vote in the election was 146,081 votes for Shunk, 128,148 for Irvin, and 11,247 for Emanuel Reigart, the Native American candidate. Philadelphia *Pennsylvanian*, October 25, 1847; Pennsylvania, *Senate Journal, 1848*, II, 85-86. See Appendix, page 225.

CHAPTER XII

The Election of 1848 and the Passing of Democratic Supremacy

WHILE politicians applied themselves to the details attending the elections of 1845, 1846, and 1847, they did not lose sight of the presidential election of 1848. Two factors contributed to arouse an unusual interest in this contest: Polk's early avowal of his determination to retire after one term; and the promise of a spirited struggle between the supporters of Buchanan and Dallas for the nomination.

Rehearsal for 1848

Buchanan's appointment as Secretary of State sent his political stock soaring; it also raised new difficulties in his path. His office was a steppingstone to the Presidency; and the aggressive foreign policy of Polk provided opportunities for his talents in the Oregon and Mexican controversies. What Polk gave with one hand, however, he took away with the other. Independent and suspicious by nature, he took pains to prevent any member of his administration from making his office a springboard to the White House. In naming his cabinet, he exacted a pledge from each appointee that he would not become an aspirant for the Presidency while holding the office.[1] And in distributing the patronage, he was on guard to avoid giving a disproportionate share of the spoils to any individual or faction. As a result, Buchanan frequently found himself rebuffed and unable to deliver offices which his friends expected.

More threatening to his future, however, than being hamstrung over appointments was the stigma of "free trade," with which his relationship to the administration inevitably associated him. Even before the introduction of the tariff in Congress, he sought an escape from the cabinet into the less controversial atmosphere of the Supreme Court. Only Polk's hesitation to make the appointment at once

[1] Polk to Buchanan, February 17, 1845, Buchanan Papers; Buchanan to Polk, February 18, 1845, *ibid.*; Quaife (ed.), *Diary of James K. Polk*, III, 350.

appears to have dissuaded him.[2] He kept the door open, however, and in June, 1846, after Polk's subsequent nominee, George W. Woodward, had been rejected by the Senate,[3] and when the tariff issue was at fever heat, he accepted the offer of the appointment from Polk.[4] But again the latter delayed in submitting his name to the Senate, with the explanation that the tariff issue made it untimely.[5] With his retreat cut off, Buchanan observed the passage of the tariff from the State Department. A few days later he announced his determination to remain at his post.

He was at once engulfed in the controversy which he had attempted to dodge. James Pollock, later to become Governor of the State, accused him in the national House of Representatives of misrepresenting Polk's tariff views in the campaign of 1844. He alleged that Buchanan had declared that Polk was a better tariff man than Clay and that the Tariff of 1842 was safe in his hands.[6] The Whig press spread Pollock's charge across the State, and Buchanan issued a countercharge of misrepresentation.[7] Recognizing his insecurity if Democrats should demand the repeal of the tariff, he launched a drive for "revision" in the editorial columns of Forney's Philadelphia *Pennsylvanian*. Buchanan's connection with these articles, of course, remained Forney's secret.[8]

The most serious threat to Buchanan's political future, however, was George M. Dallas. Back in the political arena as the result of his surprise accession to the Vice Presidency after five years of virtual retirement following his resignation as Minister to Russia, he was the logical leader of the old Van Buren element of the party in particular and the anti-Buchanan forces in general. Distinguished in appearance, polished and gracious in manner, accepted socially by Philadelphia's elite despite his adherence to the party of Jackson, favored by the Democratic press of the Philadelphia area, and well

[2] *Ibid.*, I, 46-47; Charles Warren, *The Supreme Court in United States History*, 3 vols. (Boston, 1922), II, 419-421.

[3] See pages 192-193.

[4] Buchanan to Polk, June 28, 1846, Polk Papers.

[5] Allan Nevins (ed.), *Polk: The Diary of a President, 1845-1849* (London and New York, 1952), 119, 123.

[6] In a speech delivered at Milton. Philadelphia *Pennsylvanian*, July 15, 1846.

[7] Forney to Buchanan, July 9, 12, 1846, Buchanan Papers. There is a copy of Buchanan's defense in his papers dated July 13, 1846.

[8] See page 196. Buchanan to Forney, August 1, 1846, Buchanan Papers; Forney to Buchanan, August 4, 1846, *ibid.*; Philadelphia *Pennsylvanian*, August 4, 5, 8, 19, 1846.

acquainted with leaders in Washington and Harrisburg, he became a formidable rival of Buchanan overnight.

As a competitor of Buchanan, however, Dallas had certain weaknesses. He lacked a substantial following throughout the interior. In a State-wide contest, he could rely only upon Allegheny, where he had family and political connections of long standing,[9] and possibly a few other counties outside the Philadelphia area. And his residence in the latter and the impression that he belonged to the aristocracy made the organization of a personal following in the interior extremely difficult.[10] Furthermore, he had alienated the Improvement Men by speaking out against Cameron's election to the Senate and by breaking the tie upon the Tariff Bill in the Senate.[11] His rebuke to the Democrats who evaded the caucus and his action upon the tariff, of course, won friends as well as lost them. The former gratified administration leaders surrounding Shunk, who in turn backed him in his contest with Buchanan; and the latter was popular in rural districts. Finally, Dallas lacked the zest for politics as exemplified by Cameron and Buchanan.

For a time after his election to the Vice Presidency, he engaged vigorously in the competition for the patronage, but failure dulled his interest, despite the fact that he appears to have fared as well as his rivals. For example, when Polk asked for his recommendation for Treasurer of the Mint at Philadelphia in December, 1845, Dallas preferred to make no suggestions. Instead, he aired his disappointments over the patronage. "I fear another failure, another complete checkmate," he wrote, "and I am not willing to incur again the chances of the game."[12] Six months later when a vacancy occurred on the bench of the United States District Court of Eastern Pennsylvania, Dallas was satisfied merely to forward a batch of recommendations with a brief note in which he listed four candidates who seemed to be best qualified.[13]

In November, 1847, while his friends were in the thick of the fight to make him the Pennsylvania nominee for President, he confided

[9] Dallas' brother, T. B. Dallas, had married the niece of United States Senator William Wilkins of Pittsburgh, who had headed the Eleventh Hour Men in Allegheny twenty years before.
[10] Asa Dimock to Buchanan, December 28, 1847, Buchanan Papers.
[11] See pages 191, 195.
[12] Dallas to Polk, September 3, 1845, Polk Papers.
[13] Dallas to Polk, June 9, 1846, *ibid.* He listed John K. Kane, Joel Jones, Henry D. Gilpin, and Edward King. Kane was subsequently appointed.

to Van Buren, "My personal life during the administration of Col. Polk, has but poorly compensated for the suspended enjoyments and pursuits of private and professional spheres."[14] Facing rivals who relished politics, Dallas was not equipped to engage them with their own weapons. Nevertheless, he could not be taken lightly. If an impression were made that Pennsylvania Democrats were divided between Dallas and Buchanan, the latter's bid for the nomination would inevitably fail.

One of the most exasperating problems which Buchanan faced in his drive for the nomination was the factionalism among the Democrats in Lancaster County. He had sidestepped the Wolf-Muhlenberg and the Shunk-Muhlenberg divisions, and had managed to retain the support both of the older leaders who had backed Wolf in 1835 and Shunk in 1844 and of the Muhlenberg men, headed by Simon Cameron and his brother James. Cameron's election to the Senate, however, aroused passions to a white heat and made a middle ground untenable. Buchanan attempted it, extolling the virtues of the caucus while avoiding any criticism of the legislature or of Cameron,[15] but it brought down upon him the wrath of the Caucus Men. Included were friends and neighbors of long standing—Reah Frazer, Benjamin Champneys, and Samuel C. Stambaugh. Frazer in particular took up the cudgels, overlooking no opportunity in city, county, or State conventions to denounce his former associate while advocating the candidacy of Dallas. He went so far as to circulate a report that Buchanan was no longer a resident of Lancaster, basing his claim upon the fact that he had ceased paying a personal property tax since his removal to Washington as Secretary of State. He carried the charge to the Democratic gubernatorial convention of 1847 at Harrisburg, repeating it to all who would listen. Only the frenzied efforts of the Buchanan leaders restrained him from agitating it on the convention floor.[16]

Buchanan hastily made a contribution of $240 for the purchase of wood and coal for the "poor widows and single women" of Lancaster County, explaining to the treasurer that it was the interest which had accumulated on a sum which he had invested eighteen months

---
[14] Dallas to Van Buren, November 2, 1847, Van Buren Papers.
[15] See page 191. See also Thomas Burnside to George M. Dallas, April 8, 1845, Dallas Papers.
[16] Forney to Buchanan, March 7, 1847, Buchanan Papers.

before for this purpose.[17] Forney, now in Philadelphia, worked untiringly to bring the Lancaster group back into line, but with little success. Frazer and his faction controlled the county meeting of September 1, 1847, where they adopted resolutions for Dallas for President and elected Dallas men, with a single exception, to the nominating convention.[18] Their action was at once injurious to Buchanan's pride and to his position in the State and nation.[19]

Buchanan's candidacy was weak also along the Northern Tier, especially in Bradford County. The proximity of New York State, and possibly the New England contacts and traditions in the area, contributed to nourish the Wilmot Proviso after it had lost its vitality in other parts of the State. Democrats of this region resented Buchanan's identification with the Polk administration and, more particularly, his Harvest Home letter to Berks County in which he proposed the extension of the Missouri Compromise westward. However, they also disliked Dallas' Pittsburgh declaration in support of popular sovereignty in the Southwest.[20] The one statement thus tended to neutralize the other. Lukewarm to both Buchanan and Dallas, leaders in Bradford, Luzerne, and Susquehanna counties looked again toward Van Buren.[21]

Supporters of Buchanan and Dallas attempted to fire the opening shots of their respective campaigns at the gubernatorial convention in Harrisburg in March, 1847. But opinion was so evenly divided that, after a five-hour struggle in committee, neither faction dared to risk a separate resolution for its candidate.[22]

Then for a time the Zachary Taylor boom tended to relegate both Buchanan and Dallas to the side lines. Philadelphia Whigs, with John Sergeant in the van, inaugurated the movement in April, 1847. They staged a Taylor rally and offered him their nomination for the

[17] That is, April, 1846, about the time his tax payments were discontinued. Buchanan to Michael Carpenter, October 5, 1847, *ibid*. See also Christian Bachman to Buchanan, September 12, 1847, *ibid*.; and Michael Carpenter to Buchanan, October 7, 1847, *ibid*.

[18] Forney to Buchanan, September 2, 3, 6, 1847, *ibid*.; J. L. Reynolds and J. B. Amwake to Buchanan, September 2, 1847, *ibid*.; Isaac F. Lightner to Buchanan, September 4, 1847, *ibid*.

[19] Philadelphia *North American and United States Gazette,* September 24, 1847.

[20] See page 202.

[21] Asa Dimock to Buchanan, December 3, 28, 1847, Buchanan Papers; Going, *David Wilmot,* 233.

[22] Forney to Buchanan, March 7, 1847, Buchanan Papers; J. Glancy Jones to Buchanan, March 7, 1847, *ibid*.

ELECTION OF 1848 AND DEMOCRATIC DECLINE 209

Presidency.[23] The Whig press in the city endorsed him with certain reservations, the *North American and United States Gazette*, for example, reflecting the uncertainty surrounding his politics, admitted that it was willing to await further developments.[24] Whigs in other sections assumed a "wait and see" policy. They did not act until Taylor was nominated by the national convention.

Not to be outdone with a military hero in the balance, Democrats also began to organize for Taylor. Leadership came from the Improvement Men, including former Muhlenberg and Porter supporters who were out of step with the administrations in Harrisburg and Washington. In the Philadelphia area, John M. Read, who had recently resigned from Shunk's cabinet, Samuel D. Patterson, publisher of the Norristown *Register* and formerly an editor in Harrisburg, and Richard Vaux headed the movement. In the interior, Cameron, Judge Ellis Lewis of Lancaster County, a Porter appointee and colleague of Cameron, Ovid F. Johnson, Attorney General during the Porter regime, James Peacock, postmaster of Harrisburg,[25] and Seth Salisbury took the lead.

Democratic rallies for Taylor followed, and a few Democratic editors placed his name at their mastheads.[26] Taylor Democrats also held a convention at Harrisburg on June 26, 1847, and named a state committee.[27] To satisfy doubts regarding Taylor's membership in the party, Cameron published a letter purporting to show that Taylor was a Democrat, citing opinions of his friends as evidence.[28] But Democrats, by and large, remained unconvinced, and Taylor's letters expressing his willingness to run for the Presidency, but not as a candidate of a party, sent the movement into a decline.

Even the Native Americans, now struggling to avert disintegration, rallied to the Taylor standard. After a division in their convention at Pittsburgh on May 11, 1847, over the merits of Judge John McLean, General Winfield Scott, and General Taylor, they reassembled in

[23] Richard Peters to John McLean, April 12, 1847, McLean Papers.
[24] Philadelphia *North American and United States Gazette*, April 3, 1847; Philadelphia *Pennsylvanian*, April 5, 1847.
[25] Peacock was dismissed from his office a short time later. See Peacock to Polk, October 21, November 1, 1847, Polk Papers.
[26] Democratic papers supporting Taylor included the Harrisburg *Argus*, New Berlin *Union Times*, Norristown *Register*, Chester *Democratic Journal and Jeffersonian*, and the Wilkes-Barre *Luzerne Democrat*. See *Luzerne Democrat*, August 4, 1847; and Philadelphia *Pennsylvanian*, August 31, 1847.
[27] Edwin W. Hutter to Buchanan, August 6, 1847, Buchanan Papers; Harrisburg *Argus*, July 1, 1847; Philadelphia *Pennsylvanian*, August 6, 1847.
[28] Cameron to Samuel D. Patterson, reprinted, *ibid.*, June 1, 1847.

Philadelphia on September 10 and bestowed their nomination upon the latter.[29]

With Taylor out of the way, partisans of Dallas and Buchanan prepared for a fight to the finish to control the State convention. With slight prospect of success except in scattered districts in the interior, the Dallas men concentrated upon Philadelphia city and county. And since a victory there would make Buchanan's nomination a certainty, his supporters girded themselves to meet the challenge. The contest centered upon ward elections to name the delegates to the city and county conventions, which in turn would choose the delegates to the State convention. It gave the Dallas forces a distinct advantage. They numbered in their ranks the officeholders in the customs house, inspectors, clerks and watchmen, ward and precinct committeemen—in brief, the party machinery in the city and county. Employees in the customs, for example, dug into their pockets to contribute to the expenses of the campaign and helped to swell the crowds at Dallas meetings.[30]

Buchanan men complained that the judges of the courts of common pleas in the area, especially Edward King, Anson V. Parsons, and William D. Kelley, "used the power of the Quarter Sessions in granting licenses to taverns and prosecuting for tippling so as to deprive large numbers of persons of freedom of action. Promises of licenses to applicants and threats of taking licenses away were used with an undisguised freedom."[31] Buchanan protested to Polk against the activities of James Page, Collector of the Port, and his employees, charging them with abusing him personally. Polk agreed that such a practice, if true, should not be tolerated from federal officeholders and promised to confer with Secretary Robert J. Walker. He pointed out, however, that he would take no part in the rivalry between Buchanan and Dallas for the Presidency.[32]

Lacking such a close-knit organization, the Buchanan men left no stone unturned in their search for ways and means to combat their rivals. One valuable asset was the presence of John W. Forney. After years of devoted service to Buchanan in Lancaster, where he edited

---

[29] C. Darragh to John McLean, May 12, 1847, McLean Papers; Lewis C. Levin to McLean, May 12, 1847, *ibid.*; Mueller, *Whig Party*, 144.

[30] Daniel T. Jenks to Polk, December 3, 11, 1847, Polk Papers; Forney to Buchanan, December 20, 1847, Buchanan Papers.

[31] William A. Stokes to Buchanan, January 3, 1848, *ibid.* See also James C. Van Dyke to Buchanan, January 3, 1848, *ibid.*; John M. Reed to Buchanan, January 2, 1848, *ibid.*; George Plitt to Buchanan, January 3, 1848, *ibid.*

[32] Quaife (ed.), *Diary of James K. Polk*, III, 208-209.

the *Intelligencer,* he secured with Buchanan's aid an appointment as deputy surveyor in the customs office in Philadelphia. In his own words, "The post of Deputy Surveyor is *the political office* of the customs, and it will be my own fault if I do not so conduct myself as to cause you [Buchanan] no regret, either from over-zeal or imprudence."[33]

Endowed with an enthusiastic and engaging personality, Forney was soon in the welter of Philadelphia politics and in demand on the platform. His first love, however, was journalism, and he subsequently purchased a half-interest in the Philadelphia *Pennsylvanian* despite Buchanan's refusal to assist him financially and his unfeigned misgivings lest Forney's lack of tact should embarrass him.[34] Fortunately for Buchanan, Forney was not discouraged. He made the *Pennsylvanian* the leading Democratic paper in the city, consistently supported Buchanan's political interests, and gave him an outlet for his views on the tariff, slavery in the territories, and other issues.[35] At the same time, he adhered to the party line, including the support of Dallas following his vote on the tariff in order to avoid an open break with his partisans.[36] Having become absorbed in journalism, Forney resigned from his post in the customs, but his zest for politics and his devotion to Buchanan continued unabated.[37] In the rivalry for the presidential nomination, Forney was the spearhead of the Buchanan party.

Other leaders of the Buchanan forces in Philadelphia included a sprinkling of officeholders, Henry Welsh, Naval Officer of Philadelphia, George W. Barton, Judge of the Common Pleas, and John Davis, Surveyor of the Customs; former Taylor Democrats, John M. Read, Richard Vaux, and Samuel D. Patterson; a group of young men, ambitious and dissatisfied with the older leadership, Benjamin Brewster, Thomas McCully, and James C. Van Dyke; veteran politicians seeking the comeback trail, Joel B. Sutherland and Andrew Miller; and Catholics, who were cultivated to attract the Irish vote, William A. Stokes and his brother, Doctor T. P. Stokes.[38] All in all, it was an incongruous band, united by a mutual desire to overcome the traditional Democratic leadership.

[33] Forney to Buchanan, March 21, 1845, Buchanan Papers.
[34] Forney to Buchanan, May 8, 1846, *ibid.;* Buchanan to Forney, May 10, 1846, *ibid.;* Forney to Buchanan, May 10, 11, 1846, *ibid.*
[35] Forney to Buchanan, May 22, June 7, 11, 1846, *ibid.*
[36] Forney to Buchanan, July 30, 1846, *ibid.*
[37] Forney to Buchanan, August 19, 23, 1847, *ibid.*
[38] John M. Read to Buchanan, November 27, 1847, *ibid.*

They blanketed the city and county with rallies; in Catholic districts they lingered upon Buchanan's Irish ancestry and credited him with inaugurating a movement to send a minister to Rome,[39] and in industrial areas they recruited speakers from the workingmen.[40]

Both the Dallas and Buchanan groups staged their most ambitious meetings under the aegis of war meetings. The former conducted a giant demonstration on December 1, 1847, at the Chinese Museum, where little was said about the war but much about Dallas.[41] A week later both factions attempted to organize a similar rally. It resulted in a row which continued for several hours until the Buchanan men finally obtained the chair.[42] On December 18 the Buchanan faction held its war meeting at the Chinese Museum, where Forney, Barton, and Robert Tyler delivered the principal addresses. It was crowded in spite of the last-minute efforts of the Dallas men to create a diversion by holding a meeting simultaneously at Commissioners' Hall.[43]

Buchanan men were now hopeful notwithstanding the advantages of the Dallas group in organization and money. Buchanan answered Read's Christmas day appeal for $500 "to meet the expenses of the city and so far as may be necessary to aid the county" with the sum of $200.[44] Three days later Read requested the remainder, "It must be here at once," he wrote, "or it will be too late, and the promises I have made must be unfulfilled." He added in a postscript, "The others are making desperate exertions and spending freely."[45]

The delegate elections on January 2, 1848, resulted in victories for Dallas in both the city and county. In the former, forty-seven Dallas delegates were chosen and thirty-eight Buchanan men; the popular vote

[39] James C. Van Dyke to Buchanan, November 29, 1847, *ibid.;* William A. Stokes to Buchanan, December 30, 1847, *ibid.*

[40] Stokes to Buchanan, December 14, 1847, *ibid.*

[41] John Davis to Buchanan, December 3, 1847, *ibid.;* Philadelphia *Pennsylvanian,* December 2, 1847.

[42] William A. Stokes to Buchanan, December 9, 1847, Buchanan-Johnston Papers; George Plitt to Buchanan, December 9, 1847, *ibid.;* Forney to Buchanan, December 10, 1847, Buchanan Papers.

[43] Plitt to Buchanan, December 19, 1847, Buchanan-Johnston Papers; Stokes to Buchanan, December 9, 1847, *ibid.;* James C. Van Dyke to Buchanan, December 18, 1847, Buchanan Papers; Stokes to Buchanan, December 18, 1847, *ibid.;* Robert Tyler to Buchanan, December 18, 1847, *ibid.;* John M. Read to Buchanan, December 19, 1847, *ibid.;* Forney to Buchanan, December 20, 1847, *ibid.;* Philadelphia *Pennsylvanian,* December 20, 1847.

[44] John M. Read to Buchanan, December 25, 1847, Buchanan Papers.

[45] Read to Buchanan, December 28, 1847, *ibid.*

ELECTION OF 1848 AND DEMOCRATIC DECLINE

was 1,391 for Dallas and 1,267 for Buchanan. County returns revealed a similar margin for Dallas. Buchanan leaders charged that their rivals imported voters from New Jersey, permitted Native Americans to vote, and padded the ballot boxes by polling fictitious names, and they threatened to contest the election in four wards.[46] On second thought, however, they decided to forego reprisals and to console themselves with the fact that they had defeated Dallas in his own ward and congressional district and in the Northern Liberties, "the cradle of democracy," in the county.[47]

Buchanan's defeat in Philadelphia did not prove to be disastrous. He continued to win delegate elections in the interior, and the Democrats in the legislature voted in caucus on February 1 to endorse him for the nomination. Dallas' friends could obtain but fifteen signatures to a circular criticizing the action of the caucus.[48] Even in Lancaster, his supporters defeated Frazer in the contest to nominate city officers.[49] At the State convention at Harrisburg on March 4, 1848, he scored an impressive victory. The convention instructed the delegation to the national convention to stand by him until a majority were willing to yield.[50] He thus demonstrated again that he was the favorite son despite the opposition of the leaders of the Shunk administration, the discord in Lancaster, and his defeat in Philadelphia. One of his aides did not exaggerate when he wrote with justifiable pride from Harrisburg, "It is now as clear as the sun at noon-day, that out of Philadelphia Dallas has scarce the shadow of a party."[51]

THE WHIG TIDE

Pennsylvania Democrats thus closed 1847 with the re-election of Shunk and inaugurated 1848 by giving Buchanan their official endorsement for the Presidency. Both had been made possible by the willingness of active minority elements to bow to the voice of the majority, a situation which appeared to augur well for the elections to follow. But the optimism of the Democrats receded as the year advanced.

[46] Read to Buchanan, January 3, 5, 6, 1848, *ibid.*
[47] George Plitt to Buchanan, January 6, 1848, Buchanan-Johnston Papers.
[48] Edwin W. Hutter to Buchanan, February 3, 1848, Buchanan Papers; Philadelphia *Pennsylvanian,* February 2, 1848.
[49] Hutter to Buchanan, January 20, 1848, Buchanan Papers.
[50] George Plitt to Buchanan, March 4, 1848, Buchanan-Johnston Papers.
[51] Hutter to Buchanan, March 5, 1848, Buchanan Papers.

In Washington, victories which made national heroes of Scott and Taylor shed little luster upon President Polk and his administration. Instead, they intensified the pull of sectionalism. The question of slavery in the Mexican territories now occupied by American troops was taken from the realm of speculation and oratory and dumped upon the lap of Congress for action. Democratic politicians could no longer parry the issue; they would be harassed by the fruits of Manifest Destiny to the coming of the Civil War. In November, 1847, Governor Shunk could write to Buchanan, "I do not recollect that I have expressed any opinion on the subject [of the Wilmot Proviso], to any one at any time, not having had any occasion to examine it."[52] But such an admission from one in high political station would have been anachronous a year later.

The Whig trend was made evident by the gubernatorial elections of 1847. In Polk's own state of Tennessee, in Connecticut, and in New York Whig executives replaced Democrats.[53] Shunk's re-election had been achieved in the face of this movement. But throughout Pennsylvania Democrats kept alive the factionalism which had stemmed from the rivalries of Buchanan and Dallas for the Presidency and of Muhlenberg and Shunk for the governorship. Improvement Men were out of sympathy with party chiefs aligned with southern leadership on the tariff and were hanging tenuously to the party, ready to drop at the first call of Republicanism.

While Buchanan and Dallas were competing for the role of favorite son, Whigs were not idle. Taylor men launched their campaign at a Buena Vista celebration at Philadelphia on February 22, 1848. The high light was a letter from Taylor to Joseph R. Ingersoll, in which he identified himself as a Whig. The Taylor movement made immediate headway across the State, though tariff advocates particularly in the West continued to prefer Clay or Scott.[54] At the Whig convention at Harrisburg on March 15, 1848, where senatorial delegates to the presidential nominating convention were elected, no attempt was made to pledge them to Taylor; and at the national convention at Philadelphia on June 7, Taylor received only a minority of the votes of the Pennsylvania delegation.[55]

But once Taylor and Fillmore were the party standard-bearers, Whigs rallied to support the ticket with an enthusiasm reminiscent

---

[52] Shunk to Buchanan, November 3, 1847, *ibid.*
[53] Allan Nevins, *Ordeal of the Union*, 2 vols. (New York, 1947), I, 5.
[54] Mueller, *Whig Party*, 145-147.
[55] *Ibid.*, 145-148.

of 1840. Recognizing that they would have to draw Democratic votes for victory, Whig spokesmen stressed the tariff issue in iron and coal regions of the interior and in wool growing areas such as Washington County in the West. They also bid for the proponents of the Wilmot Proviso, who were most numerous along the Northern Tier and in Allegheny and Lancaster counties. Here they portrayed the Free Soil movement as hopeless and the Democratic party as the tool of the South. In Philadelphia, Whigs held out the olive branch to the Native Americans. They supported the latter's candidate for Congress, Lewis C. Levin, and five of their nominees for the State House of Representatives. The strategy paid off when Native Americans came out for Taylor.[56]

Democrats, meanwhile, were beset with troubles. Their endorsement of Buchanan for the Presidency, his failure at the national convention at Baltimore on May 22, 1848, and the triumph of Lewis Cass left them bereft of influence in the latter's organization and apprehensive of his views on the tariff. Furthermore, Free Soilism, headed by David Wilmot, an erstwhile Democrat, encompassed the Northern Tier. The indefatigable Wilmot, a candidate for re-election to Congress, stumped the northern counties for Van Buren, the Free Soil presidential nominee, and made occasional forays into other sectors. The Free Soil party held a State convention at Reading on September 13, 1848, and formed an electoral ticket, but did not make nominations for State offices.[57]

With the Whigs belaboring the tariff issue, Democrats alleged that Taylor was not an advocate of protection and that Cass was the better tariff man of the two. But in 1844 they had said that Polk was a better tariff man than Clay only to be confronted in 1846 with the Walker Tariff. The Whigs in 1848 pointed to this Kane "fraud" and to Cass's low tariff views.[58]

In the midst of the presidential campaign, party leaders were faced with an unexpected gubernatorial election. Governor Shunk had been stricken with a lingering illness early in the year, but his condition was not diagnosed as fatal until summer. On July 9, 1848, he suddenly announced his resignation. His action made William F. Johnston, the Whig Speaker of the State Senate, the Acting Governor. Technicalities of the election laws made it possible for Johnston to hold his position until the following year, but he chose to abide by

[56] *Ibid.*, 153-155.
[57] Going, *David Wilmot*, 237-293.
[58] Eiselen, *Rise of Pennsylvanian Protectionism*, 214.

the spirit rather than the letter of the law and issued a writ on August 12, directing that an election be held to fill the vacancy on October 10, 1848, the date of the general election.[59]

Both parties moved at once to launch campaigns. The Whigs met at Harrisburg on August 31 and nominated Johnston on the first ballot. He was a logical choice. Entering politics in Armstrong County as a Democrat some fifteen years before, he was elected to the State House of Representatives where he was identified with the Improvement Men. He wore his party cloak lightly. In 1837 he joined the Coalition to defeat his party's choice for the printer of the English journal.[60] During the same session he displayed a similar unorthodoxy on the Independent Treasury, when he introduced a resolution requesting Pennsylvania's members of Congress and instructing its Senators to vote against this administration-sponsored measure.[61]

His irregularity made him a target of the Democratic press, but he retained the support of his constituents. While in the House of Representatives he worked actively behind the scenes to protect banking, and, in particular, the United States Bank of Pennsylvania.[62] Evidence that Johnston placed a high value upon his services for the United States Bank is suggested in a letter to Biddle, written a few months after his labors against the Independent Treasury, in which he sought a loan of $30,000 to speculate on land. "I need scarcely remind you," he wrote, "that I have made some personal sacrifices to sustain the 'good cause' and as this little accommodation would enable me to make a penny and as it would be of little moment to yourself, I shall most confidently expect a favorable answer." The request was refused.[63]

Three years later Johnston introduced the "Relief Bill," designed to relieve the banks and the State from embarrassment resulting from the panic. This bill, like the resolutions against the Independent

---

[59] The law required that the Acting Governor should issue a writ to fill the vacancy at least three months before the general election. Shunk resigned almost exactly three months in advance of the election, but Johnston did not arrive in Harrisburg to assume office until August 26. His writ, therefore, was a technical violation of the law. See McClure, *Old Time Notes*, I, 172-175; William C. Armor, *Lives of the Governors of Pennsylvania, . . . 1609-1873* (Philadelphia, 1872), 405-407; *Pennsylvania Archives*, 4th Series, VII, 283-285.

[60] Harrisburg *Reporter*, December 8, 1837.

[61] *Niles' Register*, LIII (February 17, 1838), 385; Philadelphia *American Sentinel*, February 14, 1838. See pages 116-118.

[62] See pages 91-92.

[63] Johnston to Biddle, October 22, 1838, Dreer Collection.

Treasury, was adopted by the legislature and became law despite the opposition of the party organization.[64]

Johnston's dislike for the Walker Tariff in 1846 finally led him to abandon his party and affiliate with the Whigs. As a member of the latter party he won an election to the State Senate in 1847, just in time, it turned out, to put him in line for the governorship. Now as a candidate for Governor he could count upon the backing of the Whigs and might anticipate support from the Improvement Men.

While the Whigs were naming Johnston, the Democrats met in convention at Harrisburg and, after a spirited contest, nominated Morris Longstreth of Montgomery County for Governor. Longstreth had carried the State the year before as a candidate for Canal Commissioner. Somewhat detached and aloof from the welter of politics, he offered a striking contrast to the colorful and opportunistic Johnston.

Not entirely overlooked in the excitement of the presidential and gubernatorial races was the contest for Canal Commissioner. For this office the Whigs at their convention at Harrisburg on March 15, 1848, nominated Ner Middleswarth of Union County. A veteran legislator of Antimasonic antecedents and a former Speaker of the State House of Representatives, he had taken a strategic role in the chartering of the Bank of the United States, the Apportionment Act, and other Coalition maneuvers. The Democrats named Israel Painter of Westmoreland County, a former member of the State House of Representatives, at their convention at Harrisburg on March 4. Painter was identified as an Improvement Democrat and had been active in the Taylor movement while it flourished among the Democrats.

The campaign was one of the most colorful of those waged during the second quarter of the century. Johnston broke precedents by vigorously stumping the State in his own behalf. He hammered away at the tariff from dozens of platforms and interjected the slavery extension issue where there was Free Soil sentiment—in Allegheny and Lancaster counties, for example, and on the Northern Tier.[65] Democrats were frequently on the defensive, especially on the tariff. Prices of coal and iron had fallen since 1847, and voters in the affected districts reflected a growing apprehension about the future.[66] In Allegheny and Philadelphia, before audiences of workingmen,

[64] Buchanan to David R. Porter, April 10, 1841, W. W. Porter Papers. See page 155.
[65] Mueller, *Whig Party*, 152-154.
[66] Eiselen, *Rise of Pennsylvania Protectionism*, 213.

Democrats stressed Middleswarth's opposition to the passage of a Ten Hour Law in the House during the previous session. It appears to have paid dividends.[67]

The October elections revealed an almost even division among the electorate. It required ten days to unravel the gubernatorial returns and to establish Johnston's victory by 297 votes out of a total of 336,747. Whigs also carried a majority of the congressional elections, seating fourteen, while the Democrats salvaged eight, Native Americans one, and Free Soil Democrats one.[68] Whigs also elected twenty-one of the thirty-three Senators, whereas the Democrats chose fifty members of the State House of Representatives, leaving forty-five to the Whigs and five to the Native Americans.[69]

In the contest for Canal Commissioner, Painter defeated Middleswarth by about 3,000 votes. The latter lost some six hundred votes in industrial Allegheny County and ran some four hundred votes behind Johnston in Wilmot's district on the Northern Tier. Painter also seems to have attracted Taylor Democrats who cast their votes for Johnston for Governor.[70]

With State elections behind them, politicians concentrated upon the presidential contest in November. The result was a decisive Whig victory. In the largest total vote to that time in Pennsylvania, Taylor defeated Cass by more than 13,000 votes. Van Buren ran a distant third, and his vote was negligible except in the Northern Tier.[71]

The explanation was to be found in the magic of a military chieftain and in the prodigious expansion in the coal and iron industries which was linking the State's future to the tariff. As one crestfallen Democratic explained, the defeat resulted from "gun powder and the tariff, which of these had the greatest influence it will be hard to ascertain." Democrats in the coal regions, he observed, could not be controlled. "They said it was bread and they would not stand to principle."[72]

[67] McClure, *Old Time Notes*, I, 177.
[68] Lewis C. Levin was the Native American and David Wilmot the Free Soil Democrat.
[69] Harrisburg *Pennsylvania Telegraph*, October 31, 1848; Pennsylvania, *Senate Journal, 1849*, II, 347-349. There were seventy-two scattered votes for Governor. See Appendix, page 226.
[70] Harrisburg *Pennsylvania Telegraph*, October 31, 1848; Mueller, *Whig Party*, 157.
[71] Taylor electors polled 186,113 votes, Cass electors received 172,661, and Van Buren electors had only 11,200. *Niles' Register*, LXXIV (December 6, 1848), 367. See Appendix, page 226.
[72] Hendrick B. Wright to Buchanan, November 13, 1848, Buchanan Papers. Wright wrote from Wilkes-Barre.

A Political Transition

The span of years between 1833 and 1848 revealed no cataclysmic political upheavals to set it apart from the decades which preceded and followed it. It was an era, nonetheless, marked by significant changes. At the outset, the factionalism which had sprung up around the national favorites, Clay, Crawford, Calhoun, Adams, and Jackson, had scarcely yielded to a new orientation—the Adams or National Republican, and the Jackson or Democratic factions; and in State politics the formidable Antimasonic party vied with the Adams and Jackson men. Long before 1848 Antimasonry had run its course. Reaching their greatest strength in 1835, the Antimasons placed Joseph Ritner in the gubernatorial chair. They failed, however, to gain control over the legislature, and "Exclusive" goals remained unfulfilled. The sole monument to commemorate their triumph was the short-lived State charter of the United States Bank, and even this was a Whig rather than an Antimasonic measure. Defeated in 1838, the party disappeared rapidly. Meanwhile, Jackson men and Adams-Clay partisans, respectively, coalesced into distinct political organizations. In so doing, they added substantially to the two-party tradition. Generally speaking, the Democrats maintained a dominant position in this period, the result of Jackson's popularity and their success in identifying themselves with the "will of the people." But the growing influence of the southern element in the nation's capital appeared to place "Pennsylvania interests" in jeopardy and enabled the Whigs to gain converts as the defenders of them. Victorious in the presidential election of 1840, the Whigs swept the State a second time in the elections of 1846 following the adoption of the Walker Tariff. By 1847-1848 the two parties were almost evenly balanced.

This era also witnessed notable transitions in political organization and management. In 1832 Pennsylvania Democrats were groping to bring themselves into conformity with principles emanating from Washington, a new and irksome responsibility; the convention was replacing the caucus so that nominations might be made by representatives "fresh" from the people; the parties were almost devoid of permanent organization. By 1848 the harmonizing of State with national party measures was an accepted, albeit unpleasant, duty which weighed heavily upon the leaders of both parties; the convention was universal on all levels of activity; parties remained loose-knit, but permanent committees, campaign chests, and other paraphernalia were contributing to give them a modern appearance.

This period brought marked changes in leadership. Failing to elect a Governor or a United States Senator or to obtain a cabinet post, the Whigs had few opportunities to gain national prominence. John Sergeant, active defender of the Bank of the United States in Congress, vice-presidential nominee in 1832, and chairman of the Constitutional Convention of 1837, was a perennial but unsuccessful candidate for the Vice Presidency and the cabinet. Few others weathered the lean years as well. Thaddeus Stevens temporarily dropped from sight; and other leaders of the Antimasonic epoch— Ritner, Ellmaker, Burrowes, and Todd—went into permanent retirement. Democrats who gravitated into the Whig party fared no better than the Antimasons. Only William F. Johnston, soon to become Governor of the State, made the transition without losing status. Among the Democrats of the 1830's, Wolf, Muhlenberg, and McKean were dead in 1848; and Porter and his associates among the Improvement Democrats were estranged from the party. Cameron with the aid of Whig and Native American votes was in the United States Senate, but he had cut off his future as a Democrat. Wilmot's Proviso likewise placed him in an untenable situation. Buchanan and Dallas, on the other hand, consistently supported the Jackson, Van Buren, and Polk administrations and thereby maintained positions of leadership in the State and nation.

Finally, new issues crowded to the fore as old ones faded into obscurity. The controversy over the Bank of the United States which had sharpened party lines and driven a wedge into Democratic ranks, the responsibility of the State for the promotion of canals, roads, and other improvements, and the relation of the State to the banks and currency tended to lose their force as the prosperity of the 1840's succeeded the panic years. Meanwhile, the tariff, dormant from 1833 until 1842, became an all-absorbing issue in 1844, 1845, 1846, and 1848, and the question of slavery in the territories began to gain momentum upon the annexation of Texas, the Mexican War, and the furor over the Wilmot Proviso.

Thus Pennsylvania politics moved from the perplexities of the Jacksonian ferment to the distractions of an ever deepening sectionalism.

Appendix

VOTE FOR GOVERNOR, 1835

VOTE FOR PRESIDENTIAL ELECTORS, 1836

VOTE FOR GOVERNOR, 1838

VOTE FOR PRESIDENTIAL ELECTORS, 1840

VOTE FOR GOVERNOR, 1841

VOTE FOR GOVERNOR, 1844

VOTE FOR PRESIDENTIAL ELECTORS, 1844

VOTE FOR GOVERNOR, 1847

VOTE FOR GOVERNOR, 1848

VOTE FOR PRESIDENTIAL ELECTORS, 1848

CONGRESSIONAL APPORTIONMENT, 1832

CONGRESSIONAL APPORTIONMENT, 1843

SENATORIAL APPORTIONMENT, 1829

SENATORIAL APPORTIONMENT, 1836

SENATORIAL APPORTIONMENT, 1843

APPENDIX

Vote for Governor, 1835[1]

County	Ritner	Wolf	Muhlenberg
Adams	1,517	406	911
Allegheny	3,848	2,854	378
Armstrong	1,100	1,874	188
Beaver	1,669	1,066	354
Bedford	2,067	1,581	46
Berks	3,016	1,743	4,194
Bradford	1,239	1,504	406
Bucks	3,584	2,534	829
Butler	1,306	1,059	237
Cambria	694	610	38
Centre	1,070	1,742	446
Chester	4,051	1,799	1,577
Clearfield	323	335	290
Columbia	767	869	1,246
Crawford	999	877	814
Cumberland	1,748	1,492	1,137
Dauphin	2,320	780	719
Delaware	1,240	699	403
Erie	1,943	164	1,280
Fayette	1,708	1,132	1,379
Franklin	2,207	1,423	1,336
Greene	1,075	366	997
Huntingdon	2,555	1,324	423
Indiana	1,524	991	14
Jefferson	246	356	3
Juniata	763	588	211
Lancaster	7,018	4,283	471
Lebanon	1,968	621	435
Lehigh	1,914	841	1,204
Luzerne	1,488	618	1,890
Lycoming	1,277	1,159	935
McKean and Potter	128	413	54
Mercer	1,694	519	878
Mifflin	866	909	109
Montgomery	3,014	1,744	1,599
Northampton	2,560	3,135	458
Northumberland	882	748	1,247
Perry	760	701	802
Philadelphia (City and County)	10,633	7,834	4,105
Pike	66	620	88
Schuylkill	833	456	1,172
Somerset	2,031	542	89
Susquehanna	594	873	789
Tioga	468	868	176
Union	2,185	578	653
Venango	613	847	467
Warren	190	397	230
Washington	3,179	2,464	379
Wayne	226	744	85
Westmoreland	2,192	2,652	757
York	2,665	1,070	1,658
Total	94,023	65,804	40,586

[1] Pennsylvania, *Senate Journal*, 1835-36, I, 42-43.

Vote for Presidential Electors, 1836[2]

County	Harrison	Van Buren
Adams	1,520	1,186
Allegheny	3,623	3,074
Armstrong	1,014	1,528
Beaver	2,077	1,075
Bedford	1,920	1,587
Berks	1,584	4,967
Bradford	1,521	1,463
Bucks	3,289	3,081
Butler	1,166	1,008
Cambria	554	450
Centre	924	1,809
Chester	3,921	3,277
Clearfield	284	499
Columbia	544	1,560
Crawford	1,232	1,614
Cumberland	1,696	1,904
Dauphin	1,993	1,372
Delaware	1,224	1,030
Erie	2,134	1,312
Fayette	1,669	2,016
Franklin	2,575	2,155
Greene	915	1,138
Huntingdon	2,628	1,340
Indiana	1,169	692
Jefferson	229	244
Juniata	596	627
Lancaster	6,250	4,144
Lebanon	1,487	1,168
Lehigh	1,784	1,987
Luzerne	938	1,705
Lycoming	1,415	2,008
Mercer	1,991	1,253
Mifflin	748	917
Monroe	166	796
Montgomery	2,409	3,446
Northampton	1,426	2,378
Northumberland	712	1,421
Perry	473	1,107
Philadelphia (City)	5,746	3,028
Philadelphia (County)	6,475	7,965
Pike	50	358
Potter and McKean	135	312
Schuylkill	687	1,380
Somerset	1,905	511
Susquehanna	856	1,145
Tioga	400	1,027
Union	1,328	1,143
Venango	600	967
Warren	254	498
Washington	2,805	2,445
Wayne	340	724
Westmoreland	1,725	2,878
York	2,005	2,756
Total	87,111	91,475

[2] *Niles' Register*, LI (November 26, 1836), 195.

APPENDIX

Vote for Governor, 1838[1]

County	Porter	Ritner
Adams	1,535	3,310
Allegheny	4,505	6,038
Armstrong	2,781	1,510
Beaver	1,931	2,457
Bedford	2,384	2,290
Berks	7,101	3,215
Bradford	2,420	2,219
Bucks	4,553	4,147
Butler	1,653	1,700
Cambria	844	762
Centre	2,589	1,467
Chester	4,527	4,971
Clearfield	792	474
Columbia	2,616	1,088
Crawford	2,304	1,957
Cumberland	2,743	2,316
Dauphin	1,944	2,843
Delaware	1,263	1,731
Erie	1,565	2,747
Fayette	2,788	1,984
Franklin	2,815	2,560
Greene	1,849	1,109
Huntingdon	2,761	3,687
Indiana	1,262	1,723
Jefferson	591	421
Juniata	1,049	863
Lancaster	5,503	8,558
Lebanon	1,553	2,228
Lehigh	2,460	2,349
Luzerne	3,132	2,592
Lycoming	2,496	1,555
McKean	219	127
Mercer	2,326	2,935
Mifflin	1,177	1,109
Monroe	1,223	366
Montgomery	4,558	3,748
Northampton	3,634	2,566
Northumberland	2,144	1,164
Perry	1,916	883
Philadelphia (City and County)	8,041	13,485
Pike	526	117
Potter	276	68
Schuylkill	2,271	1,508
Somerset	883	2,244
Susquehanna	1,530	1,264
Tioga	1,448	594
Union	1,595	2,268
Venango	1,765	828
Warren	700	542
Washington	3,461	3,528
Wayne	1,062	538
Westmoreland	4,561	2,315
York	4,196	3,257
Total	127,821	122,325

[1] Pennsylvania, Senate Journal, 1838-39, I, 42-43.

Vote for Presidential Electors, 1840[2]

County	Harrison	Van Buren
Adams	2,453	1,628
Allegheny	7,620	4,573
Armstrong	1,260	1,744
Beaver	3,143	1,710
Bedford	2,910	2,446
Berks	3,582	7,425
Bradford	2,631	2,844
Bucks	4,705	4,488
Butler	2,100	1,804
Cambria	811	920
Centre	1,447	2,242
Chester	5,643	4,882
Clarion	648	1,366
Clearfield	499	812
Clinton	637	649
Columbia	1,325	2,829
Crawford	2,469	2,908
Cumberland	2,790	2,695
Dauphin	3,124	2,187
Delaware	2,031	1,335
Erie	3,636	2,061
Fayette	2,755	3,035
Franklin	3,586	2,892
Greene	1,350	2,010
Huntingdon	3,826	2,266
Indiana	1,953	1,209
Jefferson	476	592
Juniata	966	1,043
Lancaster	9,678	5,472
Lebanon	2,369	1,402
Lehigh	2,405	2,451
Luzerne	2,774	4,119
Lycoming	1,504	2,181
McKean	262	275
Mercer	3,249	2,336
Mifflin	1,226	1,269
Monroe	345	1,447
Montgomery	4,068	4,869
Northampton	2,846	3,838
Northumberland	1,351	2,187
Perry	1,072	1,970
Philadelphia (City)	7,655	4,774
Philadelphia (County)	10,189	13,303
Pike	135	524
Potter	180	363
Schuylkill	1,881	2,184
Somerset	2,501	765
Susquehanna	1,560	2,023
Tioga	895	1,721
Union	2,423	1,518
Venango	855	1,275
Warren	827	929
Washington	4,147	3,611
Wayne	675	1,188
Westmoreland	2,778	4,704
York	3,792	4,382
Total	144,018	143,675

[2] Niles' Register, LIX (November 14, 1840), 165.

Vote for Governor, 1841[1]

County	Porter	Banks
Adams	1,599	1,941
Allegheny	4,281	5,068
Armstrong	1,756	998
Beaver	1,751	2,158
Bedford	2,550	2,261
Berks	7,495	2,925
Bradford	2,705	2,143
Bucks	4,412	4,066
Butler	1,674	1,716
Cambria	874	810
Centre	2,300	1,126
Chester	4,565	4,711
Clarion	1,500	555
Clearfield	886	419
Clinton	786	603
Columbia	2,569	1,103
Crawford	2,815	2,099
Cumberland	2,721	1,977
Dauphin	2,249	2,649
Delaware	1,289	1,578
Erie	1,855	2,956
Fayette	2,749	1,812
Franklin	2,779	2,636
Greene	1,763	949
Huntingdon	2,551	3,258
Indiana	1,195	1,557
Jefferson	678	447
Juniata	971	868
Lancaster	4,914	8,085
Lebanon	1,542	1,840
Lehigh	2,553	2,328
Luzerne	3,426	2,194
Lycoming	2,261	1,393
McKean	236	199
Mercer	2,318	2,760
Mifflin	1,324	1,124
Monroe	1,293	269
Montgomery	4,402	3,144
Northampton	3,467	2,302
Northumberland	2,162	1,143
Perry	1,827	870
Philadelphia (City and County)	15,479	13,268
Pike	540	74
Potter	365	154
Schuylkill	2,408	1,415
Somerset	792	1,853
Susquehanna	1,962	1,152
Tioga	1,598	574
Union	1,568	2,132
Venango	1,280	755
Warren	963	628
Washington	3,434	3,291
Wayne	1,167	553
Westmoreland	4,080	2,135
York	3,825	2,429
Total	136,504	113,473

[1] Pennsylvania, *Senate Journal*, 1842, I, 113-114.

Scattering votes were cast as follows:

F. J. Lemoyne	763
George F. Horton	18
Samuel L. Carpenter	4
Ellis Lewis	1

The figures and the totals listed above are given as printed, but the correct total of the county figures shown for Banks is 113,453.

Vote for Governor, 1844[2]

County	Shunk	Markle
Adams	1,848	2,4..
Allegheny	5,863	8,1..
Armstrong	1,986	1,4..
Beaver	2,093	2,7..
Bedford	2,884	3,0..
Berks	8,316	3,8..
Bradford	3,525	2,9..
Bucks	5,106	4,8..
Butler	2,054	2,1..
Cambria	1,129	9..
Carbon	784	4..
Centre	2,384	1,7..
Chester	5,475	6,1..
Clarion	1,889	7..
Clearfield	938	5..
Clinton	925	8..
Columbia	3,199	1,5..
Crawford	2,920	2,4..
Cumberland	3,008	2,9..
Dauphin	2,352	3,2..
Delaware	1,493	2,0..
Elk	132	1
Erie	2,207	3,5..
Fayette	3,304	2,8..
Franklin	3,211	3,7..
Greene	2,255	1,4..
Huntingdon	2,630	4,0..
Indiana	1,417	2,0..
Jefferson	727	6..
Juniata	1,188	1,0..
Lancaster	5,532	9,5..
Lebanon	1,748	2,4..
Lehigh	2,680	2,4..
Luzerne	3,649	2,5..
Lycoming	2,600	1,9..
McKean	416	3..
Mercer	2,744	2,7..
Mifflin	1,585	1,5..
Monroe	1,601	3..
Montgomery	5,394	4,3..
Northampton	3,466	2,4..
Northumberland	2,384	1,4..
Perry	2,246	1,3..
Philadelphia (City and County)	17,465	23,4..
Pike	643	1..
Potter	527	2..
Schuylkill	3,217	2,3..
Somerset	922	2,4..
Susquehanna	2,468	1,5..
Tioga	1,975	1,0..
Union	1,777	2,7..
Venango	1,230	8..
Warren	1,107	8..
Washington	3,958	3,9..
Wayne	1,553	8..
Westmoreland	4,704	2,7..
Wyoming	808	7..
York	4,691	3,8..
Total	160,322	156,0..

[2] Pennsylvania, *Senate Journal*, 1845, 68-69.

Scattering votes were cast as follows:

F. J. Lemoyne	2,566
J. J. Lemoyne	10
John Haney	2
James Page	1
Scattering	1

APPENDIX

Vote for Presidential Electors, 1844[1]

County	Polk	Clay
Adams	1,891	2,609
Allegheny	5,743	8,083
Armstrong	1,983	1,453
Beaver	2,172	2,792
Bedford	2,989	3,147
Berks	8,674	4,000
Bradford	3,568	3,235
Bucks	5,251	4,862
Butler	2,112	2,247
Cambria	1,123	996
Carbon	905	531
Centre	2,425	1,860
Chester	5,550	6,070
Clarion	1,883	814
Clearfield	874	544
Clinton	875	788
Columbia	3,370	1,738
Crawford	3,334	2,636
Cumberland	3,155	3,092
Dauphin	2,401	3,285
Delaware	1,466	2,090
Elk	128	101
Erie	2,226	3,621
Fayette	3,429	2,804
Franklin	3,298	3,901
Greene	2,354	1,418
Huntingdon	2,575	4,086
Indiana	1,448	2,200
Jefferson	731	591
Juniata	1,260	1,089
Lancaster	5,943	10,295
Lebanon	1,791	2,636
Lehigh	2,811	2,553
Luzerne	3,950	2,699
Lycoming	2,629	2,012
McKean	129	(majority)
Mercer	2,869	2,840
Mifflin	1,519	1,518
Monroe	1,806	414
Montgomery	5,596	4,491
Northampton	3,870	2,776
Northumberland	2,446	1,547
Perry	2,321	1,370
Philadelphia (City)	5,369	9,317
Philadelphia (County)	13,482	13,972
Pike	769	151
Potter	554	240
Schuylkill	3,404	2,571
Somerset	1,035	2,660
Susquehanna	2,697	1,802
Tioga	2,193	1,169
Union	1,765	2,788
Venango	1,377	966
Warren	1,149	899
Washington	3,973	3,872
Wayne	1,657	899
Westmoreland	4,978	2,672
Wyoming	899	814
York	5,071	4,237
Total	167,245	160,863

[1] *Niles' Register*, LXVII (November 23, 1844), 181.
The figures for Allegheny and Washington counties have been corrected from the Philadelphia *Public Ledger*, November 14, 1844.

Vote for Governor, 1847[2]

County	Shunk	Irvin	Reigart
Adams	1,558	1,946	2
Allegheny	4,453	5,753	599
Armstrong	2,136	1,518	13
Beaver	2,034	2,203	66
Bedford	2,458	2,205	
Berks	8,088	3,357	187
Blair	1,254	1,854	2
Bradford	3,058	2,520	
Bucks	4,685	4,341	17
Butler	1,931	1,860	12
Cambria	1,139	974	
Carbon	786	484	
Centre	2,477	1,782	
Chester	4,614	5,152	136
Clarion	1,607	631	5
Clearfield	867	582	2
Clinton	966	685	1
Columbia	2,913	1,506	5
Crawford	2,265	1,686	
Cumberland	2,867	2,559	7
Dauphin	1,872	2,790	212
Delaware	1,484	1,719	32
Elk	182	93	
Erie	1,728	2,586	
Fayette	2,811	2,113	
Franklin	2,762	3,219	2
Greene	1,914	880	
Huntingdon	1,641	2,012	
Indiana	1,415	2,052	1
Jefferson	709	454	
Juniata	986	975	2
Lancaster	4,931	8,741	354
Lebanon	1,600	2,149	
Lehigh	2,583	2,239	1
Luzerne	3,296	2,017	2
Lycoming	1,874	1,528	3
McKean	313	252	
Mercer	2,617	2,616	
Mifflin	1,431	1,289	27
Monroe	1,418	347	
Montgomery	5,141	3,723	178
Northampton	2,862	2,359	45
Northumberland	1,971	1,231	41
Perry	1,728	1,106	19
Philadelphia (City and County)	16,510	14,117	9,038
Pike	671	142	
Potter	530	183	
Schuylkill	3,720	2,833	229
Somerset	913	2,162	
Sullivan	317	130	
Susquehanna	2,352	1,463	4
Tioga	1,750	972	
Union	1,479	2,463	
Venango	1,326	802	
Warren	849	659	
Washington	3,531	3,335	
Wayne	1,291	686	
Westmoreland	4,525	2,337	1
Wyoming	819	653	
York	4,007	3,103	2
Castle of Perote (Soldiers in Mexico)	66	20	
Total	146,081	128,148	11,247

[2] Pennsylvania, *Senate Journal*, 1848, II, 85-86.
Scattering votes were cast as follows:
F. J. Lemoyne 1,861
Abijah Morrison 3
George M. Keim 1
Scattering 2

APPENDIX

Vote for Governor, 1848[1]

County	Johnston	Longstreth
Adams	2,331	1,806
Allegheny	8,856	6,164
Armstrong	2,094	2,133
Beaver	2,764	2,383
Bedford	2,613	2,739
Berks	4,207	8,411
Blair	2,293	1,427
Bradford	3,241	3,748
Bucks	5,084	5,245
Butler	2,410	2,308
Cambria	1,151	1,421
Carbon	768	996
Centre	1,649	2,544
Chester	5,895	5,140
Clarion	1,255	2,238
Clearfield	630	1,111
Clinton	808	1,004
Columia	1,980	3,157
Crawford	2,580	2,849
Cumberland	2,989	3,069
Dauphin	3,249	2,269
Delaware	1,975	1,500
Elk	145	283
Erie	3,500	2,087
Fayette	2,776	3,290
Franklin	3,758	2,988
Greene	1,354	2,362
Huntingdon	2,289	1,871
Indiana	2,371	1,568
Jefferson	783	992
Juniata	1,103	1,201
Lancaster	9,727	5,514
Lebanon	2,637	1,800
Lehigh	2,550	2,996
Luzerne	2,967	3,785
Lycoming	1,850	2,298
McKean	376	429
Mercer	3,643	3,109
Mifflin	1,443	1,591
Monroe	425	1,769
Montgomery	4,645	5,218
Northampton	2,551	3,476
Northumberland	1,546	2,124
Perry	1,339	2,064
Philadelphia (City and County)	25,961	21,000
Pike	126	612
Potter	278	627
Schuylkill	4,264	3,538
Somerset	2,755	1,103
Sullivan	182	360
Susquehanna	1,597	2,416
Tioga	1,219	2,077
Union	2,887	1,686
Venango	988	1,532
Warren	947	1,145
Washington	4,065	3,949
Wayne	855	1,455
Westmoreland	2,856	4,955
Wyoming	780	948
York	4,162	4,345
Total	168,522	168,225

[1] Pennsylvania, *Senate Journal, 1849*, II, 347-349.
Scattering votes were cast as follows:
E. D. Gazzam 48
Thomas Earle 7
F. J. Lemoyne 6
George W. Jackson ... 1
William Lorimer, Jr... 1
William Elder 1
E. C. Reigart 1
Scattering 7

Vote for Presidential Electors, 1848[2]

County	Taylor	Cass	Van Buren
Adams	2,576	1,762	25
Allegheny	10,112	6,591	779
Armstrong	2,030	2,126	141
Beaver	2,655	2,303	530
Bedford	2,836	2,816	1
Berks	5,082	9,485	51
Blair	2,476	1,435	4
Bradford	3,272	1,889	1,779
Bucks	5,140	5,364	163
Butler	2,505	2,247	190
Cambria	1,233	1,386	12
Carbon	889	1,181	1
Centre	1,856	2,611	4
Chester	5,949	5,360	507
Clarion	1,372	2,316	35
Clearfield	761	1,168	23
Clinton	911	967	1
Columbia	2,263	3,396	27
Crawford	2,205	2,748	624
Cumberland	3,242	3,178	25
Dauphin	3,708	2,254	34
Delaware	2,194	1,547	84
Elk	134	242	26
Erie	3,418	2,022	356
Fayette	3,045	3,441	73
Franklin	4,006	3,199	4
Greene	1,476	2,379	49
Huntingdon	2,590	1,922	25
Indiana	2,410	1,544	204
Jefferson	887	972	19
Juniata	1,179	1,212	3
Lancaster	11,390	6,080	163
Lebanon	2,996	1,862	2
Lehigh	2,978	3,199	3
Luzerne	3,516	3,991	176
Lycoming	2,036	2,357	9
McKean	367	418	22
Mercer	2,977	3,094	1,080
Mifflin	1,548	1,586	26
Monroe	518	1,830	3
Montgomery	5,040	5,627	251
Northampton	3,191	4,203	38
Northumberland	1,765	2,258	8
Perry	1,562	2,295	5
Philadelphia (City)	10,655	5,266	309
Philadelphia (County)	20,575	16,244	568
Pike	216	799	3
Potter	226	468	248
Schuylkill	4,939	3,700	35
Somerset	3,018	1,127	21
Sullivan	129	303	19
Susquehanna	1,853	2,568	301
Tioga	1,350	1,344	953
Union	3,129	1,656	25
Venango	1,061	1,538	164
Warren	948	1,088	136
Washington	3,898	3,820	468
Wayne	997	1,642	202
Westmoreland	3,124	5,197	122
Wyoming	861	892	37
York	4,838	5,151	4
Total	186,113	172,661	11,200

[2] *Niles' Register*, LXXIV (December 6, 1848), 367. The original list gave Cass only 2,197 votes in Westmoreland County. This was corrected by a reference to the figures shown in Pennsylvania, *Senate Journal, 1849*, II, 468-479. As listed above the sum of the individual county votes for Cass is 172,666 rather than the 172,661 shown.

APPENDIX

Congressional Apportionment, 1832[1]

District Number	Counties	Congressmen
1	Philadelphia County (south and west)	1
2	Philadelphia City	2
3	Philadelphia County (northeast)	1
4	Delaware, Chester, and Lancaster	3
5	Montgomery	1
6	Bucks	1
7	Northampton, Pike, and Wayne	1
8	Schuylkill and Lehigh	1
9	Berks	1
10	Dauphin and Lebanon	1
11	York	1
12	Adams and Franklin	1
13	Cumberland, Perry, and Juniata	1
14	Mifflin, Huntingdon, and Centre	1
15	Columbia and Luzerne	1
16	Union, Northumberland, and Lycoming	1
17	Susquehanna, Bradford, Tioga, Potter, and McKean	1
18	Bedford, Somerset, and Cambria	1
19	Westmoreland and Indiana	1
20	Fayette and Green	1
21	Washington	1
22	Allegheny	1
23	Clearfield, Jefferson, Armstrong, and Butler	1
24	Beaver and Mercer	1
25	Erie, Crawford, Warren, and Venango	1
	Total	28

Congressional Apportionment, 1843[2]

1	Philadelphia City and County	1
2	Philadelphia City and County	1
3	Philadelphia City and County	1
4	Philadelphia City and County	1
5	Delaware and Montgomery	1
6	Bucks and Lehigh	1
7	Chester	1
8	Lancaster	1
9	Berks	1
10	Northampton, Monroe, Pike, and Wayne	1
11	Luzerne, Columbia, and Wyoming	1
12	Susquehanna, Bradford, and Tioga	1
13	Northumberland, Lycoming, Union, and Clinton	1
14	Dauphin, Lebanon, and Schuylkill	1
15	Adams and York	1
16	Cumberland, Perry, and Franklin	1
17	Huntingdon, Centre, Juniata, and Mifflin	1
18	Somerset, Fayette, and Greene	1
19	Westmoreland, Bedford, and Cambria	1
20	Washington and Beaver	1
21	Allegheny	1
22	Crawford, Venango, and Mercer	1
23	Erie, Warren, McKean, Potter, Jefferson, and Clarion	1
24	Armstrong, Butler, Indiana, and Clearfield	1
	Total	24

[1] Pennsylvania, *Laws, 1831-1832*, pp. 560-61.
[2] Pennsylvania, *Laws, 1843*, pp. 115-17.

APPENDIX

Senatorial Apportionment, 1829[1]

District Number	Counties	Senators
1	Philadelphia City	2
2	Philadelphia County	3
3	Montgomery	1
4	Chester and Delaware	2
5	Bucks	1
6	Berks and Schuylkill	2
7	Lancaster	2
8	Dauphin and Lebanon	1
9	Northumberland and Union	1
10	Luzerne and Columbia	1
11	Susquehanna, Bradford, and Tioga	1
12	Northampton, Lehigh, Wayne, and Pike	2
13	Lycoming, Centre, Clearfield, Potter, and McKean	1
14	York and Adams	2
15	Franklin	1
16	Cumberland and Perry	1
17	Huntingdon, Mifflin, and Cambria	1
18	Westmoreland	1
19	Fayette and Greene	1
20	Washington	1
21	Allegheny	1
22	Bedford and Somerset	1
23	Erie, Crawford, and Mercer	1
24	Armstrong, Venango, Warren, Indiana, and Jefferson	1
25	Beaver and Butler	1
	Total	33

Senatorial Apportionment, 1836[2]

1	Philadelphia City	2
2	Philadelphia County	3
3	Montgomery, Chester, and Delaware	3
4	Bucks	1
5	Berks	1
6	Lancaster and York	3
7	Dauphin and Lebanon	1
8	Perry, Mifflin, Juniata, Huntingdon, and Union	2
9	Columbia and Schuylkill	1
10	Lehigh and Northampton	1
11	Luzerne, Monroe, Wayne, and Pike	1
12	Lycoming, Northumberland, and Centre	1
13	Bradford and Susquehanna	1
14	Franklin, Cumberland, and Adams	2
15	Bedford and Somerset	1
16	Westmoreland	1
17	Washington	1
18	Fayette and Greene	1
19	Allegheny and Butler	2
20	Beaver and Mercer	1
21	Crawford and Erie	1
22	Jefferson, McKean, Potter, Tioga, Warren, and Venango	1
23	Indiana, Armstrong, Cambria, and Clearfield	1
	Total	33

[1] Pennsylvania, *Laws, 1828-1829*, pp. 212-13.
[2] Pennsylvania, *Laws, 1835-1836*, pp. 794-95.

APPENDIX

Senatorial Apportionment, 1843[1]

District Number	Counties	Senators
1	Philadelphia City	2
2	Philadelphia County	3
3	Montgomery	1
4	Chester and Delaware	1
5	Berks	1
6	Bucks	1
7	Lancaster and Lebanon	2
8	Schuylkill, Monroe, Carbon, and Pike	1
9	Northampton and Lehigh	1
10	Susquehanna, Wayne, and Wyoming	1
11	Bradford and Tioga	1
12	Lycoming, Centre, and Clinton	1
13	Luzerne and Columbia	1
14	Northumberland and Dauphin	1
15	Mifflin, Juniata, and Union	1
16	Cumberland and Perry	1
17	York	1
18	Franklin and Adams	1
19	Huntingdon and Bedford	1
20	Clearfield, Indiana, Cambria, and Armstrong	1
21	Westmoreland and Somerset	1
22	Fayette and Greene	1
23	Washington	1
24	Allegheny and Butler	2
25	Beaver and Mercer	1
26	Crawford and Venango	1
27	Erie	1
28	Warren, Jefferson, Clarion, McKean, and Potter	1
	Total	33

[1] Pennsylvania, *Laws, 1843*, pp. 247-49.

Bibliography

MANUSCRIPT COLLECTIONS

AMERICAN PHILOSOPHICAL SOCIETY LIBRARY, Philadelphia:
  Henry A. Muhlenberg Papers
  Mrs. Jesse A. Wagner Papers

CARNEGIE LIBRARY OF PITTSBURGH:
  Harmar Denny Papers
  Governor George Wolf Papers

HAVERFORD COLLEGE:
  Roberts Collection

THE HISTORICAL SOCIETY OF PENNSYLVANIA, Philadelphia:
  William Bigler Papers
  James Buchanan Papers
  Conarroe Autograph Collection
  Lewis S. Coryell Correspondence
  Dallas Papers
  "Descriptive Catalogue of the Records of the Bank of North America Deposited with the Historical Society of Pennsylvania"
  Dreer Collection
  Etting Collection
  The Edward Carey Gardiner Collection
  Gilpin Papers
  Gratz Collection:
    Attorneys General of Pennsylvania
    Benjamin S. Bonsall Correspondence
    Governors of Pennsylvania
    Simon Gratz Correspondence
    William Orbison Correspondence
    Samuel D. Patterson Correspondence
  Josiah Stoddard Johnston Papers
  J. Glancy Jones Papers
  Ellis Lewis Papers
  Brigadier General William MacPherson Papers
  Meredith Papers
  Joel Roberts Poinsett Papers
  W. W. Porter Papers
  John Sergeant Papers
  Society Autograph Collection
  Vaux Papers
  John William Wallace Collection
  George Wolf Political Correspondence

LIBRARY COMPANY OF PHILADELPHIA:
  Miscellaneous Collection

BIBLIOGRAPHY

LIBRARY OF CONGRESS, Washington, D. C.:
  Nicholas Biddle Papers
  Daniel M. Brodhead Papers
  Buchanan-Johnston Papers
  John C. Calhoun Papers
  Simon Cameron Papers
  John M. Clayton Papers
  Andrew Jackson Papers
  John McLean Papers
  Edward McPherson Papers
  Personal Miscellany
  James K. Polk Papers
  Thaddeus Stevens Papers
  John Tyler Papers
  Martin Van Buren Papers
  Daniel Webster Papers

PENNSYLVANIA HISTORICAL AND MUSEUM COMMISSION, DIVISION OF PUBLIC RECORDS, Harrisburg:
  Colonel Reah Frazer Family Papers
  Miscellaneous Papers
  Secretary of the Commonwealth, Minutes and Papers, 1790-1843

UNIVERSITY OF PENNSYLVANIA LIBRARY, Philadelphia:
  Thomas H. Burrowes Letter Book
  Reah Frazer Papers

WYOMING HISTORICAL AND GEOLOGICAL SOCIETY, Wilkes-Barre:
  Hendrick B. Wright Papers

NEWSPAPERS

CHAMBERSBURG:
  Repository and Whig, 1842.

DANVILLE:
  Intelligencer, 1832-1836.

HARRISBURG:
  Antimasonic State Journal, 1836.
  Argus, 1843, 1845-1848.
  Chronicle, 1836-1840.
  Democratic Union, 1843-1846.
  Keystone, 1836-1843.
  Pennsylvania Reporter, 1835-1838.
  Telegraph, 1836-1840.

LEWISBURG:
  Chronicle, 1843-1844.
  Democrat, 1835-1836.
  Peoples' Advocate, 1838-1841.
  Standard, 1838-1839.

MILTON:
  Miltonian, 1832-1834.

BIBLIOGRAPHY

New Berlin:
: *Antimasonic Star*, 1835.
: *Union Star*, 1840.
: *Union Times*, 1844.

Philadelphia:
: *American Sentinel*, 1834-1841.
: *Gazette*, 1838.
: *Hazard's Register of Pennsylvania*, 1832-1838.
: *Inquirer*, 1834-1841.
: *National Gazette*, 1836-1838.
: *North American*, 1844-1847.
: *North American and United States Gazette*, 1847-1848.
: *Pennsylvanian*, 1833-1848.
: *Public Ledger*, 1840.
: *Spirit of the Times*, 1842.
: *United States Gazette*, 1835-1838, 1840-1846.

Pittsburgh:
: *Allegheny Democrat*, 1833-1835.
: *Daily Advocate and Advertiser*, 1834-1835, 1838-1839.
: *Gazette*, 1840-1841, 1844-1845.
: *Weekly Mercury and Manufacturer*, 1843-1844.

Pottsville:
: *Miners' Journal*, 1846.

Wilkes-Barre:
: *Luzerne Democrat*, 1847.
: *Republican Farmer and Democratic Journal*, 1835-1838, 1843, 1847.

York:
: *Democratic Press*, 1845-1847.
: *Gazette*, 1833-1835.

Baltimore, Maryland:
: *Niles' Weekly Register*, 1832-1848.

Washington, D. C.:
: *Globe*, 1833-1834.

PUBLIC DOCUMENTS

Pennsylvania:
: *Journal of the ... House of Representatives*, 1833-1849.
: *Journal of the ... Senate*, 1833-1849.
: *Laws ... of the State of Pennsylvania*, 1829-1848.
: *Pennsylvania Archives*, 4th Series. 12 vols. Harrisburg, 1900-1902.
: ———, 9th Series. 10 vols. Harrisburg, 1931-1935.
: *Proceedings and Debates of the Convention of the Commonwealth of Pennsylvania, to Propose Amendments to the Constitution, Commenced and Held at Harrisburg on the Second Day of May, 1837*. 14 vols. Harrisburg, 1837-1839.

United States:
: *Congressional Globe*, 1834-1873. Washington, 1834-1873.
: *Fifth Census; or Enumeration of the Inhabitants of the United States, 1830*. Washington, 1832.
: *Register of Debates in Congress*, 1825-1837. Washington, 1825-1837.

BIBLIOGRAPHY

Richardson, James D., comp. *A Compilation of the Messages and Papers of the Presidents, 1789-1897.* 10 vols. Washington, 1896-1900.

Sixth Census or Enumeration of the Inhabitants of the United States . . . in 1840. Washington, 1841.

Statistical View of the United States, . . . Being a Compendium of the Seventh Census. . . . Washington, 1854.

PRINTED CORRESPONDENCE

Adams, Henry, ed. *The Writings of Albert Gallatin.* 3 vols. Philadelphia, 1879.

Bassett, John S., ed. *Correspondence of Andrew Jackson.* 7 vols. Washington, 1926-1935.

Boucher, Chauncey S., and Robert P. Brooks, eds. "Correspondence Addressed to John C. Calhoun," American Historical Association, *Annual Report, 1929,* pp. 125-533. Washington, 1930.

Colton, Calvin, ed. *The Private Correspondence of Henry Clay.* New York, 1855.

————, ed. *The Works of Henry Clay, Comprising His Life, Correspondence, and Speeches.* 10 vols. New York and London, 1904.

Jameson, J. Franklin, ed. *Correspondence of John C. Calhoun,* American Historical Association, *Annual Report, 1899,* Vol. II. Washington, 1900.

"Letters of James K. Polk to Andrew J. Donelson, 1843-1848," *Tennessee Historical Magazine,* III (1917), 51-73.

"Letters of James K. Polk to Cave Johnson, 1833-1848," *Tennessee Historical Magazine,* I (1915), 209-256.

McGrane, Reginald C., ed. *The Correspondence of Nicholas Biddle Dealing with National Affairs, 1807-1844.* Boston, 1919.

Moore, John Bassett, ed. *The Works of James Buchanan, Comprising His Speeches, State Papers, and Private Correspondence.* 12 vols. Philadelphia, 1908-1911.

"Unpublished Letters of James Buchanan," Lancaster County Historical Society, *Papers,* XXXII (1928), 67-72.

Webster, Fletcher, ed. *Private Correspondence of Daniel Webster.* 2 vols. Boston, 1857.

DIARIES, MEMOIRS, AND REMINISCENCES

Adams, Charles Francis, ed. *Memoirs of John Quincy Adams, Comprising Portions of His Diary from 1795 to 1848.* 12 vols. Philadelphia, 1874-1877.

Binns, John. *Recollections of the Life of John Binns, Written by Himself. . . .* Philadelphia, 1854.

Elder, William. *A Memoir of Henry C. Carey.* Philadelphia, 1880.

Fitzpatrick, John C., ed. *The Autobiography of Martin Van Buren,* American Historical Association, *Annual Report, 1918,* Vol. II. Washington, 1920.

Forney, John W. *Anecdotes of Public Men.* New York, 1873.

Kennedy, John P. *Memoirs of the Life of William Wirt, Attorney General of the United States.* 2 vols. Philadelphia, 1849.

Klein, Philip S., ed. "Memoirs of a Senator from Pennsylvania: Jonathan Roberts, 1771-1854," *Pennsylvania Magazine of History and Biography,* LXI (1937), 446-474; LXII (1938), 64-97, 213-248, 361-409, 502-551.

BIBLIOGRAPHY

McClure, Alexander K. *Old Time Notes of Pennsylvania.* 2 vols. Philadelphia, 1905.

Nevins, Allan, ed. *The Diary of Philip Hone, 1828-1851.* 2 vols. New York, 1927.

————, ed. *Polk: The Diary of a President, 1845-1849.* London and New York, 1952.

Quaife, Milo M., ed. *The Diary of James K. Polk During His Presidency, 1845-1849.* 4 vols. Chicago, 1910.

Roberts, Thomas P. *Memoirs of John Bannister Gibson.* Pittsburg, 1890.

Sargent, Nathan. *Public Men and Events. . . .* 2 vols. Philadelphia, 1875.

Stickney, William, ed. *Autobiography of Amos Kendall.* Boston, 1872.

Weed, Harriet A., ed. *Life of Thurlow Weed, Including His Autobiography and a Memoir.* 2 vols. Boston, 1884.

POLITICAL PAMPHLETS AND CONTEMPORARY WRITINGS

Barker, Charles R. "Philadelphia in the Late Forties," Philadelphia City Historical Society, *Publications,* II (1931), 245-274.

Benton, Thomas Hart. *Thirty Years' View: or, A History of the Working of the American Government for Thirty Years, from 1820 to 1850.* 2 vols. New York, 1854-1856.

Biographical Sketch, and Services of Commodore Charles Stewart of the Navy of the United States. Philadelphia, 1838.

Biographical Sketch of George M. Dallas. n. p., n. d.

Bowen, Eli. *Locomotive Sketches . . . from Philadelphia to Pittsburg.* Philadelphia, 1854.

————. *The Pictorial Sketch-Book of Pennsylvania.* Philadelphia, 1852.

Bradford, Thomas G. *Illustrated Atlas, Geographical, Statistical, Historical, of the United States.* Boston, 1838.

Byrdsall, Fitzwilliam. *The History of the Loco-Foco or Equal Rights Party.* New York, 1842.

Carey, Mathew. *Brief View of the System of Internal Improvement of the State of Pennsylvania.* Philadelphia, 1831.

Desilver, Robert. *Desilver's United States Register and Almanac.* Philadelphia, 1833, 1835, 1836.

Duane, William J. *Narrative and Correspondence Concerning the Removal of the Deposites, and Occurrences Connected Therewith.* Philadelphia, 1838.

Eaton, Rebecca. *A Geography of Pennsylvania.* Philadelphia, 1835.

Ferguson, Russell J., ed. "Minutes of the Young Men's Whig Association of Pittsburgh, 1834," *Western Pennsylvania Historical Magazine,* XIX (1936), 213-220.

Gordon, Thomas F. *A Gazetteer of the State of Pennsylvania.* Philadelphia, 1832.

Handlin, Oscar, ed. *This Was America.* Cambridge, 1949.

Lee, John H. *The Origin and Progress of the American Party in Politics.* Philadelphia, 1855.

McElroy, A. *McElroy's Directory.* 1837, 1843.

Matthias, Benjamin. *The Politician's Register.* Philadelphia, 1835.

Political Antimasonry, Abolition and Amalgamation in Pennsylvania. Philadelphia, 1838.

Prolix, Peregrine [Philip Holbrook Nicklin]. *A Pleasant Peregrination Through the Prettiest Parts of Pennsylvania.* Philadelphia, 1836.

Sturtevant, Peleg. *The Buckshot War; or, the Last Kick of Anti-Masonry. A Burlesque, Medley, Poetic, Prosaic, Humorous, Satirical, etc.* Harrisburg, 1839.

Trego, Charles B. *A Geography of Pennsylvania.* Philadelphia, 1843.

GENERAL WORKS, MONOGRAPHS, AND ARTICLES

Adams, Henry. *History of the United States of America.* 9 vols. New York, 1889-1891.

Agnew, Daniel. "The Scotch-Irish of Pennsylvania," Scotch-Irish Congress, *Proceedings,* II (1890), 247-255.

Akagi, Roy H. "The Pennsylvania Constitution of 1838," *Pennsylvania Magazine of History and Biography,* XLVIII (1924), 301-333.

Albion, Robert G. *The Rise of New York Port.* New York, 1939.

Alexander, De Alva S. *A Political History of the State of New York.* 3 vols. New York, 1906-1909.

Andrews, J. Cutler. "The Antimasonic Movement in Western Pennsylvania," *Western Pennsylvania Historical Magazine,* XVIII (1935), 255-266.

——————. *Pittsburgh's Post-Gazette.* Boston, 1936.

Baldwin, Summerfield. "The Pennsylvania Argus: A Chapter in Westmoreland County Political Journalism," *Western Pennsylvania Historical Magazine,* XVII (1934), 77-91.

Bartlett, Marguerite G. *The Chief Phases of Pennsylvania Politics in the Jacksonian Period.* Philadelphia, 1919.

Bining, Arthur C. "The Rise of Iron Manufacture in Western Pennsylvania," *Western Pennsylvania Historical Magazine,* XVI (1933), 235-256.

Bishop, Avard L. "Corrupt Practices Connected with the Building of the State Works of Pennsylvania," *Yale Review,* XV (1907), 391-411.

——————. "The State Works of Pennsylvania," Connecticut Academy of Arts and Sciences, *Transactions,* XIII (1907), 149-297.

Blau, Joseph L., ed. *Social Theories of Jacksonian Democracy.* New York, 1947.

Bowers, Claude G. *The Party Battles of the Jackson Period.* Boston and New York, 1922.

Brunhouse, Robert L. *The Counter-Revolution in Pennsylvania, 1776-1790.* Harrisburg, 1942.

Carroll, E. Malcolm. *Origins of the Whig Party.* Durham, 1925.

Catterall, Ralph C. H. *The Second Bank of the United States.* Chicago, 1902.

Clark, Joseph S., Jr. "The Railroad Struggle for Pittsburgh: Forty-three Years of Philadelphia-Baltimore Rivalry, 1838-1871," *Pennsylvania Magazine of History and Biography,* XLVIII (1924), 1-38.

Clark, Victor S. *History of Manufactures in the United States.* 2 vols. Washington, 1916-1928.

BIBLIOGRAPHY

Cole, Arthur C. *The Whig Party in the South.* Washington, 1913.

Cornell, William M. *The History of Pennsylvania from the Earliest Discovery to the Present Time.* Philadelphia, 1876.

Crall, F. Frank. "A Half-Century of Rivalry Between Pittsburgh and Wheeling," *Western Pennsylvania Historical Magazine,* XIII (1930), 237-255.

Curti, Merle. *The Growth of American Thought.* New York and London, 1943.

Darling, Arthur B. *Political Changes in Massachusetts, 1824-1848.* New Haven, 1925.

Donehoo, George P., ed. *Pennsylvania, a History.* 7 vols. New York, 1926.

Dorfman, Joseph. *The Economic Mind in American Civilization, 1606-1865.* 2 vols. New York, 1946.

Dunaway, Wayland F. *A History of Pennsylvania.* New York, 1935.

Egle, William H. "The Buckshot War," *Pennsylvania Magazine of History and Biography,* XXIII (1899), 137-156.

Eiselen, Malcolm R. *The Rise of Pennsylvania Protectionism.* Philadelphia, 1932.

Faust, Albert B. *The German Element in the United States.* 2 vols. Boston, 1909.

Ferguson, Russell J. *Early Western Pennsylvania Politics.* Pittsburgh, 1938.

Fine, Nathan. *Labor and Farmer Parties in the United States, 1828-1928.* New York, 1928.

Fish, Carl R. *The Civil Service and the Patronage.* Harvard Historical Studies, Vol. XI. New York, 1905.

Fox, Dixon R. *The Decline of Aristocracy in the Politics of New York.* Columbia University Studies in History, Economics and Public Law, LXXXVI, No. 198. New York, 1918.

Fraser, Hugh R. *Democracy in the Making: The Jackson-Tyler Era.* Indianapolis and New York, 1938.

Geary, Sister M. Theophane. *A History of Third Parties in Pennsylvania, 1840-1860.* Washington, 1938.

Hailperin, Herman. "Pro-Jackson Sentiment in Pennsylvania, 1820-1828," *Pennsylvania Magazine of History and Biography,* L (1926), 193-240.

Hammond, Bray. *Banks and Politics in America from the Revolution to the Civil War.* Princeton, 1957.

Hartz, Louis. *Economic Policy and Democratic Thought: Pennsylvania, 1776-1860.* Cambridge, 1948.

Hewitt, Warren F. "Samuel Breck and the Pennsylvania School Law of 1834," *Pennsylvania History,* I (1934), 63-75.

Higginbotham, Sanford W. *The Keystone in the Democratic Arch: Pennsylvania Politics, 1800-1816.* Harrisburg, 1952.

Holdsworth, John Thom, and Davis R. Dewey. *The First and Second Banks of the United States.* Washington, 1910.

——————— and John S. Fisher. *Financing an Empire: History of Banking in Pennsylvania.* 4 vols. Chicago and Philadelphia, 1928.

Jenkins, Howard M., ed. *Pennsylvania, Colonial and Federal, a History, 1608-1903.* 3 vols. Philadelphia, 1903.

Kehl, James A. *Ill Feeling in the Era of Good Feeling: Western Pennsylvania Political Battles, 1815-1825.* Pittsburgh, 1956.

Klein, Philip S. "Early Lancaster County Politics," *Pennsylvania History,* III (1936), 98-114.

——————. *Pennsylvania Politics, 1817-1832: A Game Without Rules.* Philadelphia, 1940.

Klein, Theodore B. *Canals of Pennsylvania and the System of Internal Improvements.* Harrisburg, 1901.

Lambert, Oscar D. *Presidential Politics in the United States, 1841-1844.* Durham, 1936.

McCadden, Joseph J. *Education in Pennsylvania, 1801-1835, and Its Debt to Roberts Vaux.* Philadelphia, 1937.

McCarthy, Charles. "The Antimasonic Party: A Study of Political Antimasonry in the United States, 1827-1840," American Historical Association, *Annual Report, 1902,* I, 365-574. Washington, 1903.

McGrane, Reginald C. *Foreign Bondholders and American State Debts.* New York, 1935.

——————. *The Panic of 1837.* Chicago, 1924.

Madeleine, Sister M. Grace. *Monetary and Banking Theories of Jacksonian Democracy.* Philadelphia, 1943.

Miles, Edwin A. "'Fifty-four Forty or Fight'—An American Political Legend," *Mississippi Valley Historical Review,* XLIV (September, 1957), 291-309.

Mueller, Henry R. *The Whig Party in Pennsylvania.* Columbia University Studies in History, Economics and Public Law, CI, No. 2. New York, 1922.

Nevins, Allan. *Ordeal of the Union.* 2 vols. New York, 1947.

Ostrogorski, M. *Democracy and the Organization of Political Parties.* 2 vols. New York, 1902.

Robinson, Elwyn B. "The *Pennsylvanian,* Organ of the Democracy," *Pennsylvania Magazine of History and Biography,* LXII (1938), 350-360.

Schlesinger, Arthur M., Jr. *The Age of Jackson.* Boston, 1945.

Schneider, Herbert W. *A History of American Philosophy.* New York, 1946.

Scisco, Louis D. *Political Nativism in New York State.* New York, 1901.

Sharpless, Isaac. *Two Centuries of Pennsylvania History.* Philadelphia, 1900.

Simms, Henry H. *The Rise of the Whigs in Virginia, 1824-1840.* Richmond, 1929.

Smith, Walter B. *Economic Aspects of the Second Bank of the United States.* Cambridge, 1953.

Stanwood, Edward. *A History of the Presidency.* Boston and New York, 1898.

——————. *American Tariff Controversies in the Nineteenth Century.* 2 vols. Boston and New York, 1903.

Stenberg, Richard R. "The Motivation of the Wilmot Proviso," *Mississippi Valley Historical Review,* XVIII (1932), 535-541.

Sullivan, William A. "A Decade of Labor Strife," *Pennsylvania History,* XVII (1950), 23-38.

Taussig, Frank W. *The Tariff History of the United States.* New York, 1892.

Tinkcom, Harry M. *The Republicans and Federalists in Pennsylvania, 1790-1801: A Study in National Stimulus and Local Response.* Harrisburg, 1950.

Turner, Edward R. *The Negro in Pennsylvania.* Washington, 1911.

Turner, Frederick J. *The United States, 1830-1850.* New York, 1935.

Warren, Charles. *The Supreme Court in United States History.* 3 vols. Boston, 1922.

Wescott, Ralph W. *An Historical Account of the Customs Service . . . at the Port of Philadelphia.* Philadelphia, 1934.

White, Leonard D. *The Jacksonians: A Study in Administrative History, 1829-1861.* New York, 1954.

Wickersham, James P., comp. *Common School Laws of Pennsylvania.* Harrisburg, 1879.

Worthington, Thomas K. *Historical Sketch of the Finances of Pennsylvania.* American Economic Association, *Publications,* II, No. 2. Baltimore, 1887.

BIOGRAPHICAL WORKS

Alexander, Holmes M. *The American Talleyrand: The Career and Contemporaries of Martin Van Buren.* New York, 1935.

Armor, William C. *Lives of the Governors of Pennsylvania, . . . 1609-1873.* Philadelphia, 1872.

Bancroft, George. *Martin Van Buren to the End of His Public Career.* New York, 1889.

Beck, Clara A. *Kith and Kin of George Wolf, Governor of Pennsylvania, 1829-1835.* Easton, 1930.

Binney, Charles C. *The Life of Horace Binney, with Selections from His Letters.* Philadelphia, 1903.

Brigance, William N. *Jeremiah Sullivan Black.* Philadelphia, 1934.

Chitwood, Oliver P. *John Tyler, Champion of the Old South.* Philadelphia, 1939.

Clark, Bennett Champ. *John Quincy Adams, "Old Man Eloquent."* Boston, 1932.

Cleaves, Freeman. *Old Tippecanoe: William Henry Harrison and His Time.* New York, 1939.

Crippen, Lee F. *Simon Cameron, Ante-Bellum Years.* Oxford, Ohio, 1942.

Current, Richard N. "Love, Hate, and Thaddeus Stevens," *Pennsylvania History,* XIV (1947), 259-272.

Curtis, George T. *Life of James Buchanan.* 2 vols. New York, 1883.

Dyer, Brainerd. *Zachary Taylor.* Baton Rouge, 1946.

Elliott, Charles W. *Winfield Scott: The Soldier and the Man.* New York, 1937.

Fuess, Claude M. *Daniel Webster.* 2 vols. Boston, 1930.

Going, Charles B. *David Wilmot, Free-Soiler: A Biography of the Great Advocate of the Wilmot Proviso.* New York, 1924.

Hamilton, Holman. *Zachary Taylor, Soldier of the Republic.* Indianapolis, 1941.

James, Marquis. *Andrew Jackson: Portrait of a President.* Indianapolis and New York, 1937.

BIBLIOGRAPHY

Konkle, Burton A. *The Life and Speeches of Thomas Williams.* . . . 2 vols. Philadelphia, 1905.

————. *The Life of Chief Justice Ellis Lewis, 1798-1871.* . . . Philadelphia, 1907.

Korngold, Ralph. *Thaddeus Stevens.* New York, 1955.

Lewis, W. D. *Great American Lawyers.* 8 vols. Philadelphia, 1907-1909.

Lynch, Dennis T. *An Epoch and a Man: Martin Van Buren and His Times.* New York, 1929.

McCormac, Eugene I. *James K. Polk, a Political Biography.* Berkeley, 1922.

McLaughlin, Andrew C. *Lewis Cass.* Boston and New York, 1899.

Meigs, William M. *The Life of Charles Jared Ingersoll.* Philadelphia, 1897.

————. *The Life of John Caldwell Calhoun.* 2 vols. New York, 1917.

Meyer, Leland W. *The Life and Times of Colonel Richard M. Johnson of Kentucky.* New York, 1932.

Miller, Alphonse B. *Thaddeus Stevens.* New York, 1939.

Mohr, Robert L. *Thomas Henry Burrowes, 1805-1871.* Philadelphia, 1946.

Morgan, Robert J. *A Whig Embattled: The Presidency Under John Tyler.* Lincoln, 1954.

Parton, James. *Life of Andrew Jackson.* 3 vols. New York, 1860.

Poage, George R. *Henry Clay and the Whig Party.* Chapel Hill, 1936.

Sessa, Frank B. "Walter Forward in the Pennsylvania Constitutional Convention of 1837-38," *Western Pennsylvania Historical Magazine,* XX (1937), 113-122.

Simpson, Henry. *The Lives of Eminent Philadelphians, Now Deceased.* Philadelphia, 1859.

Smith, Edgar F. "Eminent Pennsylvania Germans," Pennsylvania German Society, *Proceedings,* XXXIV (1924), 37-52.

Steele, Henry J. "The Life and Services of Governor George Wolf," Pennsylvania German Society, *Proceedings,* XXXIX (1930), 5-25.

Swisher, Carl B. *Roger B. Taney.* New York, 1936.

Van Deusen, Glyndon G. *The Life of Henry Clay.* Boston, 1937.

Wallace, Paul A. W. *The Muhlenbergs of Pennsylvania.* Philadelphia, 1950.

Weisenburger, Francis P. *The Life of John McLean, a Politician on the United States Supreme Court.* Columbus, 1937.

Wiltse, Charles M. *John C. Calhoun.* 3 vols. Indianapolis and New York, 1944-1951.

Woodward, George A. *Biography of George Washington Woodward.* n. p., 1924.

Woodley, Thomas F. *Thaddeus Stevens.* Harrisburg, 1934.

LOCAL HISTORY

Auge, Moses. *Lives of the Eminent Dead and Biographical Notices of Prominent Living Citizens of Montgomery County, Pa.* Norristown, 1879.

Baldwin, Leland D. *Pittsburgh: The Story of a City.* Pittsburgh, 1938.

BIBLIOGRAPHY

Boucher, John N., ed. *A Century and a Half of Pittsburg and Her People.* 4 vols. New York, 1908.

Buck, William J. *History of Montgomery County Within the Schuylkill Valley.* Norristown, 1859.

Condit, Uzal W. *The History of Easton, Penn'a, . . . 1739-1885.* Easton, 1885.

Craig, Neville B. *The History of Pittsburgh.* Pittsburgh, 1851.

Crumrine, Boyd, ed. *History of Washington County, Pennsylvania.* Philadelphia, 1882.

Davis, William W. H. *History of Bucks County, Pennsylvania.* 3 vols. New York, 1905.

Egle, William H. *History of the Counties of Dauphin and Lebanon, in the Commonwealth of Pennsylvania.* Philadelphia, 1883.

Fox, Cyrus T., ed. *Reading and Berks County, Pennsylvania, a History.* 3 vols. New York, 1925.

[Grim, Webster]. *Historical Sketches of the Doylestown Democrat, 1816-1916.* Doylestown, 1916.

Harris, Alexander. *A Biographical History of Lancaster County.* Lancaster, 1872.

Hayden, H. E., Alfred Hand, and John W. Jordan, eds. *Genealogical and Family History of the Wyoming and Lackawanna Valleys, Pennsylvania.* 2 vols. New York, 1906.

Heathcote, Charles W., ed. *A History of Chester County, Pennsylvania.* Harrisburg, 1932.

Jackson, Joseph. *Encyclopedia of Philadelphia.* 4 vols. Harrisburg, 1931-1933.

Klein, Harry M. J., ed. *Lancaster County, Pennsylvania, a History.* 4 vols. New York, 1924.

Morgan, George H., comp. *Annals, Comprising Memoirs, Incidents and Statistics of Harrisburg.* Harrisburg, 1858.

Palmer, Charles, ed. *A History of Delaware County.* 2 vols. Harrisburg, 1932.

Prowell, George R. *History of York County, Pennsylvania.* 2 vols. Chicago, 1907.

Scharf, J. Thomas, and Thompson Westcott. *History of Philadelphia, 1609-1884.* 3 vols. Philadelphia, 1884.

Wilson, Erasmus, ed. *Standard History of Pittsburg, Pennsylvania.* Chicago, 1898.

Worner, William F. *Old Lancaster, Tales and Traditions.* Lancaster, 1927.

Index

Aaronsburg, 3
Act to Repeal the State Tax and to Continue the Improvement of the State by Railroads and Canals, 78-79
Act to Repeal the State Tax on Real and Personal Property and to Continue and Extend the Improvements of the State by Railroads and Canals, and to Charter a State Bank to be Called the United States Bank, 79
Adams, Henry, on Pennsylvania as "true democratic community," 18
Adams, John, 23, 219; and party politics, 26; support of, in Pennsylvania, 26
Adams County, 27, 56, 75, 120, 131, 196
Adjutant General, 14
Agriculture, 8
Allegheny County, 4, 41, 58, 180, 185, 215, 217, 218
Allegheny Mountains, 4, 11
Allegheny River, 3, 11; bridges over, 7
Amalgamation Men, 23-24; support Van Buren, 32-33
American Sentinel, Philadelphia, 104-105, 147, 148, 154; on McKean's opposition to national convention, 33-34; notes apathy on constitutional reform, 99
Anderson, William B., 160
Anthracite, mining of, 10
Antimasonic party, 7, 17, 19, 21, 44, 45, 46, 47, 48, 49, 53, 64-65, 70, 71, 72, 73, 75, 81, 96, 100, 107, 108, 109, 121, 124, 128, 134, 141, 142, 143, 148, 151, 152, 178, 219; and apportionment of 1836, 15; coalitionists or moderates in, 68-70; in election of 1832, 30; in election of 1835, 64-67; in election of 1838, 127-131; exclusive policy of, in Lancaster, 178; Exclusives in, 30, 68-70, 81, 219; national convention of, in 1831, 29; national convention of, in 1836, 81; national convention of, in 1838, 141; and proscriptive policy of press, 66; revived by Wolf-Muhlenberg split, 64; rise of, 27-29; sectional and racial support of, 29; State committee of, 20, 64-65; State convention of, in 1829, 28; State convention of, in 1835, 69-71, 81
Antimasonic-Whig Coalition, 30, 75, 82, 84, 85, 86, 87, 90, 92, 101-102, 103-104, 105, 106, 119, 123, 129, 131, 133-134, 140, 143, 147, 148, 149, 150; controls House, 67, 69, 74-75; controls organization of constitutional convention, 103; delays constitutional convention, 100; exploits Democratic radicalism, 100-101
Antimasonic-Whig State Committee, organized, 65-66
Antimasons; *see* Antimasonic party
Appalachian Plateau, 3, 5
Apportionment Act of 1836, 15, 74-75
Argus, Harrisburg, 203
Armstrong County, 4
Ashley, Chester, 193 n.
Association for the Abolition of Offices for Life, 97, 98
Attorney General, 14
Auditor General, 14

Bainbridge, 125
Baker, George N., 79 n.
Baldwin, Judge Henry, 17
Baldwin, Matthias W., 102
Baltimore, 3
Baltimore and Ohio Railroad, 193-194, 194 n.; rivalry of, with Pennsylvania Railroad, 202
Bank Democrats, 44-45, 46, 47, 48, 70, 85, 88, 112, 114, 118, 120, 142; aid in adopting resolutions hostile to Independent Treasury, 117-119, 136
Bank of North America, 120, 160
Bank of Pennsylvania, 162
Bank of the United States, 6, 13, 22, 23, 24, 65, 66, 112, 220; confidence in, 24; and federal deposits controversy, 35-45; Jackson's veto of charter of, 27, 35; loan reduction initiated by, 35-36; *see also* United States Bank
Banking and currency, act of 1814 on, 12; act of 1840 on, 154; act of 1842 on, 162-163; and bank panic of 1841, 153; and bank panic of 1842, 162; in Pennsylvania, 12; investigation of, 164-166; regulation urged, 113-115; and "runs" on banks, 112; and suspension of specie payments, 138
Banks, John, 174; as Whig nominee for Governor in 1841, 158, 179
Barker, James N., 122-123

243

244 INDEX

Barnard, Isaac D., 24
Barrett, Orville, as editor of Harrisburg *Keystone* and lobbyist for the United States Bank, 116
Barton, Judge George W., 146, 211, 212; in Handy case, 165
Beatty, Peggy, 129
Beaver, 46
Beaver Canal, 11
Beaver County, 27; Whig policy in, in 1835, 66
Bedford County, 4, 100, 159, 185
Bell, Thomas S., 57-58, 179-180, 182 n.
Bellefonte, 149
Bennett, James Gordon, 32-33
Benton, Thomas Hart, 73, 89, 193 n.; backed for Vice President, 144
Berks County, 4, 57-58, 60, 71, 89, 99 n., 122, 158, 172, 181, 185; harvest home celebration in, 201-202; supports Democratic party, 29
Biddle, James C., 102
Biddle, Nicholas, 33, 65, 85, 101, 106 n., 116, 117, 118, 119, 120, 125, 127, 137, 216; leaves Philadelphia during election of 1834, 48; policy of, in deposits removal controversy, 35-45; seeks State charter for United States Bank, 75-79; strategy of, to protect United States Bank, 91-95; *see also* Bank of the United States; United States Bank
Bidlack, Benjamin, 90-91, 115
Bigler, John, 182 n.
Binney, Horace, 45
Birmingham, England, 7
Blair, Francis P., on Democratic schism at Baltimore convention, 62
Blythe, Calvin, 124, 169; appointed Collector of the Port of Philadelphia, 146, 147
Boale, George, 156 n.
Borers, 13; *see also* Lobbyists
Bradford County, 5, 47, 170; unpopularity of Buchanan's views on Wilmot Proviso in, 208; unpopularity of Dallas' views on Wilmot Proviso in, 208
Brady, Jasper E., 191
Branch Men, 12
Breck, Samuel, 41, 51
Brewster, Benjamin, 211
Bristol, 125
Brodhead, Daniel M., 137, 164-165; leaves State to escape banking investigation, 165
Brodhead, Richard, opposes Wilmot Proviso in Congress, 201
Brown, Charles S., 133 n., 139
Buchanan, James, 17, 73, 85, 93, 117, 118 n., 119, 122, 136 n., 139, 145, 152, 153, 154, 157, 159, 166, 167, 170, 171-172, 181, 183, 184, 189, 193, 193 n.; advises Shunk on patronage, 198; advocates hard-money doctrine, 148-149; backed for Secretary of State, 187; backs James M. Porter for Attorney General, 144-145; backs King for Vice Presidency, 144; bids for presidential nomination in 1844, 168, 171-174; career of, to 1833, 31-32; contributes to Philadelphia delegate campaign, 212; convention backs his nomination in 1844, 172-174; defeated for Presidency in national convention, 215; elected to United States Senate, 50; embarrassed by Lancaster factions, 207; leadership of, 1833 to 1848, 220; leads party in opposition to Wilmot Proviso, 201-202; named as Secretary of State, 188; notes Porter's fall in popularity, 169; partisans of, compete for Philadelphia votes, 210-213; peacemaker in campaign of 1840, 147-148; presidential prospects of, in 1848, 204-206; protests partisanship of officeholders, 210; re-elected to Senate in 1837, 86-88; re-elected to Senate in 1843, 173-174; refuses nomination as Attorney General, 144; refuses to condemn Cameron's election to the Senate, 191-192; seeks appointment to Supreme Court, 204-205; setting up of central committee for, 172-173; urges revision rather than repeal of Tariff of 1846, 196, 198; voted favorite son in election of 1848, 213; withdraws from presidential race in 1844, 175; in Wolf-Muhlenberg split, 62-63
Bucks County, 4, 27
Buckshot War, 131-135, 136, 141, 149, 180
Buehler, Henry, 20, 172 n.; plans Wolf strategy in 1835, 56-57
Burden, Jesse, 58, 86; supports Bank charter, 77 n., 79 n.
Burns, James, elected to Canal Commission, 194, 194 n.
Burrowes, Thomas H., 127, 128, 131, 220; appointed Secretary of the Commonwealth, 68; precipitates Buckshot War, 131
Butler, Charles, 134 n.
Butler, John B., 173
Butler, Pierce, 101
Butler County, 185

INDEX

Calhoun, John C., 23-24, 25, 27, 175, 219
Cameron, James, 207
Cameron, Simon, 17, 62, 119, 120, 159, 173, 176, 184, 192, 193, 193 n., 195, 202-203; career of, prior to election to United States Senate, 189-191; elected to Senate, 189-191, 207, 220; gives tentative support to Taylor in 1848, 209; hails passage of resolutions critical of Independent Treasury, 118; opposes second term for Shunk, 199; protects banks from hostile legislation, 89, 95; seeks financial aid as bank lobbyist, 119-120
Canal Commission, 14, 111, 124, 152; election of, in 1845, 193-194; made elective, 177-178; popular election of, 170; use of, for electioneering, 125-127
Canal Convention of 1825, 12
Canals, 11-12; and electioneering, 125-127; *see also* Internal improvements; State Works
Carey, Mathew, 11
Carlisle, 133
Case, Elihu, 134 n.
Cass, Lewis, boomed for Presidency in 1844, 168, 176; defeated in State, 218; nominated for President, 215
Catholics, 185, 211; prejudice against, 67
Centre County, 3, 4
Centreville, 149
Chambersburg, 46, 142
Champion, Harrisburg, criticizes Muhlenberg in campaign of 1844, 202-203
Champneys, Benjamin, 173, 181, 191, 207; accepts appointment as Attorney General, 199; breaks with Buchanan over Cameron's election to the Senate, 199 n.; elected to State Senate in Lancaster County, 178
Chandler, Joseph R., as editor of Philadelphia *United States Gazette*, 51, 72-73, 102; refuses to testify before committee investigating Masonry, 73
Charles II, 3
Chauncey, Charles, 102
Chesapeake Bay, 3
Chester, 46
Chester County, 4, 74, 130-131
Chestnut Street, Philadelphia, 6
Christy, Robert, 72
Chronicle, Harrisburg, exploits radicalism of Democrats, 101; purchased by Biddle, 78

Church, Gaylord, 156 n.
Clarke, James, 139; appointed canal commissioner, 136
Clay, Henry, 23, 30, 43, 45, 47, 73-74, 116, 118, 142-143, 151, 178, 182-183, 219; in presidential campaign of 1844, 183-186, 187; on Wolf's Bank message, 41-42
Coal Hill, in Pittsburgh, 7
Coal mining, development of, 10
"Colonization," 12
Columbia, 11
Columbia County, 98 n.
Common School Fund, 51
Congress, apportionment for, 16, 227
Conrad, Henry W., and the bribe hoax, 79
Conrad, Robert T., 146
Constitution, frigate, as symbol, 46
Constitution, Pennsylvania, of 1776, 13; of 1790, 13, 55, 96; of 1790 defended, 96; of 1790, dissatisfaction with, 96-98; of 1838, 14, 189; of 1838 approved at polls, 109
Constitutional Convention of 1838, and currency and banking, 104, 106-107; election of delegates to, 86, 100-102; leadership in, 102; occupations represented in, 102; organization of, 103; proceedings of, 103-107; referendum on, 96-97; revisions agreed to by, 105; voted by electorate, 67
Constitutional reform, action in legislature on, 98; convention for, in 1833, 97-98; referendum of 1835 on, 99-100; support for, 59
Conventions, nominating, in 1835, 57-59, 62, 65; in 1838, 123-124; in 1840, 142-143, 145-146; in 1841, 158; in 1843, 178; in 1844, 174, 175, 179, 181-182; in 1847, 199-200; in 1848, 213, 216, 217; gubernatorial, 20-21; Lewistown Democratic, of 1835, 59; replace caucus, 15
Coonskin campaign of 1840, 147-149
Cooper, James, supported for gubernatorial nomination, 200
Cope, Caleb, 45
Cope, Thomas P., 102
Cortwright, Andrew, 156 n., 158 n.
Cotton, manufacture of, 9
County, as a political unit, 19
County seats, description of, 8
Court of Criminal Sessions, Philadelphia, 146
Courts of Common Pleas, 16
Crabb, William, elected Speaker of State House of Representatives, 151-152

INDEX

Craig, Neville B., as editor of Pittsburgh *Gazette*, 68
Crawford, William, 23, 219
Cumberland County, 4, 75
Cunningham, Thomas S., 77 n.; elected Speaker of State House of Representatives, 69; involvement of, in Buckshot War, 132-134
"Cunningham House," 132, 133, 134

Dallas, George M., 24, 72, 85, 160-161, 175, 177, 182 n.; advice of, on patronage, 53-54; before committee of House investigating Masonry, 73; breaks tie to pass tariff bill, 195; controls Philadelphia delegates to 1848 State nominating convention, 212-213; critical of Democrats voting for Cameron for United States Senator, 191; defeated by Buchanan for presidential endorsement, 213; dissatisfied with his share of patronage, 206-207; leadership of, 1822 to 1848, 220; nominated for Vice President, 177; and partisans in Philadelphia, 210-213; on Philadelphia patronage, 146; as presidential candidate in 1848, 205-207; radical statement of, exploited by Coalition, 101; refuses nomination as Attorney General, 145; rejects Wilmot Proviso, 202 n.
Dallas, T. B., 206 n.
Danville, 98, 167
Dauphin County, 4, 66, 98 n., 180, 199; convention opposes renomination of Shunk, 199
Davis, John, as Surveyor of the Customs, 211
Davis, Senator John, of Massachusetts, attacks Buchanan, 149
Delaware, state of, 128
Delaware and Hudson Canal, 10-11
Delaware Canal, 11
Delaware County, 4, 27, 54, 74; woolen factories in, 9
Delaware River, 6, 125
Democratic National Convention of 1844, 182; Pennsylvania delegates contribute to Van Buren's defeat in, 176-177
Democratic party, 17, 19, 21, 22, 27, 30, 38, 43, 44, 45, 46, 47, 48, 49, 53, 73, 74, 75, 79, 82-86, 90-91, 92, 100, 101, 103, 104, 105, 106, 107, 109, 122, 123, 128, 129, 130, 131, 135, 138-139, 148, 149, 150, 152, 153, 155, 156, 160, 162, 171-177, 182, 184, 188, 219; accepts Tariff of 1846, 201-202; in campaign of 1828, 23; campaign strategy of, in 1838, 129-130; cleavage in, aids two-thirds rule in national convention, 176; cleavage between Van Buren and Porter men in, 145-146; closes Muhlenberg-Wolf schism, 82-87; in election of 1835, 50-67; in Lancaster, 7; radical-conservative split over banking regulation in, 119-121; rejects Wilmot Proviso, 201; in senatorial election of 1834, 50; supports Constitution of 1838, 107; trend adverse to, 214; trends from 1832 to 1848, 219-220; weathers bank issue, 163
Democratic Press, Reading, supports Muhlenberg for United States Senate, 87
Democratic Press, York, 196 n.
Democratic-Republicans, 22
Democrats; *see* Democratic party
Denny, Harmar, withdraws from State Antimasonic convention, 70
Deposits controversy, 35-45
Deputy Secretary of the Commonwealth, as a political adviser, 20
Dewart, Lewis, as Speaker of the State House of Representatives protects United States Bank, 88-89, 91-92
Dickey, John, 77 n., 79 n., 142; on Canal Commission, 124 n., 125, 127; receives favors for Bank support, 78, 79
Donagan, James, 20
Doran, Joseph, 156 n.
Duane, William J., 17
Dunaway, Wayland F., on threat of repudiation, 161
Dutch, in Pennsylvania, 4
Dyottsville, 6

Earle, Thomas, 101, 104; favors constitutional reform, 97, 98; as hard-money advocate, 90
Easton, 7, 46, 125; ironmaking in, 10
Elder, Thomas, 68
Eldred, Judge Nathaniel B., 179, 188; supported for Governor, 199
Elections, Canal Commission, of 1848, 217-218
Elections, congressional, of 1834, 48-49; of 1836, 86; of 1840, 149-150; of 1846, 197; of 1848, 218
Elections, gubernatorial, of 1829, 28; of 1832, 26, 30; of 1835, 54-67; of 1838, 108, 131, 133-134; of 1841, 158-159; of 1844, 179-186; of 1847, 203, 203 n.; of 1848, 215-218

INDEX

Elections, legislative, of 1836, 86; of 1837, 115; of 1840, 149; of 1841, 159; of 1842, 177 n.; of 1843, 177 n.; of 1844, 186; of 1845, 194; of 1846, 197; of 1847, 203; of 1848, 218
Elections, presidential, of 1832, 25; of 1836, 86; of 1840, 141-150; of 1844, 182-186; of 1848, 213-218
Electoral College, 15
Electorate, characteristics of, 18-19
Eleventh Hour Men, 23-24; hostility of, toward Van Buren, 32
Ellmaker, Amos, 28-29, 68, 220
Elmira Railroad, 78
English, William, 94-95; supports constitutional revision and public school law, 60 n., 171
English element, 4
English miners, 8
Erie Canal, 6, 11
Erie County, 27, 60, 180, 199
Escheator General, 14
Espy, George R., introduces bill to repeal charter of the United States Bank, 94

Farm life, description of, 8
Farmers, and internal improvements, 9; and the tariff, 9
Farrelly, David M., 107 n.
Federalism, 22, 96; in Pittsburgh, 7
Fenn, Theophilus, as editor of Harrisburg *Telegraph*, 68, 108
Findlay, William, 23 n.; forecasts Democratic factionalism, 45
Findlayites, 23
Findley, William, 55, 96
Fore, Henry H., 77 n., 79 n.
Forney, John W., 147, 148, 159, 195 n., 203 n., 212; labors to conciliate Lancaster factions, 208; promotes Buchanan for President in 1844, 171-172; publishes Buchanan's views on tariff, 196, 205; purchases share in Philadelphia *Pennsylvanian*, 211; services of, for Buchanan in Philadelphia, 210-211
Forsyth, John, backed for Vice President, 144
Forward, Walter, 17 n.
Foster, William B., 170
Foster, William B., Jr., 170; defeated for canal commissioner, 197
Franklin County, 74, 131, 169
Frazer, Reah, 173, 181, 191; breaks with Buchanan, 207-208
Free Soil party, 215; in Allegheny and Lancaster counties, 217; along Northern Tier, 215, 217

Freeman, J. B., before committee investigating Masonry, 73
Frelinghuysen, Theodore, in campaign of 1844, 184
French, in Pennsylvania, 4
French Creek Canal, 11
Frick, Henry, 44, 46
Fullerton, David, 134 n.

Gallatin, Albert, 43; quoted, 18
Gamble, John A., 156 n., 158 n., 160
Gazette, Pittsburgh, 66
General Assembly, 43; and apportionment act of 1836, 74-75; Cameron elected to Senate by, 189-191; characteristics of, 14; election of canal commisioners voted by, 152; improvement bill adopted by, 138; and internal improvements, 10; joint committee of, to investigate Bank lobbying, 164; provides for referendum on a constitutional convention, 99; registration bill for Philadelphia adopted by, 74; resolutions of, against Independent Treasury, 152; tax bill voted by, 141
German belt, 4, 14
Germans, 5, 27; and support of Antimasonry, 29
Gerrymandering, 15; in apportionment of 1836, 74-75
Gettysburg, 46
Gettysburg Railroad, 76, 121, 130
Gibson, Chief Justice John B., opposes Constitution of 1838, 107-108
Gillis, James L., 156 n.
Gilmore, Samuel A., 95
Gilpin, Henry D., 17, 90, 146, 161, 175, 176, 206 n.; appointed Attorney General, 145; on Bank charter as a unifying force, 84; position of, on Bank of the United States, 38
Girard, Stephen, legacy of, 46
Girard Bank of Philadelphia, 92, 162; in federal deposits controversy, 37
Globe, Washington, 32-33
Gouge, William M., 89
Governor, appointive power of, 14, 96, 110-111; duties of, 13-14; tenure of, 105
Gowen, James, 48
Granger, Francis, nominated for Vice President by Antimasons, 70
Grier, Judge Robert C., 18
Grim, Jesse, 52 n.
Groves, Daniel, 45
Grundy, Felix, 144

INDEX

Hamiltonianism, 22
Handy, George, 120, 164, 166; tried for bribery, 164-165
Hard-Money Men, 85, 89, 90, 91, 94, 141, 144, 147, 154, 157, 158, 159
Harper, Francis J., 45
Harrisburg, 7, 36, 37, 38, 68, 72, 76, 82, 83, 85, 88, 97, 98, 103, 104, 105, 108, 116, 125, 127, 128, 132, 141, 142, 144, 157, 158, 159, 167, 168, 172, 176, 178-179, 185; ironmaking in, 10; State capitol in, described, 13
Harrison, William Henry, 17, 69-70, 71, 81, 141, 142-143, 179; in campaign of 1840, 148-150; carries State in 1840, 150; death of, 152; nominated for President, 142-143; nominated for President by State Antimasonic convention, 70; patronage of, 151
Hickory Club, 175
Hiester, Joseph, 23 n., 54 n.
Hiesterites, 23
Hill, John, 94, 95; heads investigation of United States Bank, 91-93
Holeman, Alexander, 156 n.
Hollidaysburg, 11, 126, 167, 194
Hone, Philip, 153
Hopkins, Uzal, 77 n., 79 n.
"Hopkins House," in Buckshot War, 132, 134
Hopkinson, Joseph, 102
Horn, Henry, 90, 175, 187; backs Muhlenberg, 61-62; rejected by Senate for Collector of the Port of Philadelphia, 193
Horton, Jesse C., 156 n., 158 n.
House of Representatives, Pennsylvania, 52, 86, 100, 103, 116, 120, 123, 131, 132-134, 138, 140, 151-152, 160; adopts improvement bill, 95; advised by Biddle on Bank bill, 76-77; Bank charter introduced in, 78-79; on bank regulatory bill, 120-121; bribe offer charged in, 79; characteristics of, 14; charter of the United States Bank introduced in, 79; charter of the United States Bank passed by, 79; on Clay's distribution bill, 73-74; committee of, investigates Masonry, 72-73; controversy in, over a printer, 115-116; defeats resolutions supporting the recharter of the Bank of the United States, 43; delays election of delegates to the constitutional convention, 100; investigates passage of the charter of the United States Bank, 91-93; occupations represented in, 15; on public education bill, 51-53; Relief Bill voted by, 154-156; resolutions on Independent Treasury voted by, 116-118; resumption bill adopted by, 162; supports immediate resumption, 139; tariff resolutions in, 195
House of Representatives, United States, 116, 195, 198, 201, 205
Hubley, Edward, 136
Huntingdon, 46, 125, 127, 136
Huntingdon County, 4, 74, 123, 185
Hutter, Edwin W., 172 n.; resigns as Porter's Deputy Secretary of the Commonwealth, 169

Improvement Democrats, 118-119, 120, 123, 124, 136, 139, 140, 157, 159, 160, 164, 166, 167, 168, 172, 180, 189, 192, 197, 198, 200, 209, 214, 217, 220; support Relief Bill, 155-156, 158; strength of, 159
Improvements; see Internal improvements; Public Works; State Works
Independent Treasury, 109, 115, 116-119, 121, 123, 124, 128, 148, 152, 184, 195, 216, 217
Indiana, state of, 97, 142
Industrial Revolution, 6
Ingersoll, Charles J., 52, 110 n.; elected to Congress, 149-150; as a hard-money advocate, 90; radical report by, on currency and banking in the constitutional convention, 104; radicalism of, exploited, 114
Ingersoll, Joseph R., 45; reveals Taylor's affiliation with Whigs, 214
Ingham, Samuel D., 23-24, 136
"Inglorious Eight," 84, 86
Intelligencer, Harrisburg, on chartering the United States Bank, 80
Intelligencer, Lancaster, 147, 148, 211
Internal improvements, 9; farmers and, 9; manufacturers and, 10; responsibility of the State for, 10; see also Public Works; State Works
Irish, 5, 8, 48, 166, 184-185, 211-212
Ironmaking, 9
Irvin, Alexander, 77 n., 79 n.; explains his support of the charter for the United States Bank, 78
Irvin, James, backed for gubernatorial nomination in 1844, 179; nominated by Whigs for Governor in 1847, 200
Irvin, William W., 68, 81 n.

Jackson, Andrew, 7, 13, 17, 23, 24, 46, 47, 48, 49, 55, 73, 82, 83, 89, 96,

INDEX

97, 139, 143, 148, 219; Bank veto by, 24-25, 35, 56, 90; and the Calhoun imbroglio, 23; in deposits removal controversy, 35-45; in election of 1832, 25; letters of, used in gubernatorial election of 1835, 61-62
Jackson Day convention of 1836, 83-84
Jacksonianism, 45
Jaudon, Samuel, 36
Jefferson, Thomas, 55, 89
Jefferson Society Men, 44
Jeffersonian Revolution, 22
Jersey City, 125
Jim Thorpe; *see* Mauch Chunk
Johnson, Ovid F., 120, 130 n., 137, 157, 165; appointed Attorney General by Porter, 136; as editor of Harrisburg *Keystone,* 123; lobbies for the United States Bank, 116, 117; supports the Taylor movement, 209
Johnson, Richard M., 144, 159, 164; boomed for Presidency by the Porter faction, 166-167, 169, 172, 175; runs for Vice President in 1840, 145, 147; tours Pennsylvania in presidential campaign of 1844, 167-168
Johnson, Walter Rogers, 51
Johnston, William F., 14 n., 119, 121, 121 n.; career of, to 1848, 216-217; dislike of, for Walker Tariff, 217; draws up Relief Bill, 155; elected Governor, 218; heads opposition to Independent Treasury, 116-119; as legislator, 91-92, 95; made acting Governor, 215-216, 216 n.; makes transition from Democrats to Whigs, 220; nominated for Governor, 216; seeks loan from United States Bank in return for services in legislature, 216; stumps State in gubernatorial campaign of 1848, 217
Jones, Joel, 206 n.; criticism of Bank of the United States by, quoted, 38
Jones, John Richter, editor of Philadelphia *Sun,* 68
Judiciary, characteristics of, 16
Juniata County, 74
Juniata region, ironmaking in, 9
Juniata River, 11, 125
Junkin, George, 73 n.

Kane, John K., 175, 206 n.; appointed Attorney General of the State, 187-188; appointed judge of district court, 198
Kane letter, 183, 215

Keating, William H., 39, 43
Keim, George, 89
Kelley, Judge William D., 210
Kendall, Amos, 89
Kensington, 6, 74; nativist riot in, 184
Kentucky, 128
Kern, Jacob, 63 n.; re-elected Speaker of Senate in 1834, 50
Keystone, Harrisburg, 87, 123, 136, 137, 139, 140, 143-144, 145, 157, 164, 165-166 169; as printer of House journal, 115; published by United States Bank lobbyists, 116; supports Bank Democrats, 117, 118
King, Judge Edward, 206 n., 210
King, Henry, 25-26
King, William R., supported for Vice President, 144-145
Kiskiminetas River, 11
Krebs, Jacob, reports bribe offer, 79
Kremer, George, as chairman of reform convention, 98

Lackawanna region, coal mining in, 10
Lafayette College, 73 n.
Lancaster, 147, 148, 149, 178; conservatism of, 7; description of, 7
Lancaster County, 4, 74, 145, 180, 181, 215, 217; Democratic factionalism in, 207; farming in, 8; support of Antimasonry by, 29-30, 64
LaPorte, John, appointed Surveyor General, 187
Lawrence, Joseph, 28, 46, 65 n.; elected State Treasurer, 69
Lebanon, ironmaking in, 10
Lebanon County, 4, 199; support of Antimasonry by, 29
Leckey, William, 41-42
Legislature; *see* General Assembly
Lehigh Coal and Navigation Company, 7, 10, 11
Lehigh County, 4
Lehigh Navigation system, 125
Levin, Lewis C., as Native American nominee for Congress, 215
Lewis, Judge Ellis, 58, 173-174; supports Taylor movement, 209
Lewistown, 58; Muhlenberg convention at, 59
Lippincott, Joshua, 45
Livingston, Edward, 38
Lobbyists, 13, 77
Locofocos, 85, 90, 91, 114, 115, 125, 128
Longstreth, Morris, elected canal commissioner, 203; nominated for Canal Commission, 200; nominated for Governor, 217; rejected by voters, 218
Lusk, Franklin, 156 n., 158 n.

INDEX

Luzerne County, 5, 90, 99 n., 110 n., 115, 145, 189, 192, 199, 208; Democratic factions in, 189
Lycoming County, 44, 78, 145, 181; decline of Antimasonry in, 64
Lycoming Gazette, Williamsport, 107
Lynch, David, 174
McAllister, J., 172 n.
McCahen, John, 133 n.
McClure, Alexander K., on Cameron's election to the United States Senate, 190-191; on Porter's veto of the Relief Bill, 156-157; on repudiation of the State debt, 161
McConkey, James, 134 n.
McCulloch, George, 52 n.
McCully, Thomas, 211
McIlvaine, Joseph, death of, 120; as lobbyist for the United States Bank, 77, 91-95
McKean, Samuel, 17, 30-31, 41, 42, 44, 47, 58, 64, 73, 124, 220; decline of, as party leader, 43; elected to the United States Senate, 31-33
McKean County, 199
McKennan, Thomas M. T., 41
McKnight, W., on consequences of retrenchment by the Bank of the United States in Pittsburgh, 36-37
McLanahan, James X., 169-170, 173
McLean, Judge John, 31, 47, 209
McLenegan, Zephaniah, 68
McMichael, Morton, 149-150
McPherson, John B., 124
McPherson, William C., describes political activities of the Canal Commission, 125-127, 128; views of, on Buckshot War, 133, 134
Madison, James, 55
Main Line Men, 12
Manayunk, 6
Mann, Jacob, 159; elected State Treasurer, 160
Manufacturers, 9; and improvements, 10
Marietta, 125
Markle, Joseph, campaign tour of, breaks precedent, 185-186; nominated for Governor in 1844, 179; supported by Whigs for nomination for Governor in 1841, 158
Maryland, 128, 153
Masons, 66, 68, 70, 81, 126; investigation of, 72-73; 103-104; and the rise of Antimasonry, 27-28
Massachusetts, 128
Mauch Chunk [Jim Thorpe], 7
May, John, 156 n.
Maysville Road veto, 27
Mercer County, 60; growth of iron production in, 198 n.

Meredith, William M., 73 n., 102; answers Stevens in constitutional convention, 103
Merrill, James, dilemma of, over acceptance of Constitution of 1838, 108-109
Mexican War, 220; popularity of, in Pennsylvania, 201, 214
Michigan, 143
Michler, Peter, 134 n.
Middlecoff, David, 77 n., 79 n.
Middleswarth, Ner, 28, 46-47, 151, 158; defeated for canal commissioner, 218; defeated for re-election to House in 1836, 86; elected Speaker of the State House of Representatives, 69; nominated for canal commissioner, 217, 218; as Speaker of the House aids United States Bank, 75
Mifflin, Benjamin, editor of Philadelphia *Pennsylvanian,* 95
Mifflin County, 4, 74, 129, 180
Miller, Abraham, 134 n.
Miller, Andrew, 211; urges repudiation of State debt, 161
Miller, Jesse, 93, 191, 202, 203 n.; appointed auditor, 83; named Secretary of the Commonwealth by Shunk, 187
Miller, Thomas C., 135 n.
Milton, 47-48
Miltonian, Milton, 44; ridicules constitutional reformers, 98
Miners' Journal, Pottsville, 197, 197 n.
Monongahela River, 3; bridges over, 7
Monroe, James, 55
Montelius, John, 134 n.
Montgomery County, 4, 74, 180, 217
Morgan, William, 130
Morris Canal, 125
Muhlenberg, Frederick A., 54 n.
Muhlenberg, Henry A.; *see* Muhlenberg, Henry Augustus Philip
Muhlenberg, Henry Augustus Philip, 20, 82, 172, 220; appointed Minister to Austria, 122; death of, 182-184; Democratic nominee for Governor in 1844, 179-182, 182 n.; as a gubernatorial candidate in 1835, 54-55, 56, 57, 58, 60, 67; in gubernatorial election of 1838, 122; protects banking from radicals, 89; seeks Buchanan's aid in election of 1835, 63; seeks election to United States Senate, 87; in senatorial election of 1833, 31-33
Muhlenberg Democrats, 59-63, 68, 69, 82, 98-99, 136, 137, 187, 188; accept electoral ticket of the Wolf faction,

250

INDEX

83; split with the Shunk faction, 188-190
National convention, accepted by Democrats, 32-33
National Republican party, origins of, 26-27
National Republicans, 24, 28, 45, 52, 64-65, 219; in election of 1832, 25; rapprochement of, with Democrats, 30-31; treatment of, by Antimasons, 30
National Gazette, Philadelphia, 107
Native Americans, 194, 215; bargain of, with Whigs in Philadelphia County in 1844, 185, 186; in gubernatorial election of 1844, 185; in Kensington riots, 184; reject Whig slate in Philadelphia, 203; support Taylor, 209-210; vote for Cameron for United States Senator, 190
Nativism, 110 n.
Naylor, Charles, 114
Negroes, 4; denied suffrage, 105
New Berlin, 108
New York City, 6, 43, 46
New York State, 3, 5, 8, 65, 97, 143, 153
Newspapers, 43-44, 85, 109, 112-113, 114, 115-117, 122, 128, 129, 130, 170, 174; Democratic, seek harmony, 82-83; reaction of, to the chartering of the United States Bank, 80; *see also* Press
Niles' Register, Baltimore, on constitutional convention, 104; reports money panic, 35
Norristown, ironmaking in, 10
North American, Philadelphia, 184-185
North American and United States Gazette, Philadelphia, 208; foments Shunk-Muhlenberg feud, 202, 203 n.
Northampton County, 4
Northern Liberties, Philadelphia County, 131, 132, 213
Northumberland County, 44, 47, 74, 99 n.

Ohio, 8, 142
Ohio River, 3, 5
Old Ironsides Club, supports Stewart for President, 171
Omnibus Bill, 76, 107; *see also* United States Bank
Original Jackson Men, 23, 50, 54, 55, 61

Packer, William F., appointed canal commissioner, 136; as editor of Harrisburg *Keystone*, 123

Page, James, charged with partisanship for Dallas, 210; named Collector of the Port of Philadelphia, 193
Painter, Israel, 194 n.; elected to Canal Commission, 218; nominated for canal commissioner, 217
Panic of 1819, 11, 123
Panic of 1837, 10, 80, 109, 112, 182; issues regarding, in legislature, 115
Parke, Samuel, 81 n.
Parkesburg, 149
Parsons, Judge Anson V., 210; appointed Secretary of the Commonwealth, 164
Patronage, federal, 17-18, 146, 152, 169-170, 177, 192-193, 206, 210-211; State, 14, 53, 96, 110-111, 125, 187-188
Patterson, General Robert, in Buckshot War, 133; promotes United States Bank among Democratic electors, 88
Patterson, Samuel D., 209, 211; as editor of Harrisburg *Reporter*, 117, 164, 172 n.
Patterson, William, 44
Patton, Joseph H., as Whig nominee for Canal Commission, 200
Paynter, Lemuel, elected to Congress, 86
Peacock, James, as postmaster of Harrisburg, 209
Penniman, Edward, 156, 166
Pennsylvania, appointive officials of, 17-18; banking in, 12-13; capital of, 13; cities of, 5-7; coal trade in, 10; electorate of, 18-19; executive department of, 13-14; farming in, 8-9; geography of, 3-4; government of, 13-16; internal improvements of, 11-12; judiciary of, 16; legislative branch of, 15-16; manufacturing in, 9; nationalities in, 4-5; political methods in, 19-22; political parties in, 22-30; representation of, in Congress, 16-17; towns of, 7-8
Pennsylvania Canal, 11; *see also* Public Works; State Works
Pennsylvania Dutch, 4, 29
Pennsylvania Railroad, rivalry of, with Baltimore and Ohio Railroad, 202
Pennsylvania Society for the Promotion of Public Improvements, 11
Pennsylvania Society for the Promotion of Public Schools, 51-52
Pennsylvania State Works, 7; *see also* Internal improvements; Public Works; State Works
Pennsylvanian, Philadelphia, 40, 55, 56, 87, 95, 99, 105, 150, 162, 196,

205; edited by James G. Bennett, 32-33; opposes charter for United States Bank, 79, 84; proposes concessions to Wolf faction, 82; purchased by Forney, 211
Pennypacker, Elijah, 124 n., 125
Penrose, Charles B., 77 n., 79 n., 139, 142; in Buckshot War, 132; receives favors for support of United States Bank, 78, 79
Pentland, Judge Ephraim, 72; before House committee investigating Masonry, 73
Perry County, 74
Petriken, Henry, 20, 202; resigns as Porter's Deputy Secretary, 163
Pettit, Thomas M., 52
Philadelphia, 3-4, 5-6, 10-12, 30, 33, 35, 37, 42, 44, 45, 46, 48, 51, 59, 60, 67, 76, 82, 83, 90, 97, 98, 100, 104, 109, 125, 128, 137, 146, 147, 153, 159, 160-161, 172, 180, 185, 193; agriculture in area of, 8; bank panic in, 37; celebration of Whig victory in 1834 in, 46; cotton manufacture in, 9; Dallas and Buchanan compete for delegates to State convention in, 210-213; leadership of, 6; registration law of 1836 in, 19; woolen manufacture in, 9
Philadelphia and Columbia Railroad, 16
Philadelphia and Reading Railroad Company, 12
Philadelphia Common Councils, 45
Philadelphia County, 4, 56, 86, 98 n., 101, 131, 133, 145
Phoenixville, ironmaking in, 10
Piedmont region, 3
Pike County, 199
Pittsburgh, 3, 11-12, 27, 30, 46, 48, 51, 64, 66, 67, 73, 137, 147, 148, 159, 180, 185; Bank of the United States in, 36-37; as "Gateway to the West," 7; ironmaking in, 9-10; leadership of, 6
Plitt, George, 173
Polk, James K., 17, 110, 182, 183, 193 n.; disapproves partisanship among Philadelphia officeholders, 210; foreign policy of, popular in State, 198; nominated for President, 177; nominates Woodward for Supreme Court, 192-193; and Pennsylvania patronage, 192-193; in presidential campaign of 1844, 183-185, 186, 187; seeks Dallas' views on appointments, 206; suspicious of Buchanan's presidential ambitions, 204

Pollock, James, scores Buchanan for insincerity on tariff, 205
Population, density of, 3
Porter, David R., 14, 20, 116, 124 n., 125, 126 n., 129 n., 131, 132, 135, 136, 139, 145, 147, 148, 152, 153, 154, 158, 159, 162, 164, 166, 167, 168 n., 172, 174, 177, 178, 180, 194, 220; as an administrator, 137; bids for radical support, 153; career of, to 1838, 123; elected to State Senate, 86; intercedes in newspaper quarrel, 117; nominated for Governor, 124; obtains loan for Public Works, 137-138; opposes repudiation of State debt, 161; patronage of, 136, 145, 146; political decline of, 163-170; protects banks, 139-141; renominated for Governor, 158; role in Bank investigation, 165-166; supports Tyler's bid for President, 169; vetoes banking bill of 1841, 154-155; vetoes Relief Bill, 155-156, 157, 159
Porter, James M., 17 n., 107 n., 144-145, 165; nominated by Tyler as Secretary of War, 169-170; nomination rejected by Senate, 170
Porter, John, 129
Porter Men, 143, 147, 148, 152
Pottsville, description of, 7-8; ironmaking in, 10
Power, Alexander, 192
Power, James M., elected to Canal Commission, 197
Presbyterians, 27
Press, coverage of legislature by, 16; and politics, 21; see also Newspapers
Protectionism, 10; see also Tariff
Public Education Law, 51-53, 59
Public Works, 11-12, 43, 60, 125, 155, 202; unpopularity of, 29, 51; see also Internal improvements; State Works

Quakers, 27, 149

Radicalism, in Constitutional Convention of 1838, 101, 104, 106
Radicals, 13, 140, 153, 159; rally of, in Independence Square, 113; see also Hard-Money Men; Locofocos
Randall, Archibald, 107 n.
Randall, Judge Josiah, 45, 72
Read, John M., 176, 209, 211, 212; appointed Attorney General of the State, 198-199
Reading, 20, 87; description of, 7; ironmaking in, 10

INDEX

Reed, Samuel F., 121
Reed, William B., 101; appointed Attorney General of the State, 130; lobbies for the United States Bank, 93
Registry Law of 1836, 74, 75
Relief Bill, 155-157, 159, 160, 216
Reporter, Harrisburg, 137, 164, 165-166; combines with *State Journal*, 83; on constitutional reform, 99; defends McKean, 32-33; rejected as printer of House journal, 115; supports Independent Treasury, 117, 118-119
Republican Farmer, Wilkes-Barre, 172
Republican Farmer and Democratic Journal, Wilkes-Barre, quoted, 90
Repudiation of State debt, movement for, 160; legislative resolutions against, 161
Rhode Island, 97, 128
Richards, Benjamin Wood, 52
Ritner, Joseph, 14, 20, 21, 69, 75, 76, 77, 87, 108, 121, 124, 125, 130, 131, 132, 135, 138, 141, 151, 219, 220; appointed Treasurer of Mint, 152; in Buckshot War, 133-135; in campaign of 1835, 66-67; career of, to 1835, 71-72; charged with abolitionism, 130; deserts Jackson, 26; in election of 1829, 28-29; in election of 1832, 25, 30; enters Antimasonic party, 28; nominated for Governor, 65; precipitates Buckshot War, 131-132; qualifications of, for Governor, 72; reaction of, to Panic of 1837, 112; renominated for Governor, 124; seeks resumption of specie payments in campaign of 1838, 127-128; signs bill chartering United States Bank, 79; vetoes improvement bill, 95
Ritner, Peter, as lobbyist for banks, 77
Roberts, Jonathan, as Collector of the Port of Philadelphia, 152; quarrels with Tyler, 177
Robinson, William, as lobbyist for United States Bank, 77, 91
Ross, William S., 189, 192
Rush, Richard, 171

Safe Harbor, ironmaking in, 9
Salisbury, Seth, 169; charges Shunk leaders with abusive articles about Muhlenberg, 202-203; supports Taylor movement, 209
Sangston, John A., 52 n.
Schuylkill Canal, 7
Schuylkill County, 4, 57-58, 99 n., 145
Schuylkill Navigation Company, 10-11

Schuylkill River, 6, 10, 11
Schuylkill Valley, ironmaking in, 9-10
Scotch-Irish, 4-5, 27; leadership of, in judiciary, 16; as politicians, 5, 14; support of Antimasonry by, 29; support of Democratic party by, 29
Scots, as miners, 8
Scott, John M., 102
Scott, General Winfield, 142, 209; boomed for President by Antimasons, 178-179
Second Bank of the United States; *see* Bank of the United States
Secret societies, 68, 103
Senate, Pennsylvania, 51, 52, 79, 100, 111, 115, 118, 121, 123, 124, 131, 132, 133, 134, 139, 151; on the Bank of the United States and the restoration of deposits, 43; characteristics of, 14; Democratic minority in, supports charter of the United States Bank, 79, 84; election of delegates to constitutional convention delayed by, 100; improvement bill adopted by, 95; internal improvements offered for support of Bank charter by, 77-78; Relief Bill voted by, 154-156; resumption bill in, 140; resumption bill voted by, 162; school law repeal voted by, 52-53; tariff resolutions in, 195
Senate, United States, 73-74, 116, 148, 195; procedure followed in the election of members of, 16-17
Sentinel, Philadelphia, accepts two-term principle for governors, 82
Sergeant, John, 45, 47, 52, 151, 208; elected president of constitutional convention, 103; rejects Constitution of 1838, 107; in senatorial election of 1833, 30-31; as Whig leader, 220; on Wolf's Bank message, 41
Sevier, Ambrose H., 193 n.
Sharswood, George, 165
Shulze, John A., 26, 46, 54 n., 124; opposes acceptance of Constitution of 1838, 108; as a vice president of the Whig National Convention of 1840, 142
Shunk, Francis R., 14, 137, 187; appointed Secretary of the Commonwealth by Porter, 136; appointments of, as Governor, 187-188; on the Bible in public schools, 185; in the campaign of 1847, 186; death of, 215; on the effects of the Constitution of 1838 upon the patronage, 110; elected Governor

in 1844, 186, 187; in gubernatorial campaigns of 1844, 179-182, 182 n., 184-186, 187; gains re-election, 203; ignores Wilmot Proviso, 214; opposed for a second term, 199; renominated for Governor, 199-200; resigns as Governor, 215, 216 n.; resigns as Secretary of the Commonwealth, 163-164
Signal, Harrisburg, 169
Simpson, Stephen, 51
Slavery, in territories becomes political issue, 220
Smilie, John, 55, 66
Smith, Joseph B., 45
Smith, R. Penn, 73 n.
Smithfield, 101
Snowden, J. Ross, elected Speaker of the State House of Representatives, 160; elected State Treasurer, 188
Snyder, Simon, 13, 50
Snyder County, 29 n.
Society of Mechanics and Workingmen, supports Muhlenberg for Governor in Philadelphia, 60
Somerset County, 100, 185
Southwark, Philadelphia County, 50, 56, 74, 152, 184
Specie Circular, 88, 90, 112, 115, 127
Specie payments, resumption of, 127-129
Spirit of the Times, Philadelphia, 147, 157, 161, 162-163, 171
Spring Garden, Philadelphia, 56, 184
Stambaugh, Samuel C., 207
Star, Gettysburg, supports Antimasonic national convention in 1836, 81
State Capital Gazette, Harrisburg, 138-139, 166
State Capitol, 13
State Journal, Harrisburg, combines with *Reporter,* 83
State Librarian, 14
State Works, 10-11, 25, 137, 161, 194; see also Internal improvements; Public Works
States' Rights Men, 44
States' Rights Party of Pennsylvania, 85
Sterigere, John B., 180 n.
Stevens, Thaddeus, 81, 108, 120, 121, 124 n., 127, 130, 134, 151, 178, 220; appointed to Canal Commission, 124; in Buckshot War, 132-134; in campaign of 1835, 66; defeated for House in 1836, 86; defends public education law, 52; efforts of, to strengthen Coalition in Constitutional Convention of 1838, 100; elected to State House of Representatives, 64-65; guides charter of United States Bank in legislature, 76-79; initiates investigation of secret societies in constitutional convention, 103; investigates Masonry, 71, 72-73; leadership of, in constitutional convention, 102; leadership of, in legislature, 70, 72; moves to limit Philadelphia's membership in State House of Representatives, 103; opposes concessions to Whigs, 70-71; supports national convention, 70; testifies in banking investigation, 92-93; turns Canal Commission into electioneering device, 125, 127, 129
Stevenson, Samuel, introduces bank regulatory bill, 120-121
Stewart, Commodore Charles, 116; boomed for President, 143-144, 159, 168, 171
Stoever, Jacob, 52 n.
Stokes, Dr. T. P., 211
Stokes, William A., 211
Strohm, John, 134 n.
Sturdevant, John, 134 n.
Sturgeon, Daniel, 124, 152, 170, 179, 182 n., 183, 195; elected to United States Senate, 139; re-elected to Senate, 188
Suffrage, in Constitution of 1790, 18; in Constitution of 1838, 105
Sun, Philadelphia, 65
Supreme Court, of Pennsylvania, 16
Susquehanna County, 5, 208
Susquehanna River, 3, 11, 74, 125; North Branch of, 10, 126; West Branch of, 10
Susquehanna Valley, 3, 7, 128; ironmaking in, 9
Sutherland, Joel B., 48, 49, 152, 169, 211; defeated for Congress, 86; defeated for the Senate, 50; as a Wolf partisan, 54, 56, 59 n.

Taney, Roger B., 89
"Tapeworm," 76, 130; see also Gettysburg Railroad
Tariff, of 1833, 182-183; of 1842, 183, 190, 192, 194-197; of 1846, 195-198; as all-absorbing interest of Pennsylvania by 1848, 220; convention on, at Hollidaysburg, 194; in election of 1844, 182; and McKay Bill of 1844, 183, 195
Taylor, John, 89
Taylor, General Zachary, boomed by Whigs for President, 208-209; defeats Cass in State, 218; identified as Whig at Philadelphia rally, 214; presidential support for, among

INDEX

Democrats, 209; receives Whig backing for Presidency, 214-215
Tax Law of 1840, 141
Telegraph, Harrisburg, 103, 110, 114, 122, 129
Texas, annexation of, popular in State, 176; in campaign of 1844, 182
Thompson, James, 58; elected Speaker of State House of Representatives in 1834, 50
Times, Pittsburgh, supports Antimasonic national convention in 1836, 81
Tioga County, 5
Todd, James, 220; appointed Attorney General by Ritner, 69; lobbies for United States Bank, 77; opposes an Antimasonic national convention, 70
Toland, George W., 52
Tunkhannock, 126
Turnpikes, 10-11
Tyler, John, 17, 158; backed for President by Porter faction, 169; dismisses Jonathan Roberts as Collector of the Port of Philadelphia, 177; nominated for Vice President, 143; patronage of, in Philadelphia, 177; succeeds to the Presidency, **152**
Tyler, Robert, 212

Union, Lancaster, 178
Union Canal, 11
Union County, 4, 48, 74, 98 n., 109, 158, 180, 199, 217; opposition to school law in, 52, 60, 114; supports Antimasonry, 29
United States Bank, 90, 106, 107, 109, 115, 121, 125, 138, 140, 153, 155, 156, 164-165, 184, 216, 219; amendments to prevent veto of charter of, 78; chartering of, 75-79; cost of the charter of, 78; failure of, 80; loss of prestige of, 154; terms of charter of, 80; unpopularity of, in Philadelphia, 153; vote on bill to charter, 79; *see also* Bank of the United States
United States Gazette, Philadelphia, 142, 162, 163, 186; resists Antimasonic leadership in Coalition, 66

Van Buren, Martin, 17, 24, 48, **56,** 58, 61, 66, 67, 69, 70, 71, 82, 84, 122, 126, 141, 143, 144, 147, 148, 152, 166, 179, 182; accepted by State Democrats for President, 32; at Baltimore Convention, 62-63; in campaign of 1840, 148; elected Vice President, 24, 27; supported along Northern Tier for President in 1848, 208; supported for President in 1844, 174-175; supported by Free Soil party, 215; Texas letter of, displeases Democrats, 176
Van Buren Men, 143, 146, 147, 148, 152, 160, 172, 174-175, 193
Van Dyke, James C., 211
Vaux, Richard, 171, 209, 211
Vaux, Roberts, 52; describes Bank rally, 42, 51; in election of 1835, 63
Venango County, 158
Vermont, 143
Virginia, 128, 153

Walker, Robert J., as Secretary of the Treasury, 210
Walker Tariff; *see* Tariff of 1846
Wallace, John B., 70; as lobbyist for the United States Bank, 77, 91
Wallace, Joseph, 201; as chairman of the Antimasonic State Committee, 64-66, 68; named Deputy Secretary of the Commonwealth by Ritner, 68
Washington, D. C., 36, 37, 42, 46
Washington, George, 55
Washington County, 4, 9, 29, 41, 71
Watmough, John G., 45
Wayne County, 199
Weaver, John, 156 n.
Webster, Daniel, 69, 71, 141, 143, 151, 185; on Wolf's Bank message, 40-41
Weed, Thurlow, 28, **142**
Welsh, 4
Welsh, Henry, as Naval Officer of Philadelphia, 211
Welsh miners, 8
Wescott, James D., 193 n.
Westmoreland County, 185, 217
Wetherill, John P., 45
Wharton, Lloyd, 59 n., 89
Whig party, 17, 19, 26, 44, 45, 46, 47, 48, 49, 53, 65, 68, 70, 71, 72, 81, 96, 100, 101, 104, 105, 112, 116, 121, 124, 128, 130, 132, 133, 134, 141, 142, 148, 149, 151, 152, 154-156, 160, 162, 177-179, 184, 188, 194, 219-220; adoption of party label by, 45; ascendancy of, in the Coalition, 80-81; in election of 1835, 66; encouraged by the Wolf-Muhlenberg feud, 64; endorses Native American nominees in Philadelphia, 215; fails to capitalize on tariff, 200-203; in gubernatorial campaign of 1844, 179-186; leadership of, in Constitutional Con-

vention of 1838, 102; national convention of, in 1839, 142; nomination of Harrison and Tyler by, at Harrisburg, 143; opposes Wilmot Proviso, 201; organization of, in interior of State, 47-48; in presidential campaign of 1844, 177-179; rejects Constitution of 1838, 107-108; seeks political capital from Tariff of 1846, 196-198; strategy of, in 1836, 71, 73; supports Cameron for United States Senator, 190; trend favors success of, 214

Whigs; see Whig party

Wilkes-Barre, 98, 157, 158 n.

Wilkins, Senator William, 7, 17, 36, 38, 206 n.; appointed Minister to Russia, 50; defends Wolf's Bank message, 41; receives Pennsylvania electoral vote for Vice President in 1832, 24

Williamsport, 46, 167

Wilmot, David, 193 n., 194, 195, 197, 220; motives of, in offering Wilmot Proviso, 196 n.; re-elected to Congress, 197; supports Walker Tariff, 195, 196, 196 n.; stumps Northern Tier for Van Buren and Free Soilism, 215

Wilmot Proviso, 196, 215, 220; rejected by Democrats, 201

Wirt, William, 29

Wolf, George, 14, 20, 72, 73 n., 83, 122, 124, 154, 220; administrations of, evaluated, 50-51; appointed Collector of the Port of Philadelphia, 123; appointed Comptroller of the Treasury, 83; criticizes Bank of the United States, 39-41, 44, 61; death of, 146, 179; defends Bank of the United States, 37; in election of 1829, 25, 28; in election of 1832, 25, 30-31; in election of 1835, 44, 50-51, 56, 57, 58, 60-67; as an Eleventh Hour Man, 24; patronage of, 53; praises Constitution of 1790, 99; and public education law, 51-53; refuses to amplify criticism of Bank of the United States, 43-44; resigns as comptroller, 122; supports Bank of the United States, 24-25, 56

Wolf Democrats, 50, 82, 83, 98-99, 100, 122, 137; acknowledge irregularities at gubernatorial convention, 83, 136

Woodward, George W., 192; charged with nativism, 189; in Constitutional Convention of 1838, 110 n.; defeated for United States Senator, 188-190; nominated for United States Supreme Court, 192-193; rejected by Senate, 205

Woolens, manufacture of, 9

Woolens Bill, 26, 28

Wright, Hendrick B., 156 n., 159, 172, 187, 189; assailed for his vote on the Relief Bill, 158; named chairman of the Internal Improvements Committee, 160; as president of the National Democratic Convention, 176

Wright, Silas, 177

York, 7, 46

York County, 74, 180, 196

Young Men's Democratic Convention, 85

Yulee, David L., 193 n.